MIKE MIGNOLA RICHARD PACE
writers

TROY NIXEY
penciller

DENNIS JANKE
inker

DAVE STEWART
colorist

BILL OAKLEY
letterer

MIKE MIGNOLA
Collection and series cover artist

BATMAN created by BOB KANE with BILL FINGER

BATMAN:
the DOOM that came to GOTHAM

Archie Goodwin, Mike Carlin
Editors - Original Series

Jeb Woodard
Group Editor - Collected Editions

Damian Ryland
Publication Design

Bob Harras
Senior VP - Editor-in-Chief, DC Comics

Diane Nelson
President

Dan DiDio and Jim Lee
Co-Publishers

Geoff Johns
Chief Creative Officer

Amit Desai
Senior VP - Marketing & Global Franchise Management

Nairi Gardiner
Senior VP - Finance

Sam Ades
VP - Digital Marketing

Bobbie Chase
VP - Talent Development

Mark Chiarello
Senior VP - Art, Design & Collected Editions

John Cunningham
VP - Content Strategy

Anne DePies
VP - Strategy Planning & Reporting

Don Falletti
VP - Manufacturing Operations

Lawrence Ganem
VP - Editorial Administration & Talent Relations

Alison Gill
Senior VP - Manufacturing & Operations

Hank Kanalz
Senior VP - Editorial Strategy & Administration

Jay Kogan
VP - Legal Affairs

Derek Maddalena
Senior VP - Sales & Business Development

Jack Mahan
VP - Business Affairs

Dan Miron
VP - Sales Planning & Trade Development

Nick Napolitano
VP - Manufacturing Administration

Carol Roeder
VP - Marketing

Eddie Scannell
VP - Mass Account & Digital Sales

Courtney Simmons
Senior VP - Publicity & Communications

Jim (Ski) Sokolowski
VP - Comic Book Specialty & Newsstand Sales

Sandy Yi
Senior VP - Global Franchise Management

BATMAN: THE DOOM THAT CAME TO GOTHAM

DC Comics, 2900 W. Alameda Ave, Burbank, CA 91505
Printed by RR Donnelley, Salem, VA, USA. 11/13/15. First Printing.
ISBN: 978-1-4012-5806-1

Library of Congress Cataloging-in-Publication Data

Mignola, Michael.
Batman : the doom that came to Gotham / Mike Mignola, Troy Nixey.
pages cm
ISBN 978-1-4012-5806-1 (paperback)
1. Graphic novels. I. Nixey, Troy, illustrator. II. Title
PN6728.B36M44 2015
741.5'973-dc23
2015031178

PEFC Certified
Printed on paper from sustainably managed forests and controlled sources
PEFC
PEFC/29-31-75
www.pefc.org

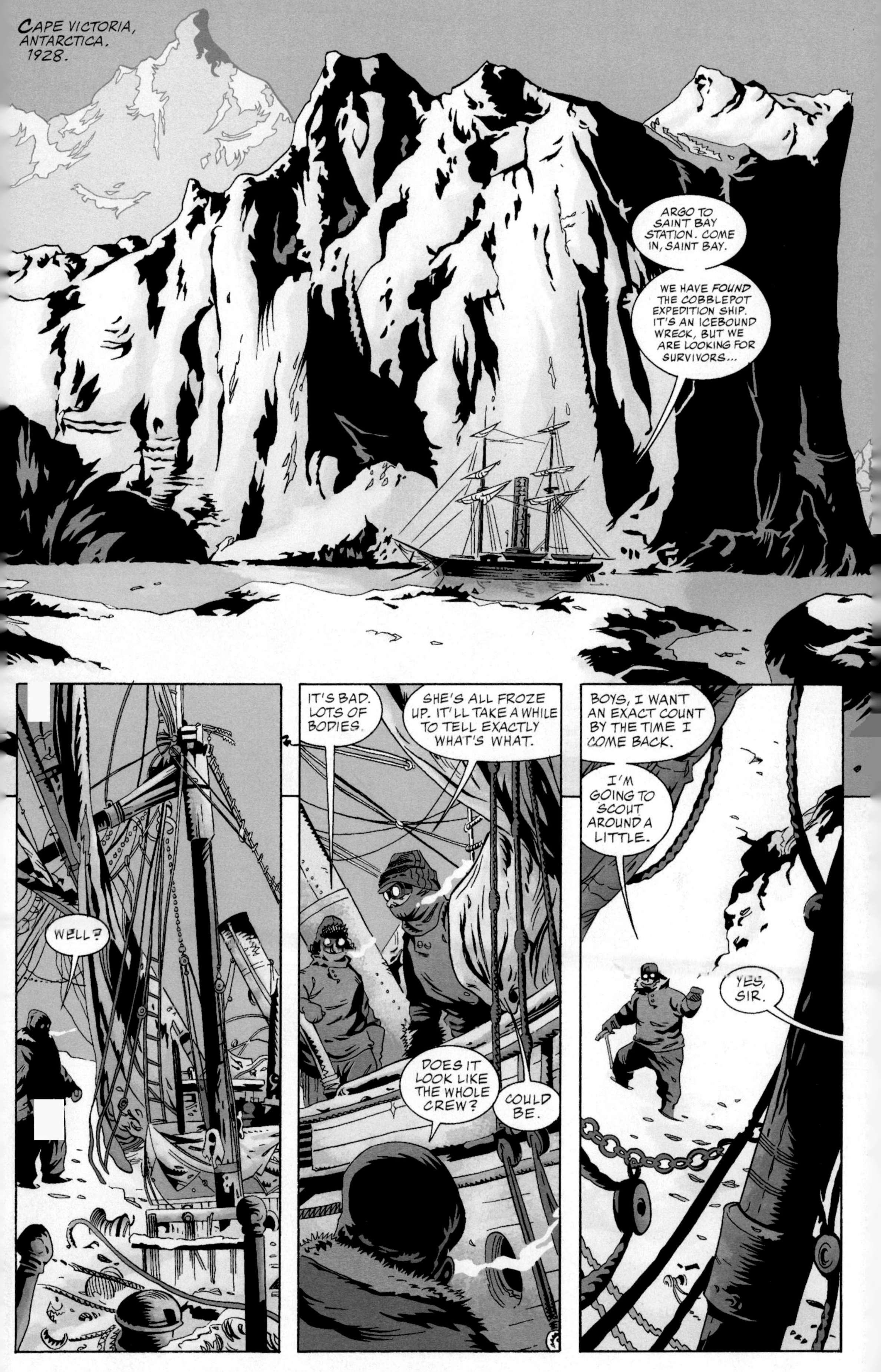
CAPE VICTORIA, ANTARCTICA, 1928.
ARGO TO SAINT BAY STATION. COME IN, SAINT BAY.
WE HAVE FOUND THE COBBLEPOT EXPEDITION SHIP. IT'S AN ICEBOUND WRECK, BUT WE ARE LOOKING FOR SURVIVORS...
WELL?
IT'S BAD. LOTS OF BODIES.
SHE'S ALL FROZE UP. IT'LL TAKE A WHILE TO TELL EXACTLY WHAT'S WHAT.
DOES IT LOOK LIKE THE WHOLE CREW?
COULD BE.
BOYS, I WANT AN EXACT COUNT BY THE TIME I COME BACK.
I'M GOING TO SCOUT AROUND A LITTLE.
YES, SIR.

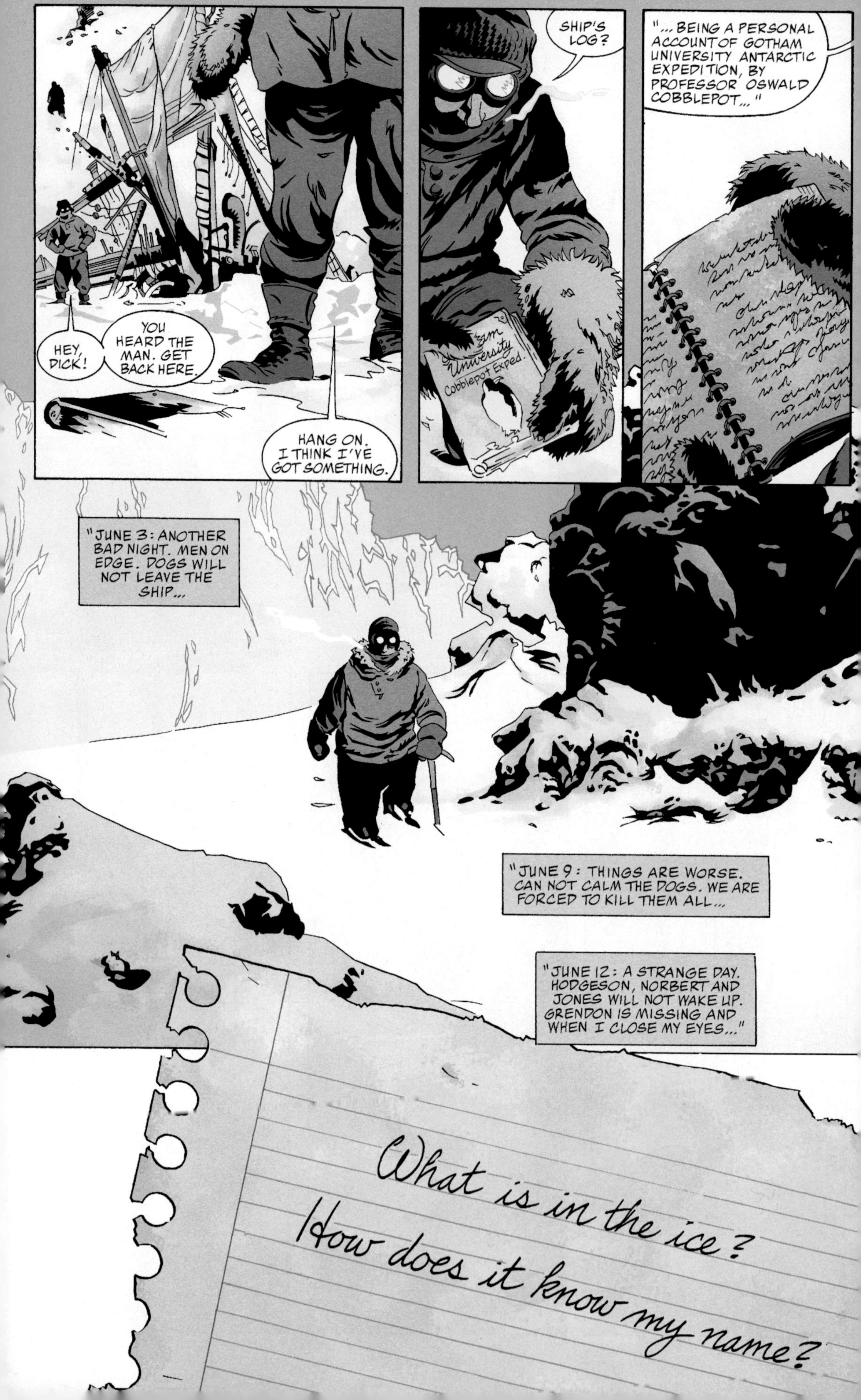

HEY, DICK!
YOU HEARD THE MAN. GET BACK HERE.
HANG ON. I THINK I'VE GOT SOMETHING.
SHIP'S LOG?
University
Cobblepot Exped.
"... BEING A PERSONAL ACCOUNT OF GOTHAM UNIVERSITY ANTARCTIC EXPEDITION, BY PROFESSOR OSWALD COBBLEPOT..."
"JUNE 3: ANOTHER BAD NIGHT. MEN ON EDGE. DOGS WILL NOT LEAVE THE SHIP...
"JUNE 9: THINGS ARE WORSE. CAN NOT CALM THE DOGS. WE ARE FORCED TO KILL THEM ALL...
"JUNE 12: A STRANGE DAY. HODGESON, NORBERT AND JONES WILL NOT WAKE UP. GRENDON IS MISSING AND WHEN I CLOSE MY EYES..."
What is in the ice?
How does it know my name?

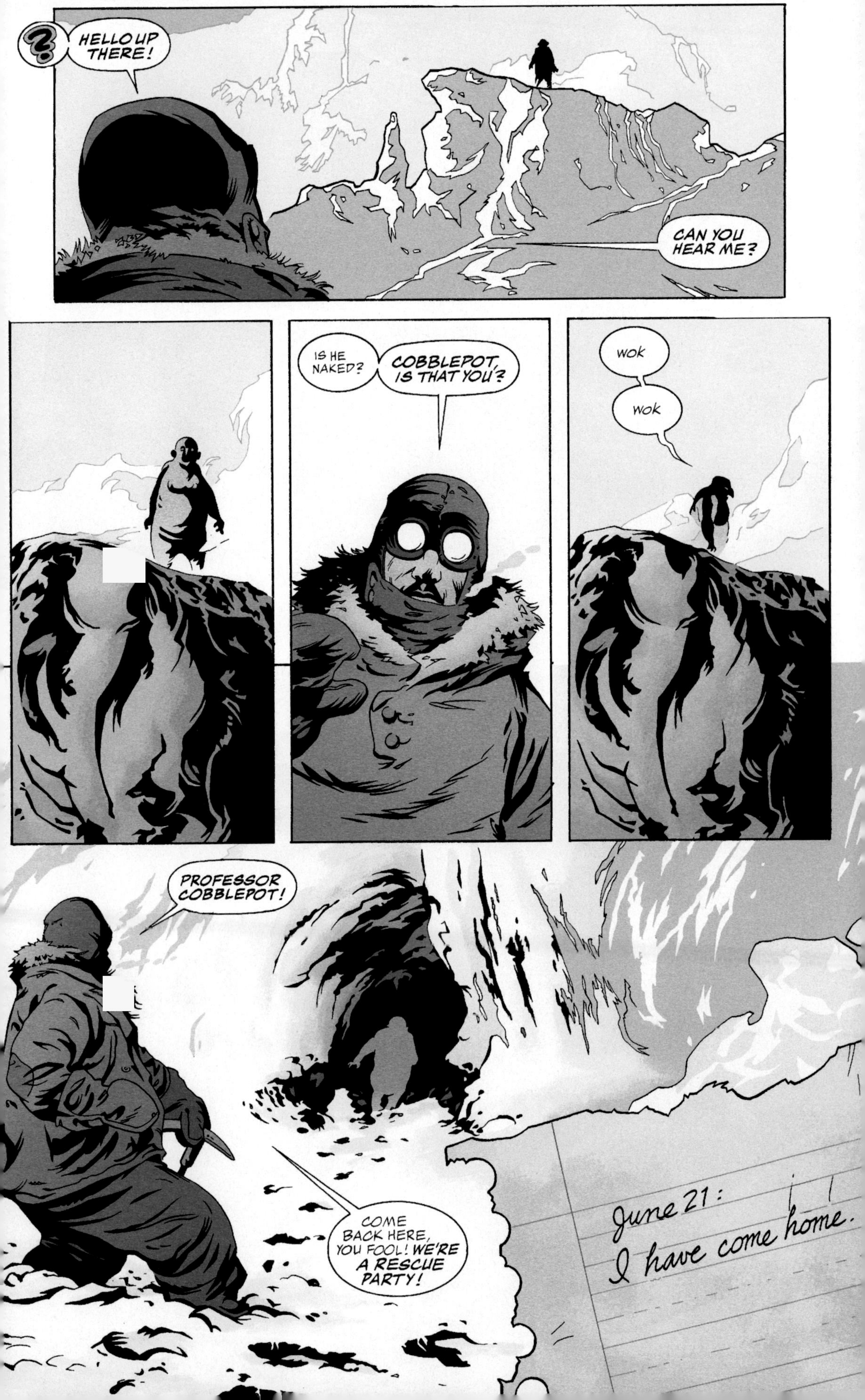
HELLO UP THERE!
CAN YOU HEAR ME?
IS HE NAKED?
COBBLEPOT, IS THAT YOU?
wok
wok
PROFESSOR COBBLEPOT!
COME BACK HERE, YOU FOOL! WE'RE A RESCUE PARTY!
June 21:
I have come home.

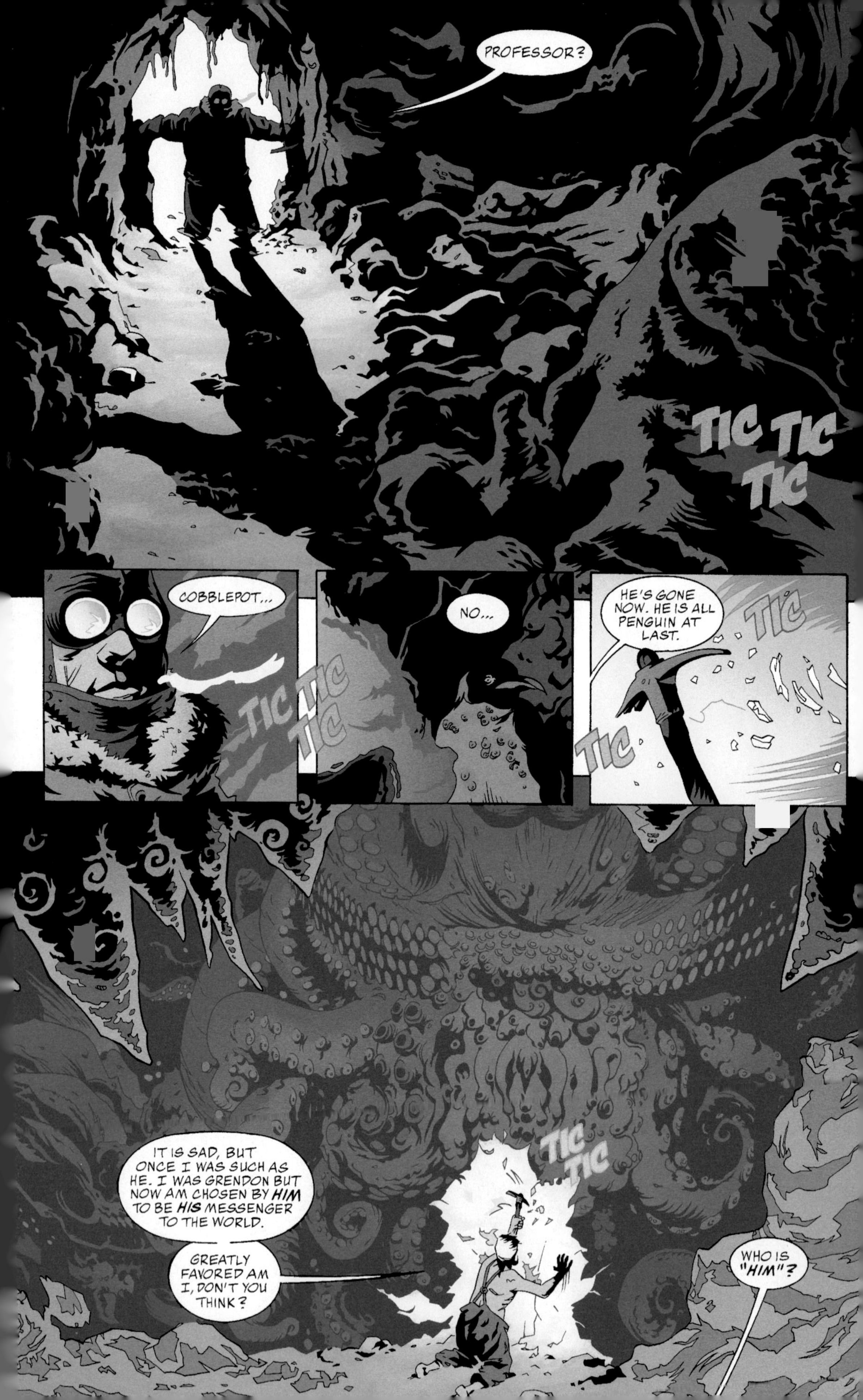
PROFESSOR?
TIC TIC
TIC
COBBLEPOT...
TIC TIC
TIC
NO...
HE'S GONE NOW. HE IS ALL PENGUIN AT LAST.
TIC
TIC
TIC
TIC
IT IS SAD, BUT ONCE I WAS SUCH AS HE. I WAS GRENDON BUT NOW AM CHOSEN BY *HIM* TO BE *HIS* MESSENGER TO THE WORLD.
GREATLY FAVORED AM I, DON'T YOU THINK?
WHO IS "*HIM*"?

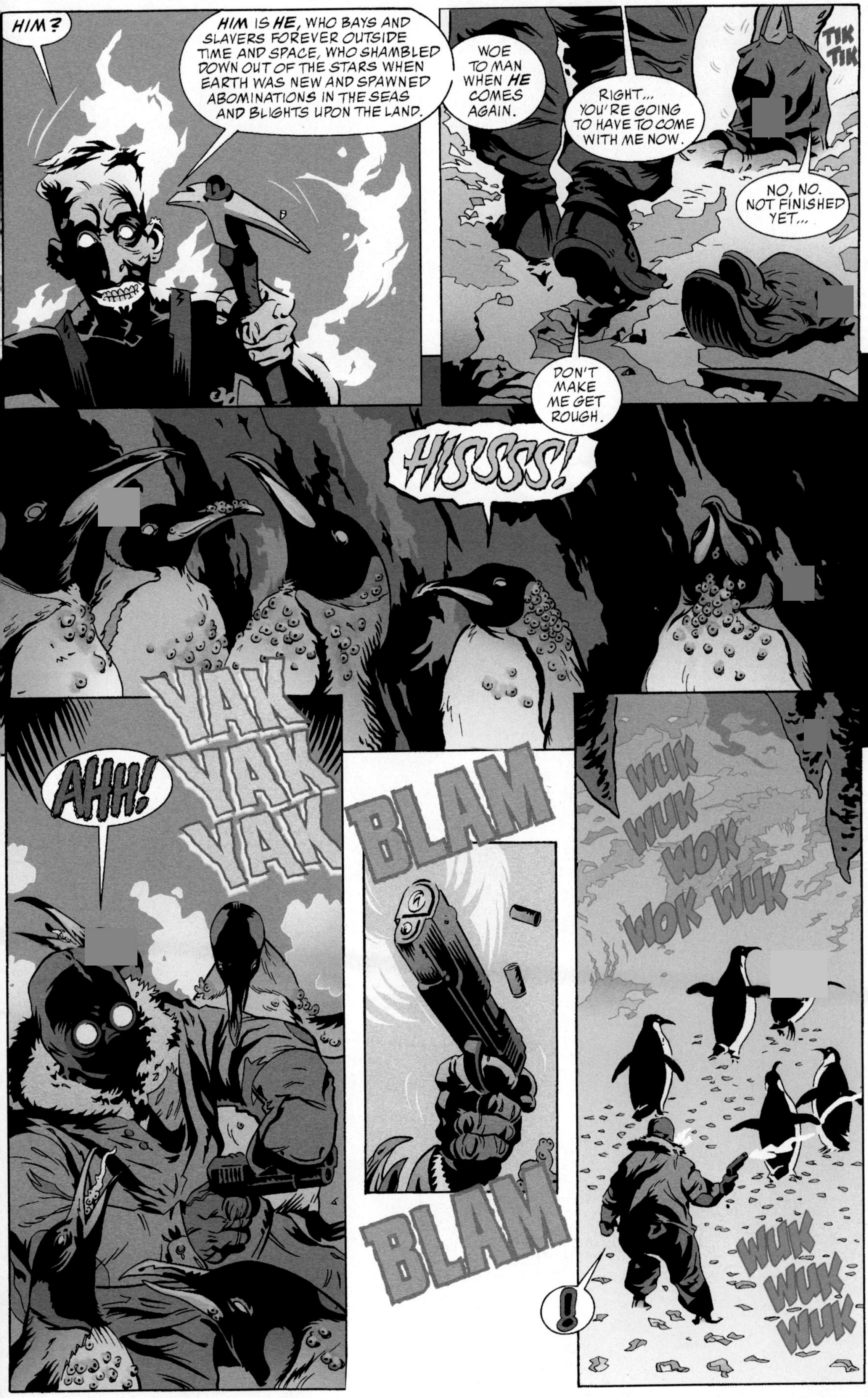
HIM?
HIM IS HE, WHO BAYS AND SLAVERS FOREVER OUTSIDE TIME AND SPACE, WHO SHAMBLED DOWN OUT OF THE STARS WHEN EARTH WAS NEW AND SPAWNED ABOMINATIONS IN THE SEAS AND BLIGHTS UPON THE LAND.
WOE TO MAN WHEN HE COMES AGAIN.
RIGHT... YOU'RE GOING TO HAVE TO COME WITH ME NOW.
TIK TIK
NO, NO. NOT FINISHED YET...
DON'T MAKE ME GET ROUGH.
HISSSS!
YAK YAK YAK
AHH!
BLAM
BLAM
WUK WUK WOK WOK WUK
!
WUK WUK WUK

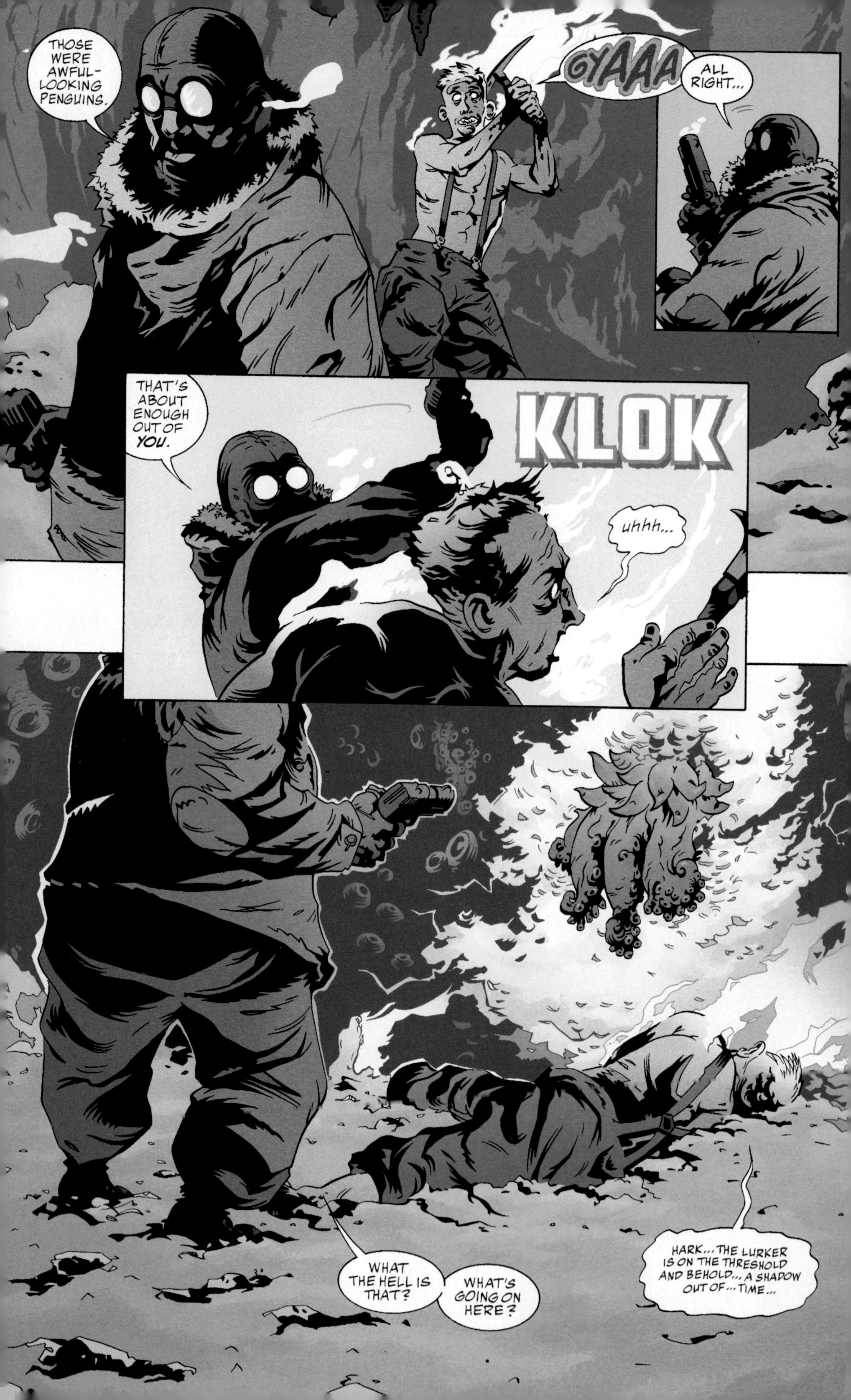
THOSE WERE AWFUL-LOOKING PENGUINS.
GYAAA
ALL RIGHT...
THAT'S ABOUT ENOUGH OUT OF YOU.
KLOK
uhhh...
WHAT THE HELL IS THAT?
WHAT'S GOING ON HERE?
HARK... THE LURKER IS ON THE THRESHOLD AND BEHOLD... A SHADOW OUT OF... TIME...

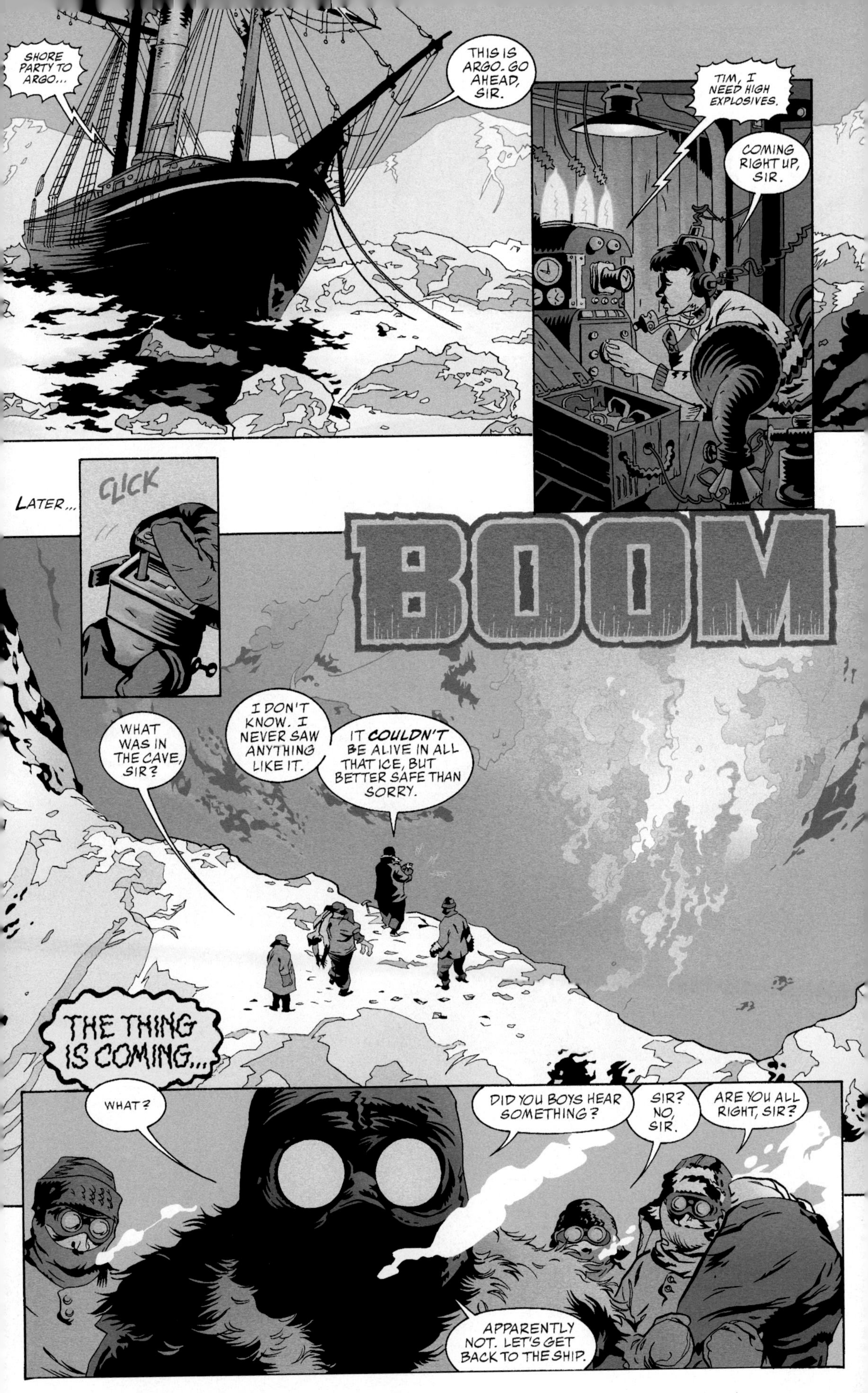
SHORE PARTY TO ARGO...
THIS IS ARGO. GO AHEAD, SIR.
TIM, I NEED HIGH EXPLOSIVES.
COMING RIGHT UP, SIR.
LATER...
CLICK
BOOM
WHAT WAS IN THE CAVE, SIR?
I DON'T KNOW. I NEVER SAW ANYTHING LIKE IT.
IT COULDN'T BE ALIVE IN ALL THAT ICE, BUT BETTER SAFE THAN SORRY.
THE THING IS COMING...
WHAT?
DID YOU BOYS HEAR SOMETHING?
SIR? NO, SIR.
ARE YOU ALL RIGHT, SIR?
APPARENTLY NOT. LET'S GET BACK TO THE SHIP.

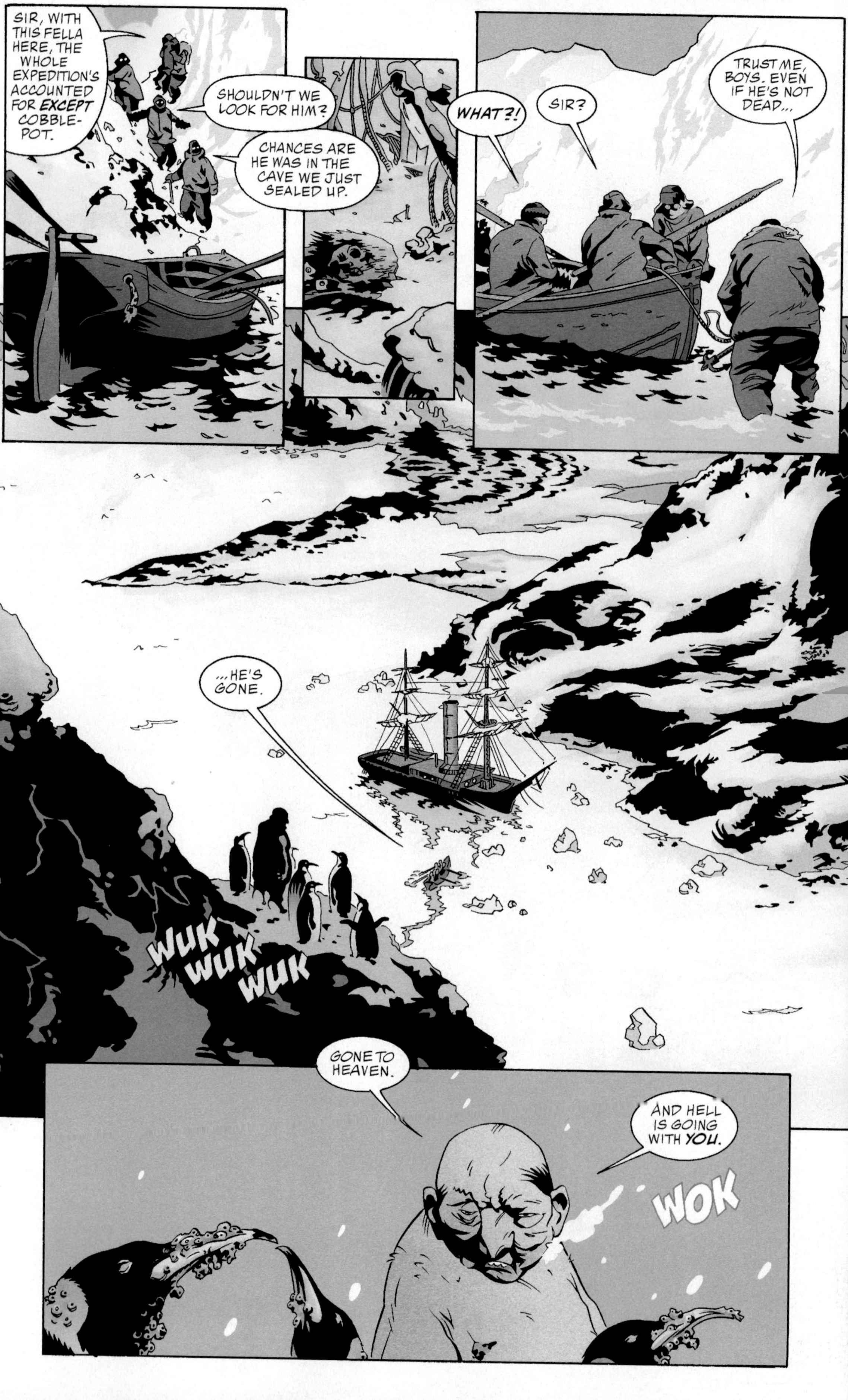
SIR, WITH THIS FELLA HERE, THE WHOLE EXPEDITION'S ACCOUNTED FOR EXCEPT COBBLE-POT.
SHOULDN'T WE LOOK FOR HIM?
CHANCES ARE HE WAS IN THE CAVE WE JUST SEALED UP.
WHAT?!
SIR?
TRUST ME, BOYS. EVEN IF HE'S NOT DEAD...
...HE'S GONE.
WUK WUK WUK
GONE TO HEAVEN.
AND HELL IS GOING WITH YOU.
WOK

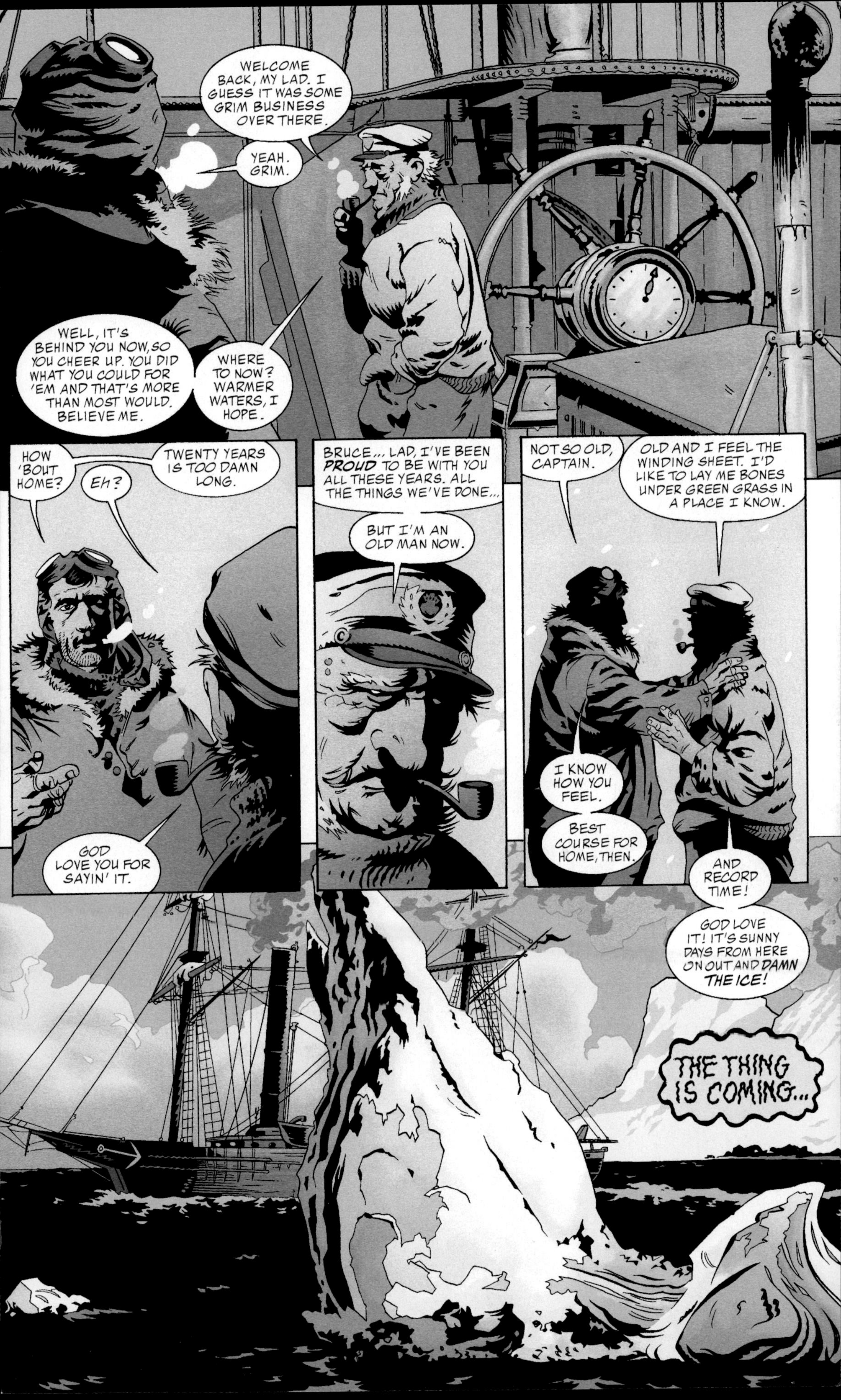
WELCOME BACK, MY LAD. I GUESS IT WAS SOME GRIM BUSINESS OVER THERE.
YEAH. GRIM.
WELL, IT'S BEHIND YOU NOW, SO YOU CHEER UP. YOU DID WHAT YOU COULD FOR 'EM AND THAT'S MORE THAN MOST WOULD. BELIEVE ME.
WHERE TO NOW? WARMER WATERS, I HOPE.
HOW 'BOUT HOME?
EH?
TWENTY YEARS IS TOO DAMN LONG.
GOD LOVE YOU FOR SAYIN' IT.
BRUCE... LAD, I'VE BEEN PROUD TO BE WITH YOU ALL THESE YEARS. ALL THE THINGS WE'VE DONE...
BUT I'M AN OLD MAN NOW.
NOT SO OLD, CAPTAIN.
OLD AND I FEEL THE WINDING SHEET. I'D LIKE TO LAY ME BONES UNDER GREEN GRASS IN A PLACE I KNOW.
I KNOW HOW YOU FEEL.
BEST COURSE FOR HOME, THEN.
AND RECORD TIME!
GOD LOVE IT! IT'S SUNNY DAYS FROM HERE ON OUT AND DAMN THE ICE!
THE THING IS COMING...

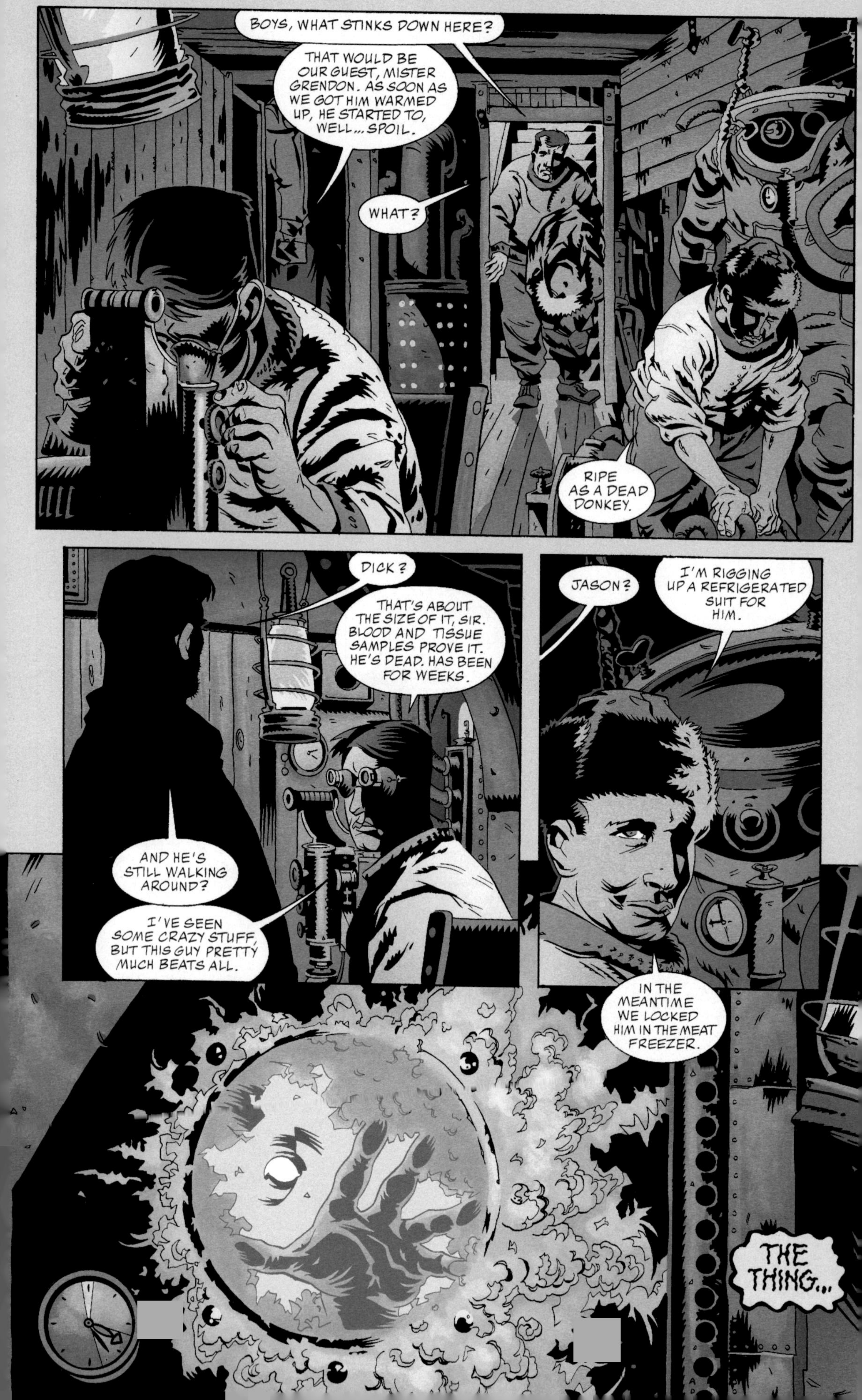
BOYS, WHAT STINKS DOWN HERE?
THAT WOULD BE OUR GUEST, MISTER GRENDON. AS SOON AS WE GOT HIM WARMED UP, HE STARTED TO, WELL... SPOIL.
WHAT?
RIPE AS A DEAD DONKEY.
DICK?
THAT'S ABOUT THE SIZE OF IT, SIR. BLOOD AND TISSUE SAMPLES PROVE IT. HE'S DEAD. HAS BEEN FOR WEEKS.
AND HE'S STILL WALKING AROUND?
I'VE SEEN SOME CRAZY STUFF, BUT THIS GUY PRETTY MUCH BEATS ALL.
JASON?
I'M RIGGING UP A REFRIGERATED SUIT FOR HIM.
IN THE MEANTIME WE LOCKED HIM IN THE MEAT FREEZER.
THE THING...

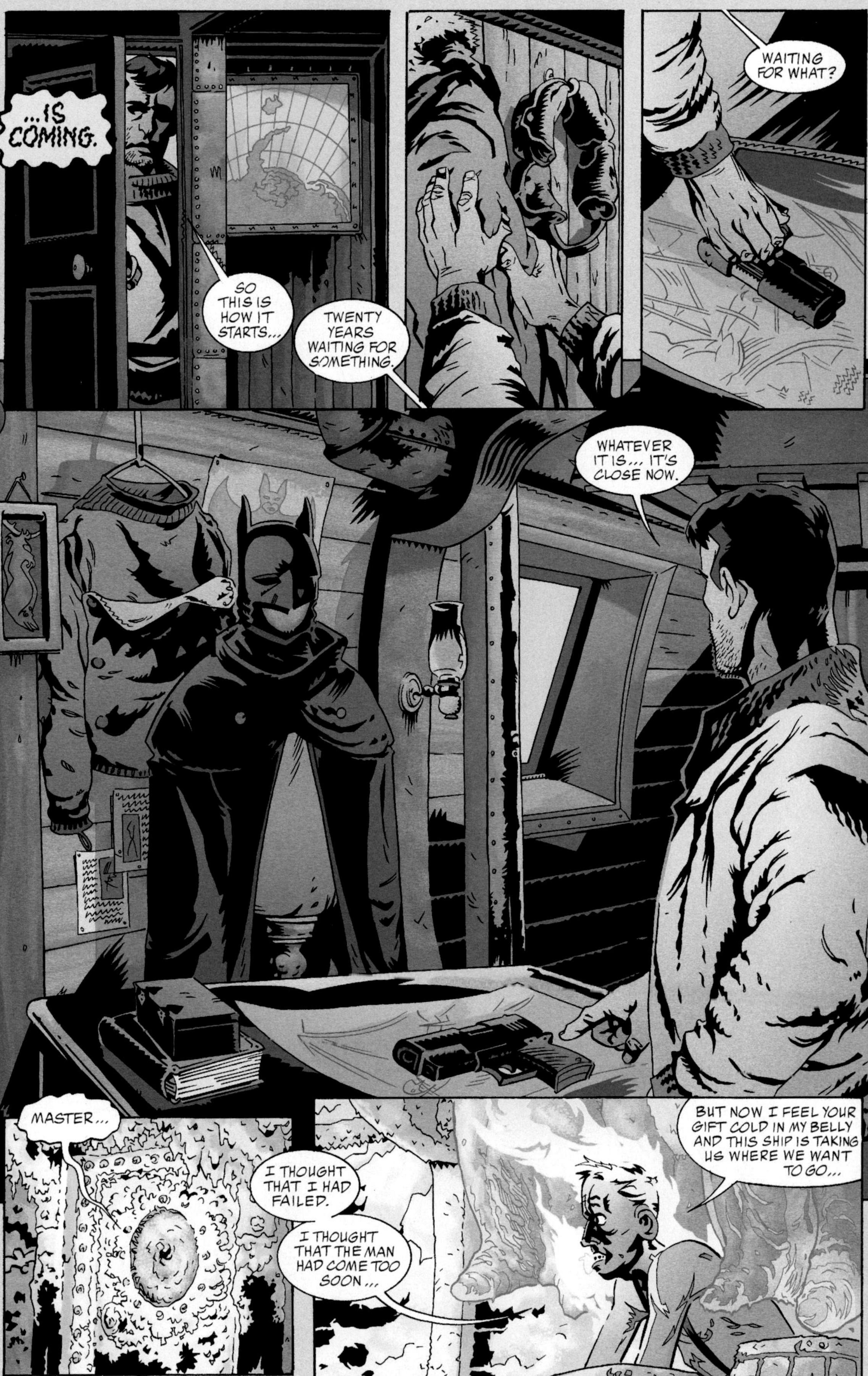

...IS COMING.
SO THIS IS HOW IT STARTS...
TWENTY YEARS WAITING FOR SOMETHING.
WAITING FOR WHAT?
WHATEVER IT IS... IT'S CLOSE NOW.
MASTER...
I THOUGHT THAT I HAD FAILED.
I THOUGHT THAT THE MAN HAD COME TOO SOON...
BUT NOW I FEEL YOUR GIFT COLD IN MY BELLY AND THIS SHIP IS TAKING US WHERE WE WANT TO GO...

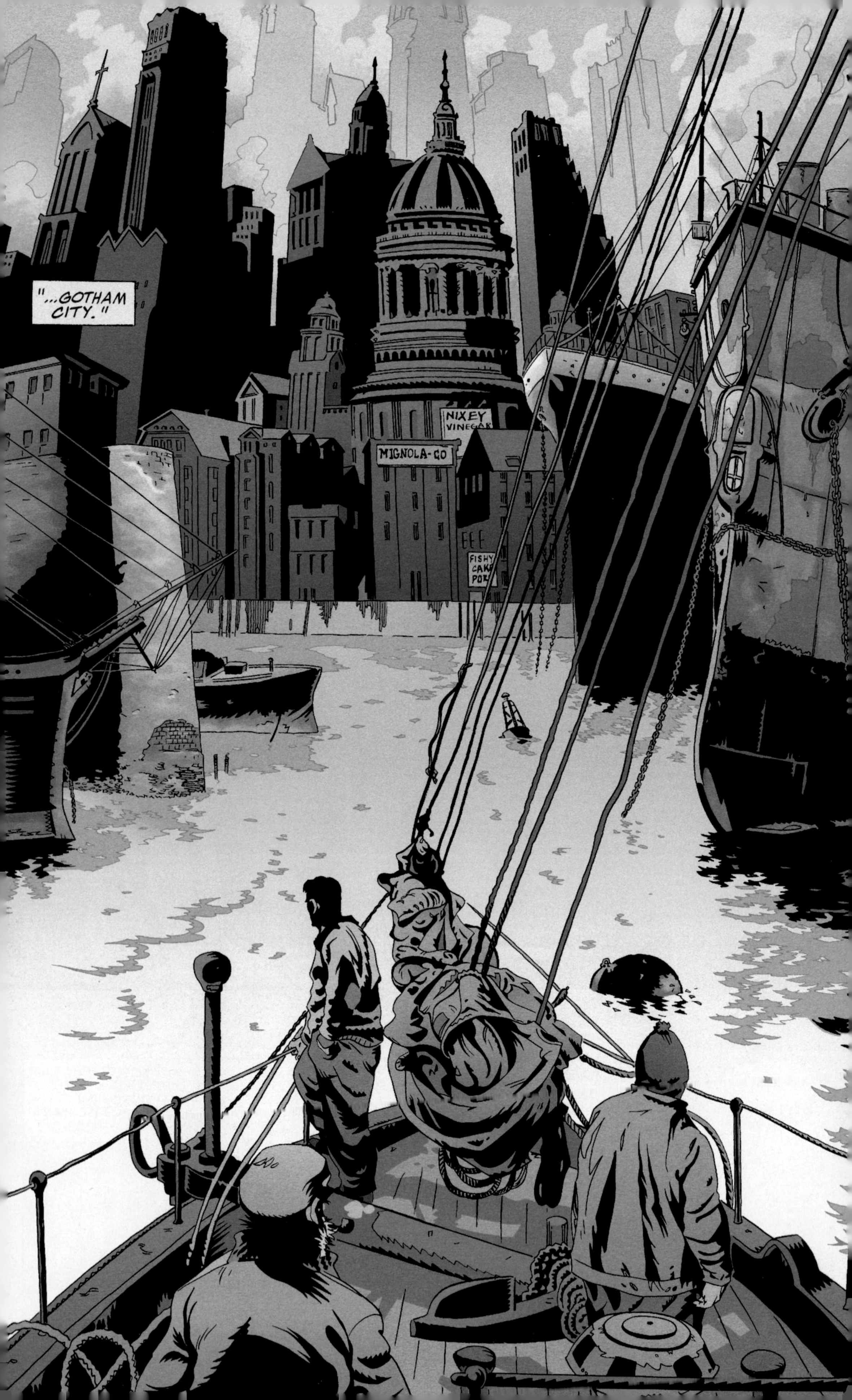
"...GOTHAM CITY."
NIXEY
MIGNOLA-CO
FISHY

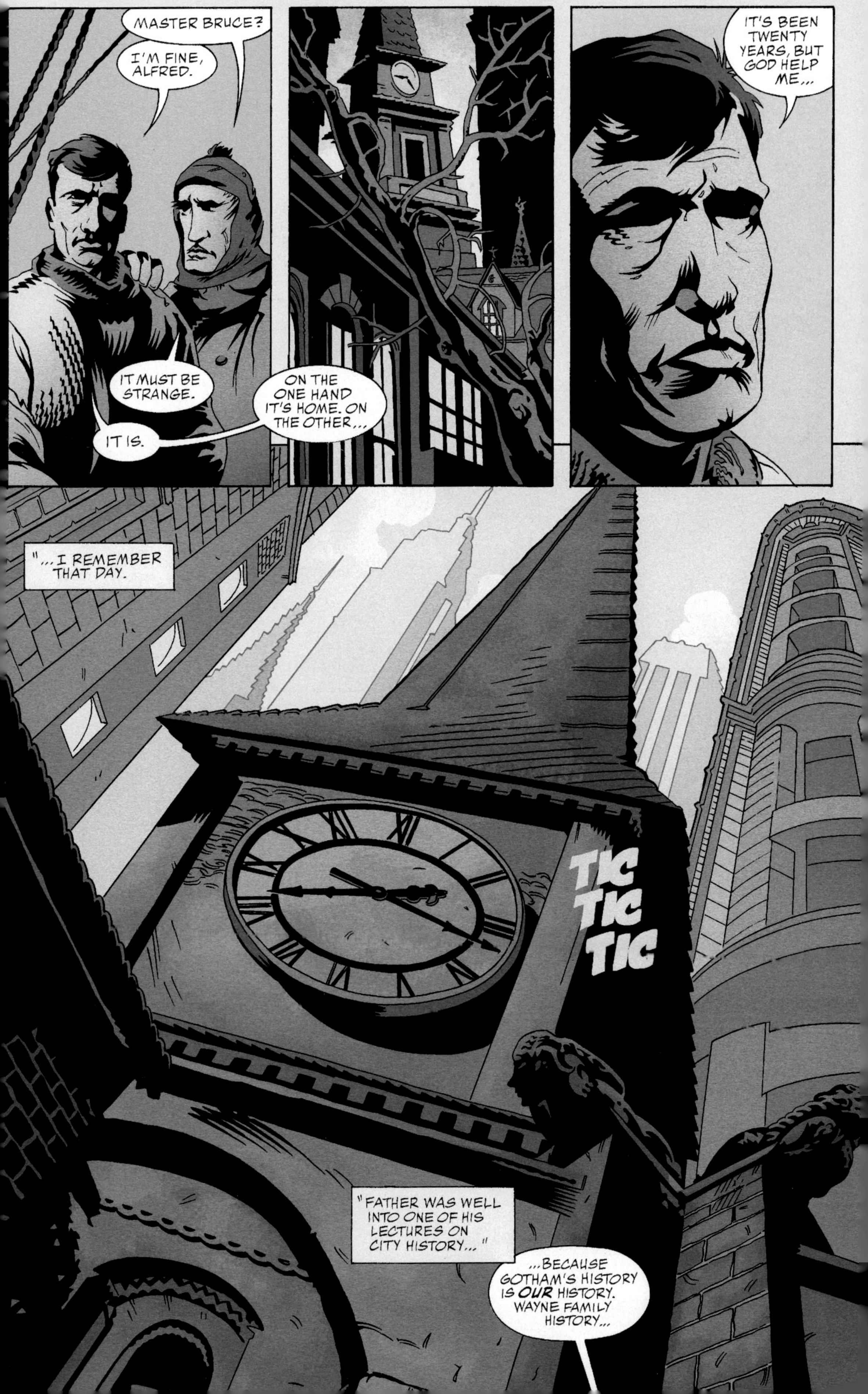
MASTER BRUCE?
I'M FINE, ALFRED.
IT MUST BE STRANGE.
IT IS.
ON THE ONE HAND IT'S HOME. ON THE OTHER...
IT'S BEEN TWENTY YEARS, BUT GOD HELP ME...
"...I REMEMBER THAT DAY.
TIC TIC TIC
"FATHER WAS WELL INTO ONE OF HIS LECTURES ON CITY HISTORY..."
...BECAUSE GOTHAM'S HISTORY IS OUR HISTORY. WAYNE FAMILY HISTORY...

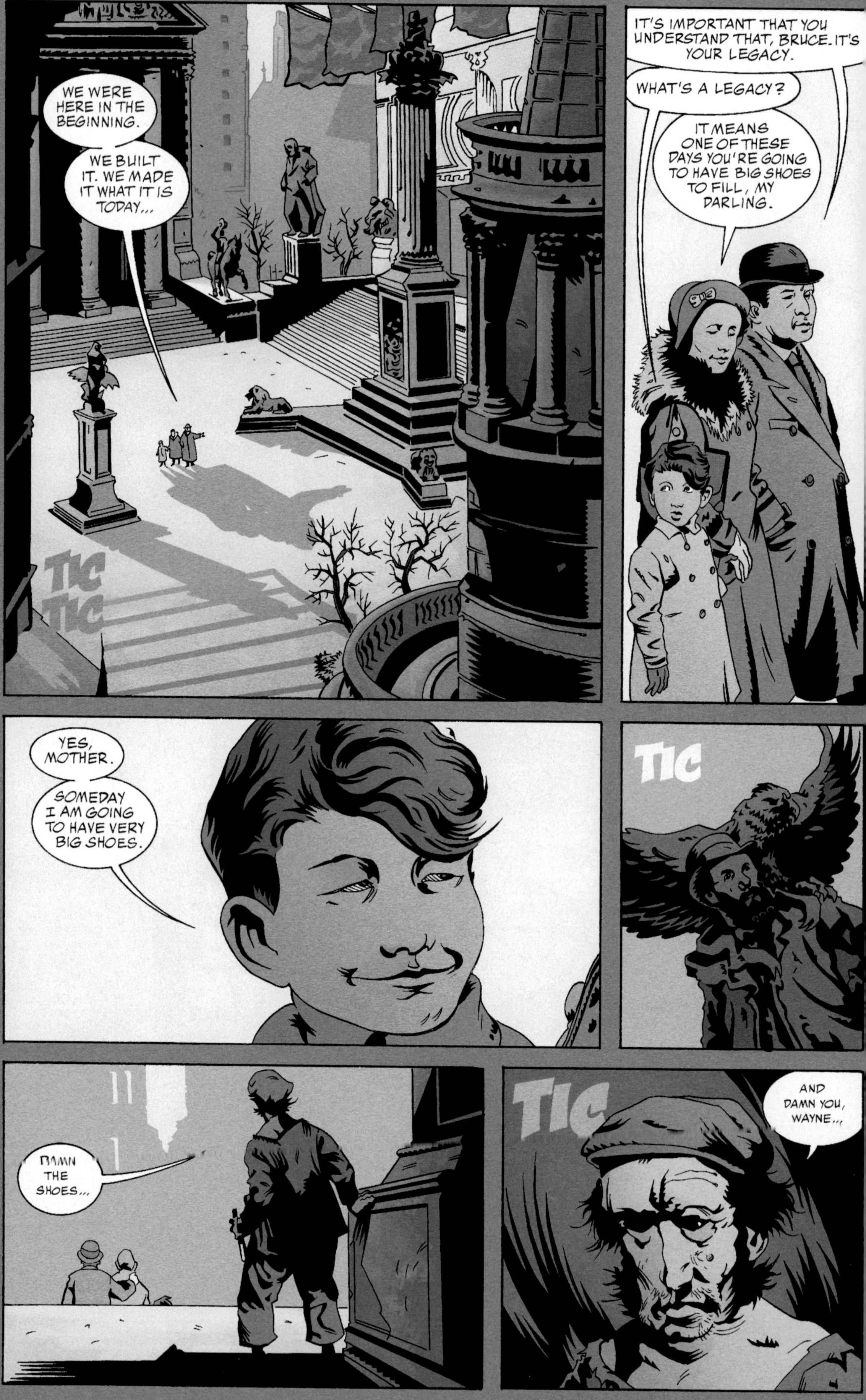
WE WERE HERE IN THE BEGINNING.
WE BUILT IT. WE MADE IT WHAT IT IS TODAY...
TIC
TIC
IT'S IMPORTANT THAT YOU UNDERSTAND THAT, BRUCE. IT'S YOUR LEGACY.
WHAT'S A LEGACY?
IT MEANS ONE OF THESE DAYS YOU'RE GOING TO HAVE BIG SHOES TO FILL, MY DARLING.
YES, MOTHER.
SOMEDAY I AM GOING TO HAVE VERY BIG SHOES.
TIC
DAMN THE SHOES...
TIC
AND DAMN YOU, WAYNE...

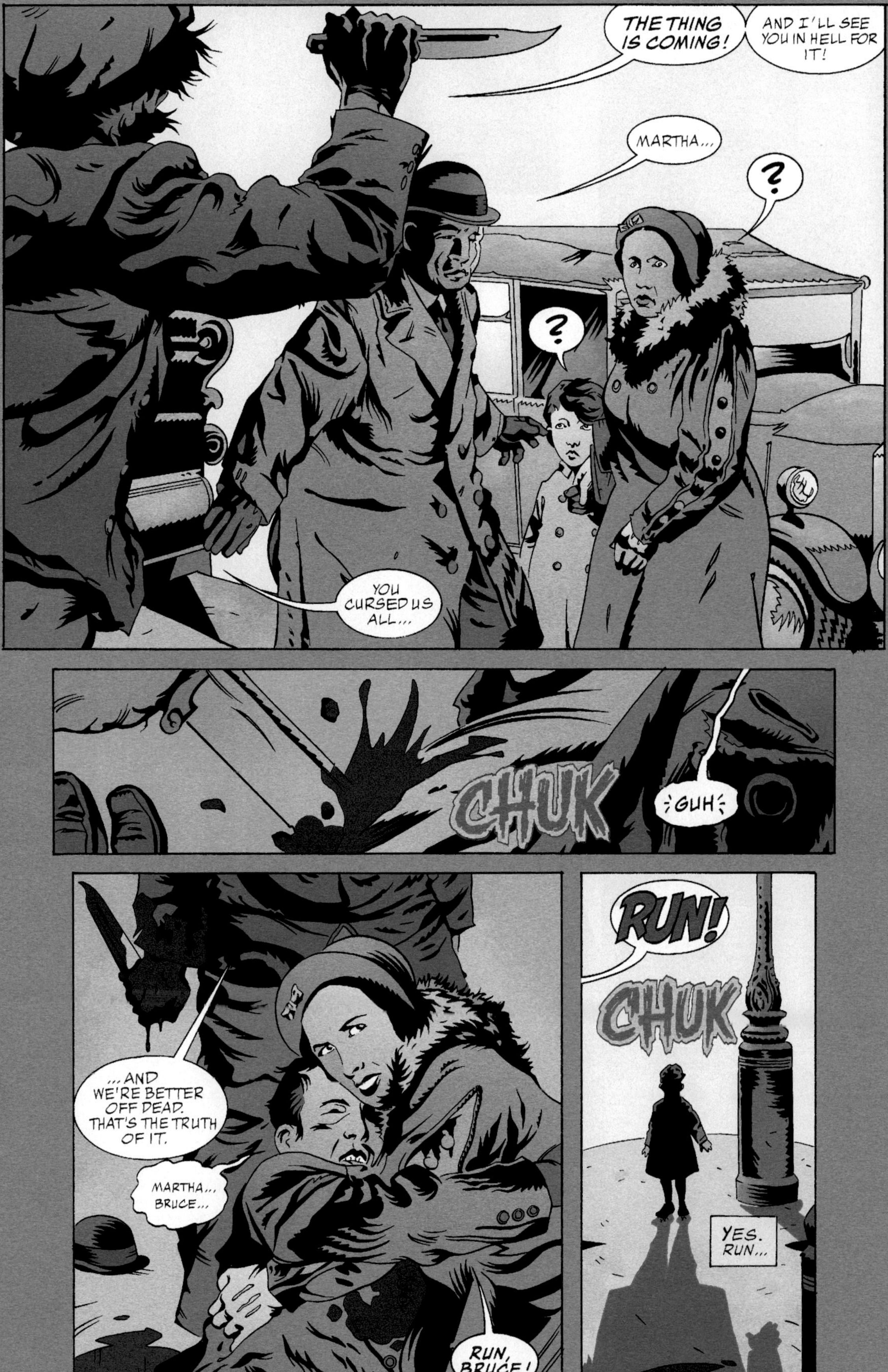
THE THING IS COMING!
AND I'LL SEE YOU IN HELL FOR IT!
MARTHA...
?
?
YOU CURSED US ALL...
CHUK
GUH
...AND WE'RE BETTER OFF DEAD. THAT'S THE TRUTH OF IT.
MARTHA... BRUCE...
RUN, BRUCE!
RUN!
CHUK
YES. RUN...

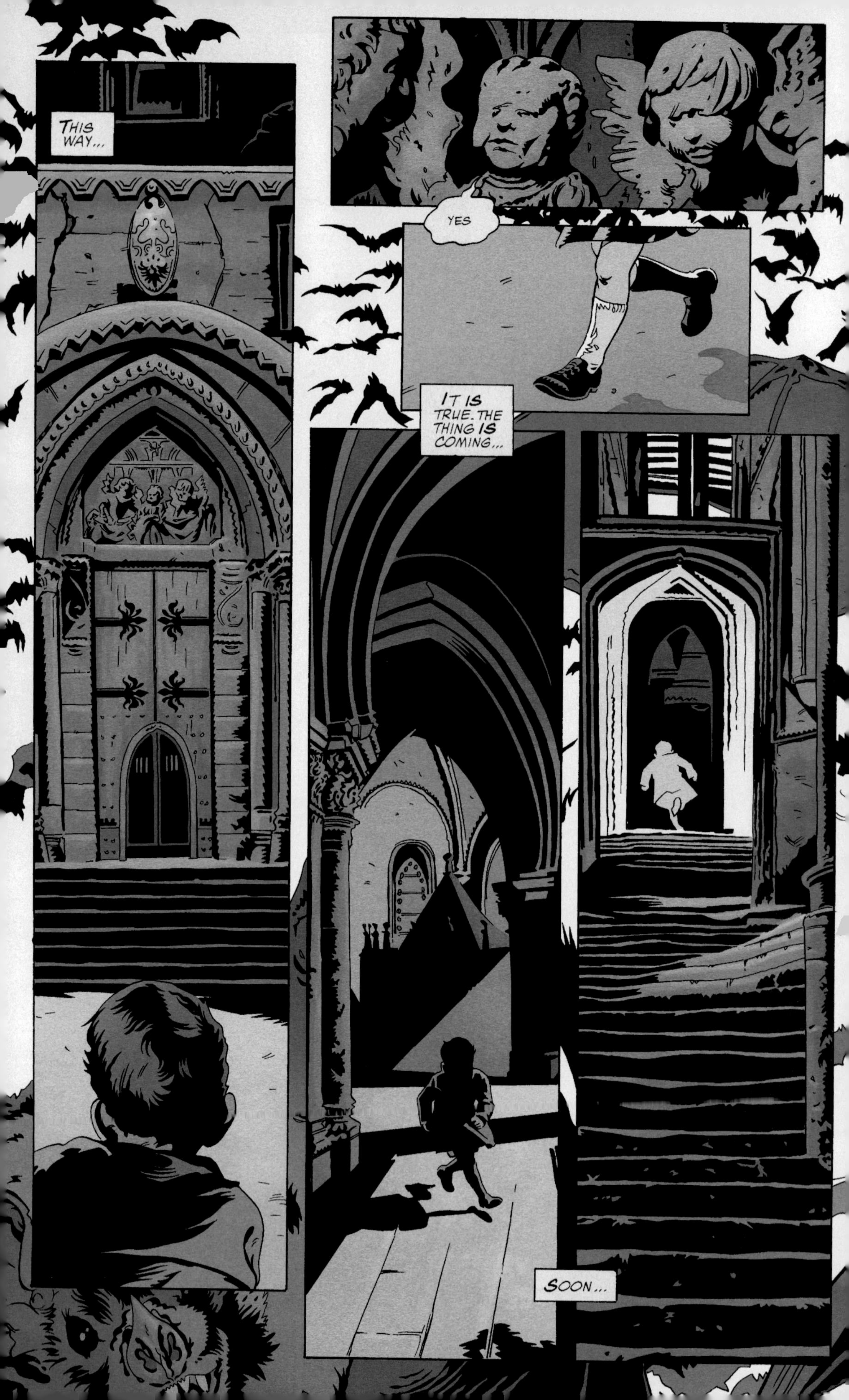
THIS WAY...
YES
IT IS TRUE. THE THING IS COMING...
SOON...

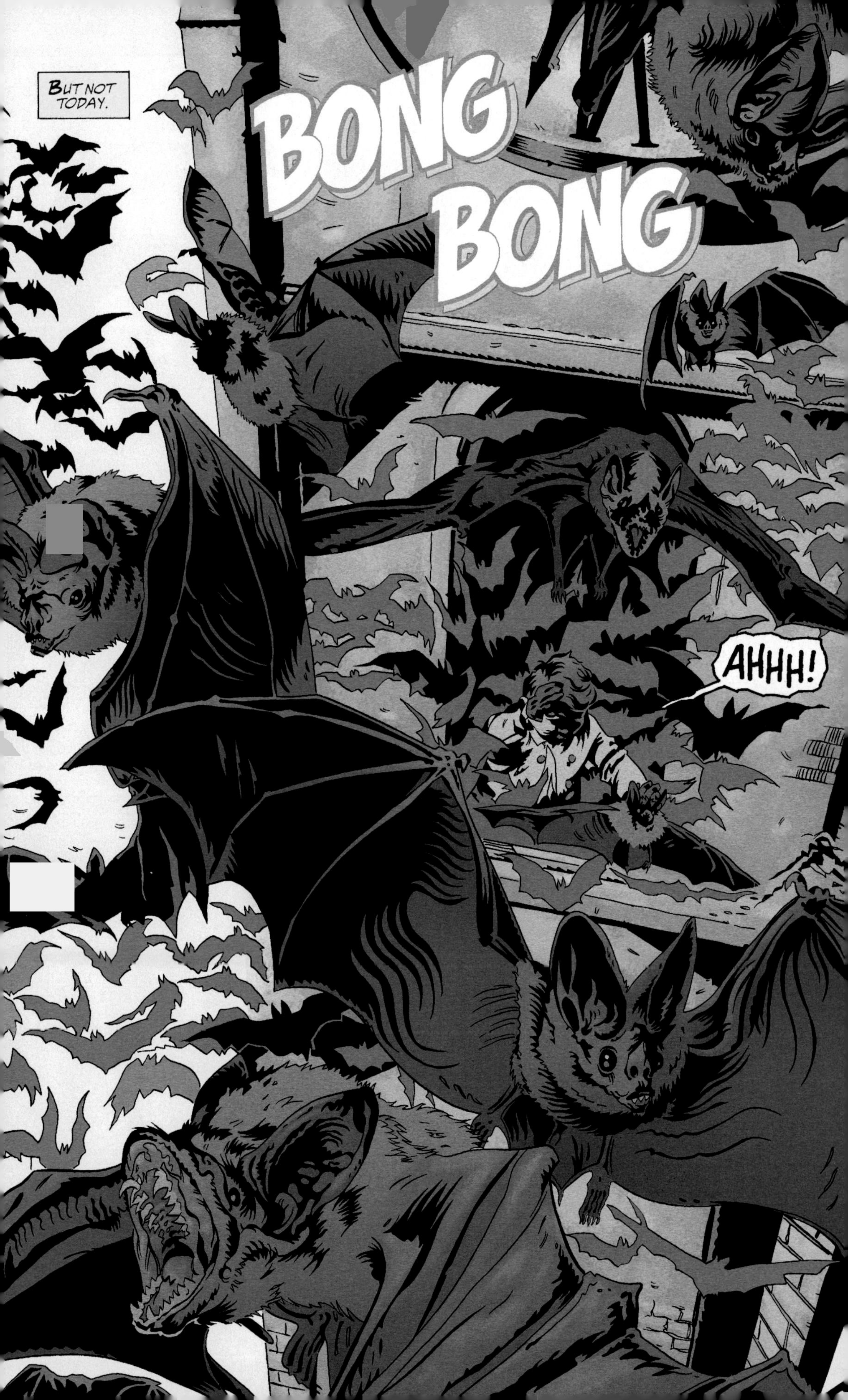
BUT NOT TODAY.
BONG
BONG
AHHH!

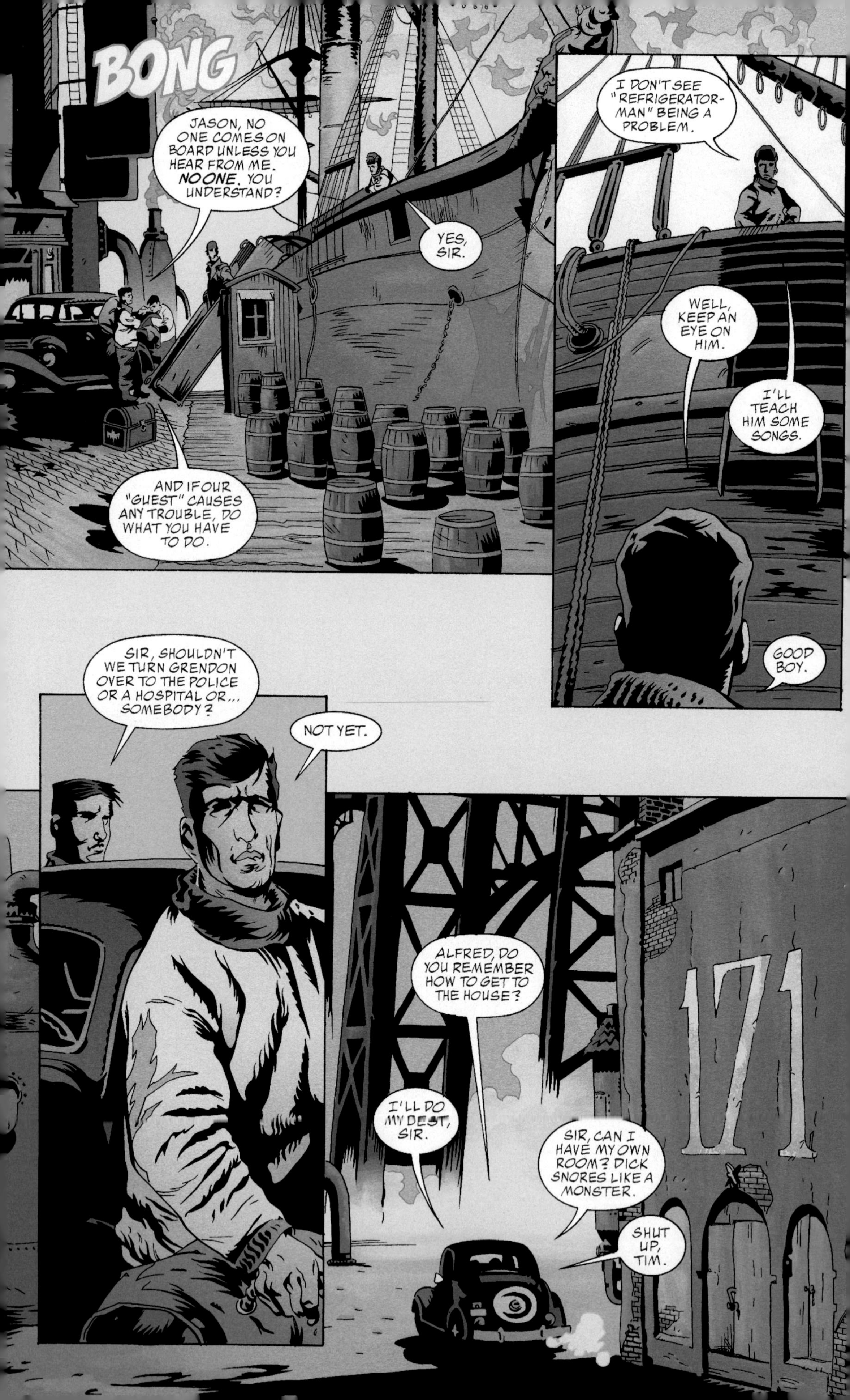
BONG
JASON, NO ONE COMES ON BOARD UNLESS YOU HEAR FROM ME. NO ONE. YOU UNDERSTAND?
YES, SIR.
AND IF OUR "GUEST" CAUSES ANY TROUBLE, DO WHAT YOU HAVE TO DO.
I DON'T SEE "REFRIGERATOR-MAN" BEING A PROBLEM.
WELL, KEEP AN EYE ON HIM.
I'LL TEACH HIM SOME SONGS.
GOOD BOY.
SIR, SHOULDN'T WE TURN GRENDON OVER TO THE POLICE OR A HOSPITAL OR... SOMEBODY?
NOT YET.
ALFRED, DO YOU REMEMBER HOW TO GET TO THE HOUSE?
I'LL DO MY BEST, SIR.
171
SIR, CAN I HAVE MY OWN ROOM? DICK SNORES LIKE A MONSTER.
SHUT UP, TIM.

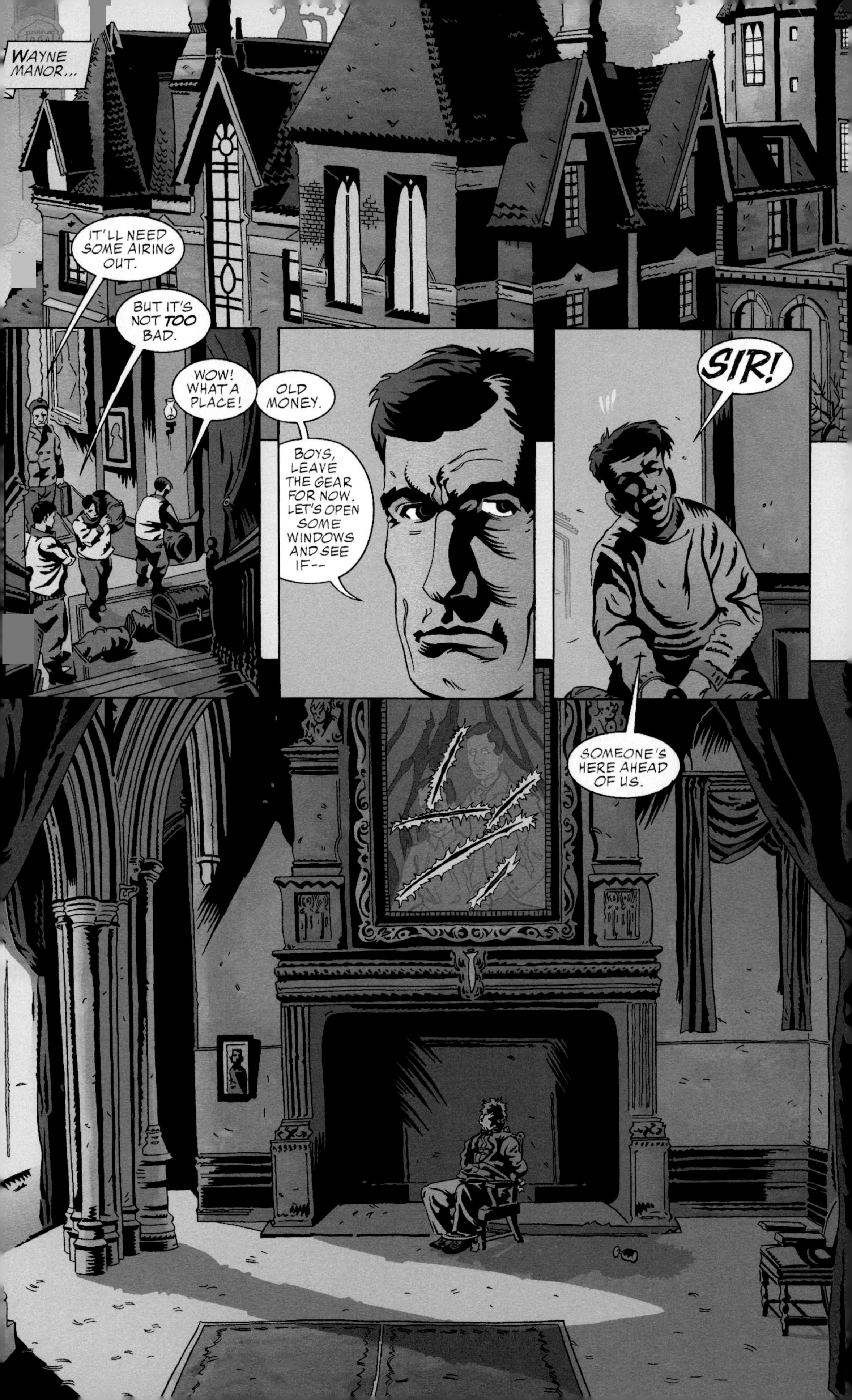
WAYNE MANOR...
IT'LL NEED SOME AIRING OUT.
BUT IT'S NOT TOO BAD.
WOW! WHAT A PLACE!
OLD MONEY.
BOYS, LEAVE THE GEAR FOR NOW. LET'S OPEN SOME WINDOWS AND SEE IF--
SIR!
SOMEONE'S HERE AHEAD OF US.

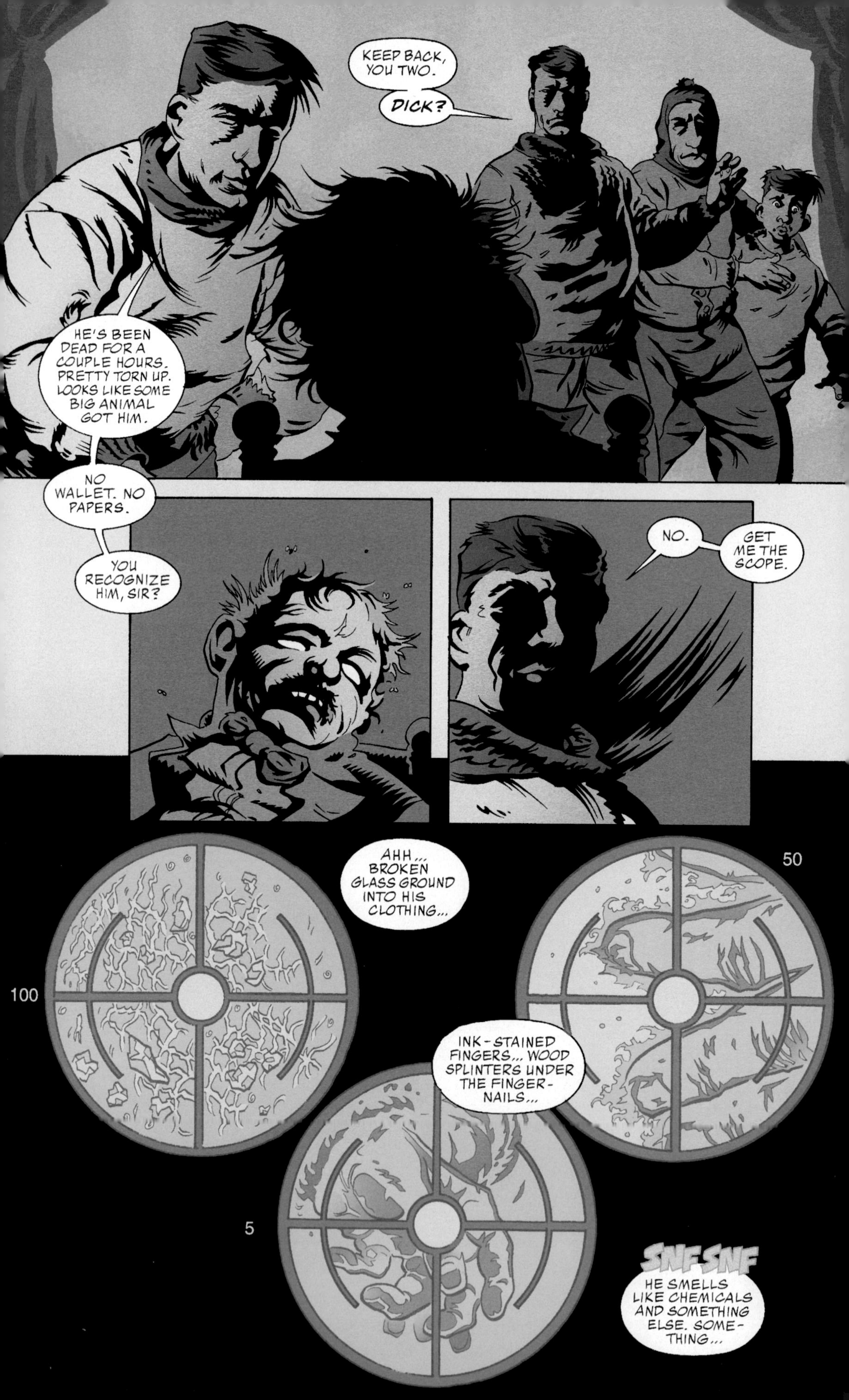
KEEP BACK, YOU TWO.
DICK?
HE'S BEEN DEAD FOR A COUPLE HOURS. PRETTY TORN UP. LOOKS LIKE SOME BIG ANIMAL GOT HIM.
NO WALLET. NO PAPERS.
YOU RECOGNIZE HIM, SIR?
NO.
GET ME THE SCOPE.
AHH... BROKEN GLASS GROUND INTO HIS CLOTHING...
50
100
INK-STAINED FINGERS... WOOD SPLINTERS UNDER THE FINGER-NAILS...
5
SNF SNF
HE SMELLS LIKE CHEMICALS AND SOMETHING ELSE. SOME-THING...

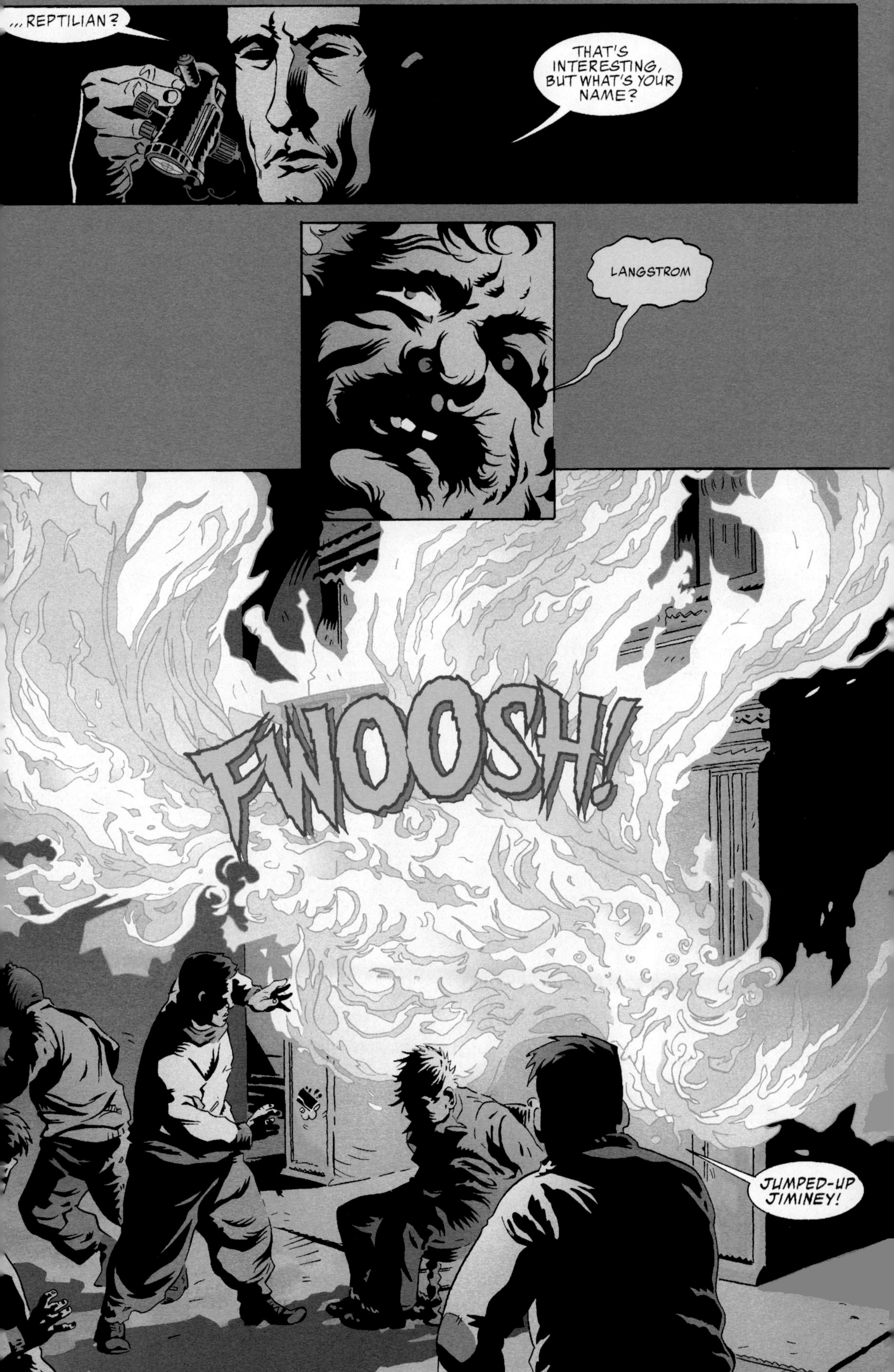
...REPTILIAN?
THAT'S INTERESTING, BUT WHAT'S YOUR NAME?
LANGSTROM
FWOOSH!
JUMPED-UP JIMINEY!

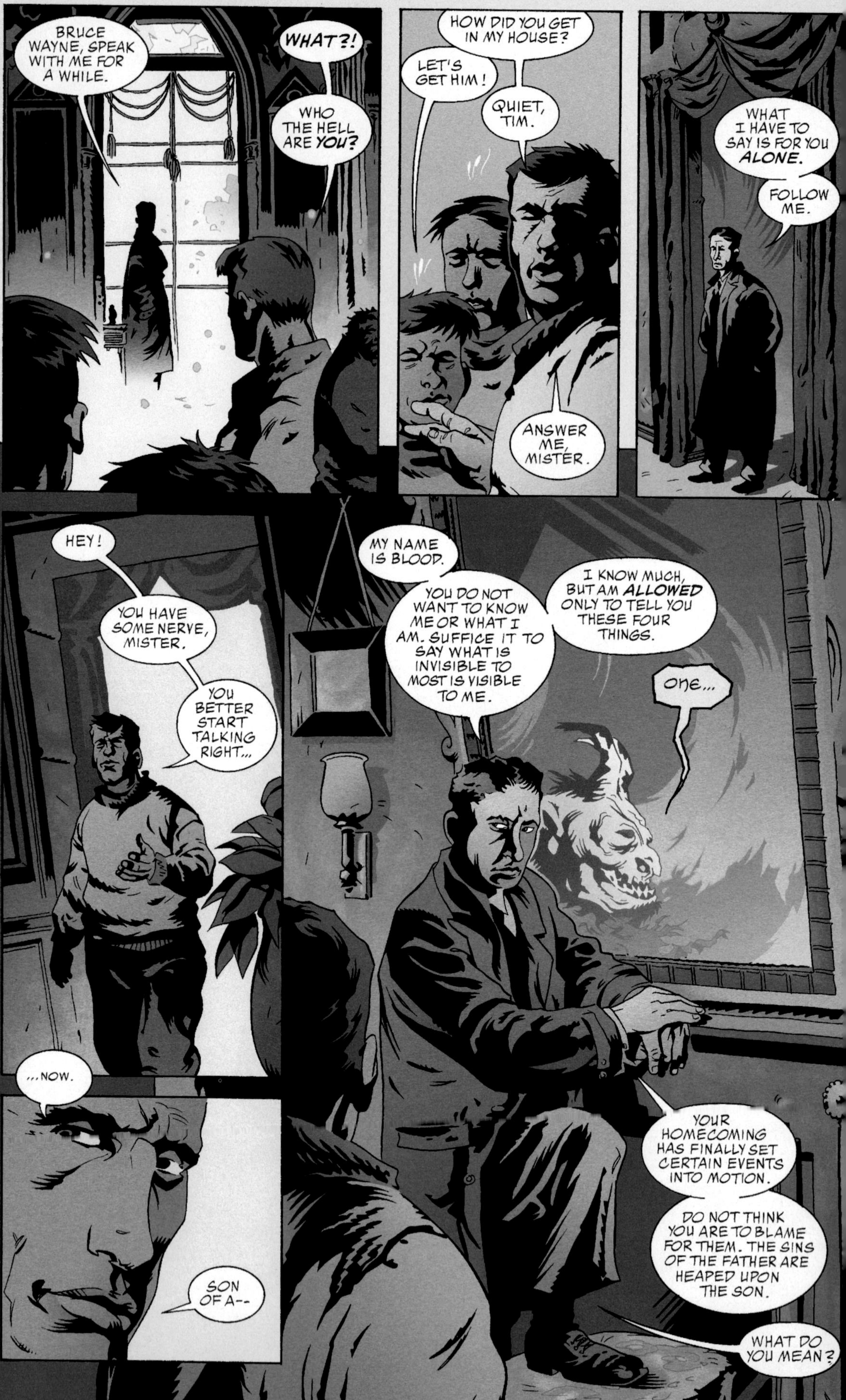
BRUCE WAYNE, SPEAK WITH ME FOR A WHILE.
WHAT?!
WHO THE HELL ARE YOU?
HOW DID YOU GET IN MY HOUSE?
LET'S GET HIM!
QUIET, TIM.
ANSWER ME, MISTER.
WHAT I HAVE TO SAY IS FOR YOU ALONE.
FOLLOW ME.
HEY!
YOU HAVE SOME NERVE, MISTER.
YOU BETTER START TALKING RIGHT...
...NOW.
SON OF A--
MY NAME IS BLOOD.
YOU DO NOT WANT TO KNOW ME OR WHAT I AM. SUFFICE IT TO SAY WHAT IS INVISIBLE TO MOST IS VISIBLE TO ME.
I KNOW MUCH, BUT AM ALLOWED ONLY TO TELL YOU THESE FOUR THINGS.
ONE...
YOUR HOMECOMING HAS FINALLY SET CERTAIN EVENTS INTO MOTION.
DO NOT THINK YOU ARE TO BLAME FOR THEM. THE SINS OF THE FATHER ARE HEAPED UPON THE SON.
WHAT DO YOU MEAN?

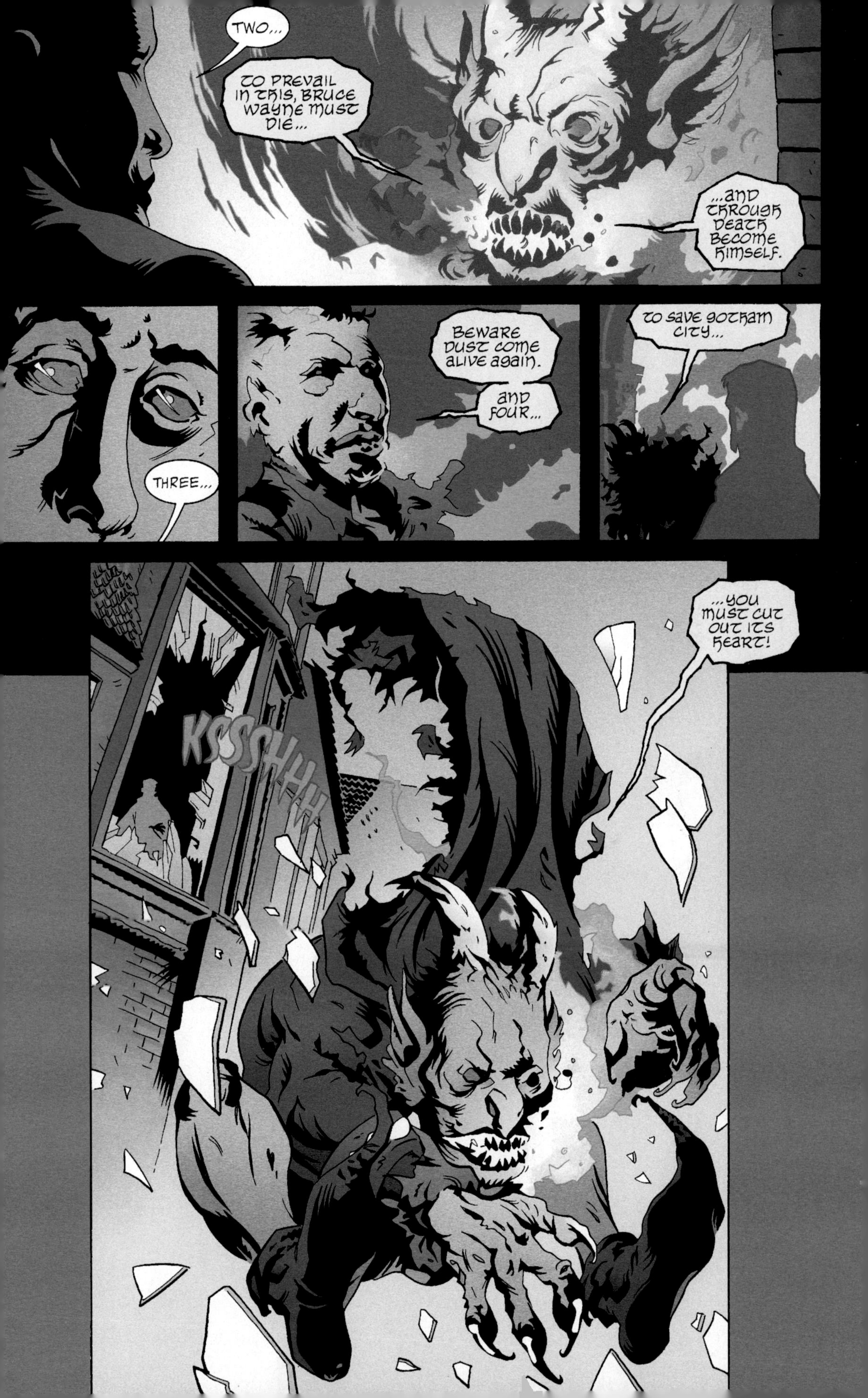
TWO,...
TO PREVAIL IN THIS, BRUCE WAYNE MUST DIE...
...AND THROUGH DEATH BECOME HIMSELF.
THREE...
BEWARE DUST COME ALIVE AGAIN.
AND FOUR...
TO SAVE GOTHAM CITY...
KSSSHHH
...YOU MUST CUT OUT ITS HEART!

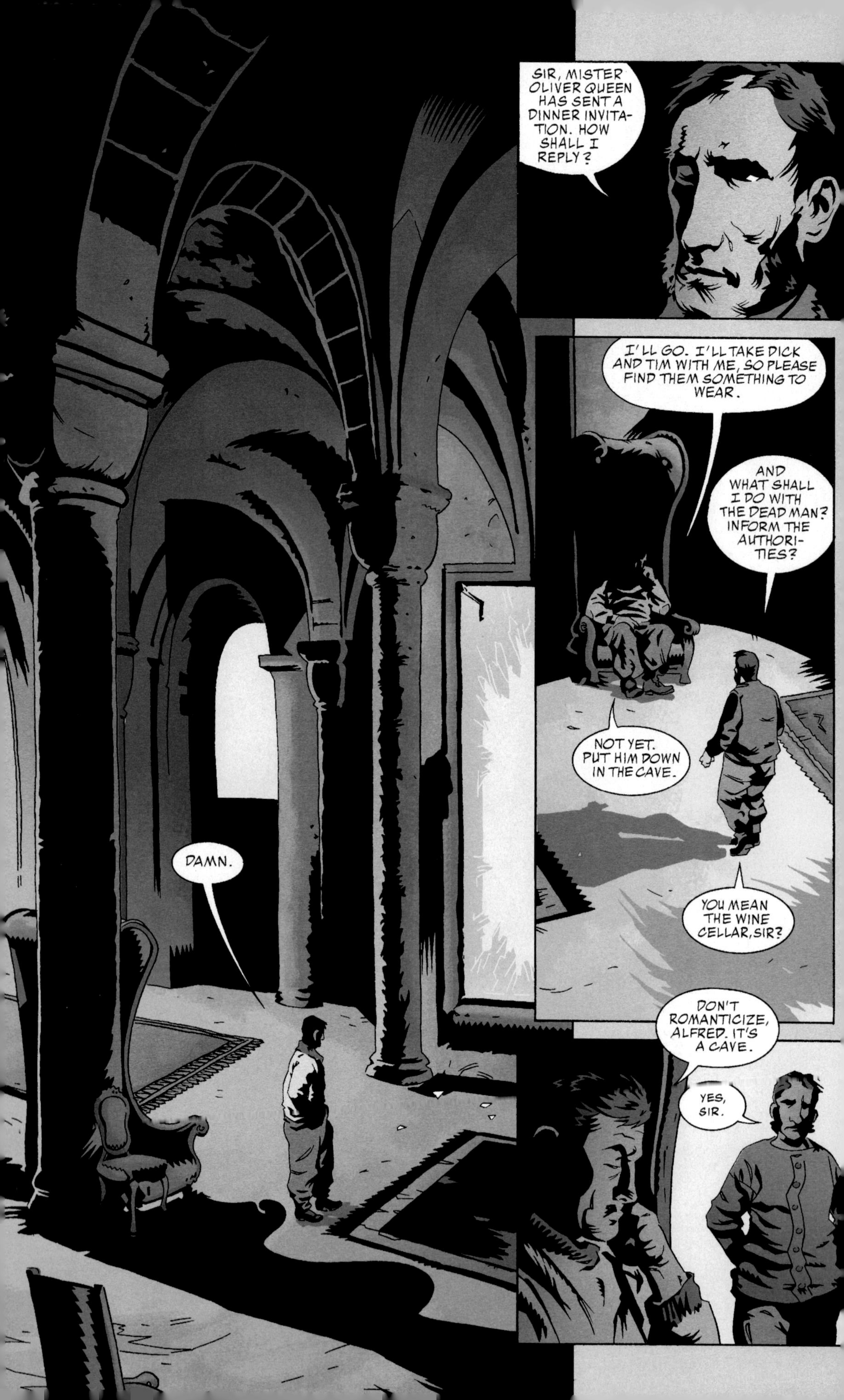
SIR, MISTER OLIVER QUEEN HAS SENT A DINNER INVITATION. HOW SHALL I REPLY?
I'LL GO. I'LL TAKE DICK AND TIM WITH ME, SO PLEASE FIND THEM SOMETHING TO WEAR.
AND WHAT SHALL I DO WITH THE DEAD MAN? INFORM THE AUTHORITIES?
NOT YET. PUT HIM DOWN IN THE CAVE.
YOU MEAN THE WINE CELLAR, SIR?
DON'T ROMANTICIZE, ALFRED. IT'S A CAVE.
YES, SIR.
DAMN.

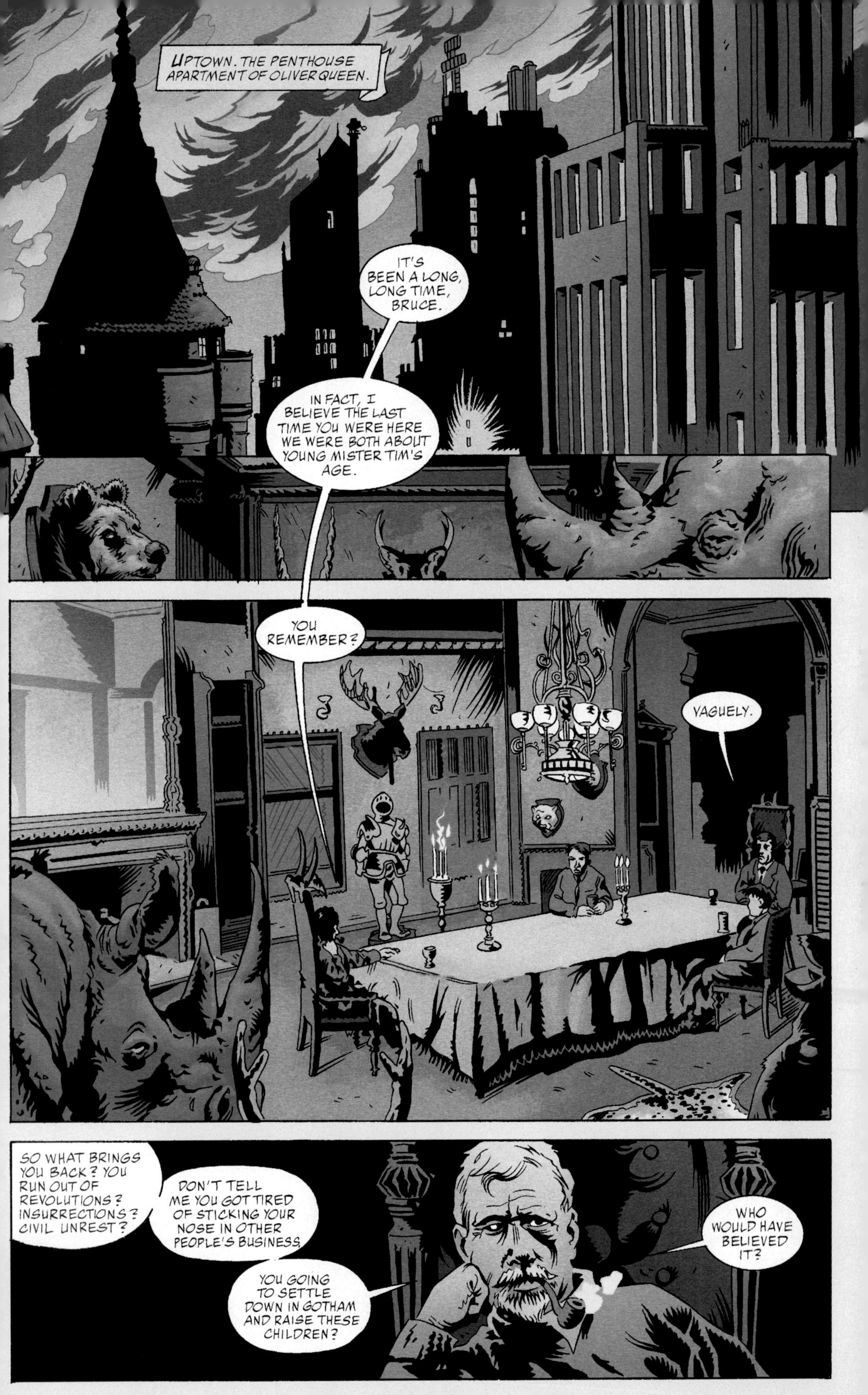
UPTOWN. THE PENTHOUSE APARTMENT OF OLIVER QUEEN.
IT'S BEEN A LONG, LONG TIME, BRUCE.
IN FACT, I BELIEVE THE LAST TIME YOU WERE HERE WE WERE BOTH ABOUT YOUNG MISTER TIM'S AGE.
YOU REMEMBER?
VAGUELY.
SO WHAT BRINGS YOU BACK? YOU RUN OUT OF REVOLUTIONS? INSURRECTIONS? CIVIL UNREST?
DON'T TELL ME YOU GOT TIRED OF STICKING YOUR NOSE IN OTHER PEOPLE'S BUSINESS.
YOU GOING TO SETTLE DOWN IN GOTHAM AND RAISE THESE CHILDREN?
WHO WOULD HAVE BELIEVED IT?

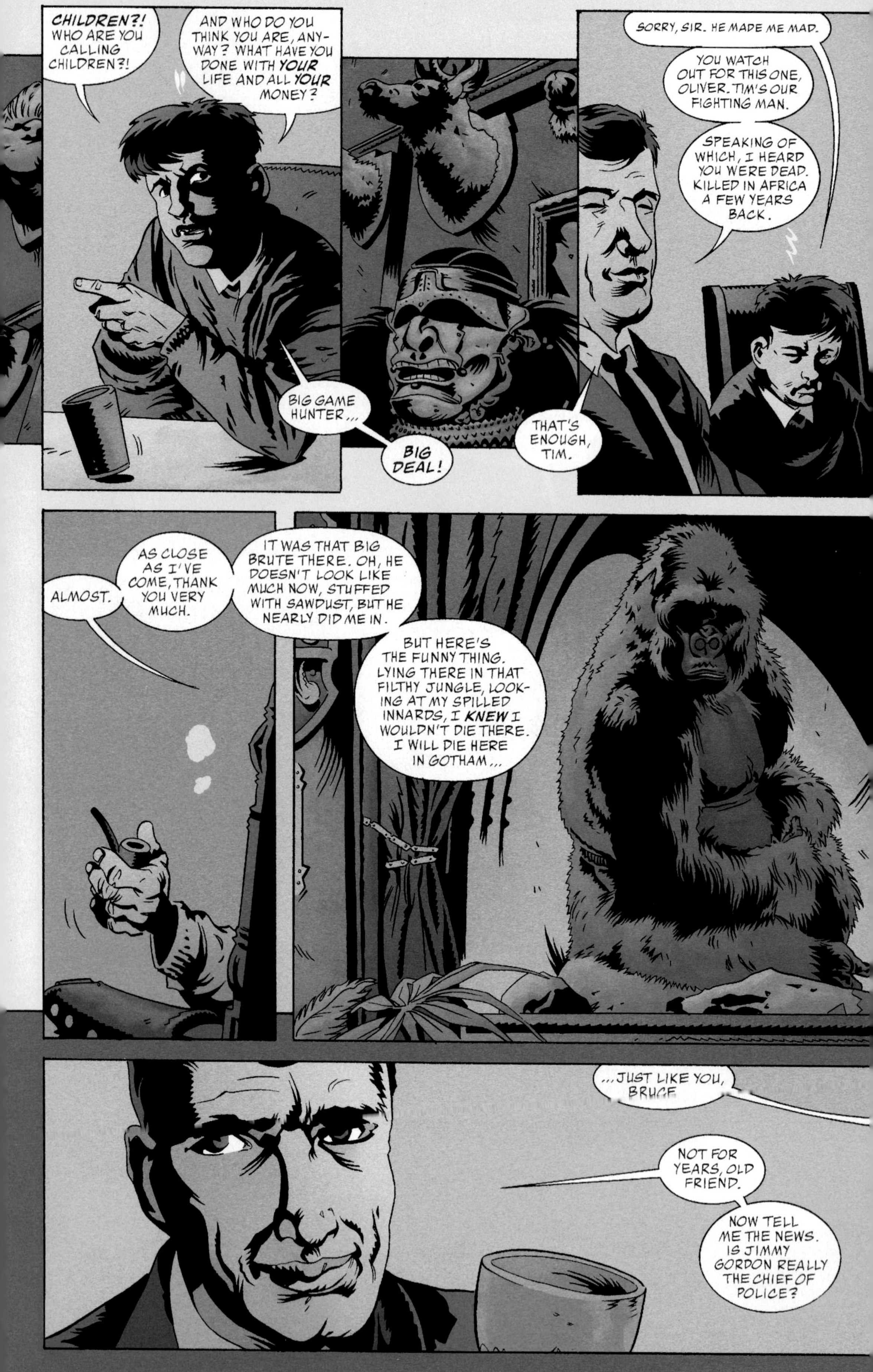
CHILDREN?! WHO ARE YOU CALLING CHILDREN?!
AND WHO DO YOU THINK YOU ARE, ANYWAY? WHAT HAVE YOU DONE WITH YOUR LIFE AND ALL YOUR MONEY?
BIG GAME HUNTER...
BIG DEAL!
THAT'S ENOUGH, TIM.
SORRY, SIR. HE MADE ME MAD.
YOU WATCH OUT FOR THIS ONE, OLIVER. TIM'S OUR FIGHTING MAN.
SPEAKING OF WHICH, I HEARD YOU WERE DEAD. KILLED IN AFRICA A FEW YEARS BACK.
ALMOST.
AS CLOSE AS I'VE COME, THANK YOU VERY MUCH.
IT WAS THAT BIG BRUTE THERE. OH, HE DOESN'T LOOK LIKE MUCH NOW, STUFFED WITH SAWDUST, BUT HE NEARLY DID ME IN.
BUT HERE'S THE FUNNY THING. LYING THERE IN THAT FILTHY JUNGLE, LOOKING AT MY SPILLED INNARDS, I KNEW I WOULDN'T DIE THERE. I WILL DIE HERE IN GOTHAM...
...JUST LIKE YOU, BRUCE.
NOT FOR YEARS, OLD FRIEND.
NOW TELL ME THE NEWS. IS JIMMY GORDON REALLY THE CHIEF OF POLICE?

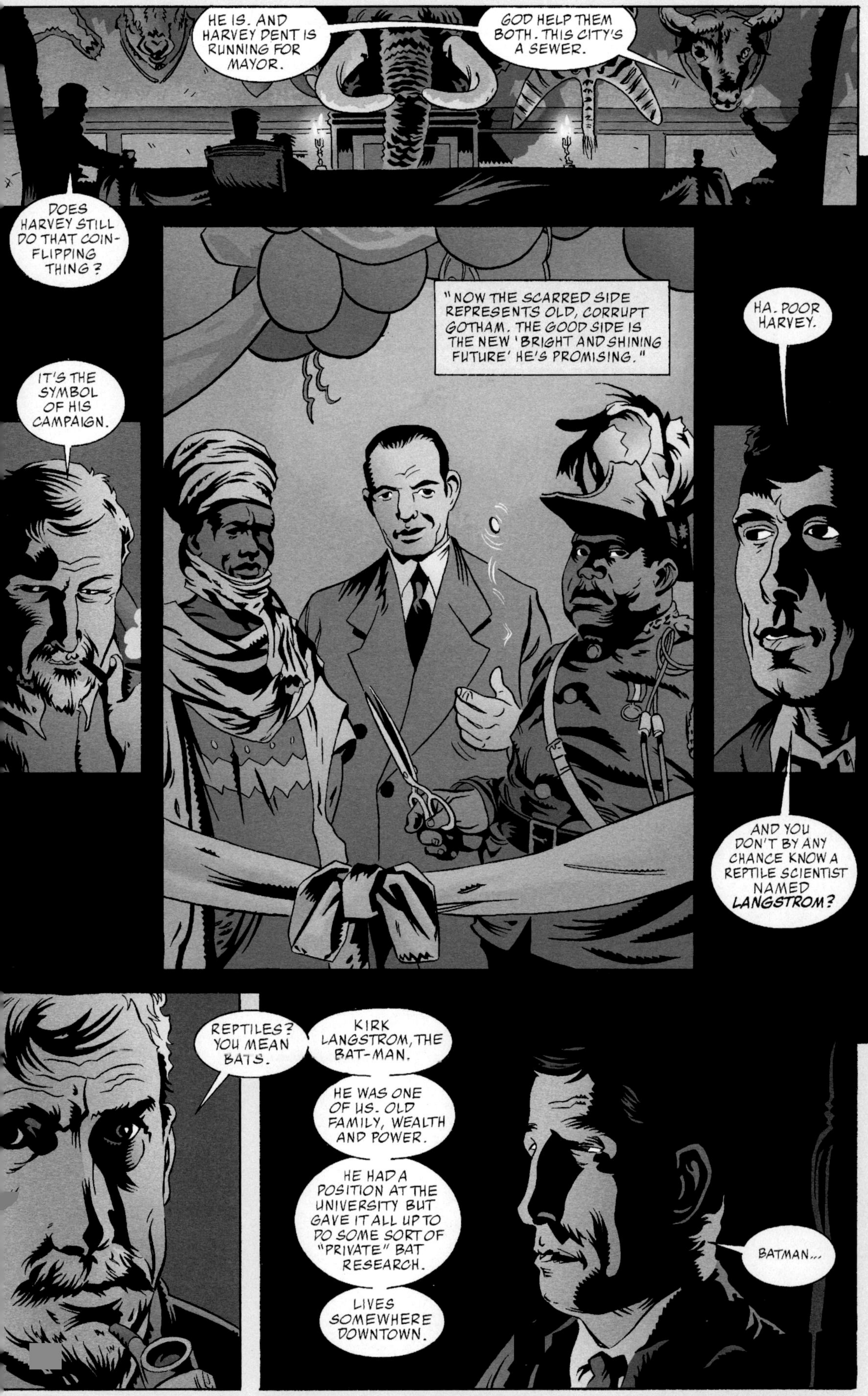
HE IS. AND HARVEY DENT IS RUNNING FOR MAYOR.
GOD HELP THEM BOTH. THIS CITY'S A SEWER.
DOES HARVEY STILL DO THAT COIN-FLIPPING THING?
"NOW THE SCARRED SIDE REPRESENTS OLD, CORRUPT GOTHAM. THE GOOD SIDE IS THE NEW 'BRIGHT AND SHINING FUTURE' HE'S PROMISING."
HA. POOR HARVEY.
IT'S THE SYMBOL OF HIS CAMPAIGN.
AND YOU DON'T BY ANY CHANCE KNOW A REPTILE SCIENTIST NAMED LANGSTROM?
REPTILES? YOU MEAN BATS.
KIRK LANGSTROM, THE BAT-MAN.
HE WAS ONE OF US. OLD FAMILY, WEALTH AND POWER.
HE HAD A POSITION AT THE UNIVERSITY BUT GAVE IT ALL UP TO DO SOME SORT OF "PRIVATE" BAT RESEARCH.
LIVES SOMEWHERE DOWNTOWN.
BATMAN...

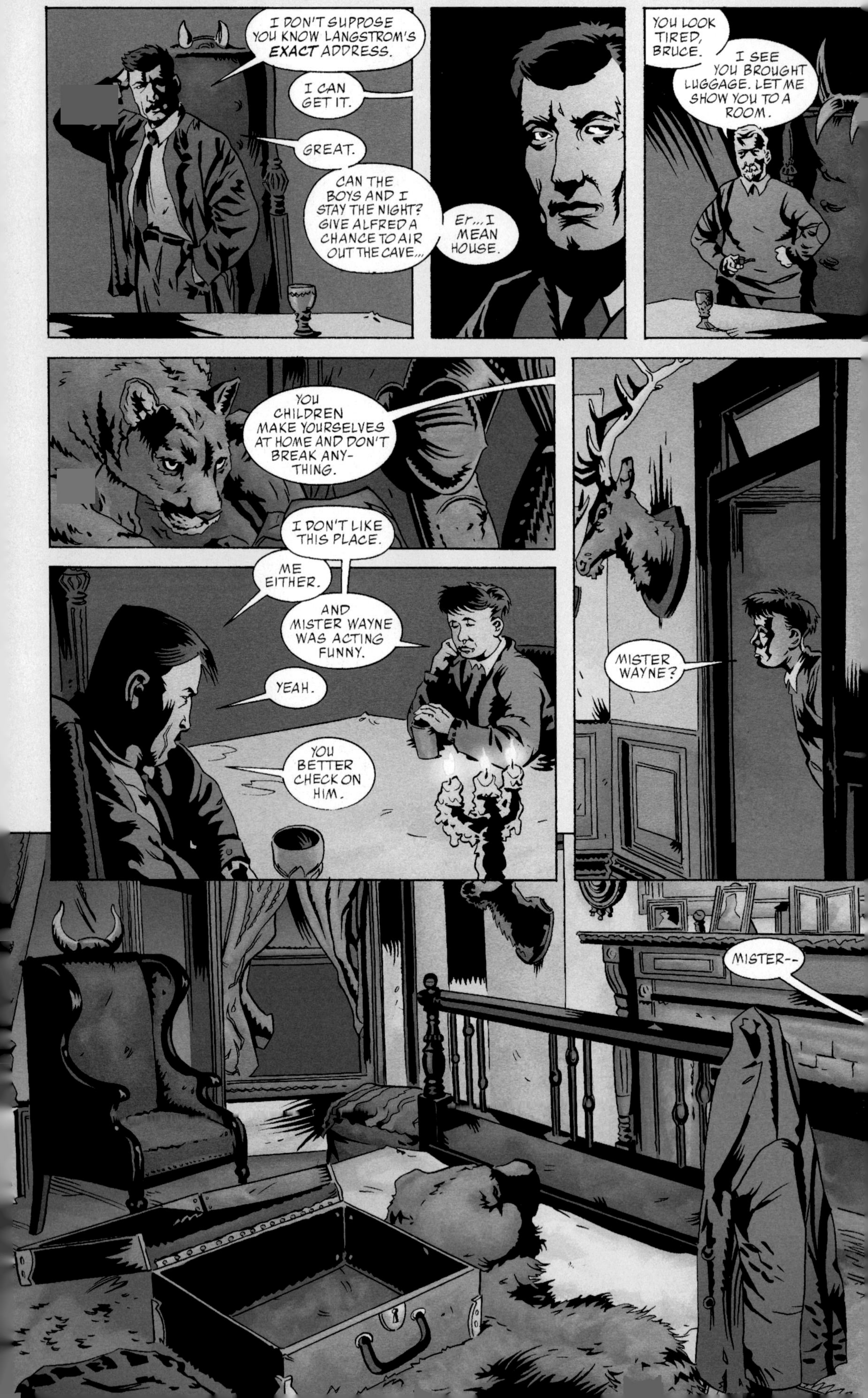
I DON'T SUPPOSE YOU KNOW LANGSTROM'S **EXACT** ADDRESS.
I CAN GET IT.
GREAT.
CAN THE BOYS AND I STAY THE NIGHT? GIVE ALFRED A CHANCE TO AIR OUT THE CAVE...
Er... I MEAN HOUSE.
YOU LOOK TIRED, BRUCE.
I SEE YOU BROUGHT LUGGAGE. LET ME SHOW YOU TO A ROOM.
YOU CHILDREN MAKE YOURSELVES AT HOME AND DON'T BREAK ANY-THING.
I DON'T LIKE THIS PLACE.
ME EITHER.
AND MISTER WAYNE WAS ACTING FUNNY.
YEAH.
YOU BETTER CHECK ON HIM.
MISTER WAYNE?
MISTER--

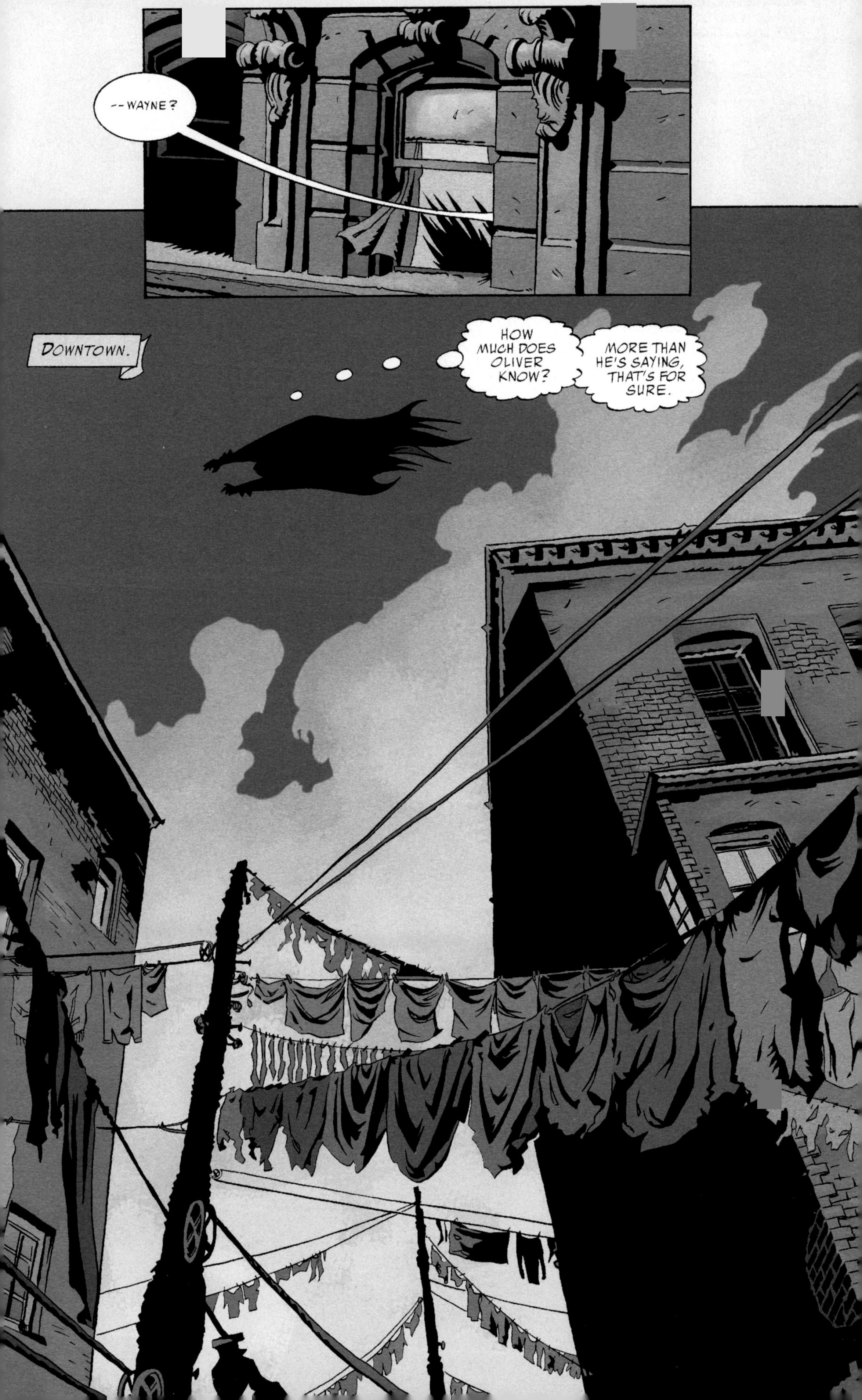
--WAYNE?
DOWNTOWN.
HOW MUCH DOES OLIVER KNOW?
MORE THAN HE'S SAYING, THAT'S FOR SURE.

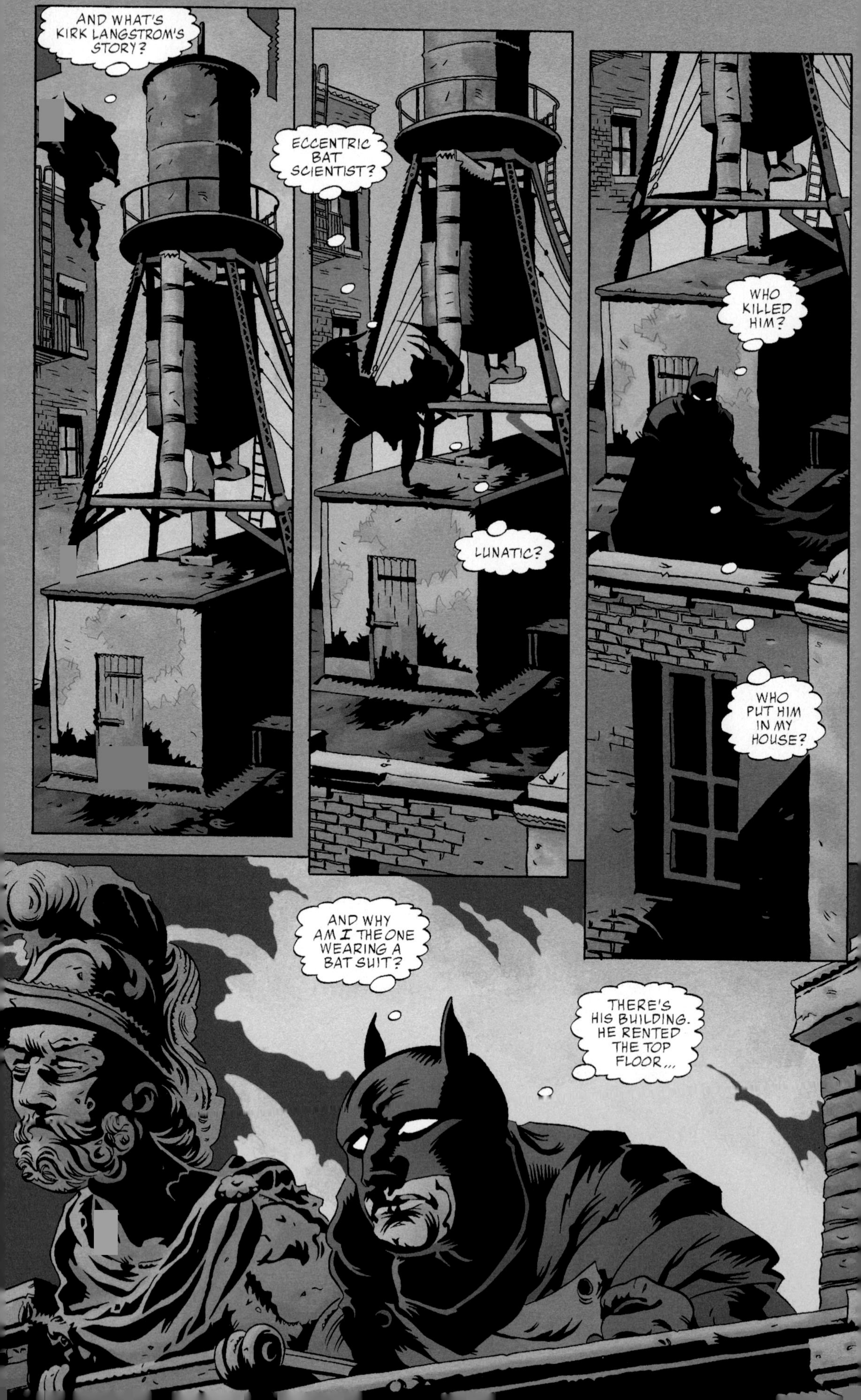
AND WHAT'S KIRK LANGSTROM'S STORY?
ECCENTRIC BAT SCIENTIST?
LUNATIC?
WHO KILLED HIM?
WHO PUT HIM IN MY HOUSE?
AND WHY AM I THE ONE WEARING A BAT SUIT?
THERE'S HIS BUILDING. HE RENTED THE TOP FLOOR...

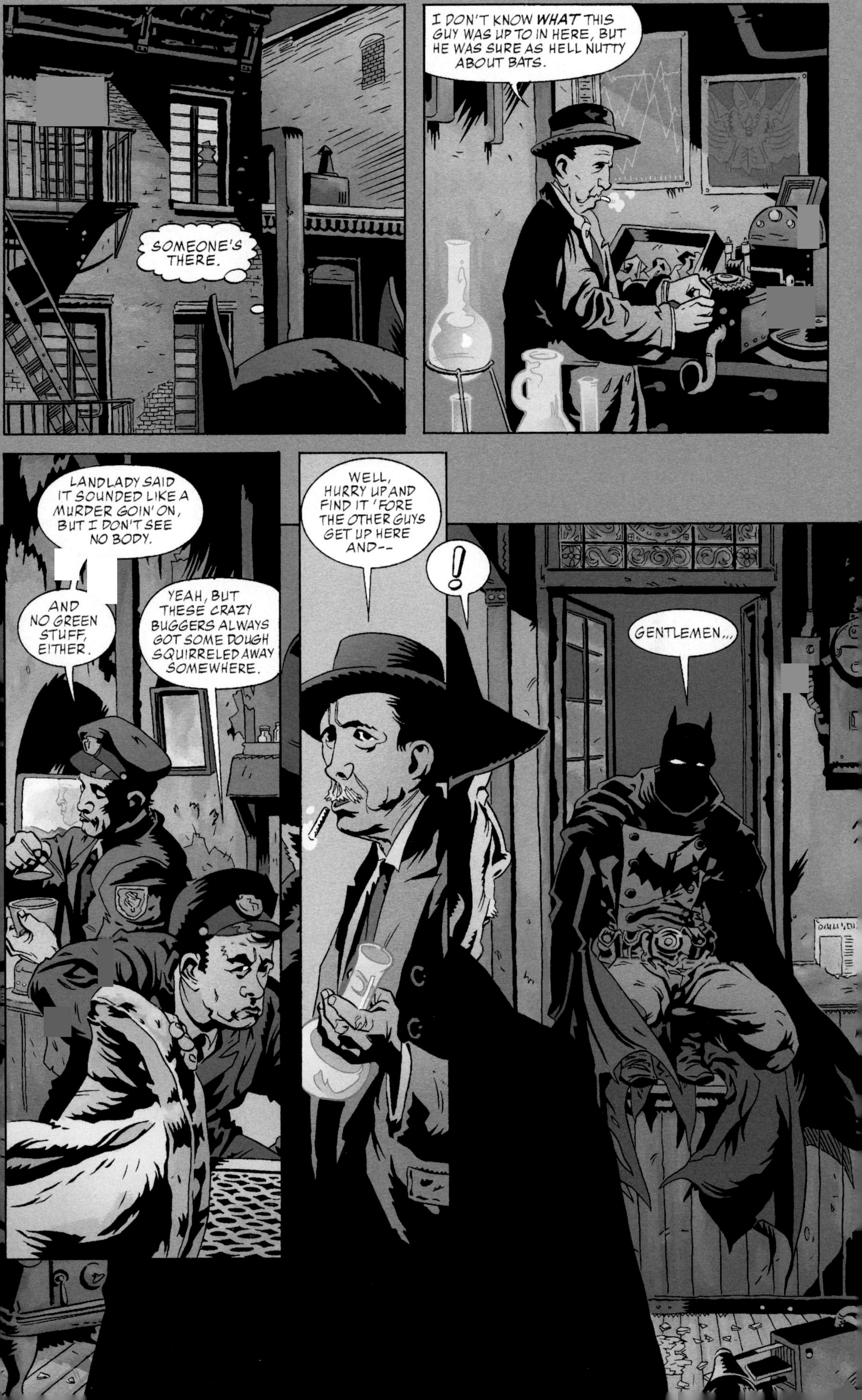
SOMEONE'S THERE.
I DON'T KNOW WHAT THIS GUY WAS UP TO IN HERE, BUT HE WAS SURE AS HELL NUTTY ABOUT BATS.
LANDLADY SAID IT SOUNDED LIKE A MURDER GOIN' ON, BUT I DON'T SEE NO BODY.
AND NO GREEN STUFF, EITHER.
YEAH, BUT THESE CRAZY BUGGERS ALWAYS GOT SOME DOUGH SQUIRRELED AWAY SOMEWHERE.
WELL, HURRY UP AND FIND IT 'FORE THE OTHER GUYS GET UP HERE AND--
!
GENTLEMEN...

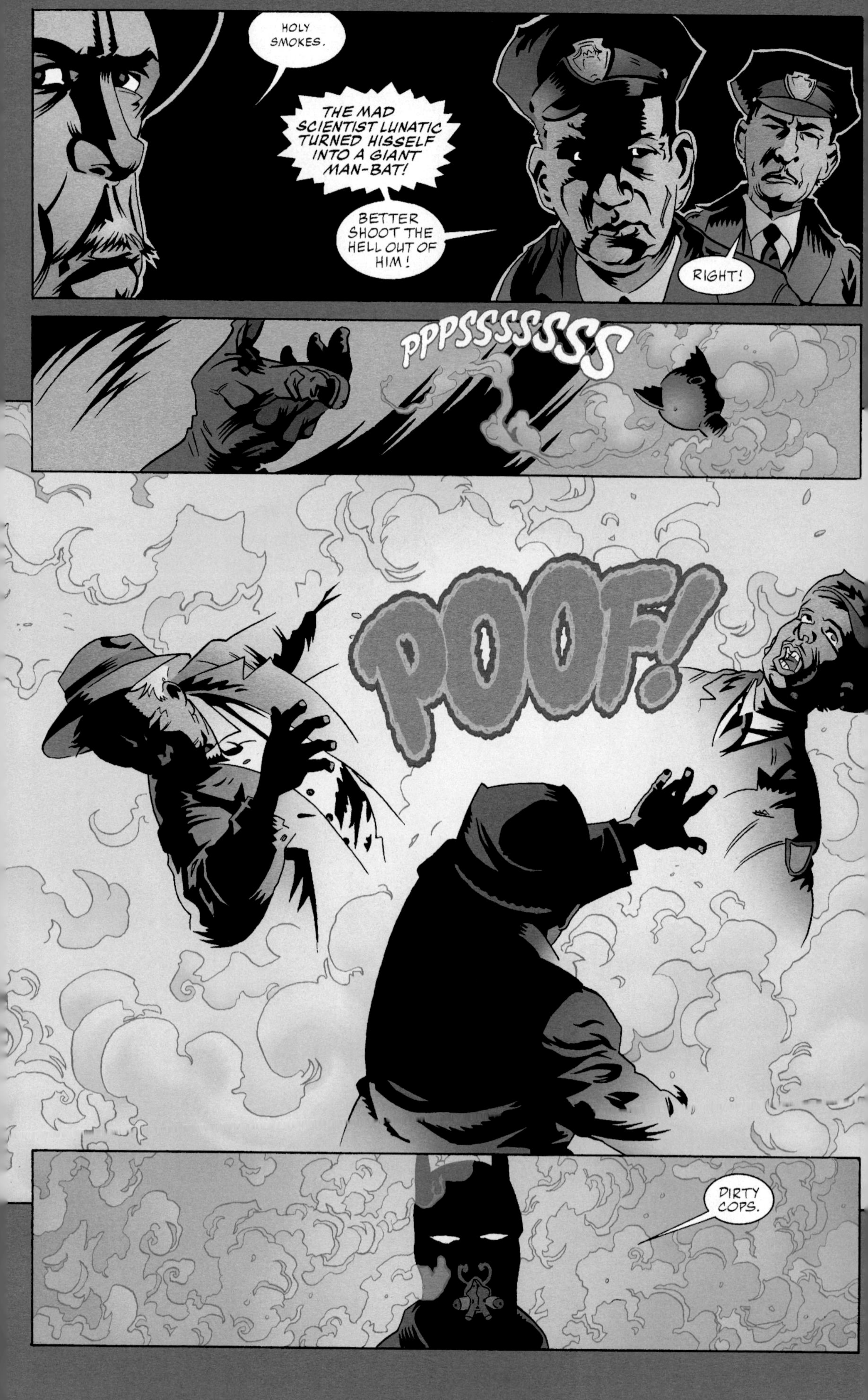
HOLY SMOKES.
THE MAD SCIENTIST LUNATIC TURNED HISSELF INTO A GIANT MAN-BAT!
BETTER SHOOT THE HELL OUT OF HIM!
RIGHT!
PPPSSSSSSSS
POOF!
DIRTY COPS.

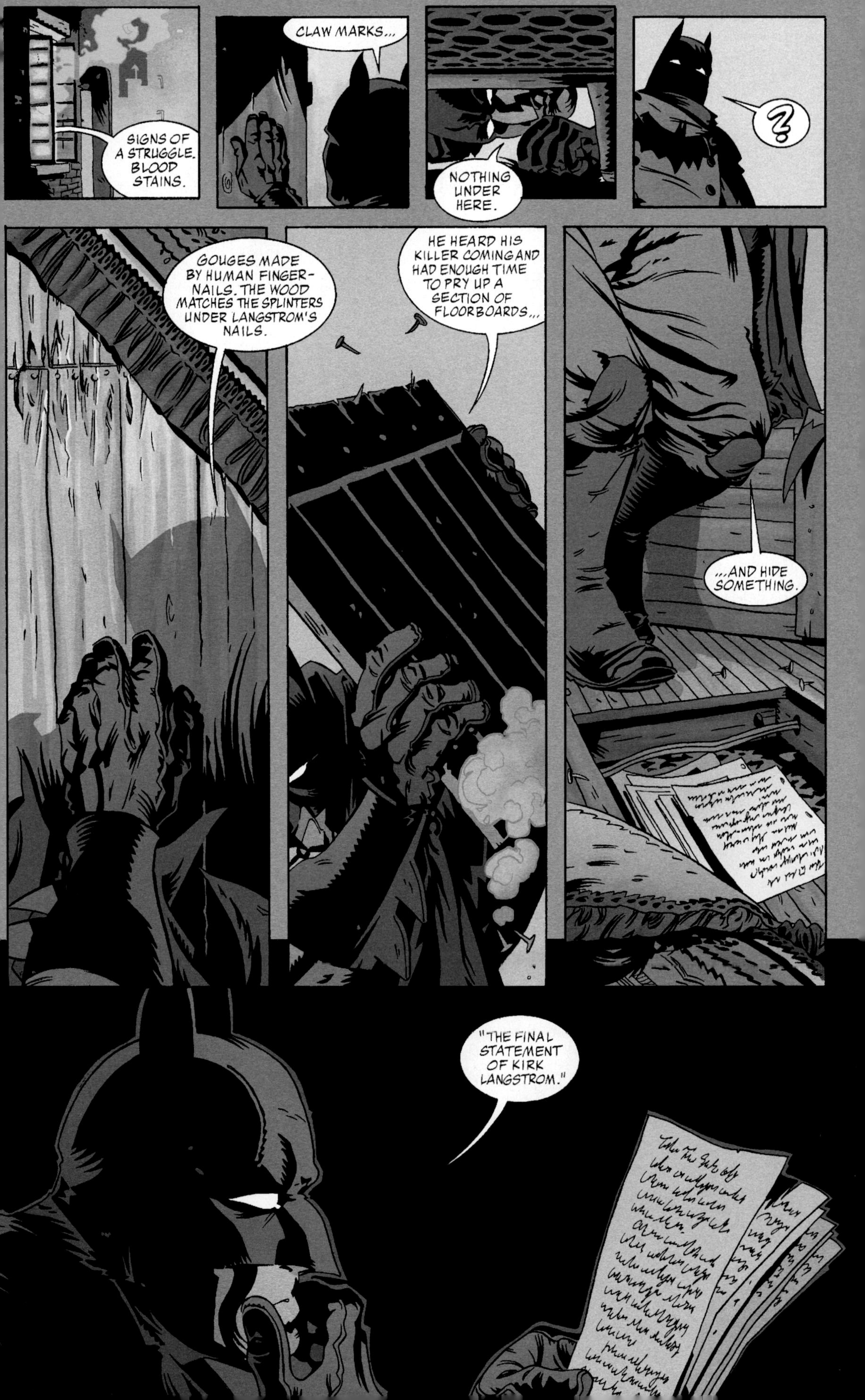
SIGNS OF A STRUGGLE. BLOOD STAINS.
CLAW MARKS...
NOTHING UNDER HERE.
?
GOUGES MADE BY HUMAN FINGER-NAILS. THE WOOD MATCHES THE SPLINTERS UNDER LANGSTROM'S NAILS.
HE HEARD HIS KILLER COMING AND HAD ENOUGH TIME TO PRY UP A SECTION OF FLOORBOARDS...
...AND HIDE SOMETHING.
"THE FINAL STATEMENT OF KIRK LANGSTROM."

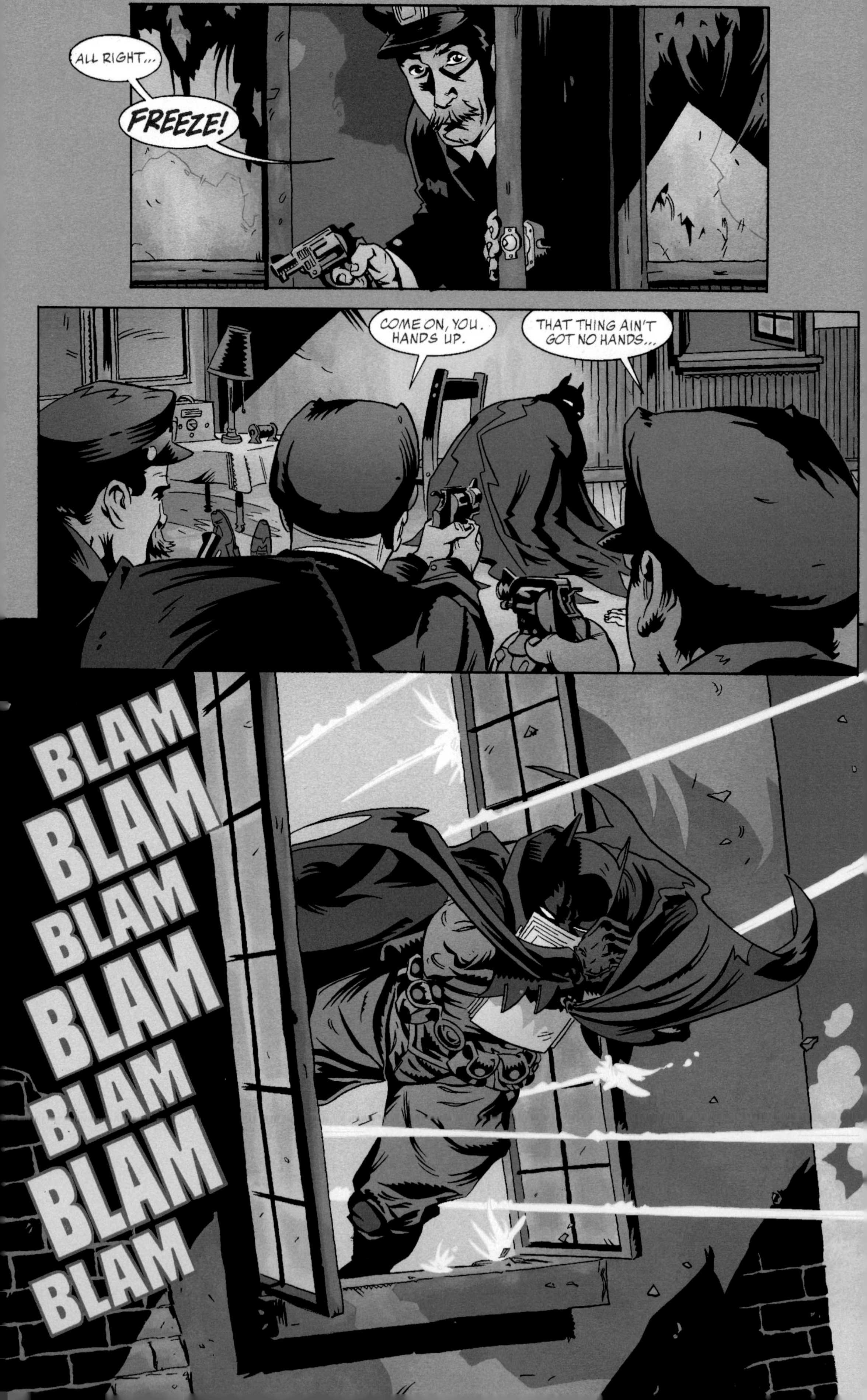
ALL RIGHT...
FREEZE!
COME ON, YOU. HANDS UP.
THAT THING AIN'T GOT NO HANDS...
BLAM
BLAM
BLAM
BLAM
BLAM
BLAM
BLAM
BLAM
BLAM
BLAM

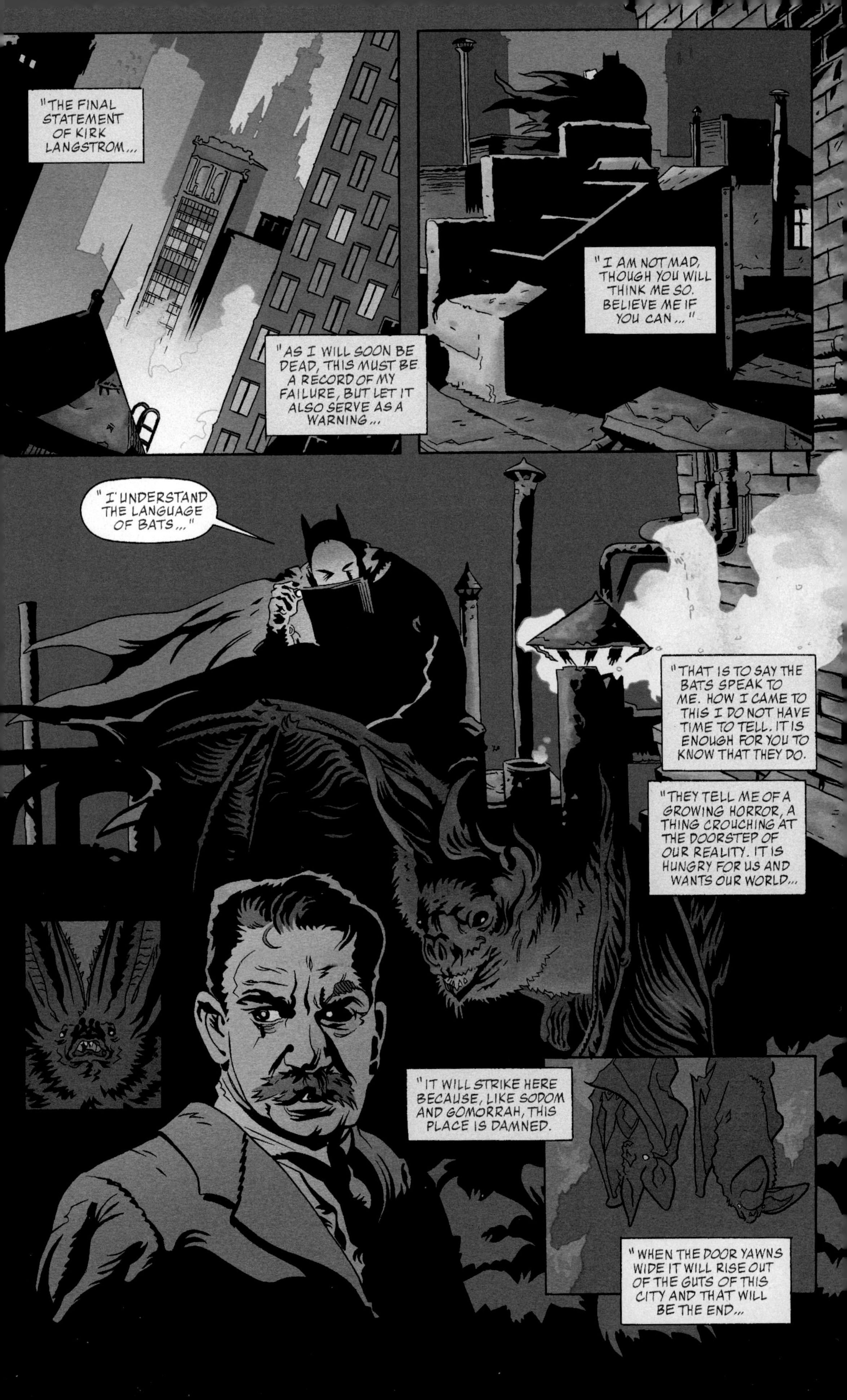
"THE FINAL STATEMENT OF KIRK LANGSTROM...
"AS I WILL SOON BE DEAD, THIS MUST BE A RECORD OF MY FAILURE, BUT LET IT ALSO SERVE AS A WARNING...
"I AM NOT MAD, THOUGH YOU WILL THINK ME SO. BELIEVE ME IF YOU CAN..."
"I UNDERSTAND THE LANGUAGE OF BATS..."
"THAT IS TO SAY THE BATS SPEAK TO ME. HOW I CAME TO THIS I DO NOT HAVE TIME TO TELL. IT IS ENOUGH FOR YOU TO KNOW THAT THEY DO.
"THEY TELL ME OF A GROWING HORROR, A THING CROUCHING AT THE DOORSTEP OF OUR REALITY. IT IS HUNGRY FOR US AND WANTS OUR WORLD...
"IT WILL STRIKE HERE BECAUSE, LIKE SODOM AND GOMORRAH, THIS PLACE IS DAMNED.
"WHEN THE DOOR YAWNS WIDE IT WILL RISE OUT OF THE GUTS OF THIS CITY AND THAT WILL BE THE END...

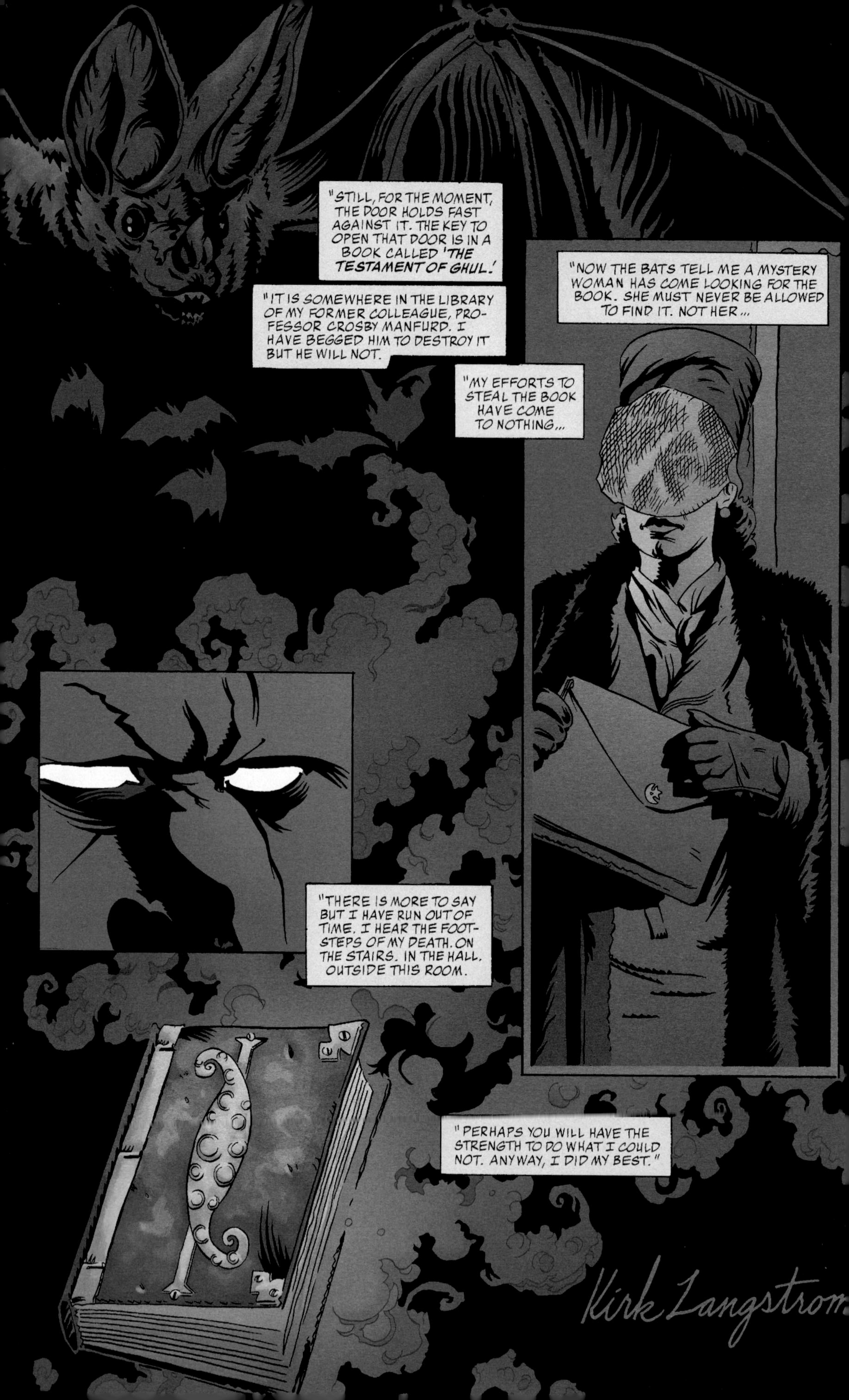
"STILL, FOR THE MOMENT, THE DOOR HOLDS FAST AGAINST IT. THE KEY TO OPEN THAT DOOR IS IN A BOOK CALLED 'THE TESTAMENT OF GHUL.'
"IT IS SOMEWHERE IN THE LIBRARY OF MY FORMER COLLEAGUE, PRO-FESSOR CROSBY MANFURD. I HAVE BEGGED HIM TO DESTROY IT BUT HE WILL NOT.
"NOW THE BATS TELL ME A MYSTERY WOMAN HAS COME LOOKING FOR THE BOOK. SHE MUST NEVER BE ALLOWED TO FIND IT. NOT HER...
"MY EFFORTS TO STEAL THE BOOK HAVE COME TO NOTHING...
"THERE IS MORE TO SAY BUT I HAVE RUN OUT OF TIME. I HEAR THE FOOT-STEPS OF MY DEATH. ON THE STAIRS. IN THE HALL. OUTSIDE THIS ROOM.
"PERHAPS YOU WILL HAVE THE STRENGTH TO DO WHAT I COULD NOT. ANYWAY, I DID MY BEST."
Kirk Langstrom

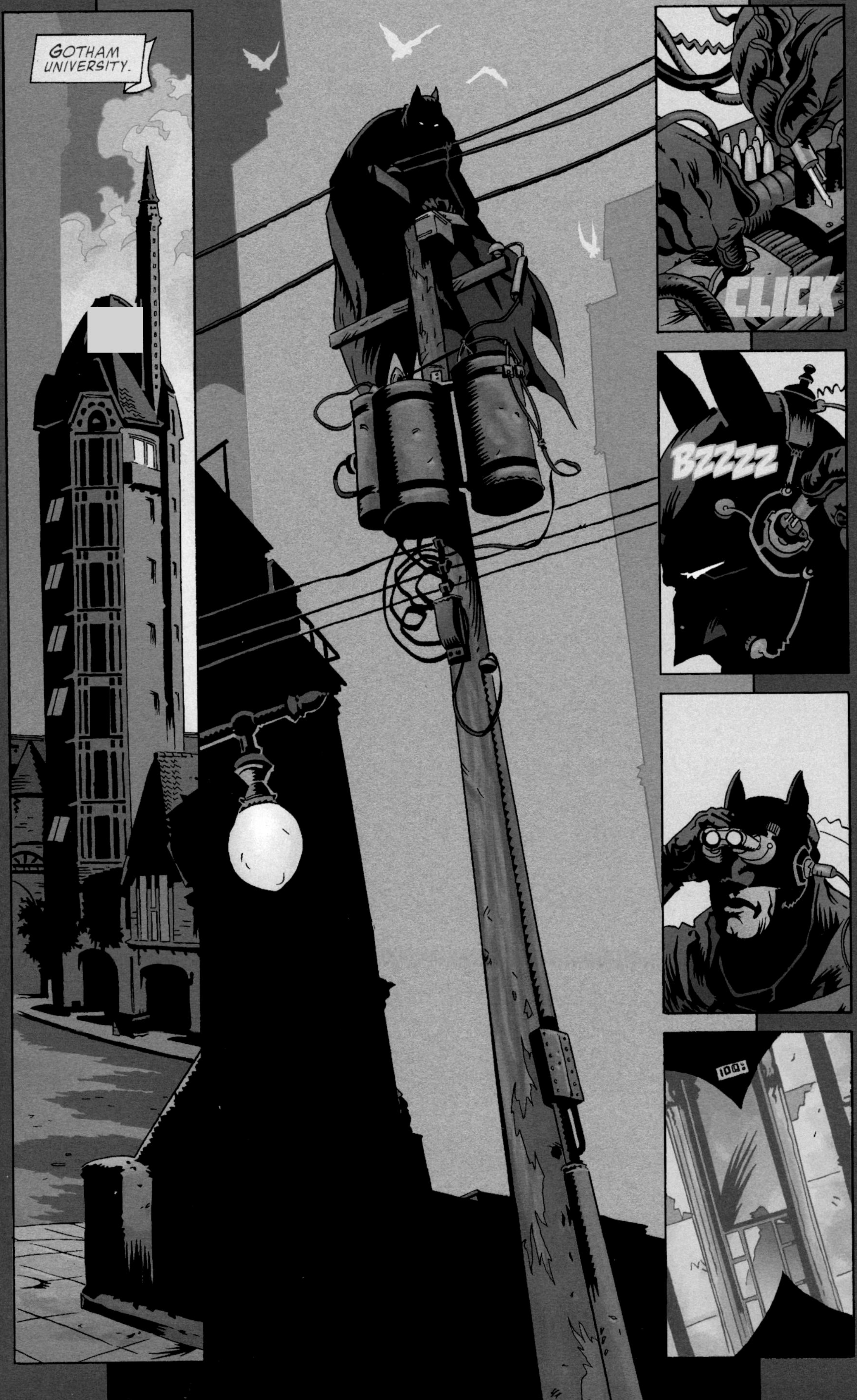
GOTHAM UNIVERSITY.
CLICK
BZZZZ

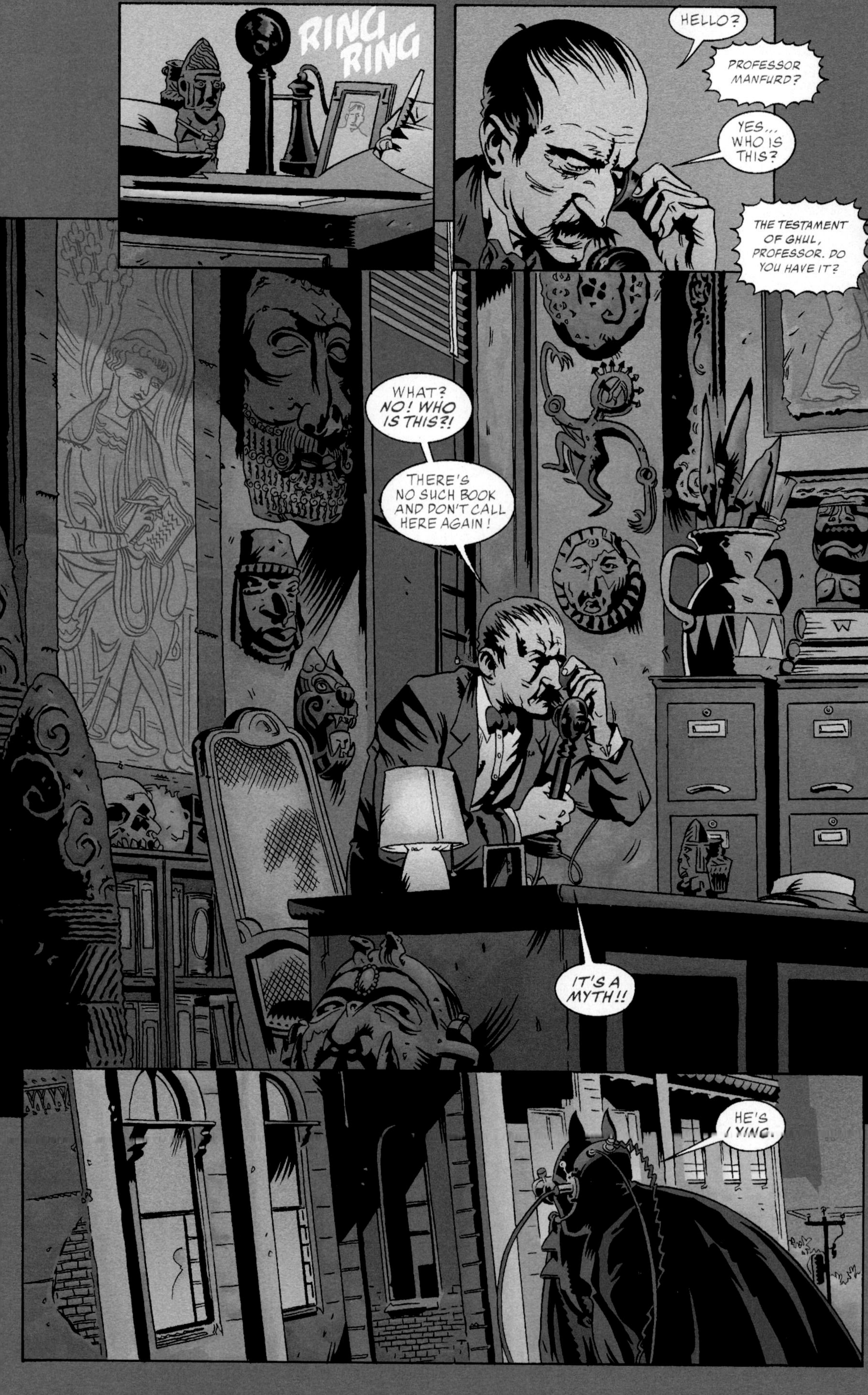
RING RING
HELLO?
PROFESSOR MANFURD?
YES... WHO IS THIS?
THE TESTAMENT OF GHUL, PROFESSOR. DO YOU HAVE IT?
WHAT? NO! WHO IS THIS?!
THERE'S NO SUCH BOOK AND DON'T CALL HERE AGAIN!
IT'S A MYTH!!
HE'S LYING.

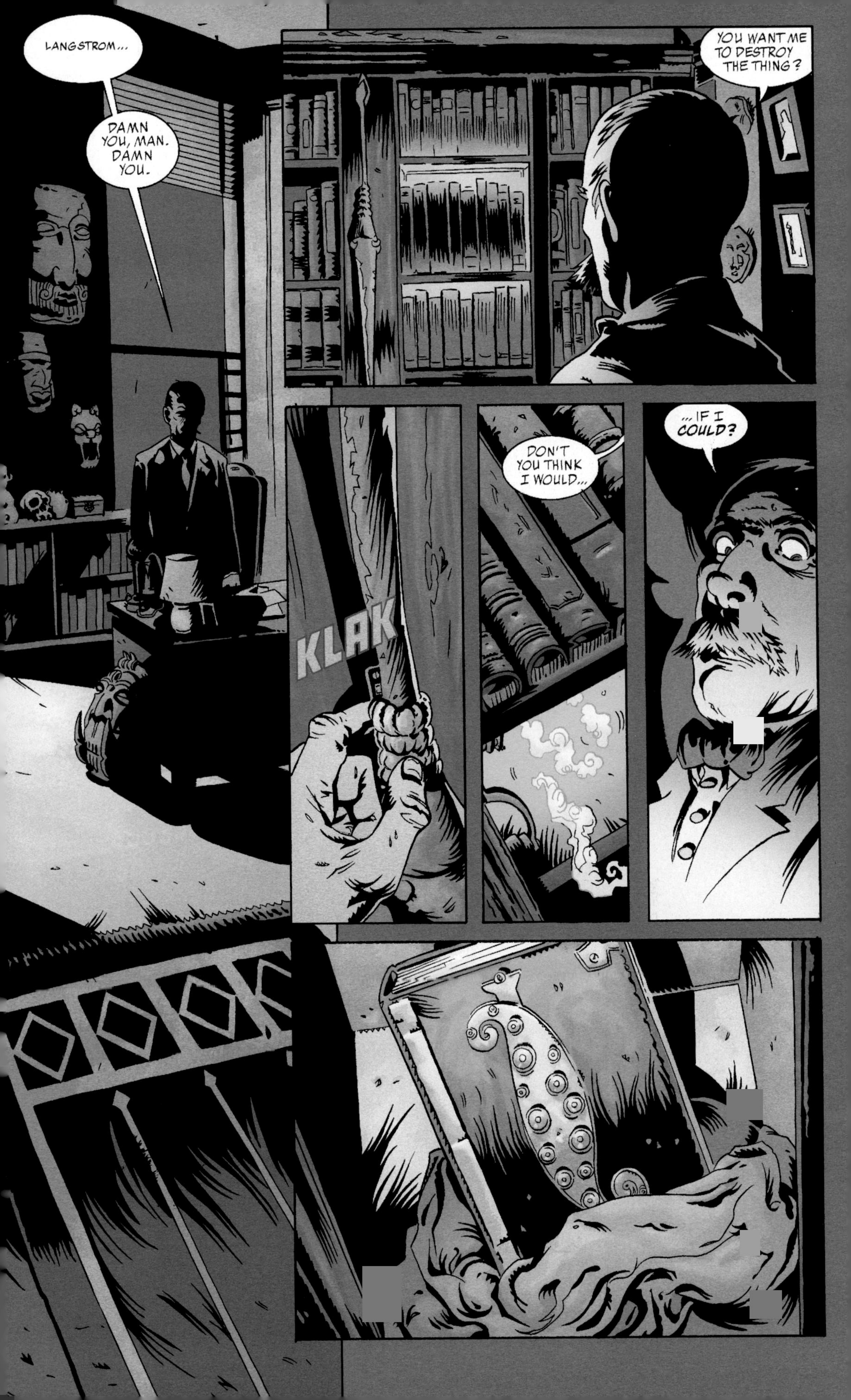
LANGSTROM...
DAMN YOU, MAN. DAMN YOU.
YOU WANT ME TO DESTROY THE THING?
KLAK
DON'T YOU THINK I WOULD...
...IF I COULD?

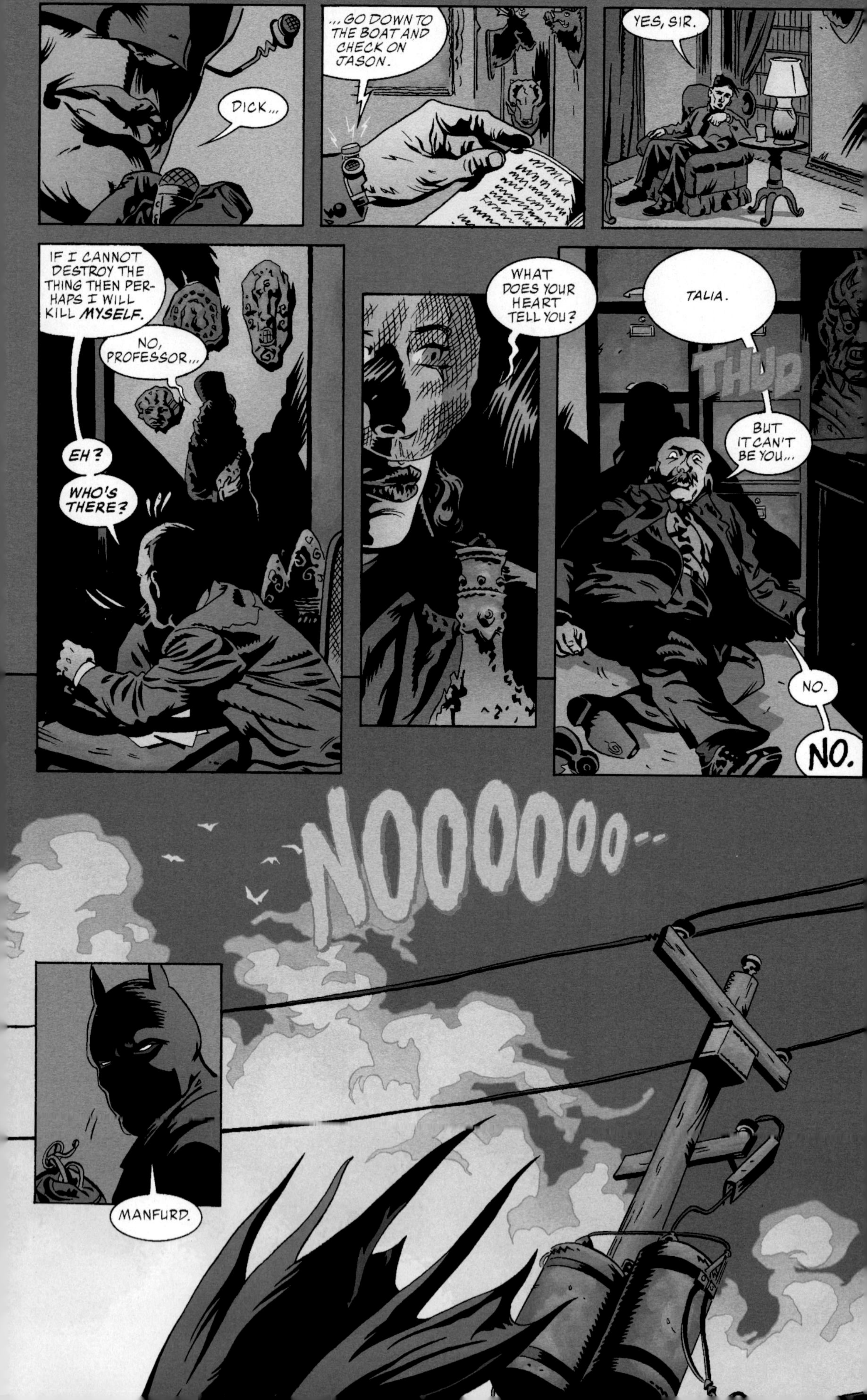
DICK...
...GO DOWN TO THE BOAT AND CHECK ON JASON.
YES, SIR.
IF I CANNOT DESTROY THE THING THEN PERHAPS I WILL KILL MYSELF.
NO, PROFESSOR...
EH?
WHO'S THERE?
WHAT DOES YOUR HEART TELL YOU?
TALIA.
THUD
BUT IT CAN'T BE YOU...
NO.
NO.
NOOOOOO--
MANFURD.

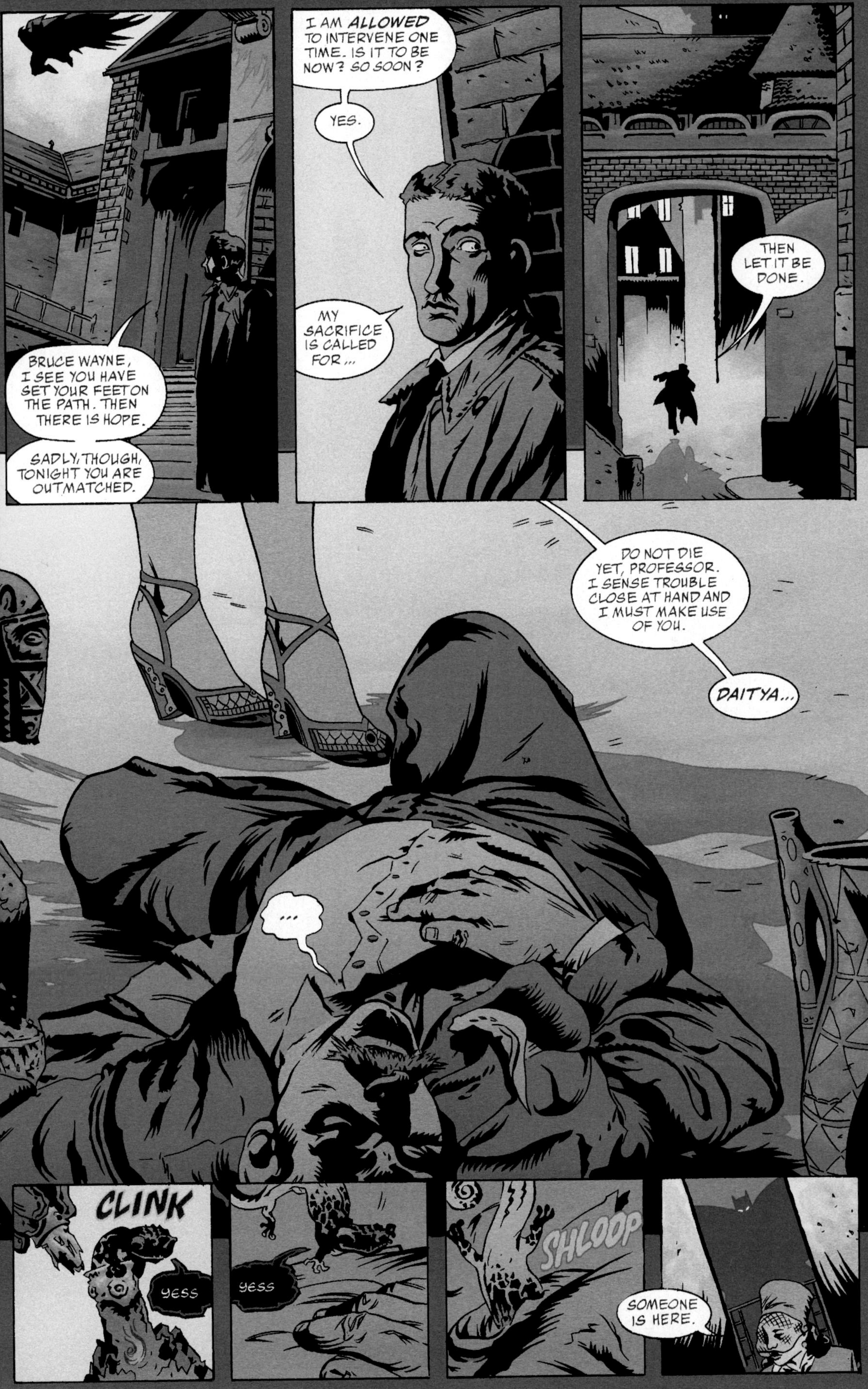
BRUCE WAYNE, I SEE YOU HAVE SET YOUR FEET ON THE PATH. THEN THERE IS HOPE.
SADLY, THOUGH, TONIGHT YOU ARE OUTMATCHED.
I AM ALLOWED TO INTERVENE ONE TIME. IS IT TO BE NOW? SO SOON?
YES.
MY SACRIFICE IS CALLED FOR...
THEN LET IT BE DONE.
DO NOT DIE YET, PROFESSOR. I SENSE TROUBLE CLOSE AT HAND AND I MUST MAKE USE OF YOU.
DAITYA...
...
CLINK
YESS
YESS
SHLOOP
SOMEONE IS HERE.

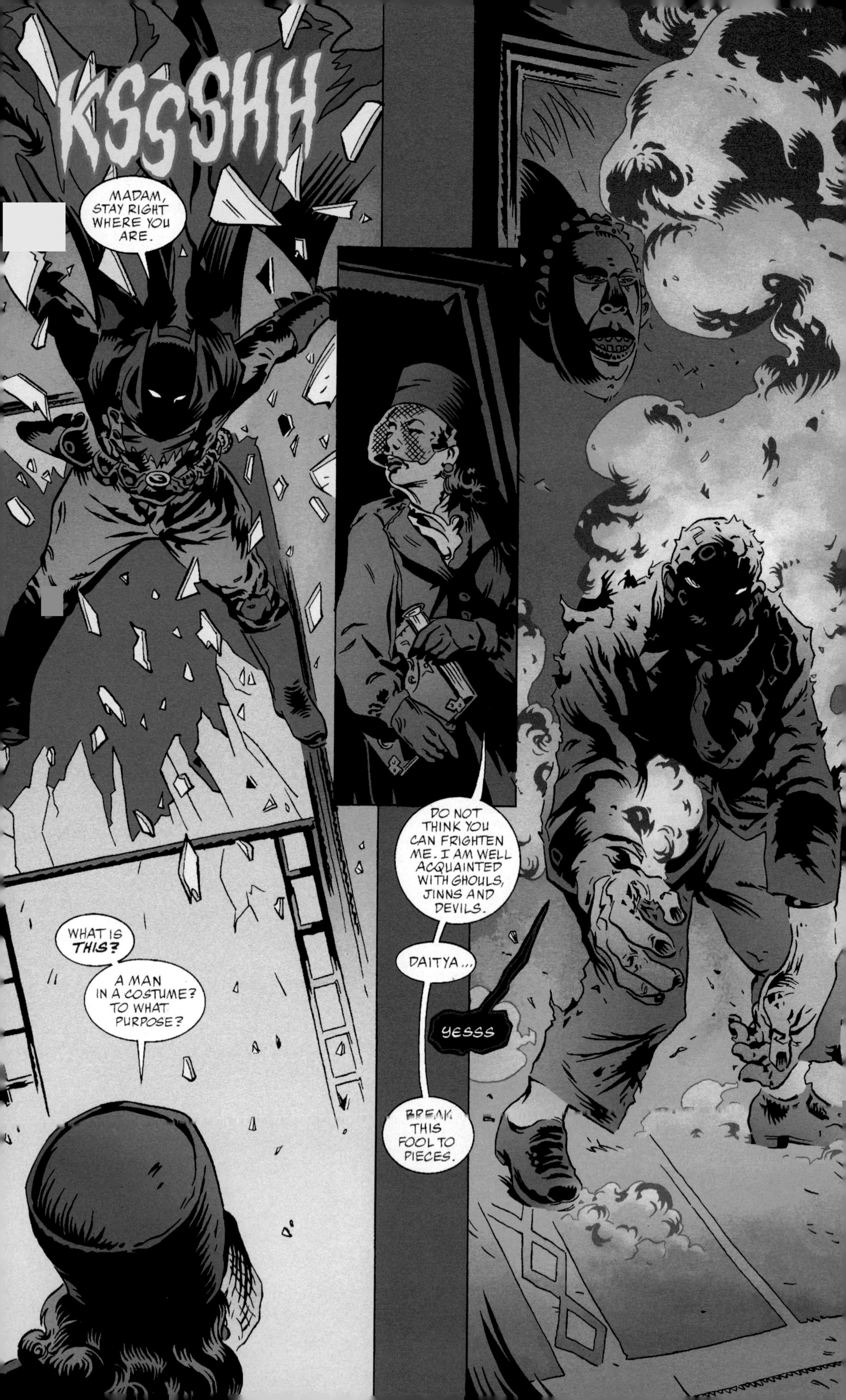
KSSSHH
MADAM, STAY RIGHT WHERE YOU ARE.
WHAT IS THIS?
A MAN IN A COSTUME? TO WHAT PURPOSE?
DO NOT THINK YOU CAN FRIGHTEN ME. I AM WELL ACQUAINTED WITH GHOULS, JINNS AND DEVILS.
DAITYA...
YESSS
BREAK THIS FOOL TO PIECES.

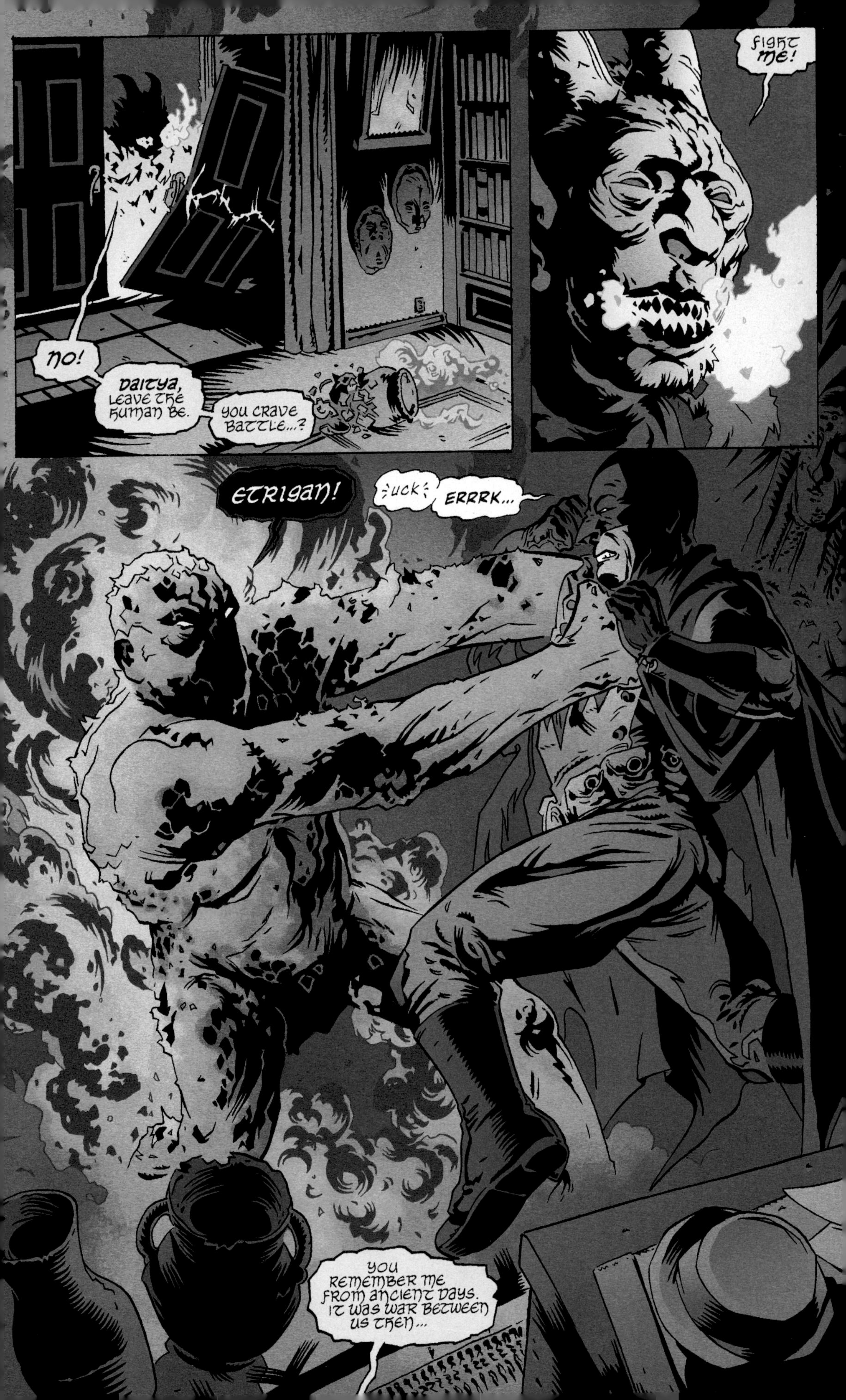
NO!
DAITYA, LEAVE THE HUMAN BE.
YOU CRAVE BATTLE...?
FIGHT ME!
ETRIGAN!
UCK
ERRRK...
YOU REMEMBER ME FROM ANCIENT DAYS. IT WAS WAR BETWEEN US THEN...

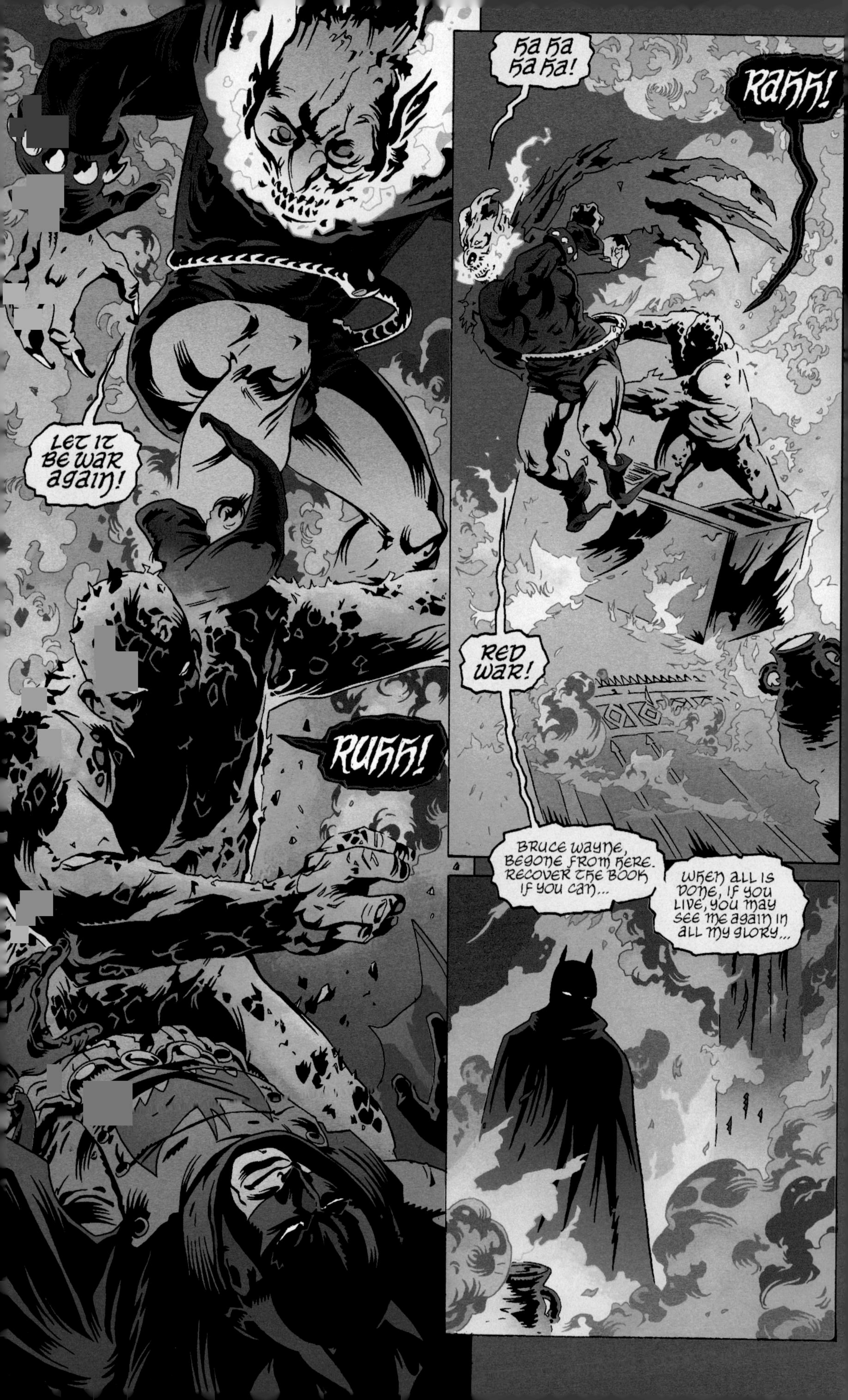
LET IT BE WAR AGAIN!
RUHH!
HA HA HA HA!
RAHH!
RED WAR!
BRUCE WAYNE, BEGONE FROM HERE. RECOVER THE BOOK IF YOU CAN...
WHEN ALL IS DONE, IF YOU LIVE, YOU MAY SEE ME AGAIN IN ALL MY GLORY...

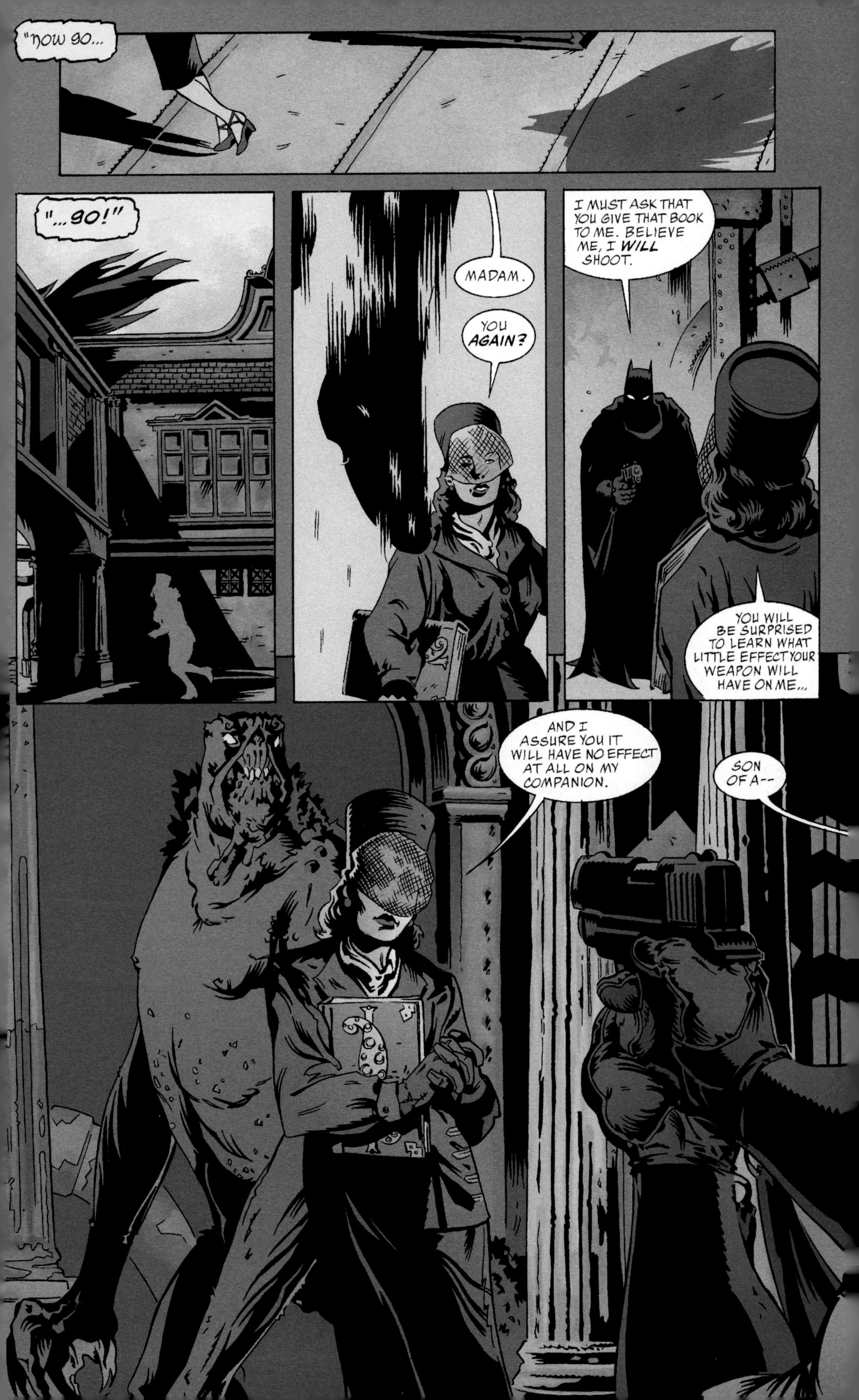
"NOW GO...
"...GO!"
MADAM.
YOU AGAIN?
I MUST ASK THAT YOU GIVE THAT BOOK TO ME. BELIEVE ME, I WILL SHOOT.
YOU WILL BE SURPRISED TO LEARN WHAT LITTLE EFFECT YOUR WEAPON WILL HAVE ON ME...
AND I ASSURE YOU IT WILL HAVE NO EFFECT AT ALL ON MY COMPANION.
SON OF A--

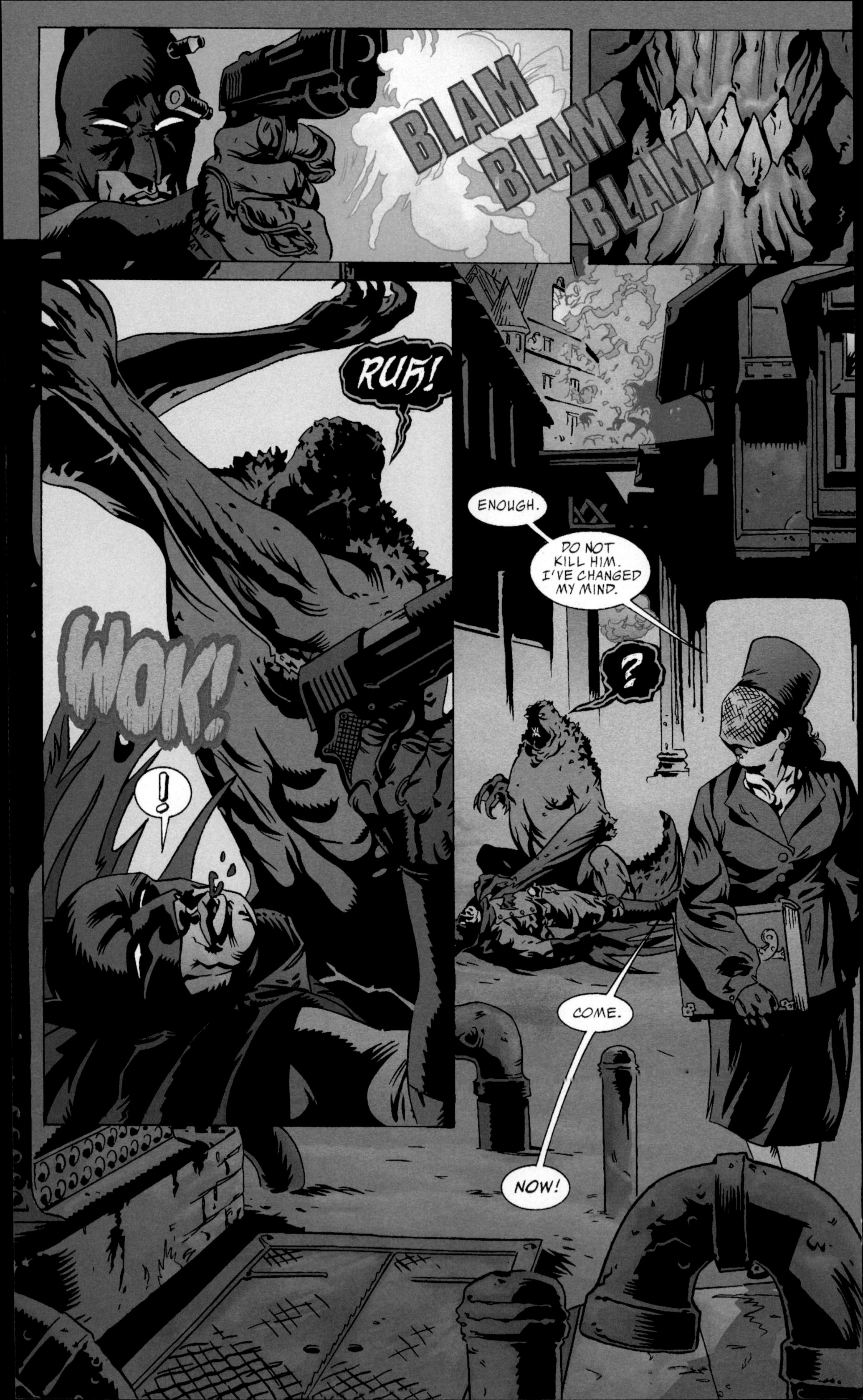

BLAM
BLAM
BLAM
RUH!
WOK!
!
ENOUGH.
DO NOT KILL HIM. I'VE CHANGED MY MIND.
?
COME.
NOW!

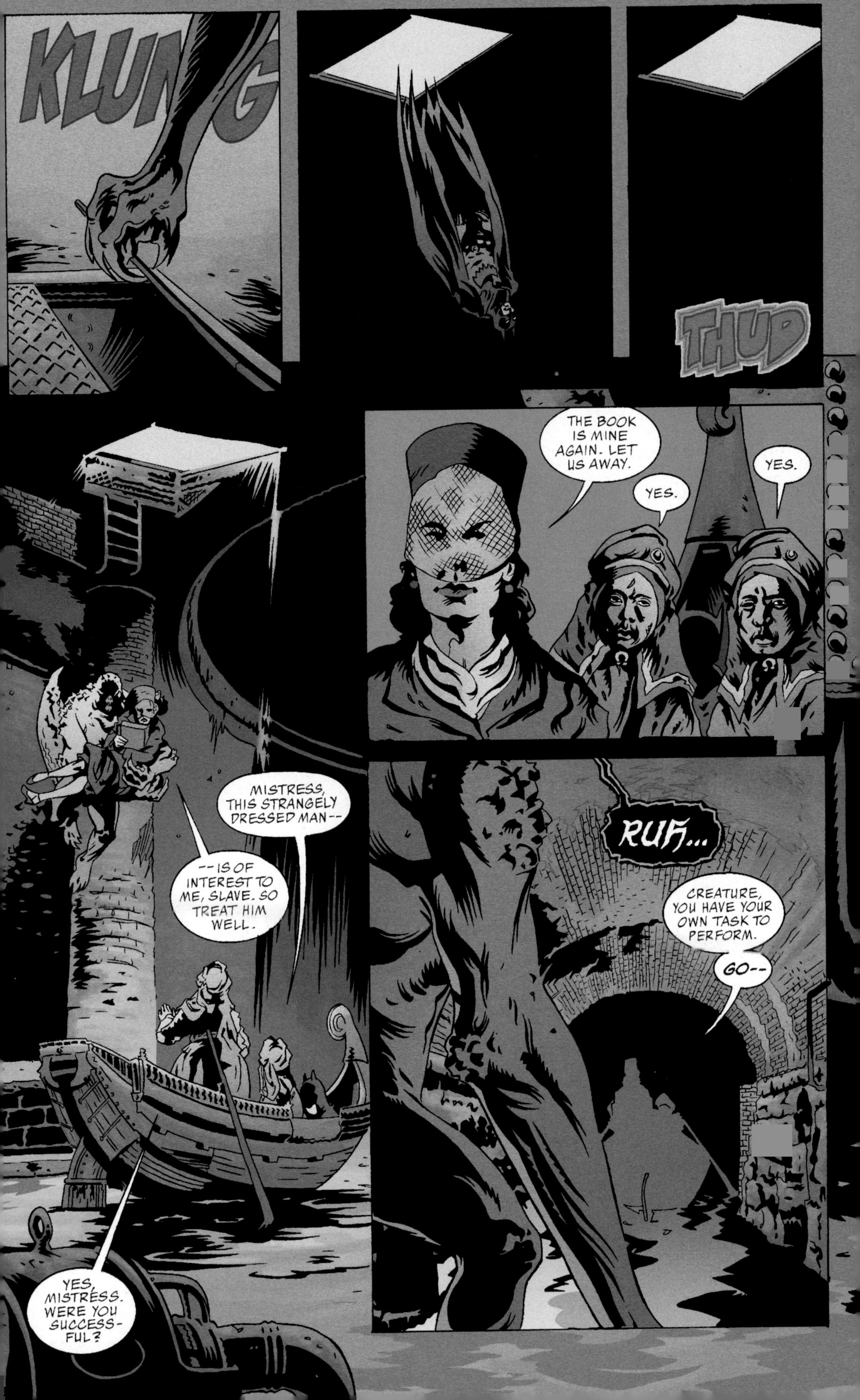
KLUNG
THUD
THE BOOK IS MINE AGAIN. LET US AWAY.
YES.
YES.
MISTRESS, THIS STRANGELY DRESSED MAN--
--IS OF INTEREST TO ME, SLAVE. SO TREAT HIM WELL.
YES, MISTRESS. WERE YOU SUCCESS-FUL?
RUH...
CREATURE, YOU HAVE YOUR OWN TASK TO PERFORM.
GO--

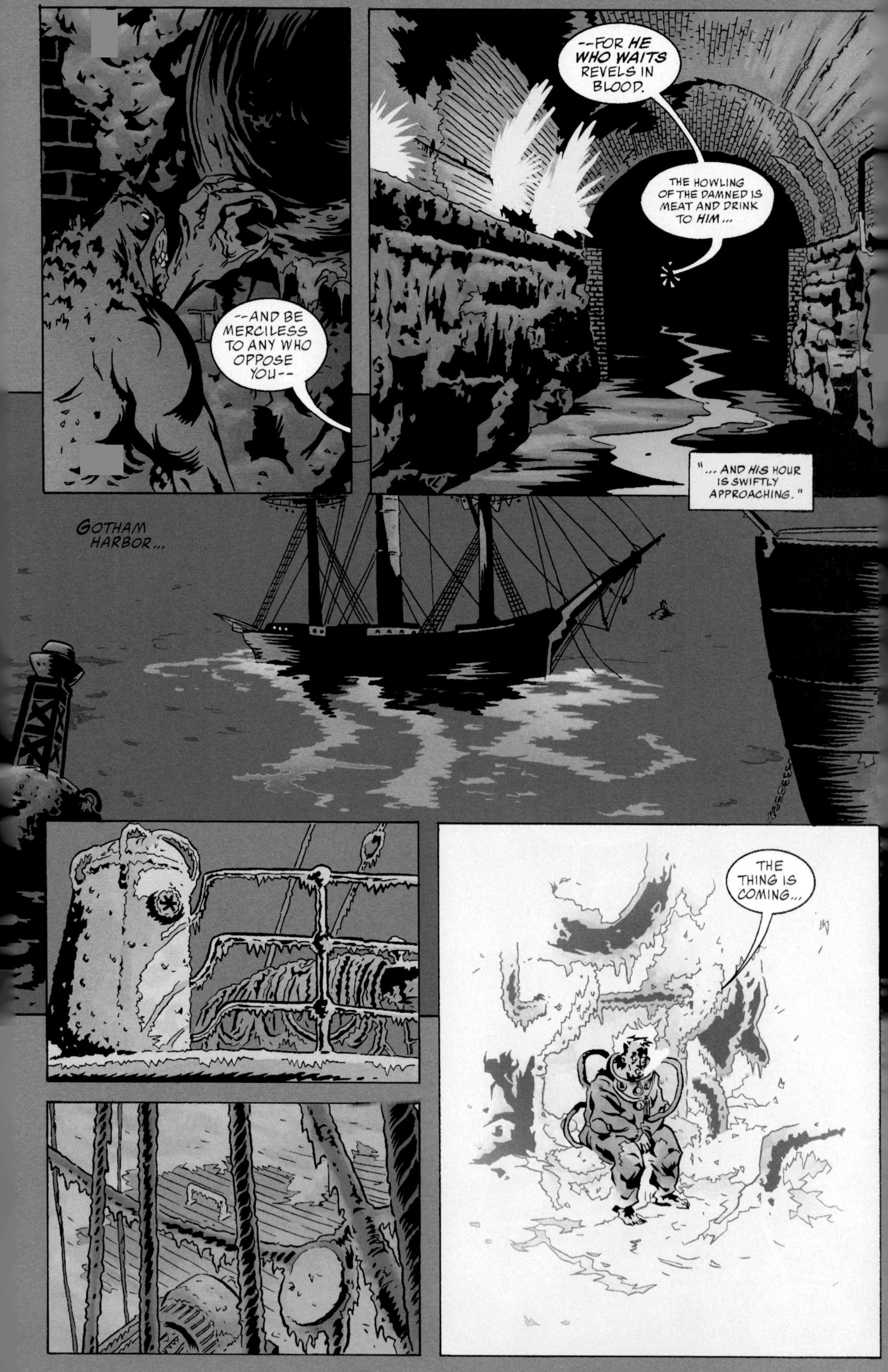
--AND BE MERCILESS TO ANY WHO OPPOSE YOU--
--FOR HE WHO WAITS REVELS IN BLOOD.
THE HOWLING OF THE DAMNED IS MEAT AND DRINK TO HIM...
"...AND HIS HOUR IS SWIFTLY APPROACHING."
GOTHAM HARBOR...
THE THING IS COMING...

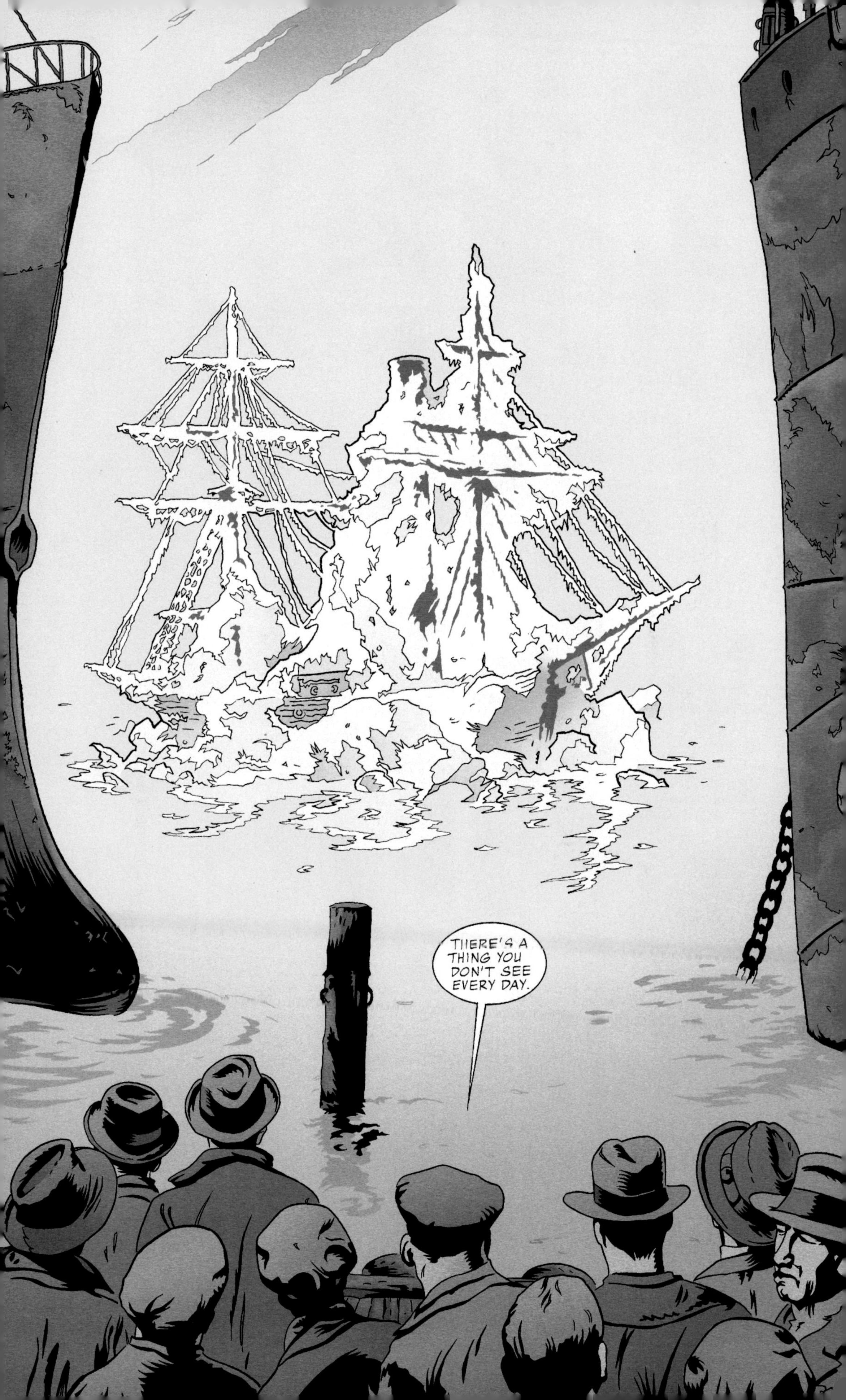
THERE'S A THING YOU DON'T SEE EVERY DAY.

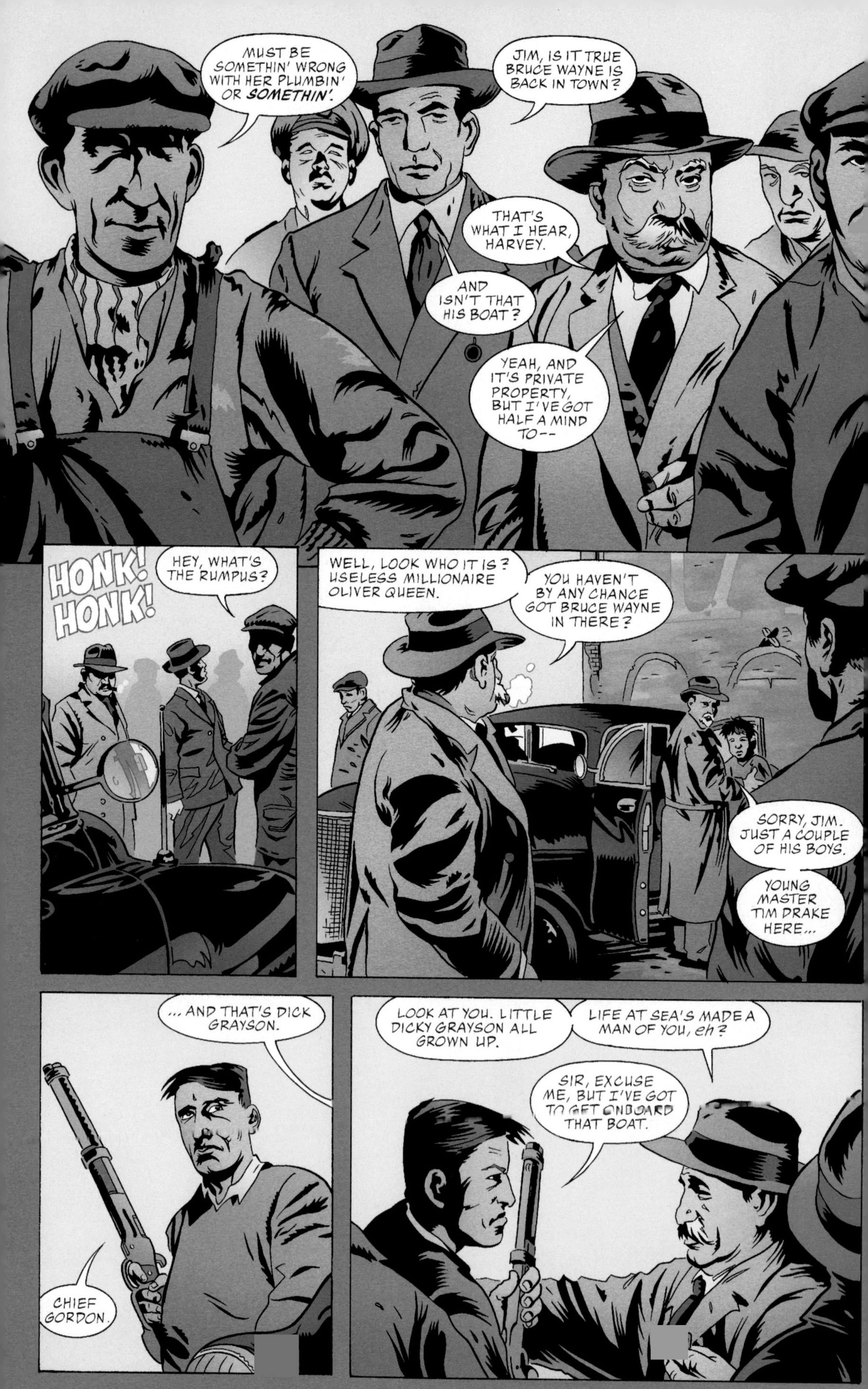
MUST BE SOMETHIN' WRONG WITH HER PLUMBIN' OR SOMETHIN'.
JIM, IS IT TRUE BRUCE WAYNE IS BACK IN TOWN?
THAT'S WHAT I HEAR, HARVEY.
AND ISN'T THAT HIS BOAT?
YEAH, AND IT'S PRIVATE PROPERTY, BUT I'VE GOT HALF A MIND TO--
HONK! HONK!
HEY, WHAT'S THE RUMPUS?
WELL, LOOK WHO IT IS? USELESS MILLIONAIRE OLIVER QUEEN.
YOU HAVEN'T BY ANY CHANCE GOT BRUCE WAYNE IN THERE?
SORRY, JIM. JUST A COUPLE OF HIS BOYS.
YOUNG MASTER TIM DRAKE HERE...
...AND THAT'S DICK GRAYSON.
CHIEF GORDON.
LOOK AT YOU. LITTLE DICKY GRAYSON ALL GROWN UP.
LIFE AT SEA'S MADE A MAN OF YOU, eh?
SIR, EXCUSE ME, BUT I'VE GOT TO GET ONBOARD THAT BOAT.

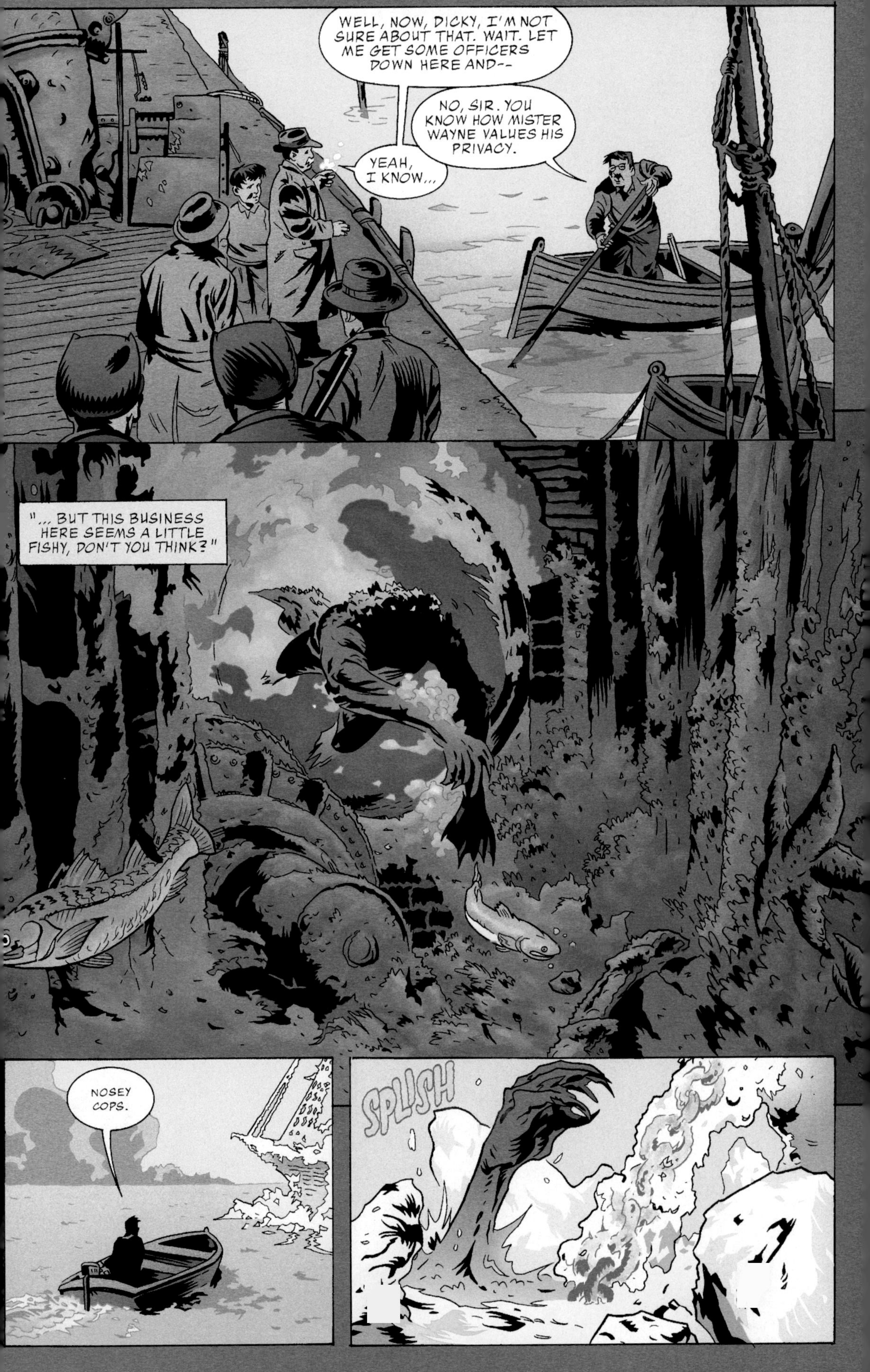
WELL, NOW, DICKY, I'M NOT SURE ABOUT THAT. WAIT. LET ME GET SOME OFFICERS DOWN HERE AND--
NO, SIR. YOU KNOW HOW MISTER WAYNE VALUES HIS PRIVACY.
YEAH, I KNOW...
"... BUT THIS BUSINESS HERE SEEMS A LITTLE FISHY, DON'T YOU THINK?"
NOSEY COPS.
SPLISH

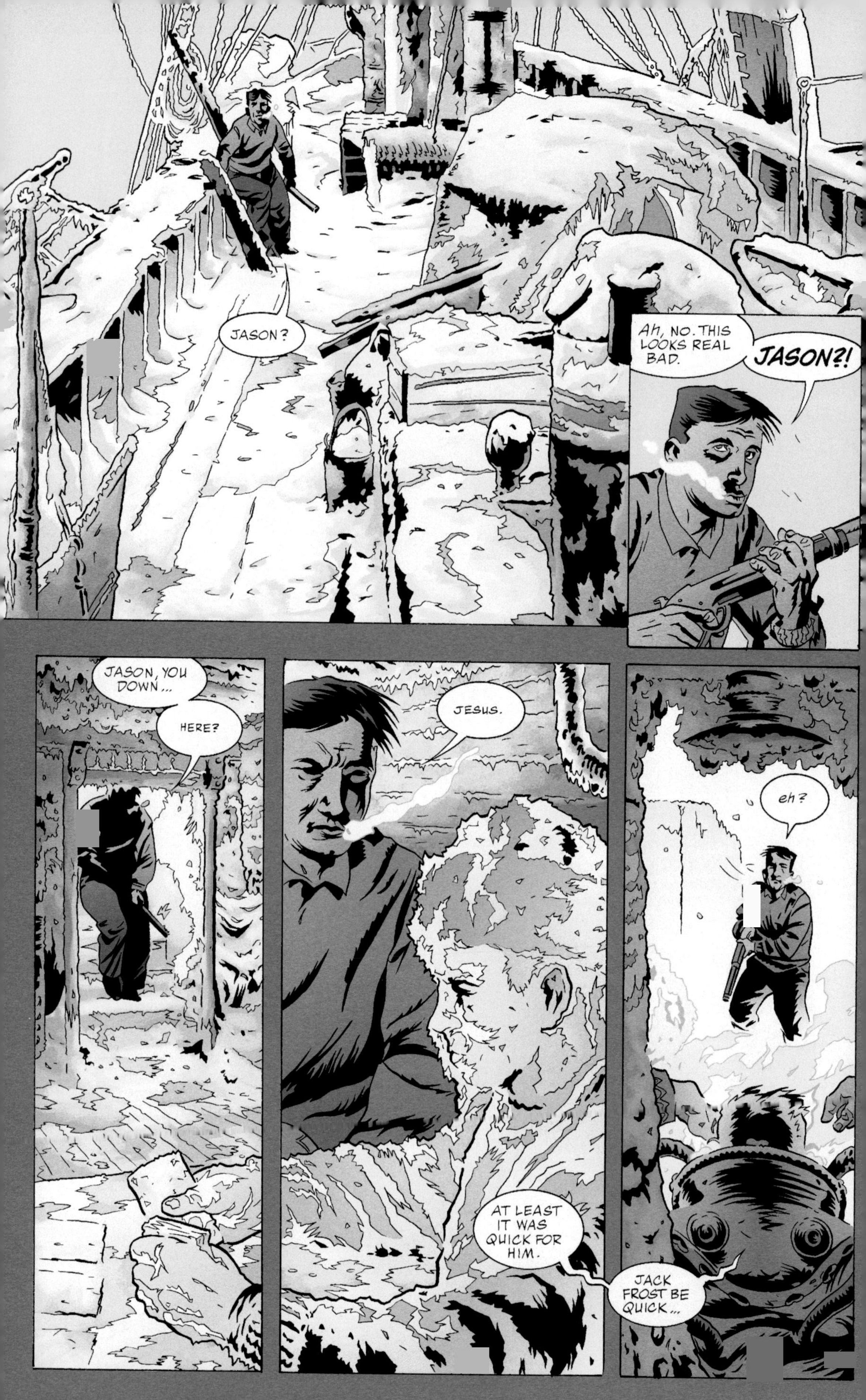
JASON?
AH, NO. THIS LOOKS REAL BAD.
JASON?!
JASON, YOU DOWN...
HERE?
JESUS.
AT LEAST IT WAS QUICK FOR HIM.
eh?
JACK FROST BE QUICK...

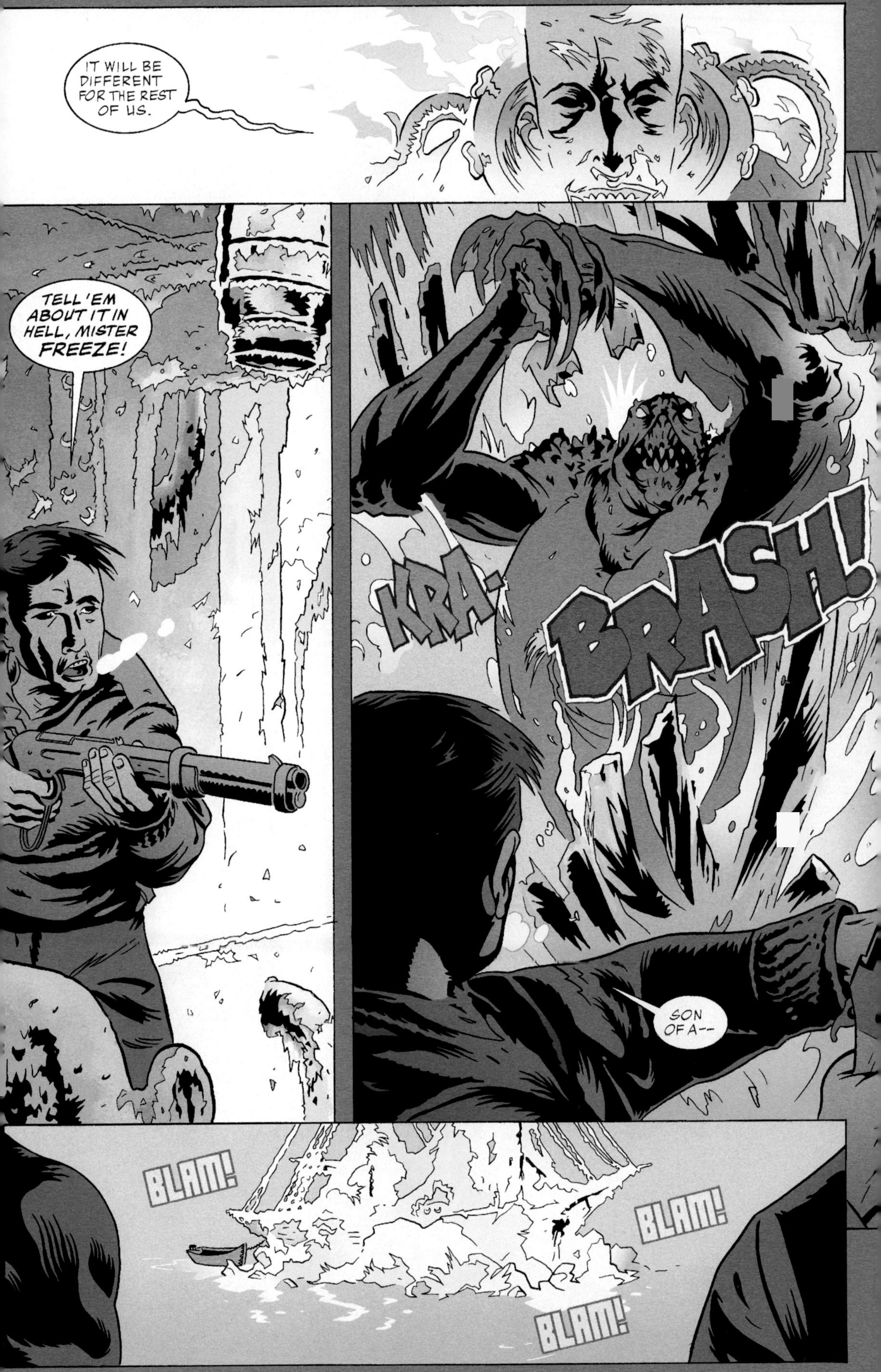
IT WILL BE DIFFERENT FOR THE REST OF US.
TELL 'EM ABOUT IT IN HELL, MISTER FREEZE!
KRA-
BRASH!
SON OF A--
BLAM!
BLAM!
BLAM!

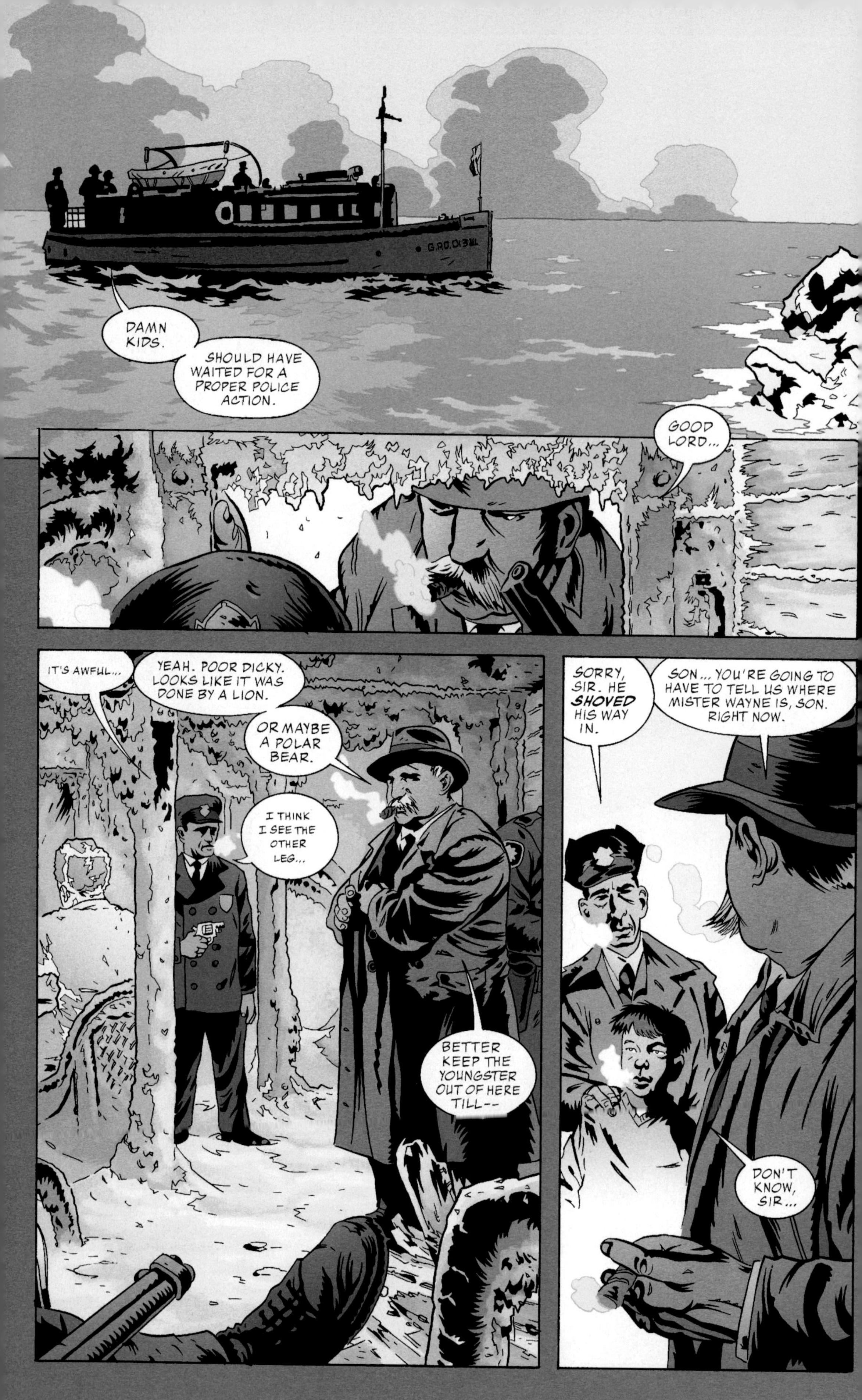

DAMN KIDS.
SHOULD HAVE WAITED FOR A PROPER POLICE ACTION.
GOOD LORD...
IT'S AWFUL...
YEAH. POOR DICKY. LOOKS LIKE IT WAS DONE BY A LION.
OR MAYBE A POLAR BEAR.
I THINK I SEE THE OTHER LEG...
BETTER KEEP THE YOUNGSTER OUT OF HERE TILL--
SORRY, SIR. HE SHOVED HIS WAY IN.
SON... YOU'RE GOING TO HAVE TO TELL US WHERE MISTER WAYNE IS, SON. RIGHT NOW.
DON'T KNOW, SIR...

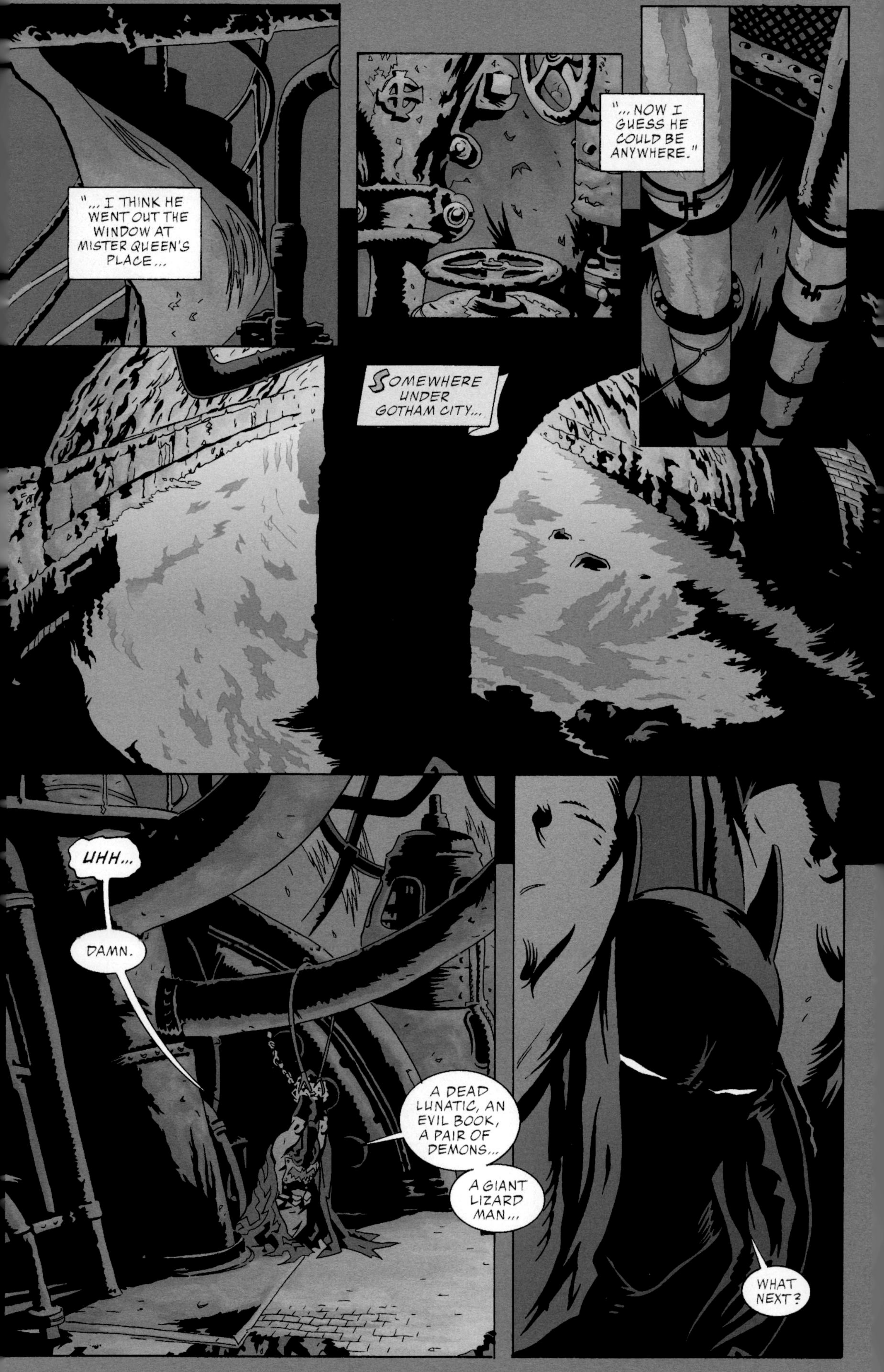
"... I THINK HE WENT OUT THE WINDOW AT MISTER QUEEN'S PLACE...
"... NOW I GUESS HE COULD BE ANYWHERE."
SOMEWHERE UNDER GOTHAM CITY...
UHH...
DAMN.
A DEAD LUNATIC, AN EVIL BOOK, A PAIR OF DEMONS...
A GIANT LIZARD MAN...
WHAT NEXT?

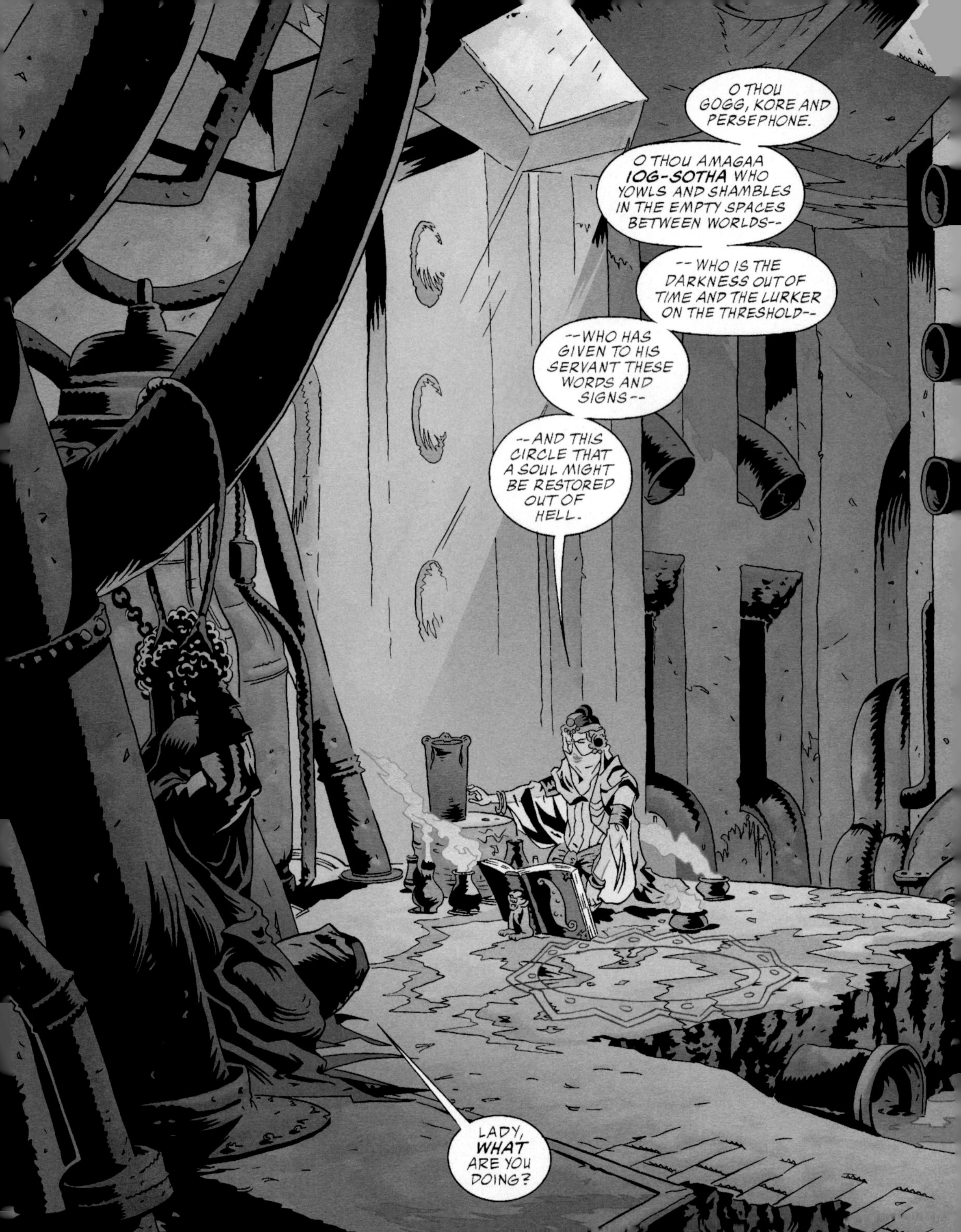
O THOU GOGG, KORE AND PERSEPHONE.
O THOU AMAGAA IOG-SOTHA WHO YOWLS AND SHAMBLES IN THE EMPTY SPACES BETWEEN WORLDS--
-- WHO IS THE DARKNESS OUT OF TIME AND THE LURKER ON THE THRESHOLD--
--WHO HAS GIVEN TO HIS SERVANT THESE WORDS AND SIGNS--
--AND THIS CIRCLE THAT A SOUL MIGHT BE RESTORED OUT OF HELL.
LADY, WHAT ARE YOU DOING?

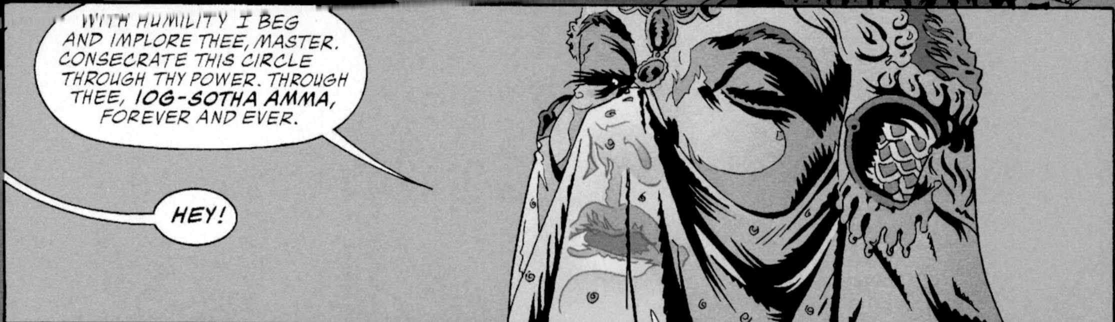
WITH HUMILITY I BEG AND IMPLORE THEE, MASTER. CONSECRATE THIS CIRCLE THROUGH THY POWER. THROUGH THEE, IOG-SOTHA AMMA, FOREVER AND EVER.
HEY!

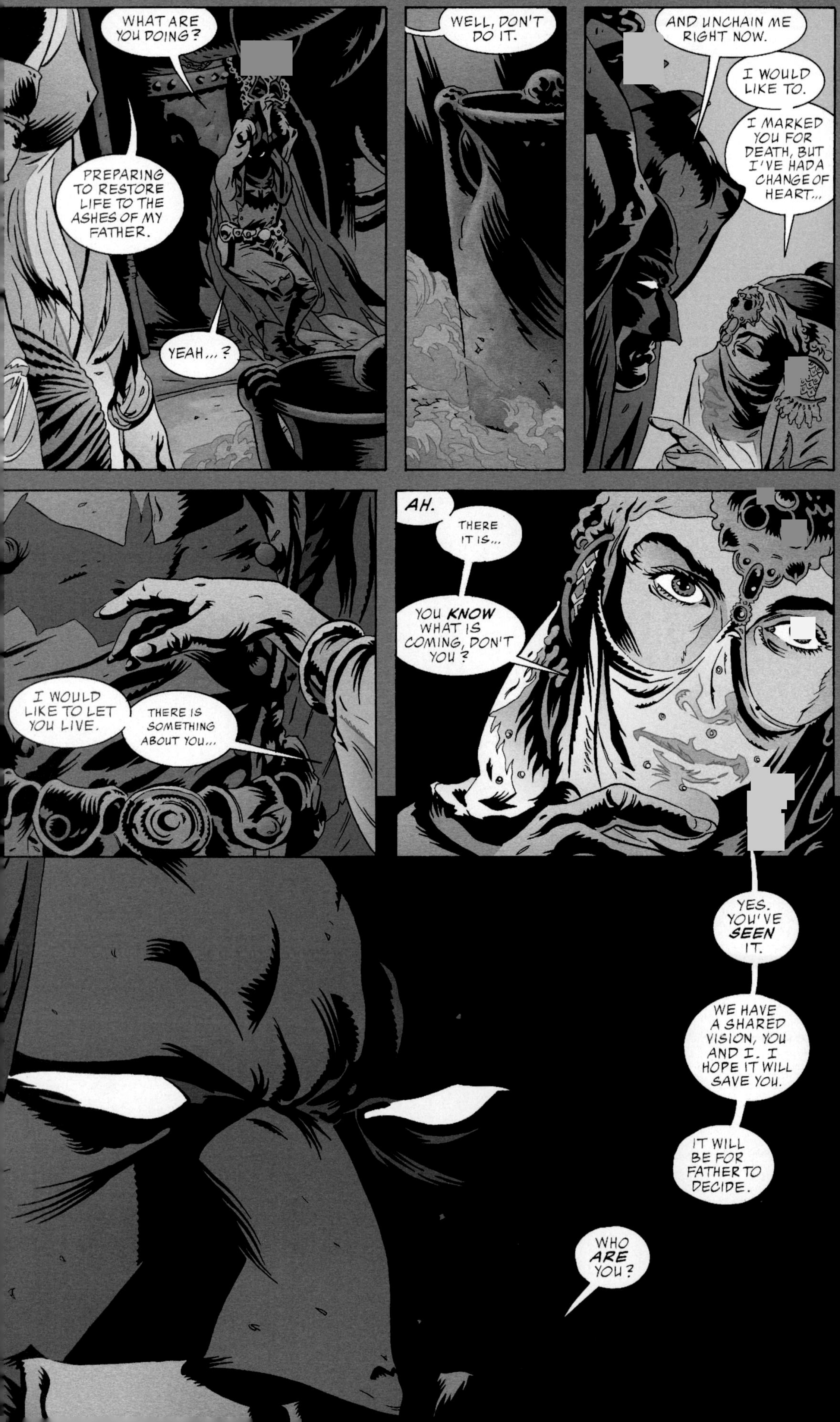
WHAT ARE YOU DOING?
PREPARING TO RESTORE LIFE TO THE ASHES OF MY FATHER.
YEAH...?
WELL, DON'T DO IT.
AND UNCHAIN ME RIGHT NOW.
I WOULD LIKE TO.
I MARKED YOU FOR DEATH, BUT I'VE HAD A CHANGE OF HEART...
I WOULD LIKE TO LET YOU LIVE.
THERE IS SOMETHING ABOUT YOU...
AH.
THERE IT IS...
YOU KNOW WHAT IS COMING, DON'T YOU?
YES. YOU'VE SEEN IT.
WE HAVE A SHARED VISION, YOU AND I. I HOPE IT WILL SAVE YOU.
IT WILL BE FOR FATHER TO DECIDE.
WHO ARE YOU?

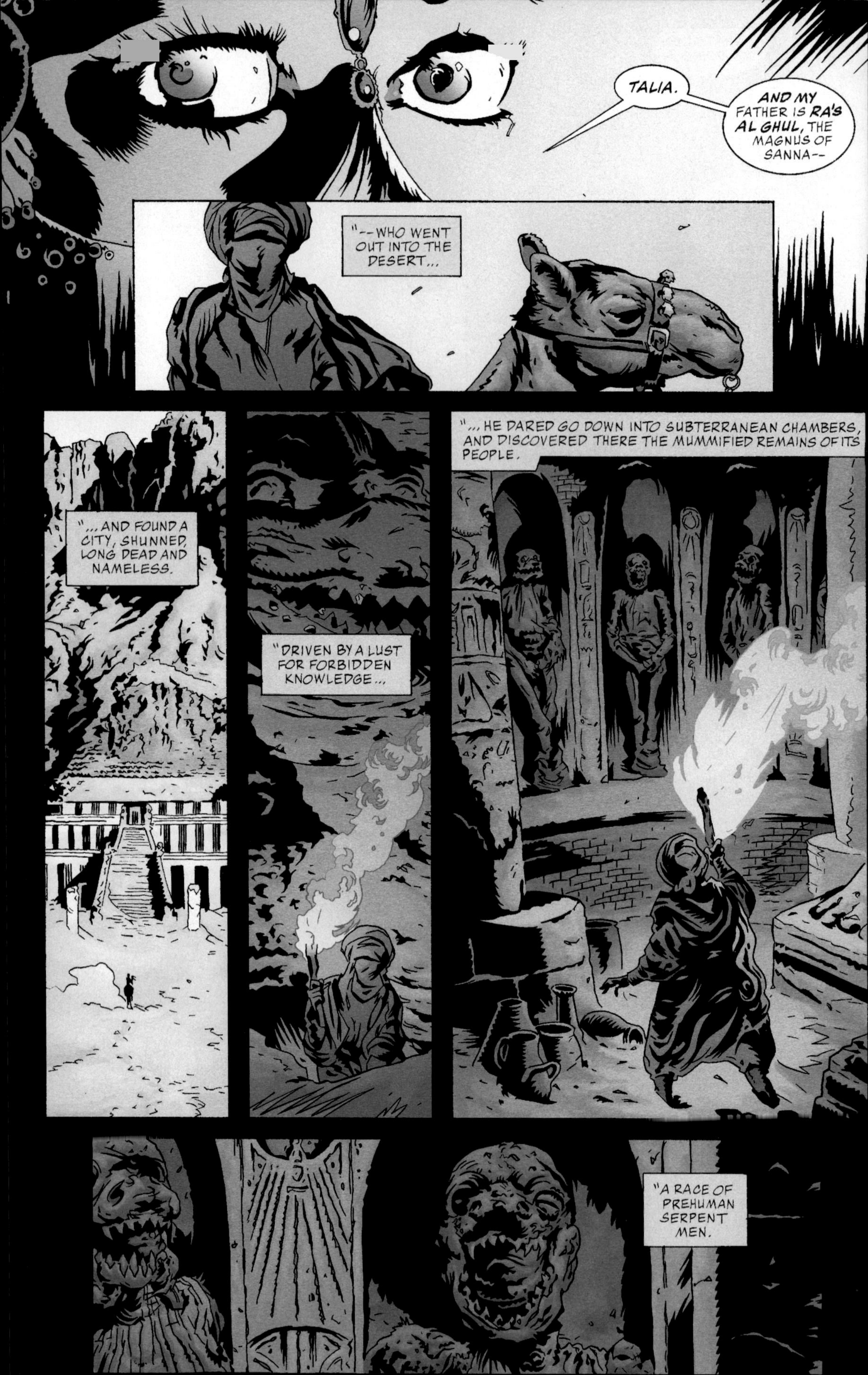
TALIA.
AND MY FATHER IS RA'S AL GHUL, THE MAGNUS OF SANNA--
"--WHO WENT OUT INTO THE DESERT...
"...AND FOUND A CITY, SHUNNED, LONG DEAD AND NAMELESS.
"DRIVEN BY A LUST FOR FORBIDDEN KNOWLEDGE...
"...HE DARED GO DOWN INTO SUBTERRANEAN CHAMBERS, AND DISCOVERED THERE THE MUMMIFIED REMAINS OF ITS PEOPLE.
"A RACE OF PREHUMAN SERPENT MEN.

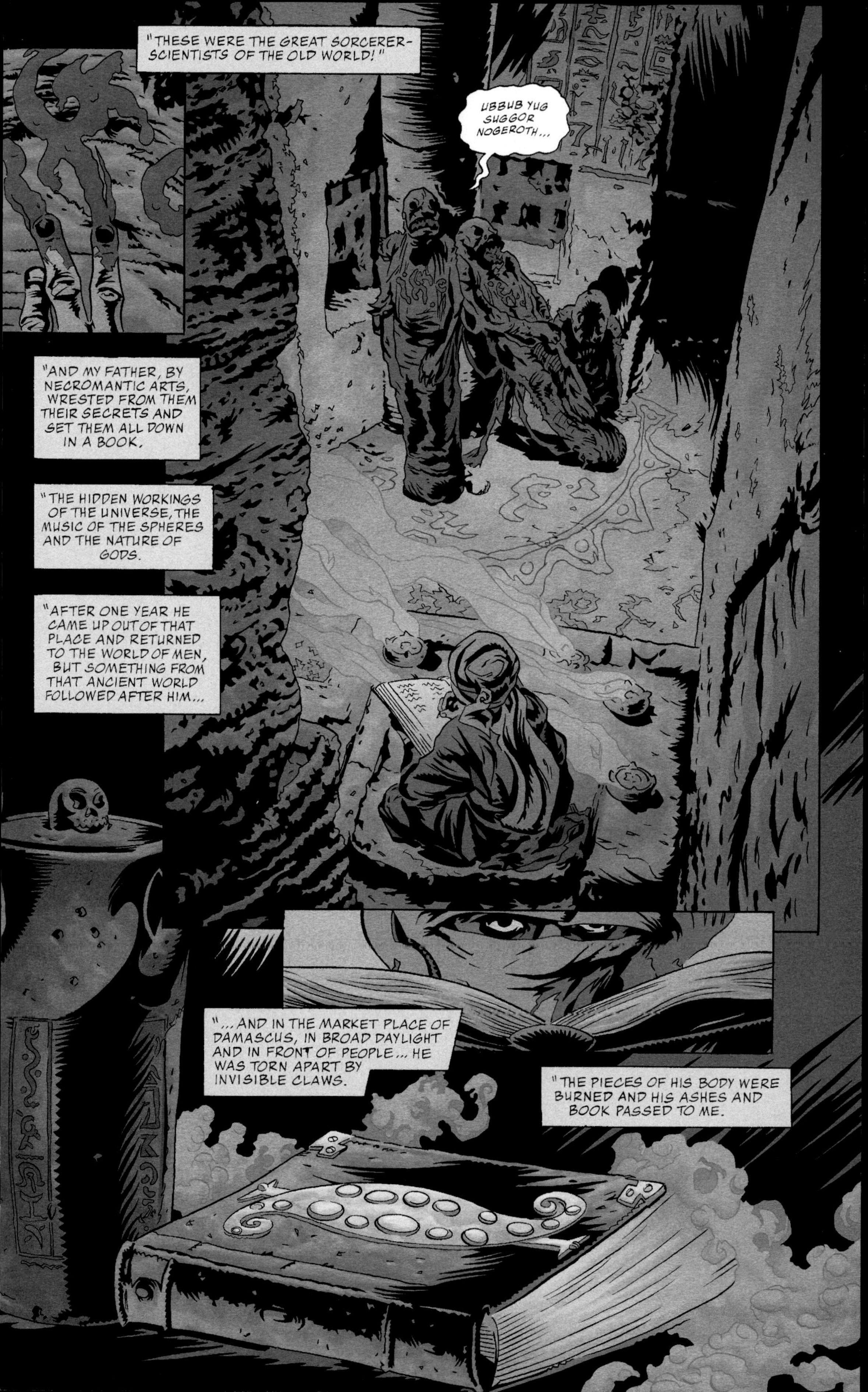
"THESE WERE THE GREAT SORCERER-SCIENTISTS OF THE OLD WORLD!"
UBBUB YUG SUGGOR NOGEROTH...
"AND MY FATHER, BY NECROMANTIC ARTS, WRESTED FROM THEM THEIR SECRETS AND SET THEM ALL DOWN IN A BOOK.
"THE HIDDEN WORKINGS OF THE UNIVERSE, THE MUSIC OF THE SPHERES AND THE NATURE OF GODS.
"AFTER ONE YEAR HE CAME UP OUT OF THAT PLACE AND RETURNED TO THE WORLD OF MEN, BUT SOMETHING FROM THAT ANCIENT WORLD FOLLOWED AFTER HIM...
"...AND IN THE MARKET PLACE OF DAMASCUS, IN BROAD DAYLIGHT AND IN FRONT OF PEOPLE... HE WAS TORN APART BY INVISIBLE CLAWS.
"THE PIECES OF HIS BODY WERE BURNED AND HIS ASHES AND BOOK PASSED TO ME.

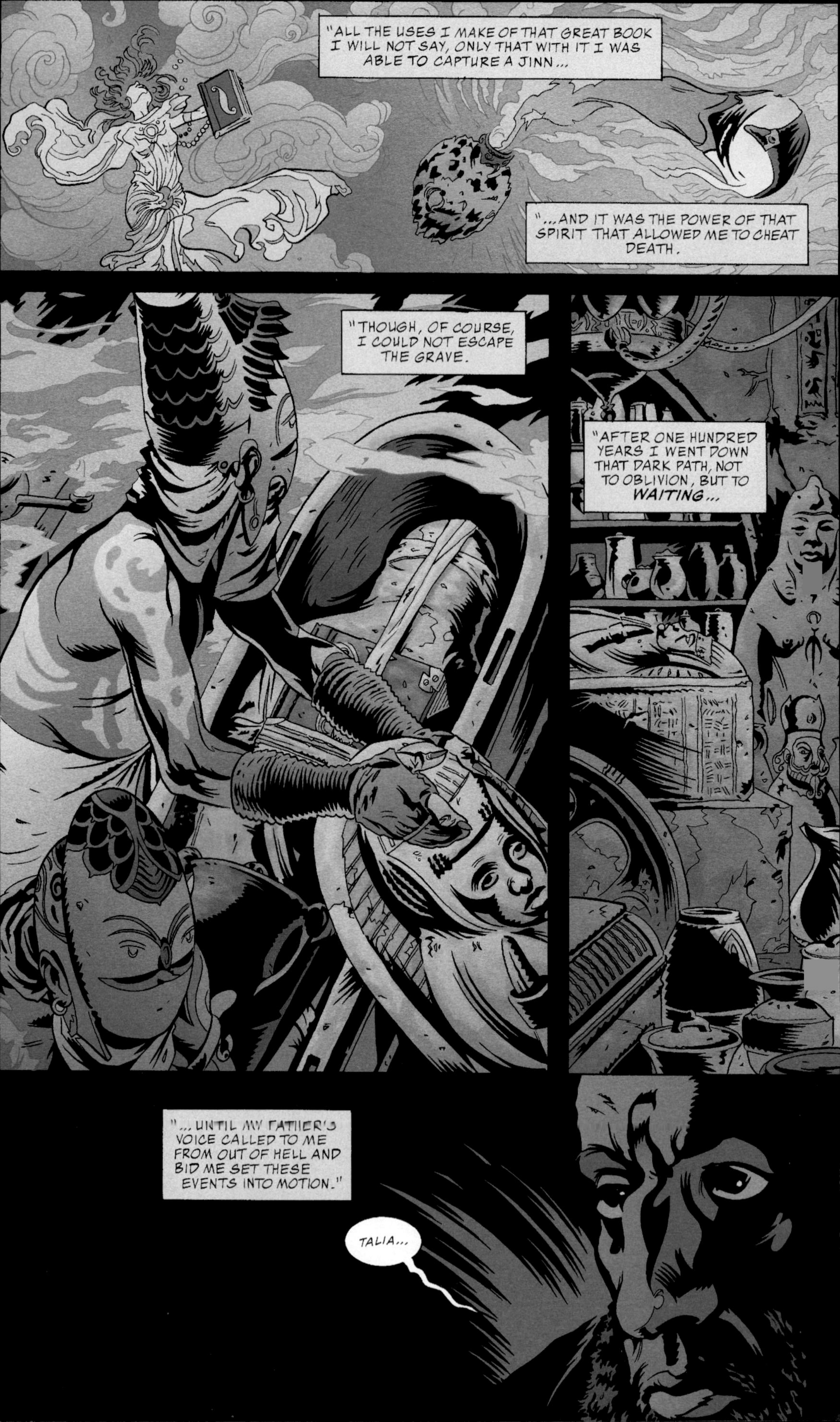
"ALL THE USES I MAKE OF THAT GREAT BOOK I WILL NOT SAY, ONLY THAT WITH IT I WAS ABLE TO CAPTURE A JINN...
"...AND IT WAS THE POWER OF THAT SPIRIT THAT ALLOWED ME TO CHEAT DEATH.
"THOUGH, OF COURSE, I COULD NOT ESCAPE THE GRAVE.
"AFTER ONE HUNDRED YEARS I WENT DOWN THAT DARK PATH, NOT TO OBLIVION, BUT TO WAITING...
"...UNTIL MY FATHER'S VOICE CALLED TO ME FROM OUT OF HELL AND BID ME SET THESE EVENTS INTO MOTION."
TALIA...

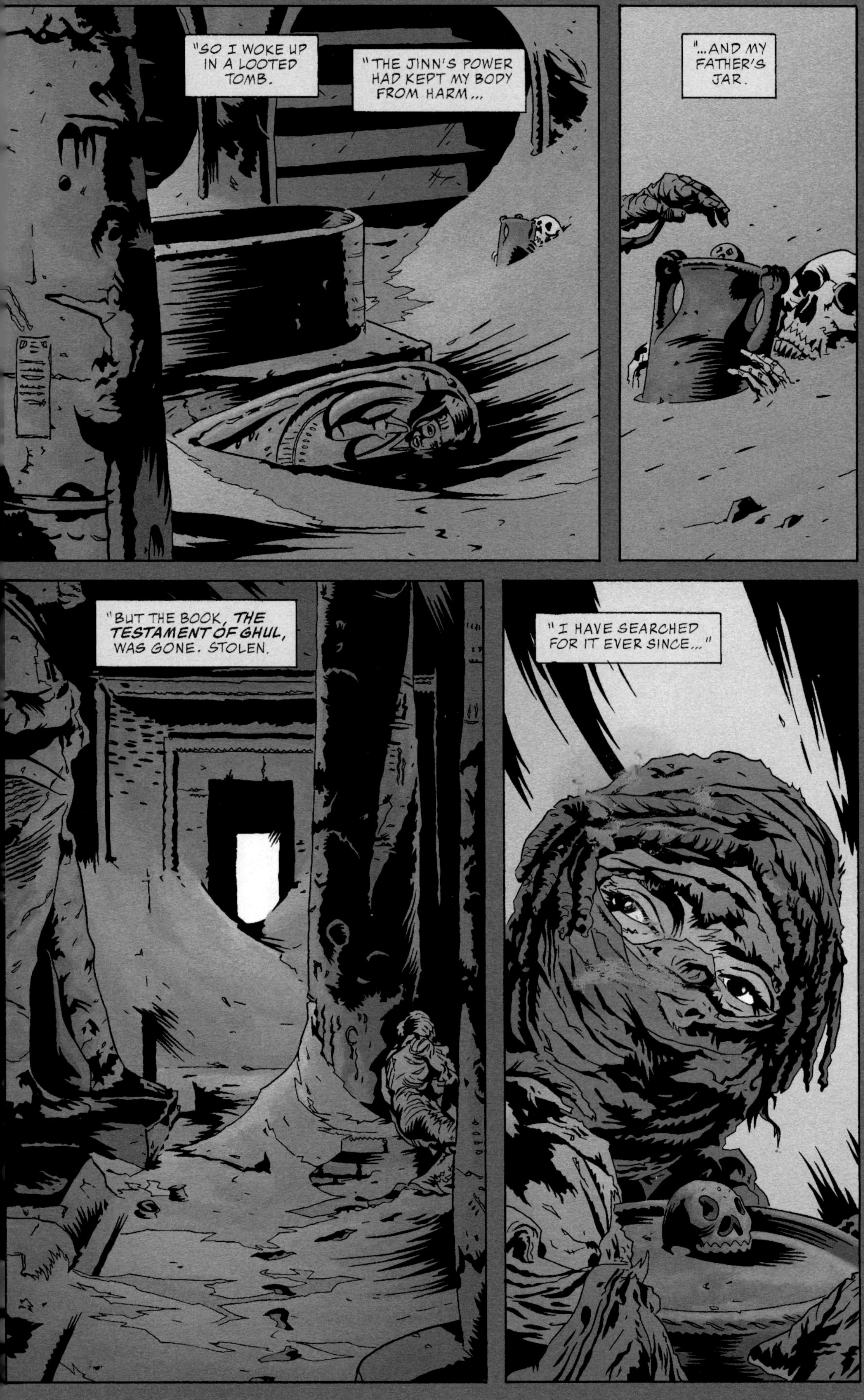
"SO I WOKE UP IN A LOOTED TOMB.
"THE JINN'S POWER HAD KEPT MY BODY FROM HARM...
"...AND MY FATHER'S JAR.
"BUT THE BOOK, *THE TESTAMENT OF GHUL,* WAS GONE. STOLEN.
"I HAVE SEARCHED FOR IT EVER SINCE..."

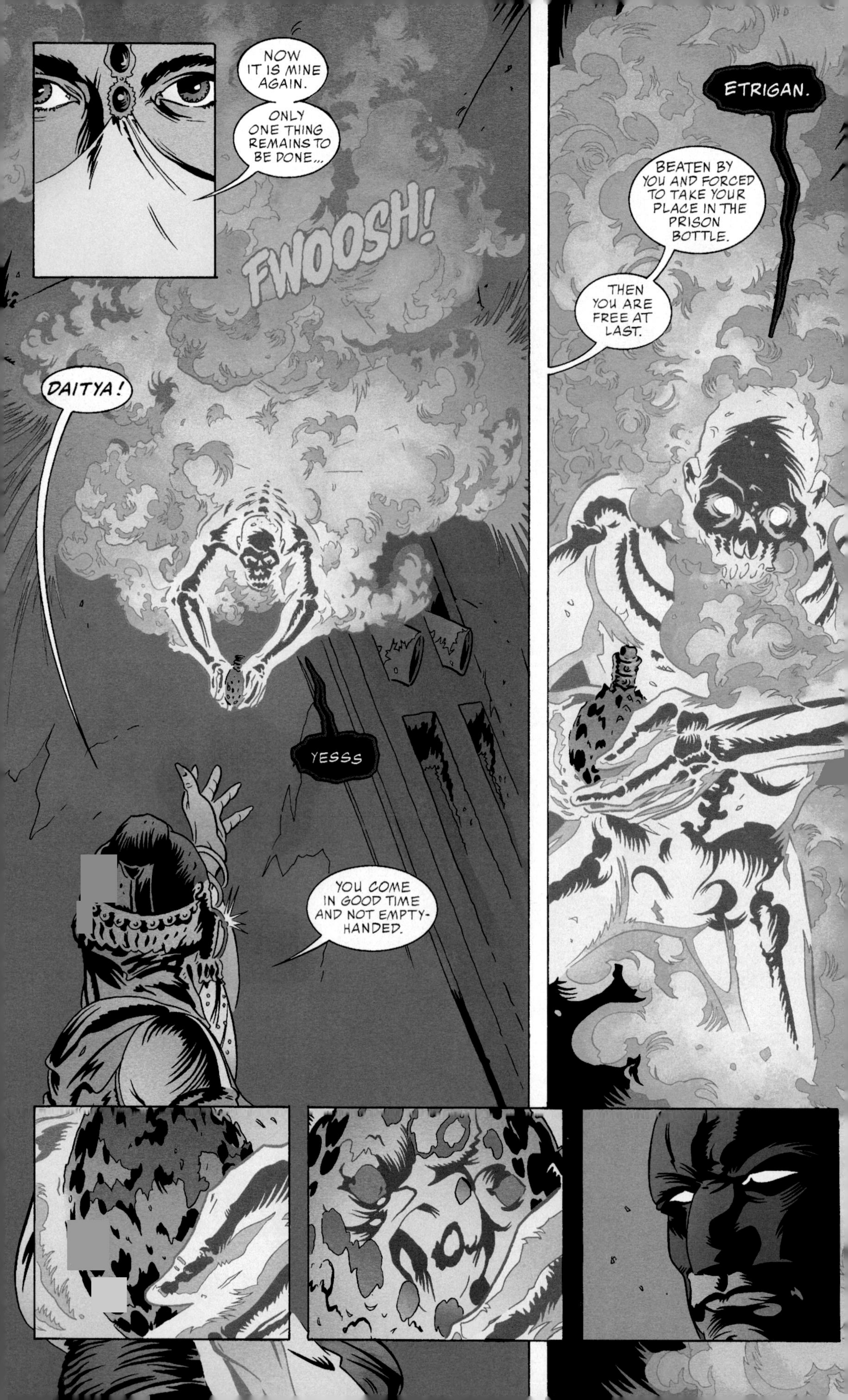
NOW IT IS MINE AGAIN.
ONLY ONE THING REMAINS TO BE DONE...
FWOOSH!
DAITYA!
YESSS
YOU COME IN GOOD TIME AND NOT EMPTY-HANDED.
ETRIGAN.
BEATEN BY YOU AND FORCED TO TAKE YOUR PLACE IN THE PRISON BOTTLE.
THEN YOU ARE FREE AT LAST.

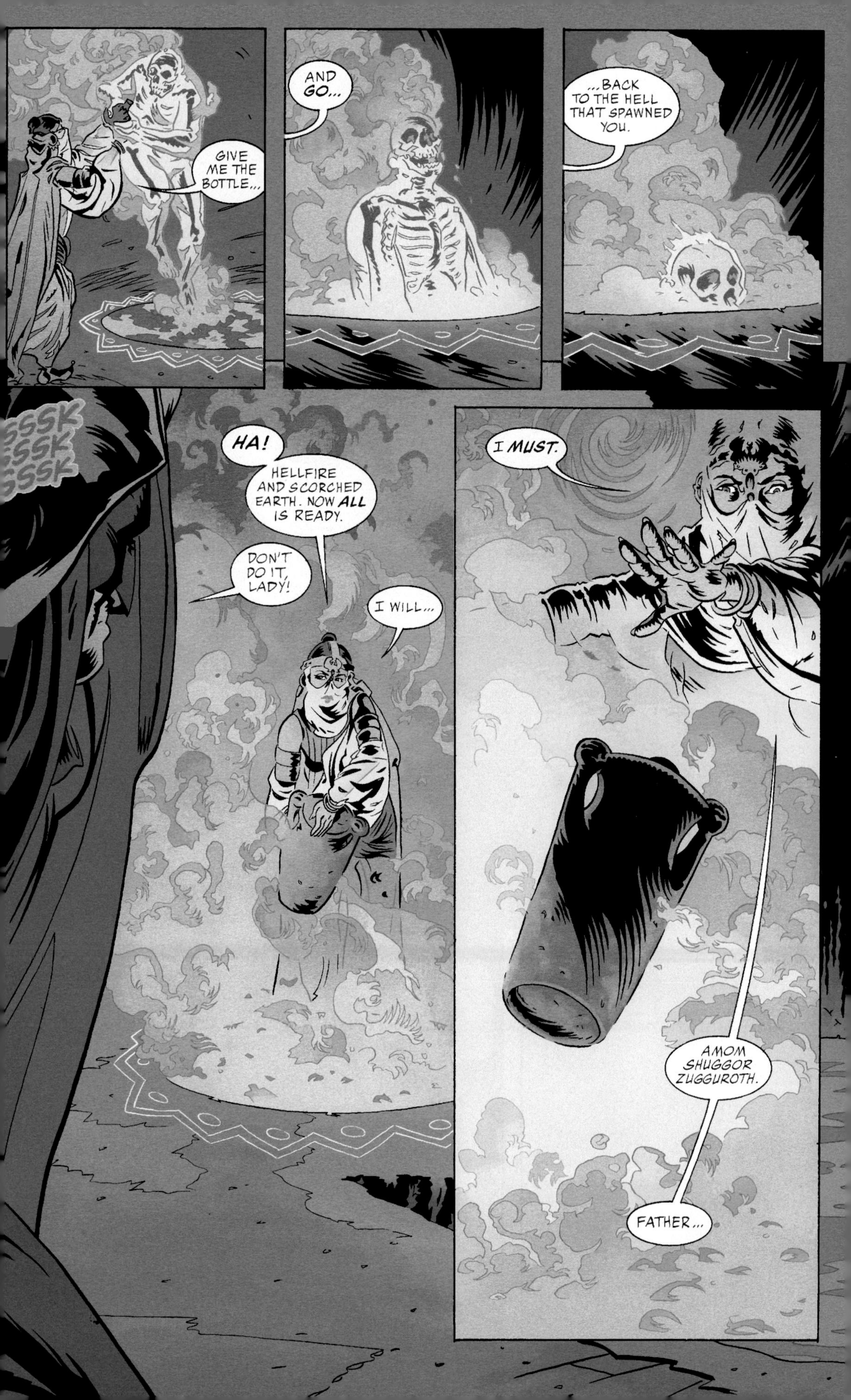
GIVE ME THE BOTTLE...
AND GO...
...BACK TO THE HELL THAT SPAWNED YOU.
SSSK SSSK SSSK
HA!
HELLFIRE AND SCORCHED EARTH. NOW ALL IS READY.
DON'T DO IT, LADY!
I WILL...
I MUST.
AMOM SHUGGOR ZUGGUROTH.
FATHER...

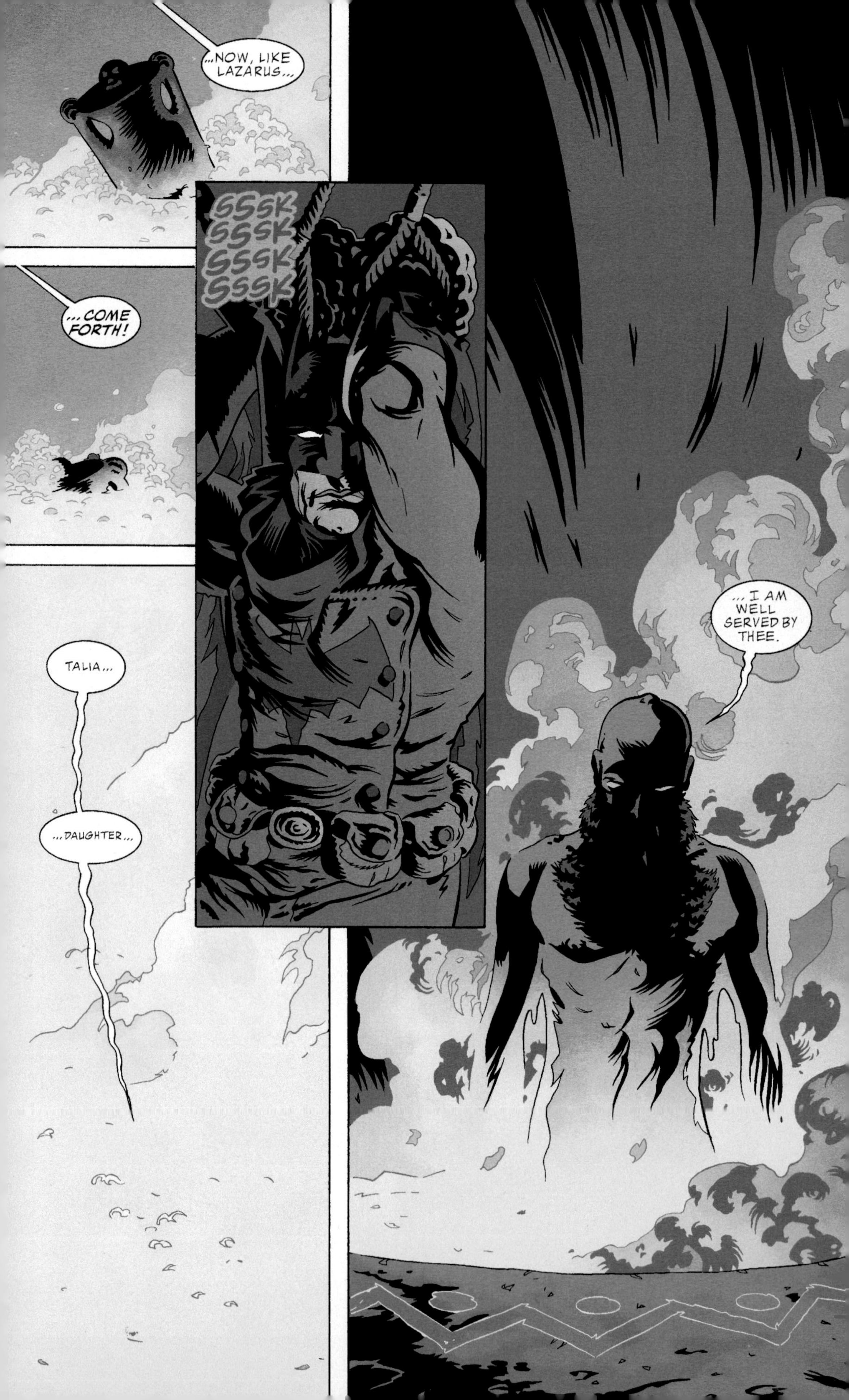
...NOW, LIKE LAZARUS...
...COME FORTH!
SSSK SSSK SSSK SSSK
TALIA...
...DAUGHTER...
...I AM WELL SERVED BY THEE.

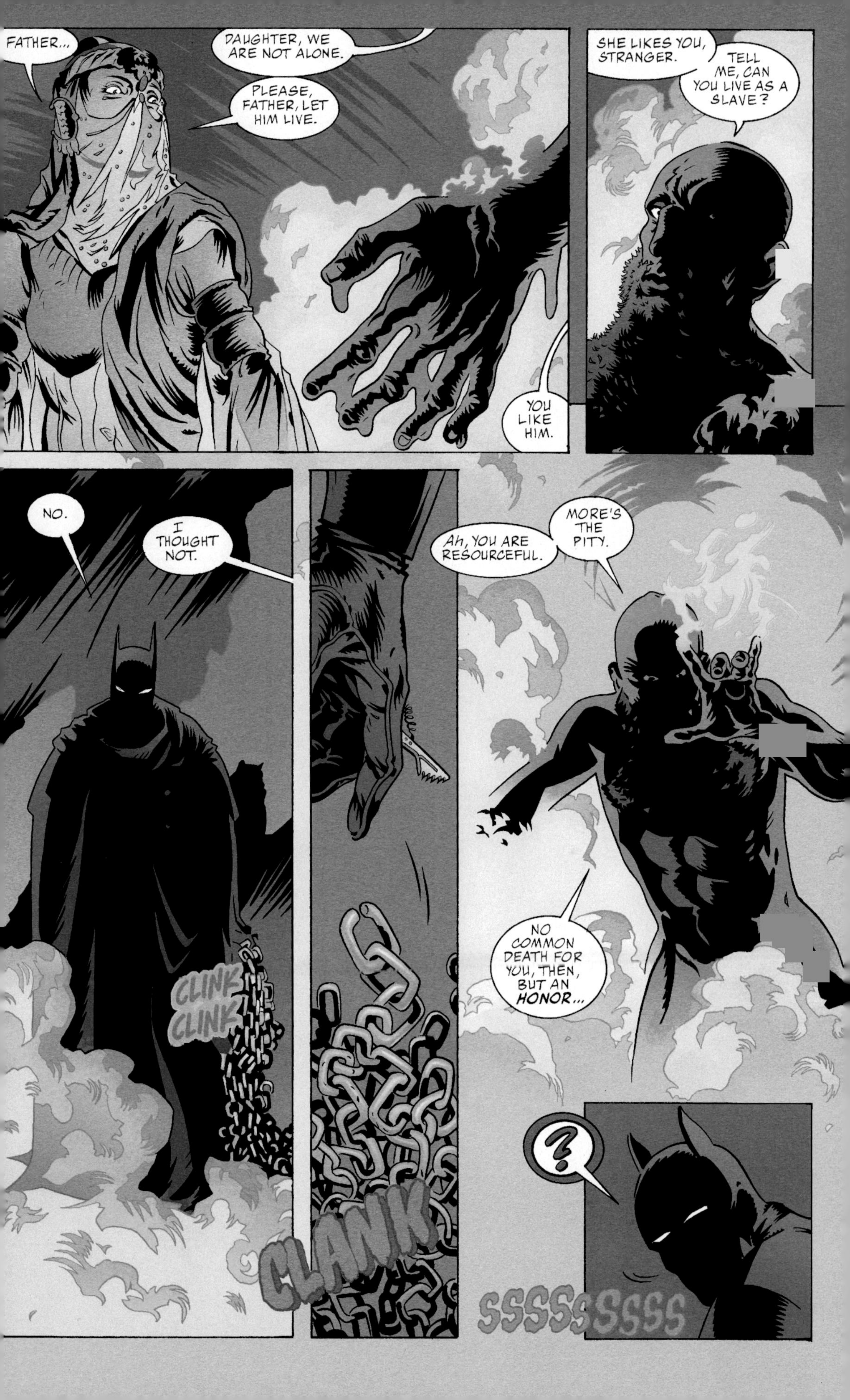

FATHER...
DAUGHTER, WE ARE NOT ALONE.
PLEASE, FATHER, LET HIM LIVE.
YOU LIKE HIM.
SHE LIKES YOU, STRANGER.
TELL ME, CAN YOU LIVE AS A SLAVE?
NO.
I THOUGHT NOT.
CLINK CLINK
CLANK
Ah, YOU ARE RESOURCEFUL.
MORE'S THE PITY.
NO COMMON DEATH FOR YOU, THEN, BUT AN HONOR...
?
SSSSSSSSS

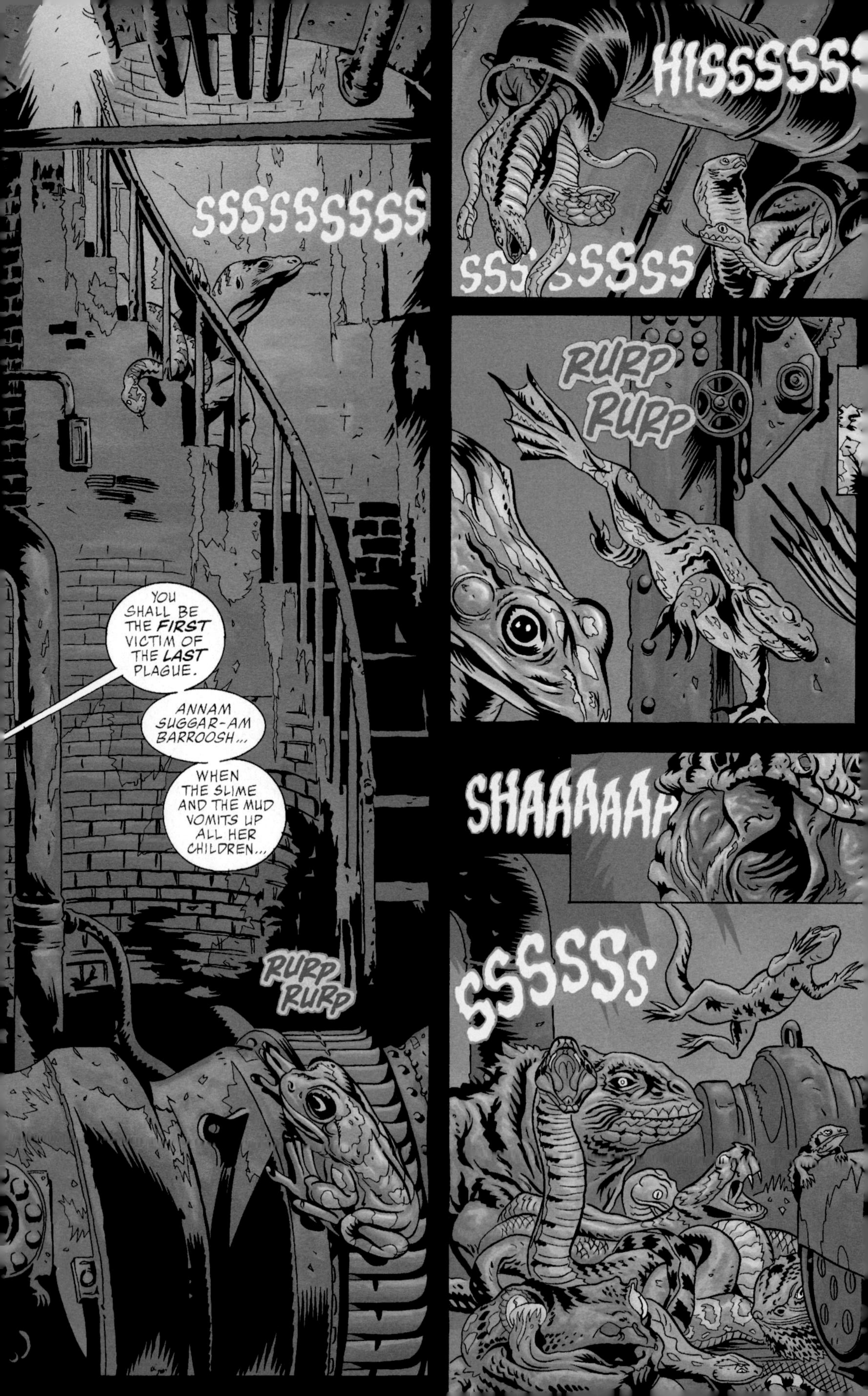
SSSSSSSSSS
YOU SHALL BE THE FIRST VICTIM OF THE LAST PLAGUE.
ANNAM SUGGAR-AM BARROOSH...
WHEN THE SLIME AND THE MUD VOMITS UP ALL HER CHILDREN...
RURP RURP
HISSSSSS
RURP RURP
SHAAAAAP
SSSSSs

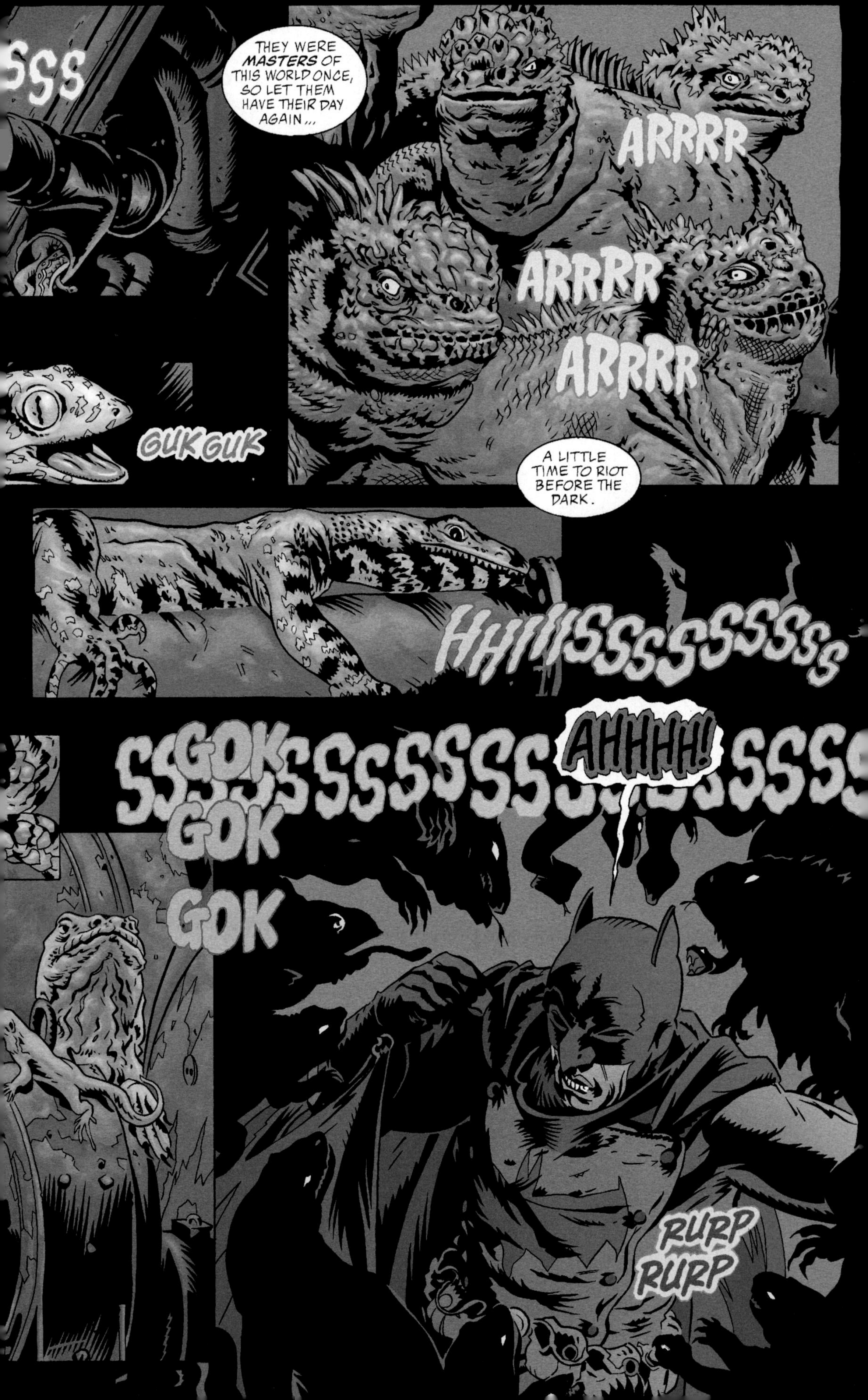
SSS
THEY WERE MASTERS OF THIS WORLD ONCE, SO LET THEM HAVE THEIR DAY AGAIN...
ARRRR
ARRRR
ARRRR
GUK GUK
A LITTLE TIME TO RIOT BEFORE THE DARK.
HHHSSSSSSSS
SSSSSSSSSSSSSSSSSSSS
AHHHH!
GOK
GOK
GOK
RURP
RURP

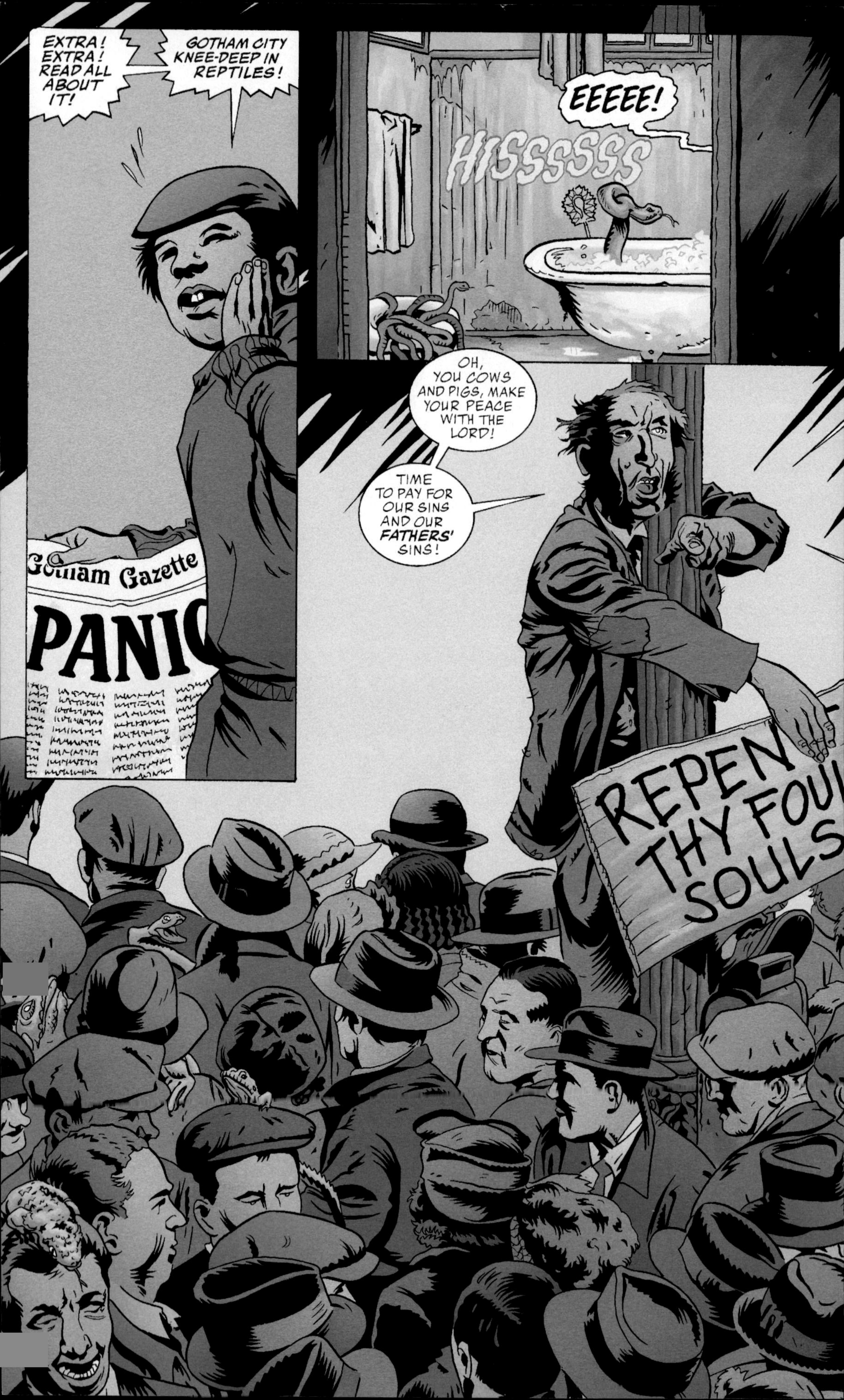
EXTRA! EXTRA! READ ALL ABOUT IT!
GOTHAM CITY KNEE-DEEP IN REPTILES!
Gotham Gazette
PANIC
EEEEE!
HISSSSSS
OH, YOU COWS AND PIGS, MAKE YOUR PEACE WITH THE LORD!
TIME TO PAY FOR OUR SINS AND OUR FATHERS' SINS!
REPEN
THY FOU
SOULS

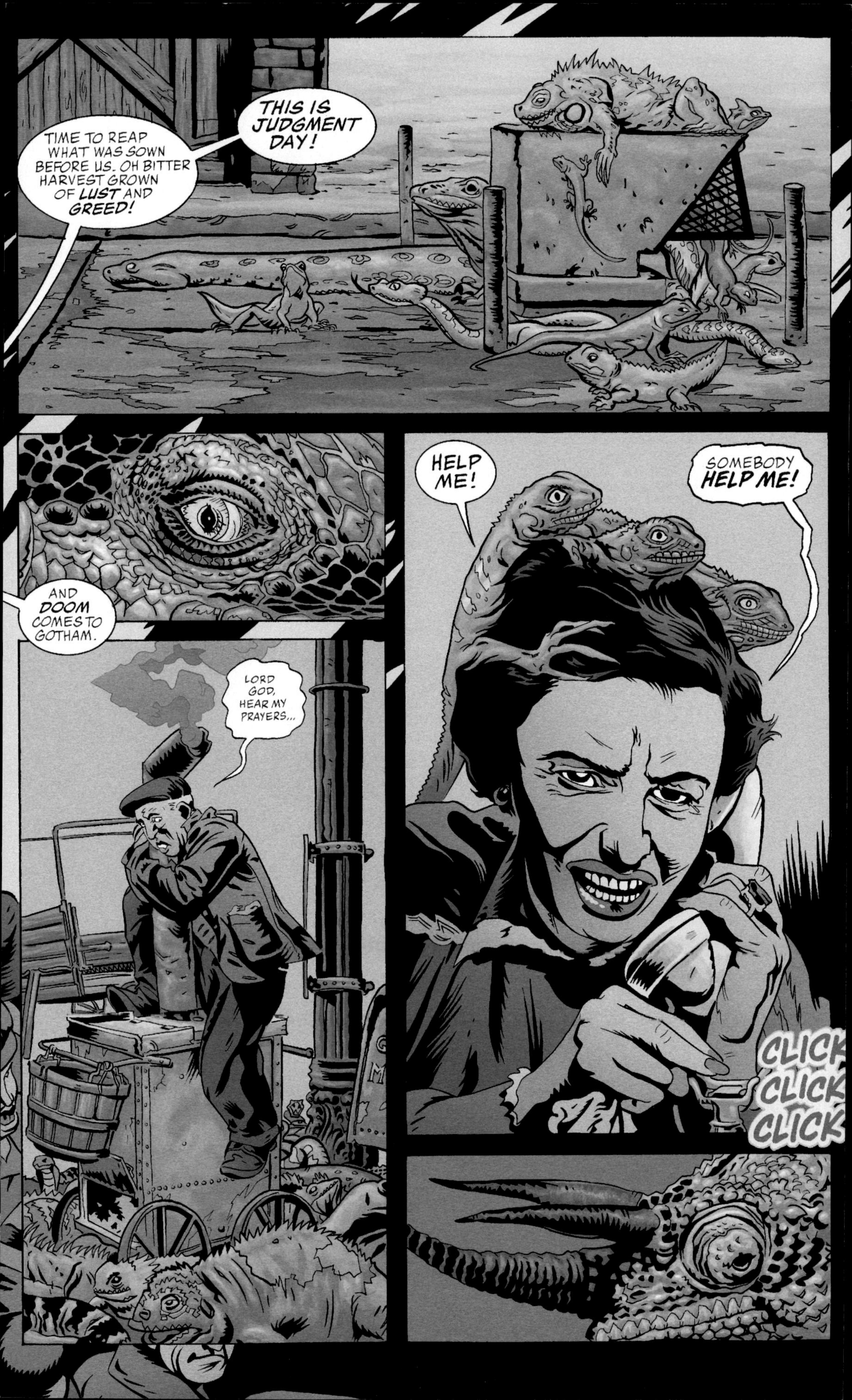
TIME TO REAP WHAT WAS SOWN BEFORE US. OH BITTER HARVEST GROWN OF LUST AND GREED!
THIS IS JUDGMENT DAY!
AND DOOM COMES TO GOTHAM.
HELP ME!
SOMEBODY HELP ME!
LORD GOD, HEAR MY PRAYERS...
CLICK CLICK CLICK

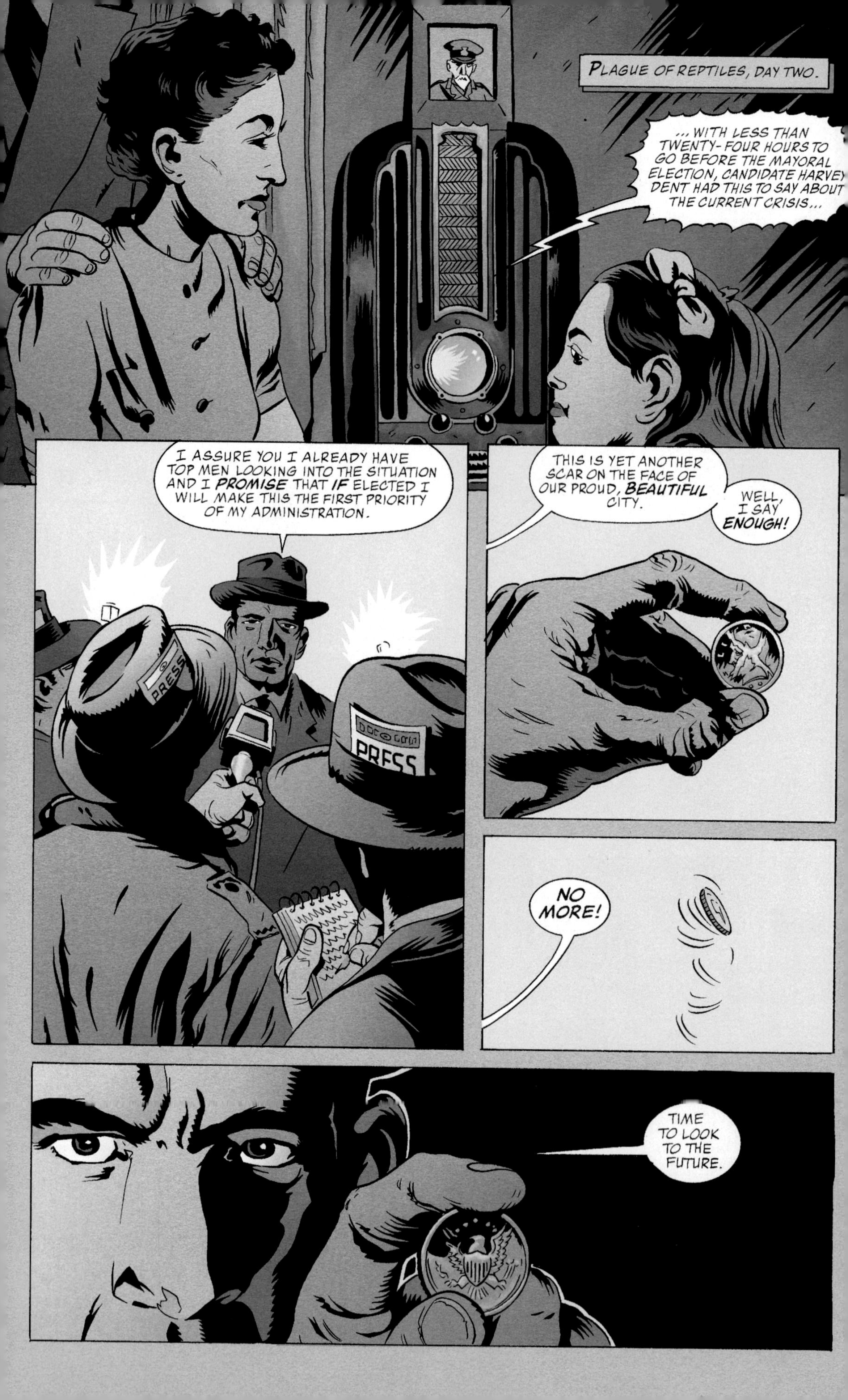
PLAGUE OF REPTILES, DAY TWO.
...WITH LESS THAN TWENTY-FOUR HOURS TO GO BEFORE THE MAYORAL ELECTION, CANDIDATE HARVEY DENT HAD THIS TO SAY ABOUT THE CURRENT CRISIS...
I ASSURE YOU I ALREADY HAVE TOP MEN LOOKING INTO THE SITUATION AND I PROMISE THAT IF ELECTED I WILL MAKE THIS THE FIRST PRIORITY OF MY ADMINISTRATION.
PRESS
PRESS
THIS IS YET ANOTHER SCAR ON THE FACE OF OUR PROUD, BEAUTIFUL CITY.
WELL, I SAY ENOUGH!
NO MORE!
TIME TO LOOK TO THE FUTURE.

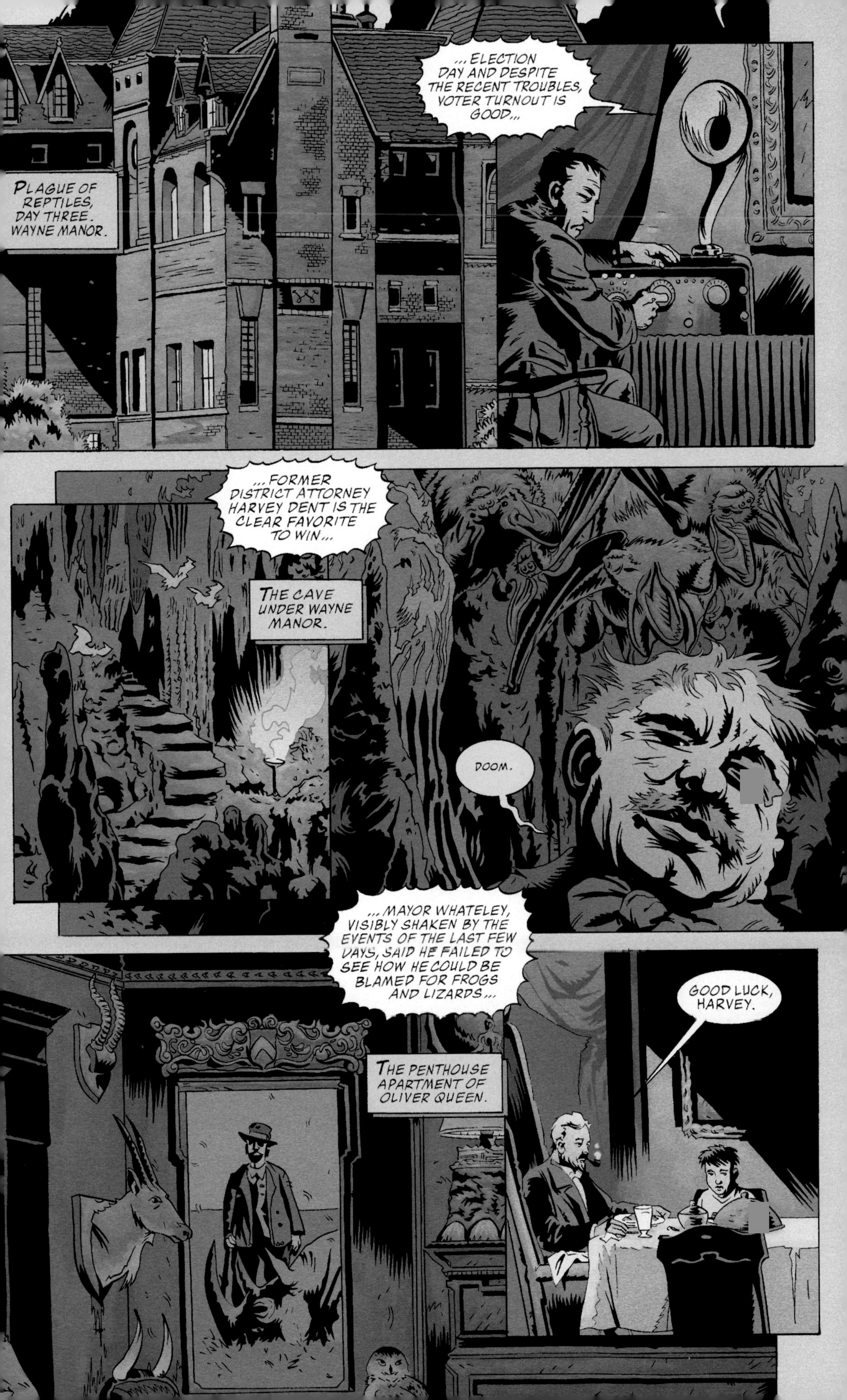
PLAGUE OF REPTILES, DAY THREE. WAYNE MANOR.
...ELECTION DAY AND DESPITE THE RECENT TROUBLES, VOTER TURNOUT IS GOOD...
...FORMER DISTRICT ATTORNEY HARVEY DENT IS THE CLEAR FAVORITE TO WIN...
THE CAVE UNDER WAYNE MANOR.
DOOM.
...MAYOR WHATELEY, VISIBLY SHAKEN BY THE EVENTS OF THE LAST FEW DAYS, SAID HE FAILED TO SEE HOW HE COULD BE BLAMED FOR FROGS AND LIZARDS...
THE PENTHOUSE APARTMENT OF OLIVER QUEEN.
GOOD LUCK, HARVEY.

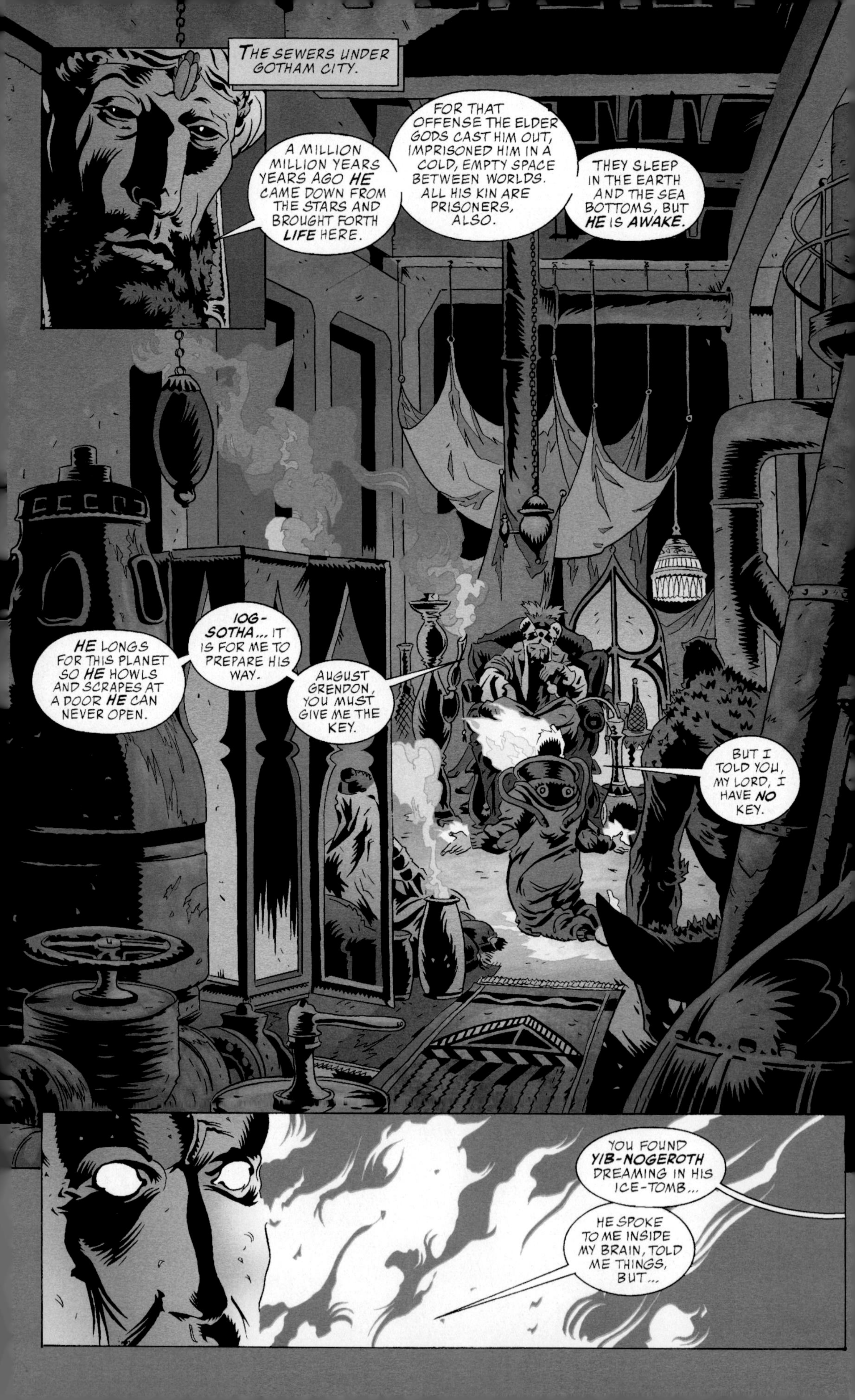
THE SEWERS UNDER GOTHAM CITY.
A MILLION MILLION YEARS AGO HE CAME DOWN FROM THE STARS AND BROUGHT FORTH LIFE HERE.
FOR THAT OFFENSE THE ELDER GODS CAST HIM OUT, IMPRISONED HIM IN A COLD, EMPTY SPACE BETWEEN WORLDS. ALL HIS KIN ARE PRISONERS, ALSO.
THEY SLEEP IN THE EARTH AND THE SEA BOTTOMS, BUT HE IS AWAKE.
HE LONGS FOR THIS PLANET SO HE HOWLS AND SCRAPES AT A DOOR HE CAN NEVER OPEN.
IOG-SOTHA... IT IS FOR ME TO PREPARE HIS WAY.
AUGUST GRENDON, YOU MUST GIVE ME THE KEY.
BUT I TOLD YOU, MY LORD, I HAVE NO KEY.
YOU FOUND YIB-NOGEROTH DREAMING IN HIS ICE-TOMB...
HE SPOKE TO ME INSIDE MY BRAIN, TOLD ME THINGS, BUT...

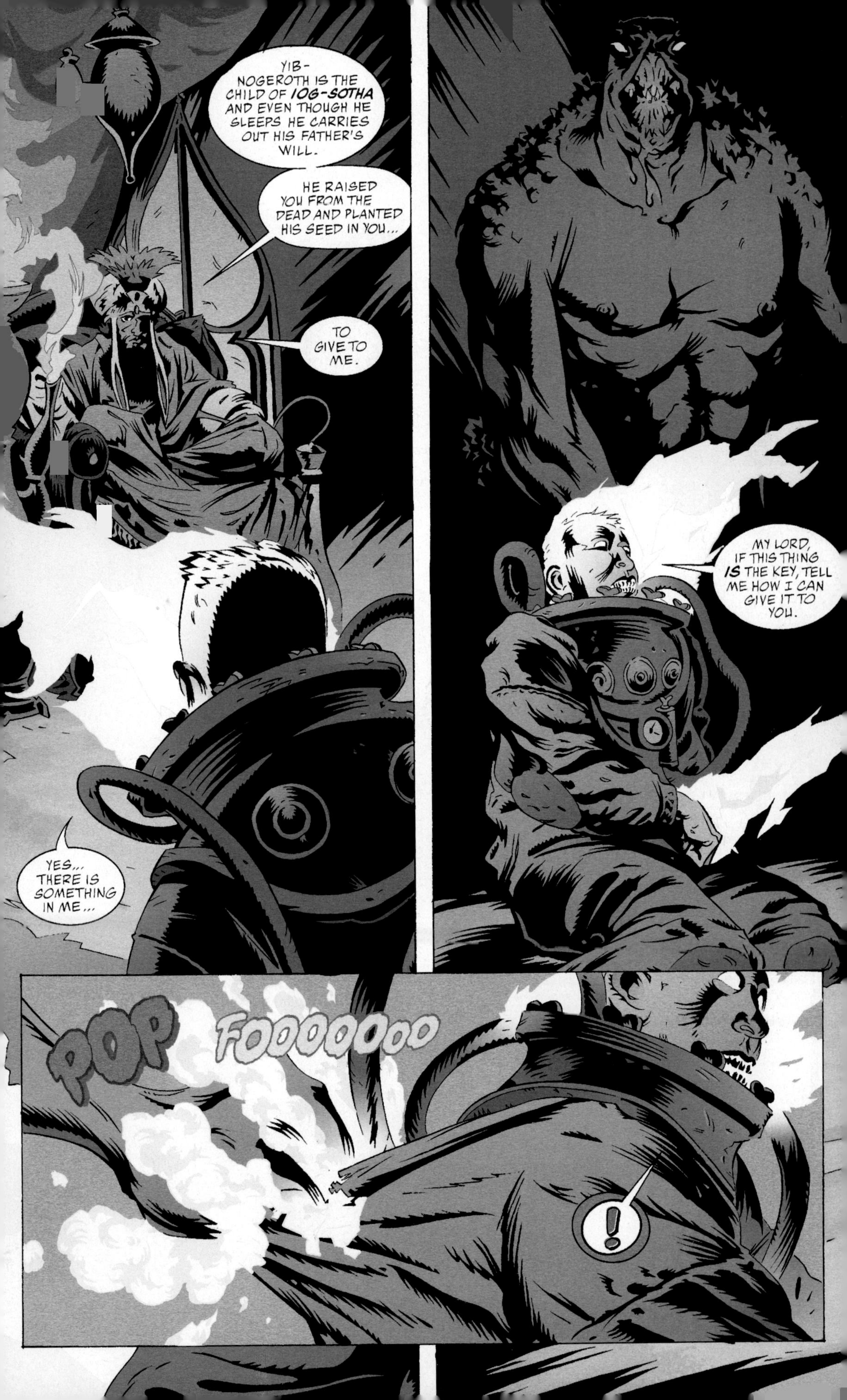
YIB-NOGEROTH IS THE CHILD OF IOG-SOTHA AND EVEN THOUGH HE SLEEPS HE CARRIES OUT HIS FATHER'S WILL.
HE RAISED YOU FROM THE DEAD AND PLANTED HIS SEED IN YOU...
TO GIVE TO ME.
MY LORD, IF THIS THING IS THE KEY, TELL ME HOW I CAN GIVE IT TO YOU.
YES... THERE IS SOMETHING IN ME...
POP
FOOOOOOO
!

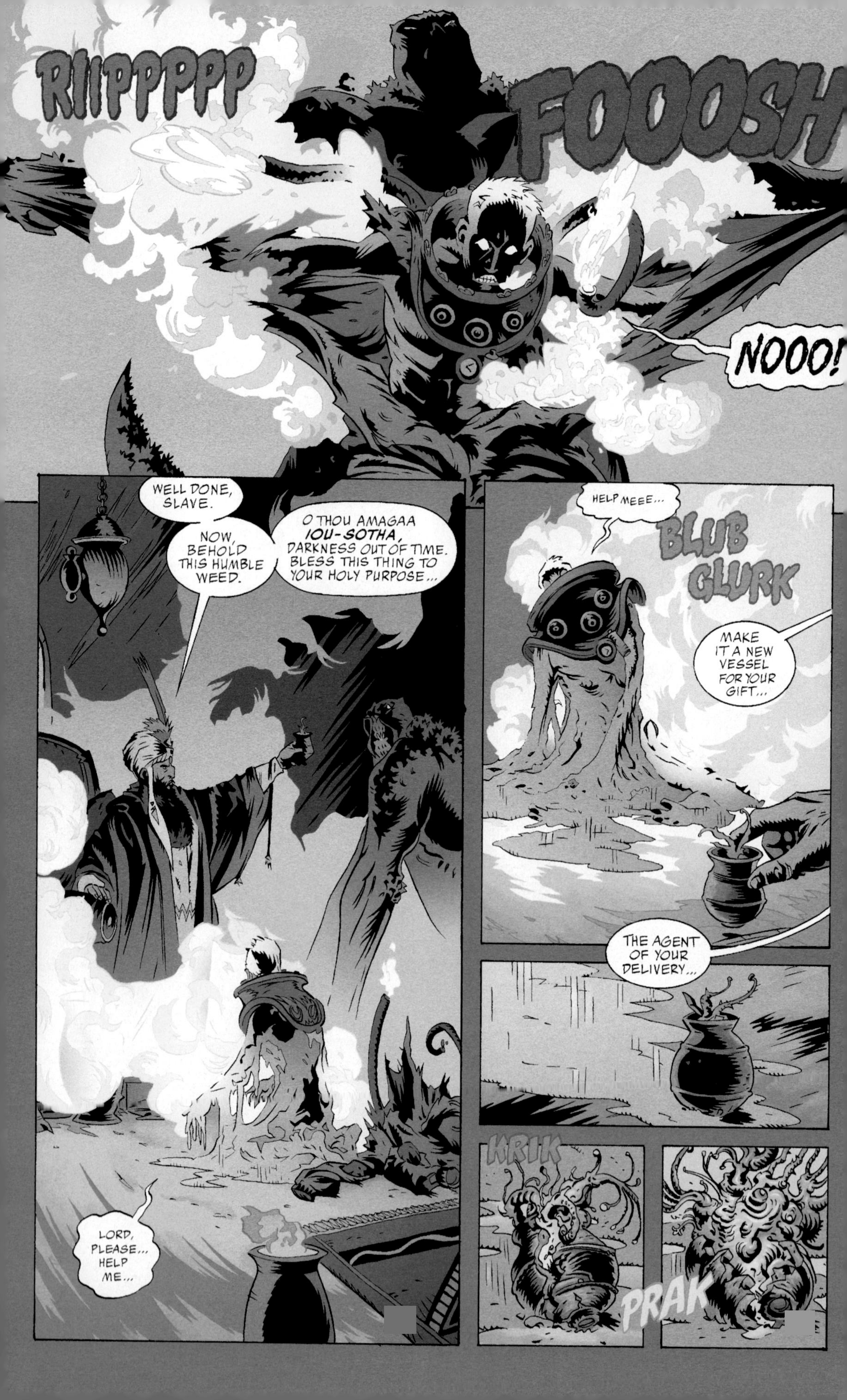

RIIPPPPP
FOOOSH
NOOO!
WELL DONE, SLAVE.
NOW, BEHOLD THIS HUMBLE WEED.
O THOU AMAGAA IOU-SOTHA, DARKNESS OUT OF TIME. BLESS THIS THING TO YOUR HOLY PURPOSE...
LORD, PLEASE... HELP ME...
HELP MEEE...
BLUB GLURK
MAKE IT A NEW VESSEL FOR YOUR GIFT...
THE AGENT OF YOUR DELIVERY...
KRIK
PRAK

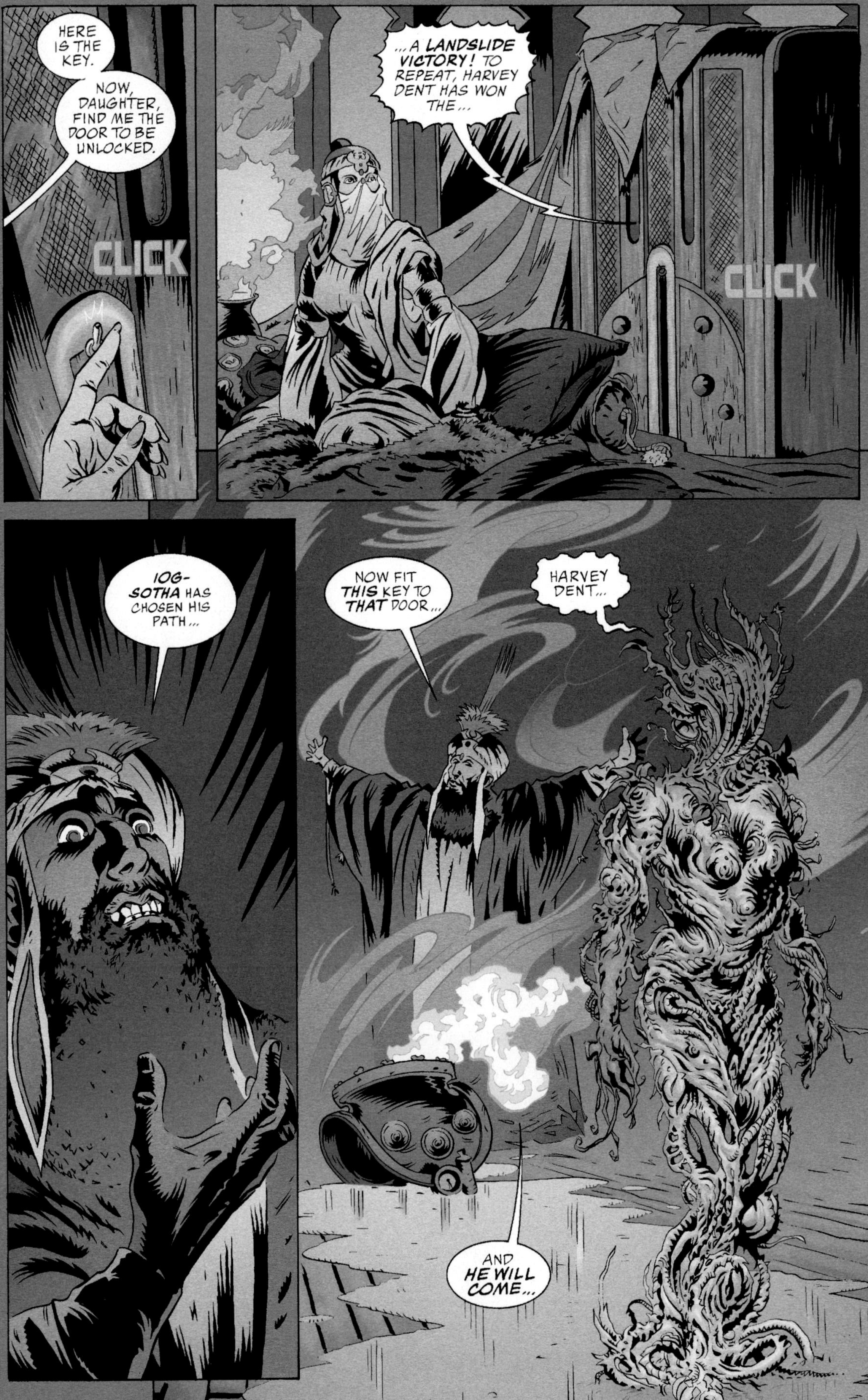
HERE IS THE KEY.
NOW, DAUGHTER, FIND ME THE DOOR TO BE UNLOCKED.
CLICK
...A LANDSLIDE VICTORY! TO REPEAT, HARVEY DENT HAS WON THE...
CLICK
IOG-SOTHA HAS CHOSEN HIS PATH...
NOW FIT THIS KEY TO THAT DOOR...
HARVEY DENT...
AND HE WILL COME...

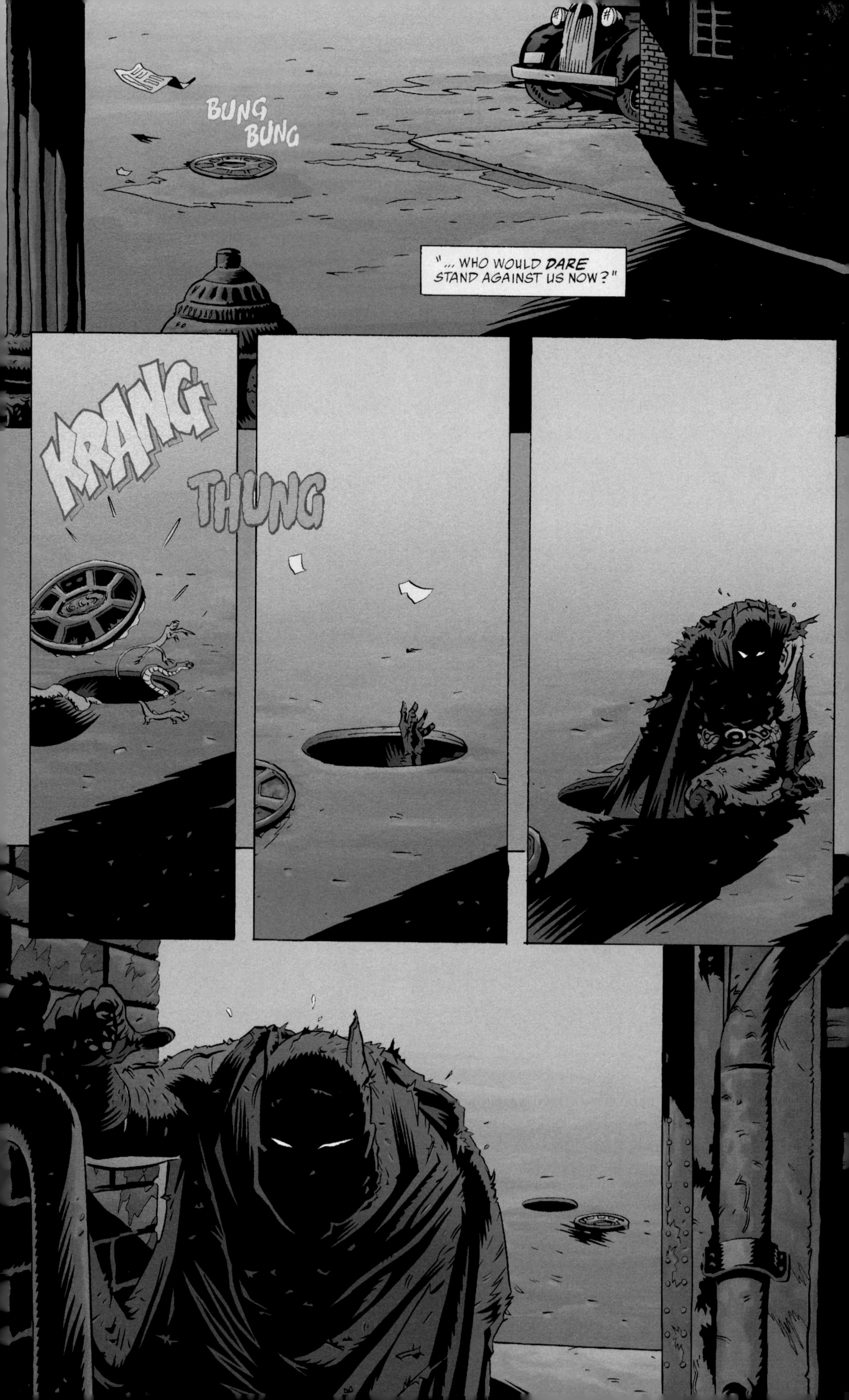
BUNG
BUNG
"... WHO WOULD DARE STAND AGAINST US NOW?"
KRANG
THUNG

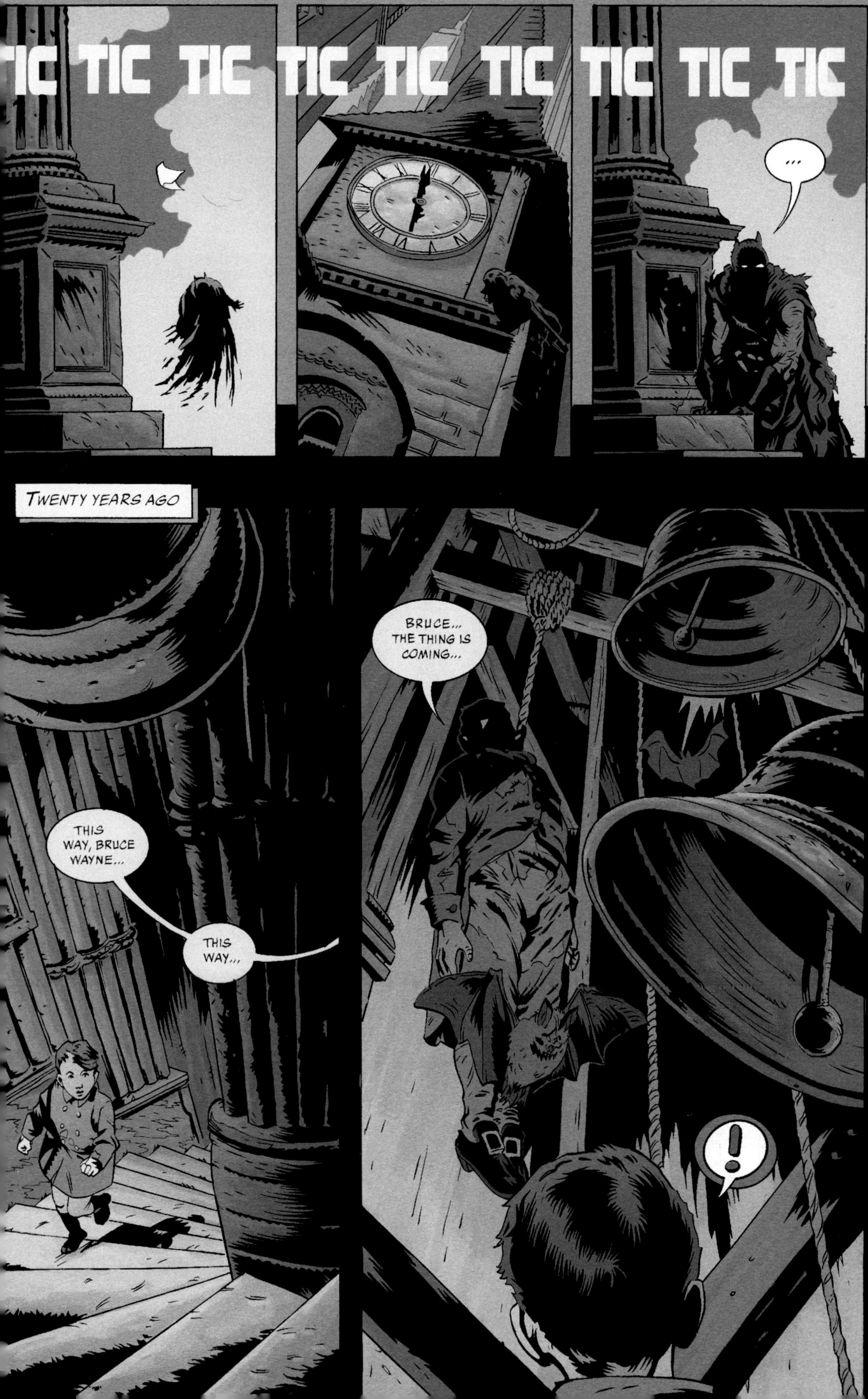
TIC TIC TIC TIC TIC TIC TIC TIC TIC
...
TWENTY YEARS AGO
THIS WAY, BRUCE WAYNE...
THIS WAY...
BRUCE... THE THING IS COMING...
!

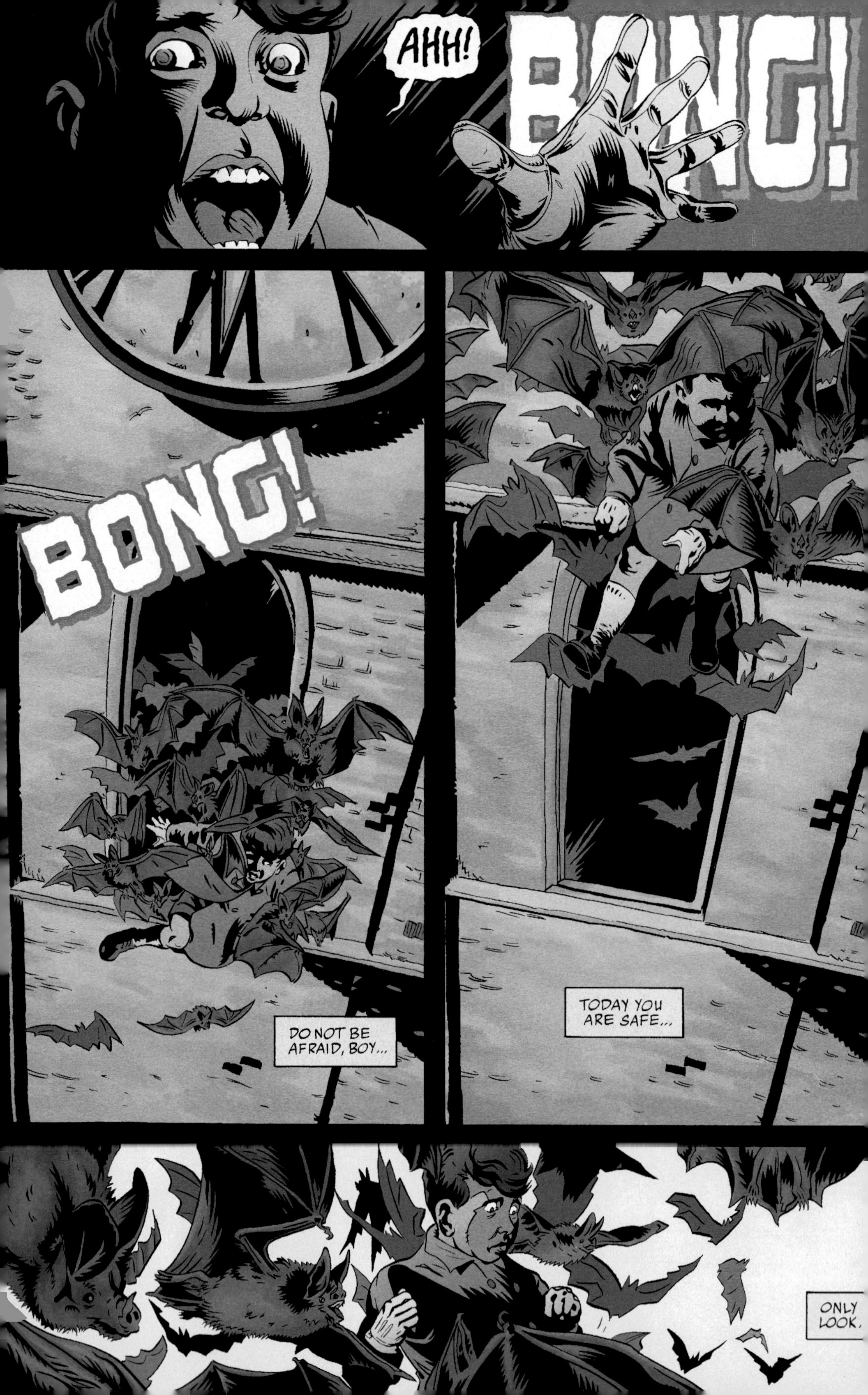
AHH!
BONG!
BONG!
DO NOT BE AFRAID, BOY...
TODAY YOU ARE SAFE...
ONLY LOOK.

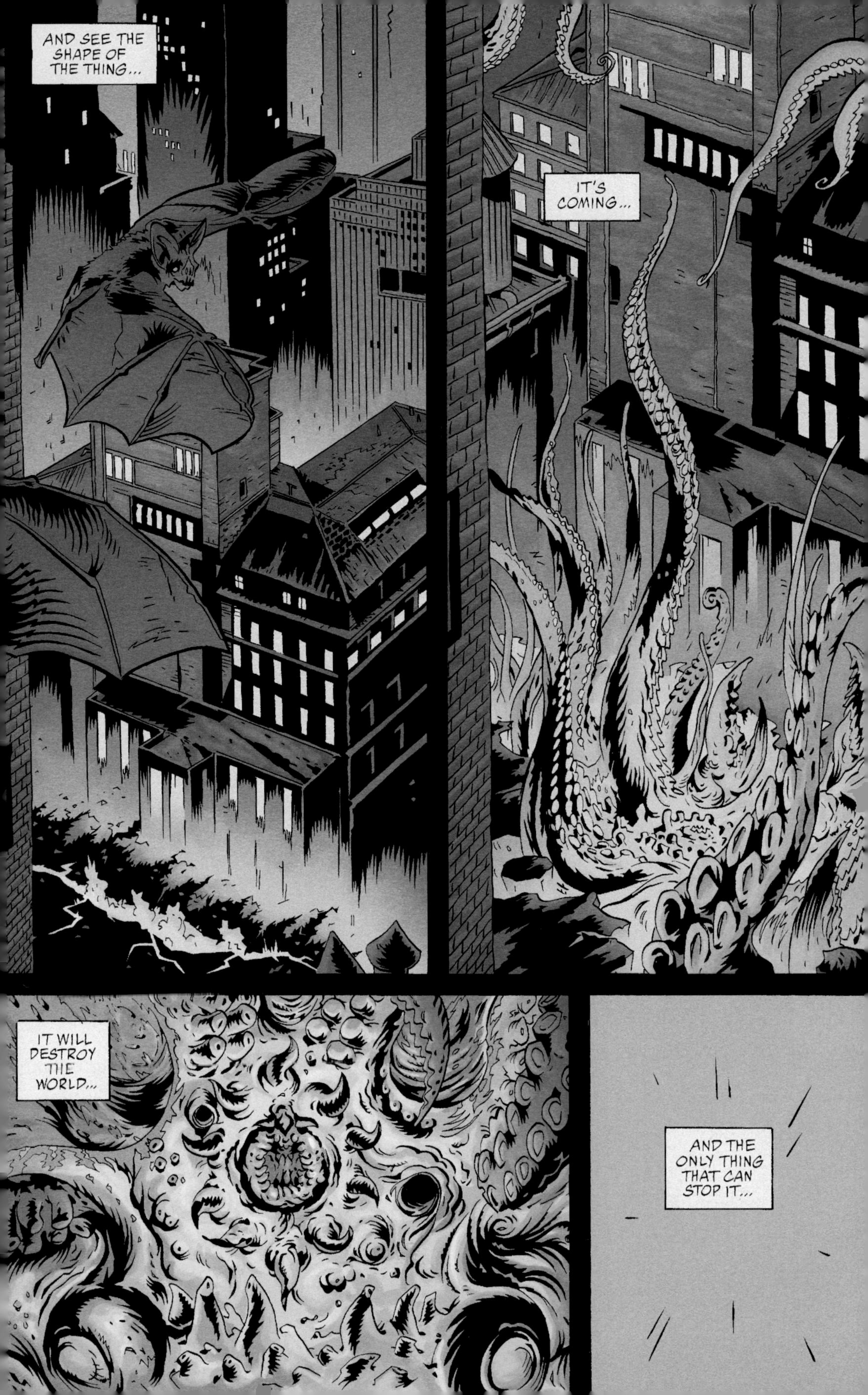
AND SEE THE SHAPE OF THE THING...
IT'S COMING...
IT WILL DESTROY THE WORLD...
AND THE ONLY THING THAT CAN STOP IT...

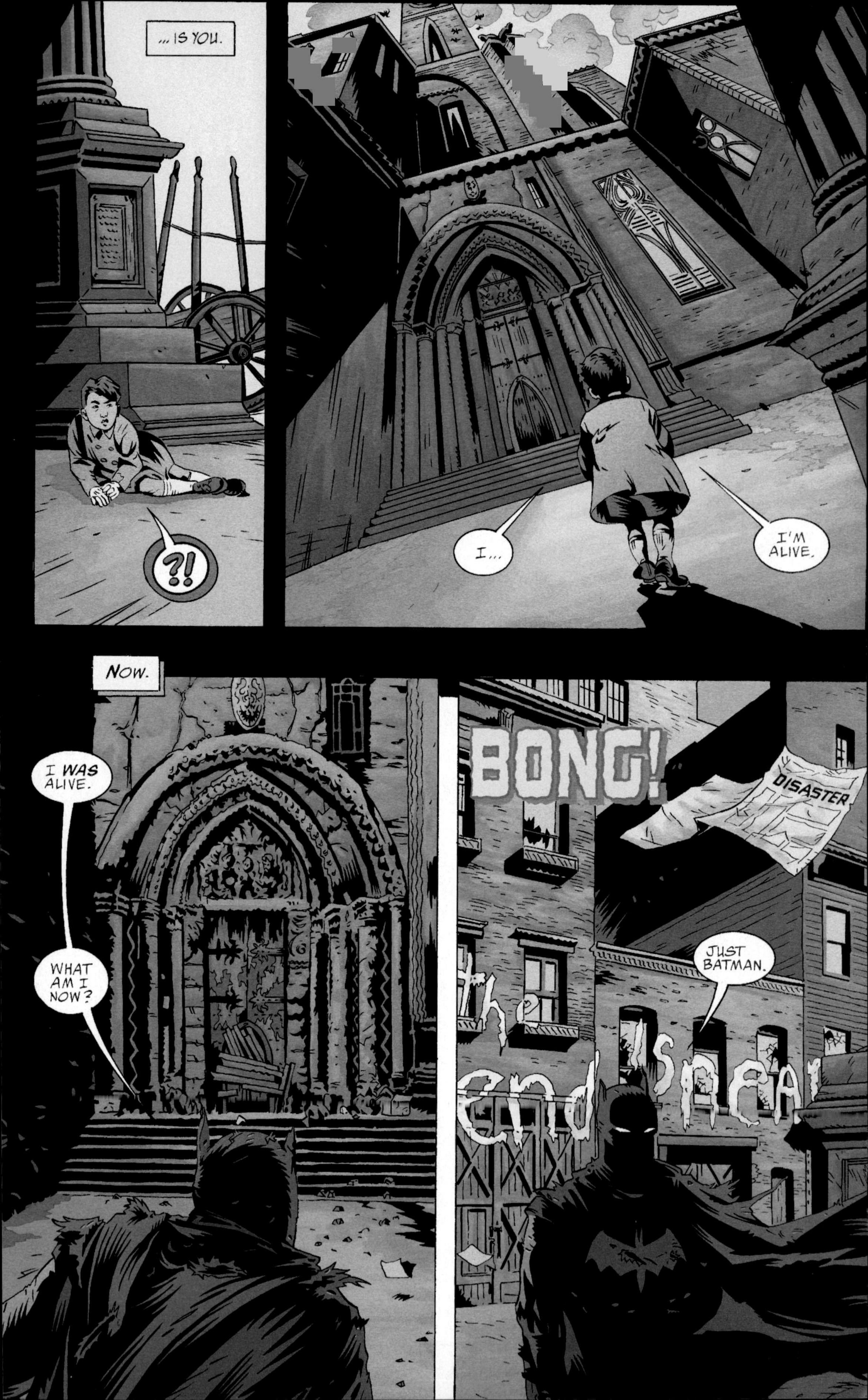
...IS YOU.
?!
I...
I'M ALIVE.
NOW.
I WAS ALIVE.
WHAT AM I NOW?
BONG!
DISASTER
JUST BATMAN.

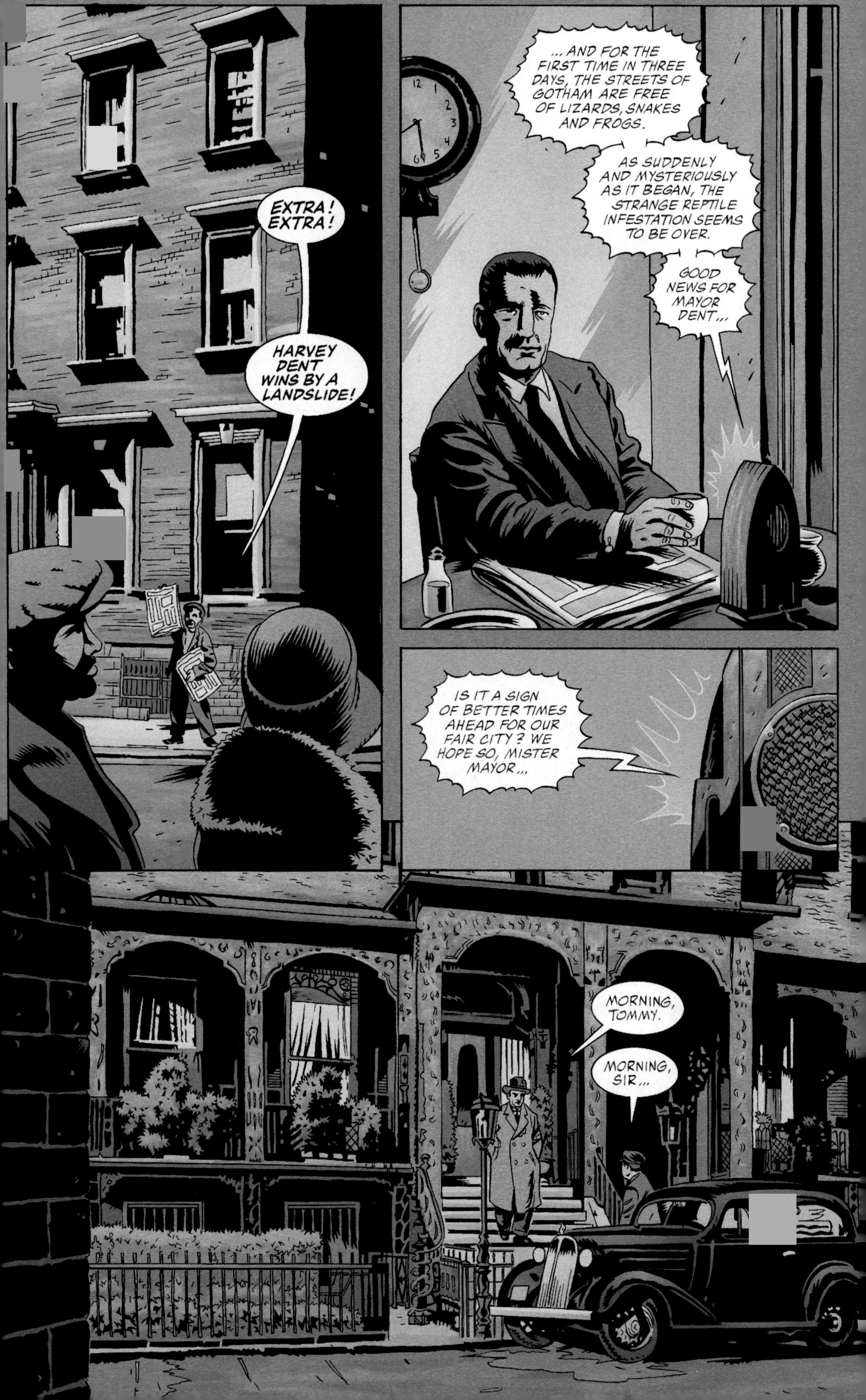
EXTRA! EXTRA!
HARVEY DENT WINS BY A LANDSLIDE!
... AND FOR THE FIRST TIME IN THREE DAYS, THE STREETS OF GOTHAM ARE FREE OF LIZARDS, SNAKES AND FROGS.
AS SUDDENLY AND MYSTERIOUSLY AS IT BEGAN, THE STRANGE REPTILE INFESTATION SEEMS TO BE OVER.
GOOD NEWS FOR MAYOR DENT...
IS IT A SIGN OF BETTER TIMES AHEAD FOR OUR FAIR CITY? WE HOPE SO, MISTER MAYOR...
MORNING, TOMMY.
MORNING, SIR...

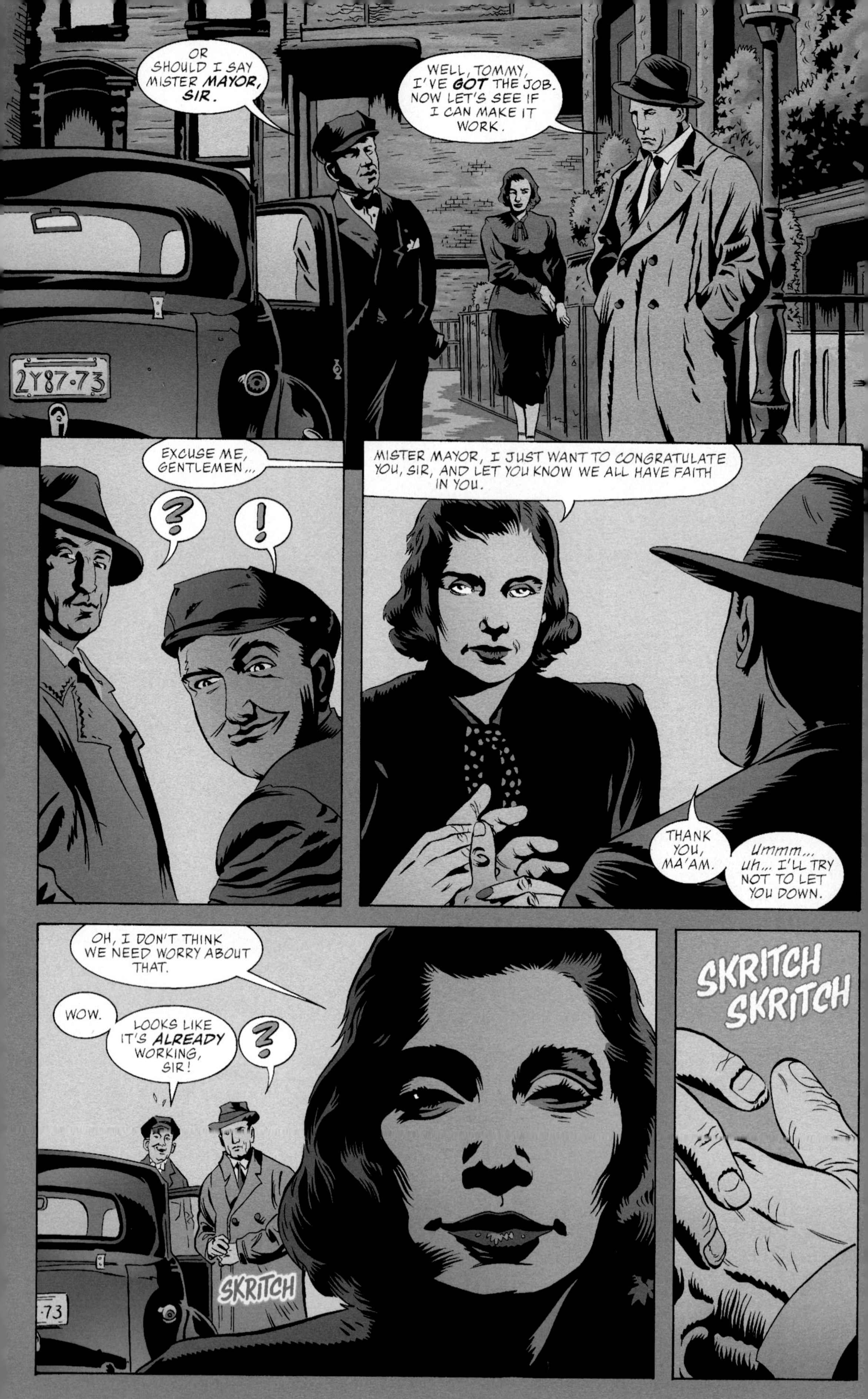
OR SHOULD I SAY MISTER MAYOR, SIR.
WELL, TOMMY, I'VE GOT THE JOB. NOW LET'S SEE IF I CAN MAKE IT WORK.
2Y87-73
EXCUSE ME, GENTLEMEN...
?
!
MISTER MAYOR, I JUST WANT TO CONGRATULATE YOU, SIR, AND LET YOU KNOW WE ALL HAVE FAITH IN YOU.
THANK YOU, MA'AM.
Ummm... uh... I'LL TRY NOT TO LET YOU DOWN.
OH, I DON'T THINK WE NEED WORRY ABOUT THAT.
WOW.
LOOKS LIKE IT'S ALREADY WORKING, SIR!
?
SKRITCH
SKRITCH SKRITCH

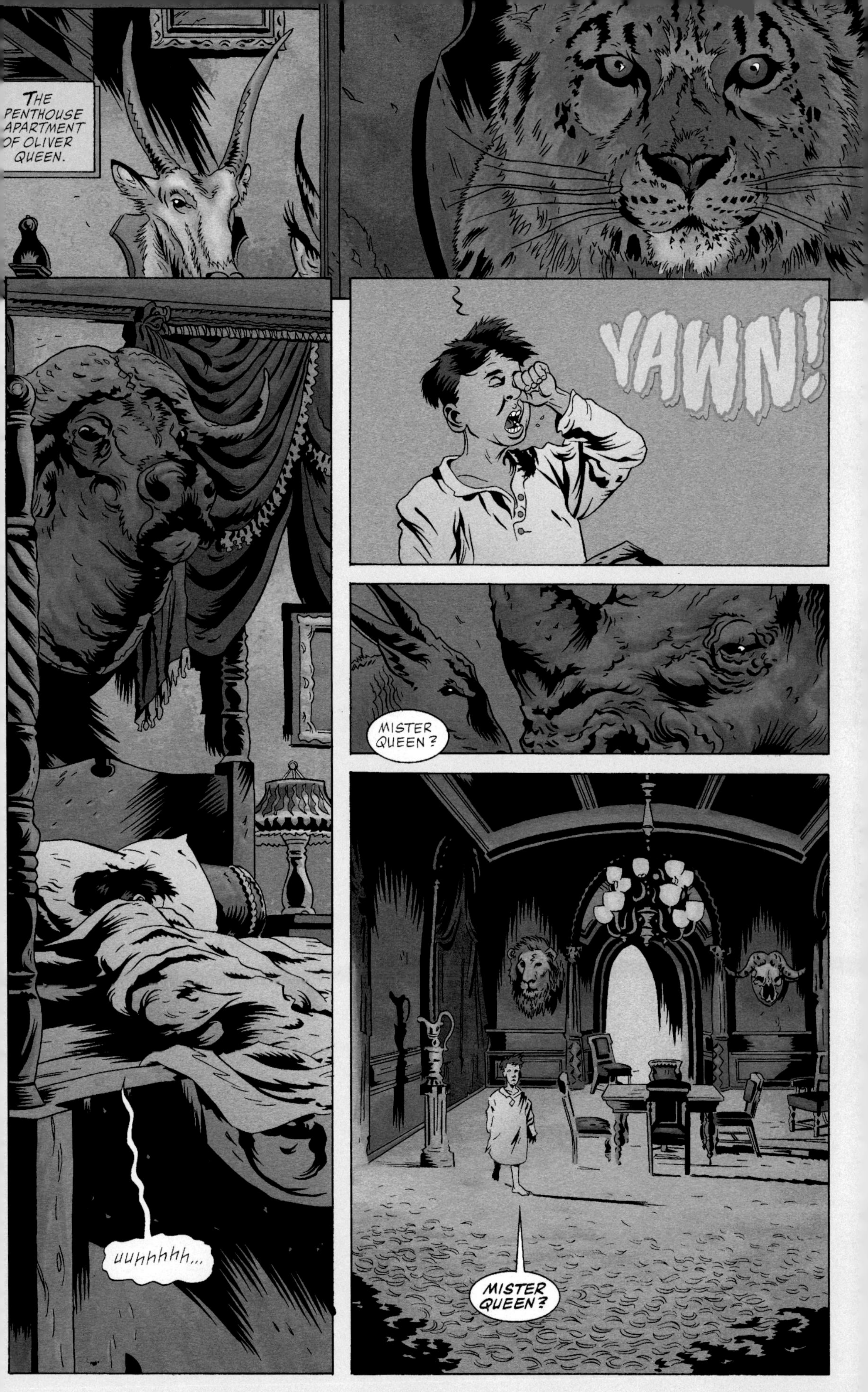
THE PENTHOUSE APARTMENT OF OLIVER QUEEN.
YAWN!
uuhhhhh...
MISTER QUEEN?
MISTER QUEEN?

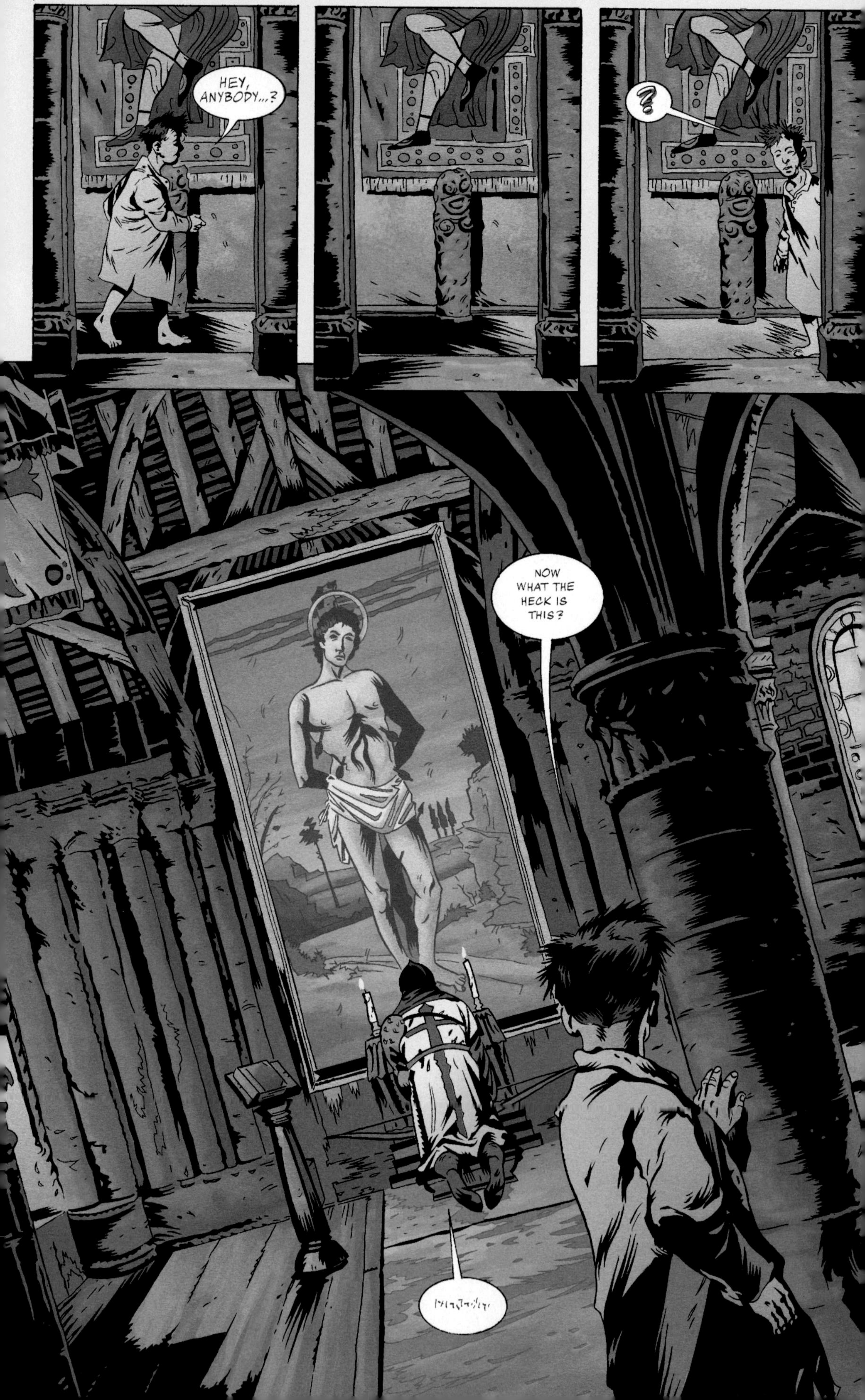
HEY, ANYBODY...?
?
NOW WHAT THE HECK IS THIS?

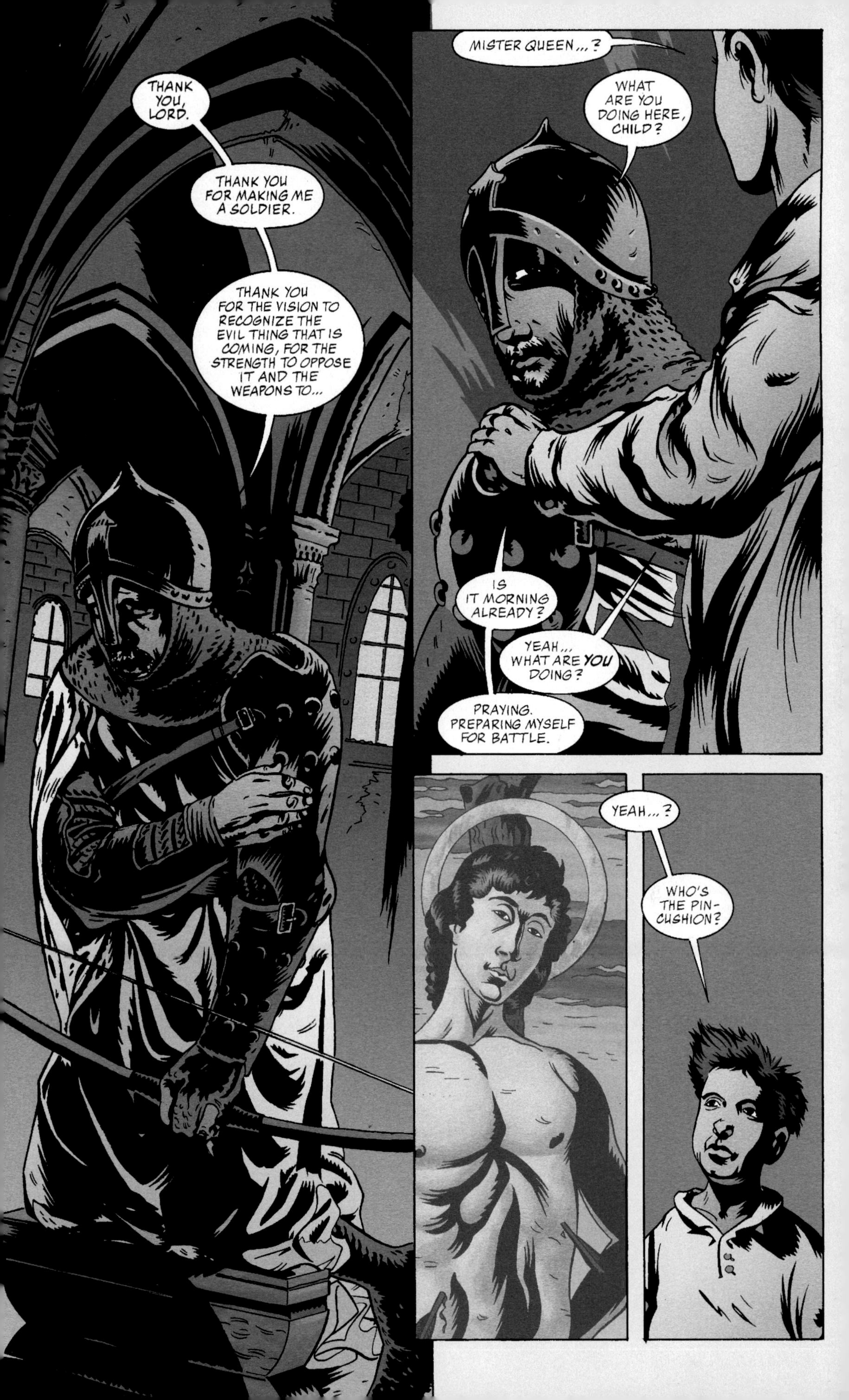
THANK YOU, LORD.
THANK YOU FOR MAKING ME A SOLDIER.
THANK YOU FOR THE VISION TO RECOGNIZE THE EVIL THING THAT IS COMING, FOR THE STRENGTH TO OPPOSE IT AND THE WEAPONS TO...
MISTER QUEEN...?
WHAT ARE YOU DOING HERE, CHILD?
IS IT MORNING ALREADY?
YEAH... WHAT ARE *YOU* DOING?
PRAYING. PREPARING MYSELF FOR BATTLE.
YEAH...?
WHO'S THE PIN-CUSHION?

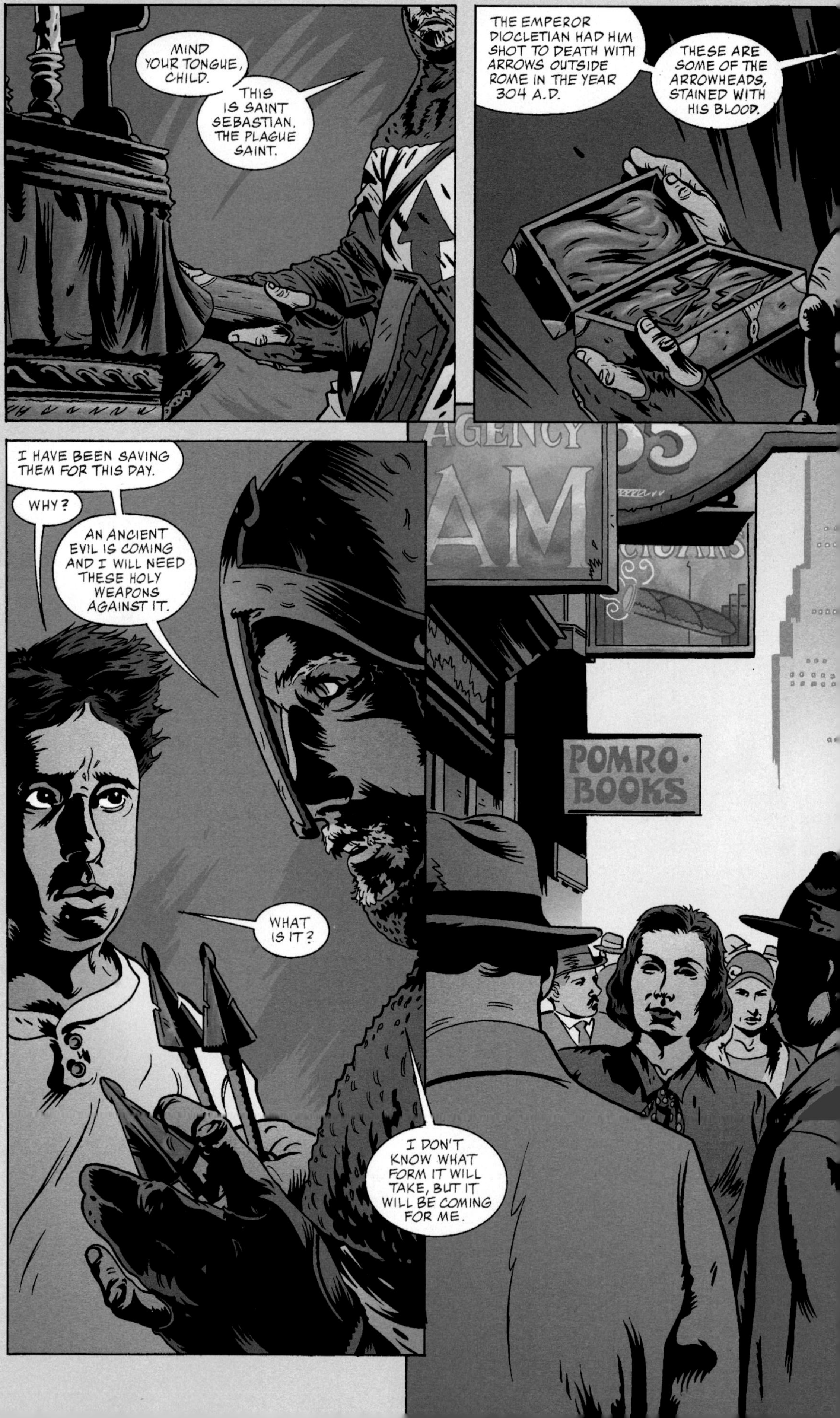
MIND YOUR TONGUE, CHILD.
THIS IS SAINT SEBASTIAN. THE PLAGUE SAINT.
THE EMPEROR DIOCLETIAN HAD HIM SHOT TO DEATH WITH ARROWS OUTSIDE ROME IN THE YEAR 304 A.D.
THESE ARE SOME OF THE ARROWHEADS, STAINED WITH HIS BLOOD.
AGENCY
POMRO· BOOKS
I HAVE BEEN SAVING THEM FOR THIS DAY.
WHY?
AN ANCIENT EVIL IS COMING AND I WILL NEED THESE HOLY WEAPONS AGAINST IT.
WHAT IS IT?
I DON'T KNOW WHAT FORM IT WILL TAKE, BUT IT WILL BE COMING FOR ME.

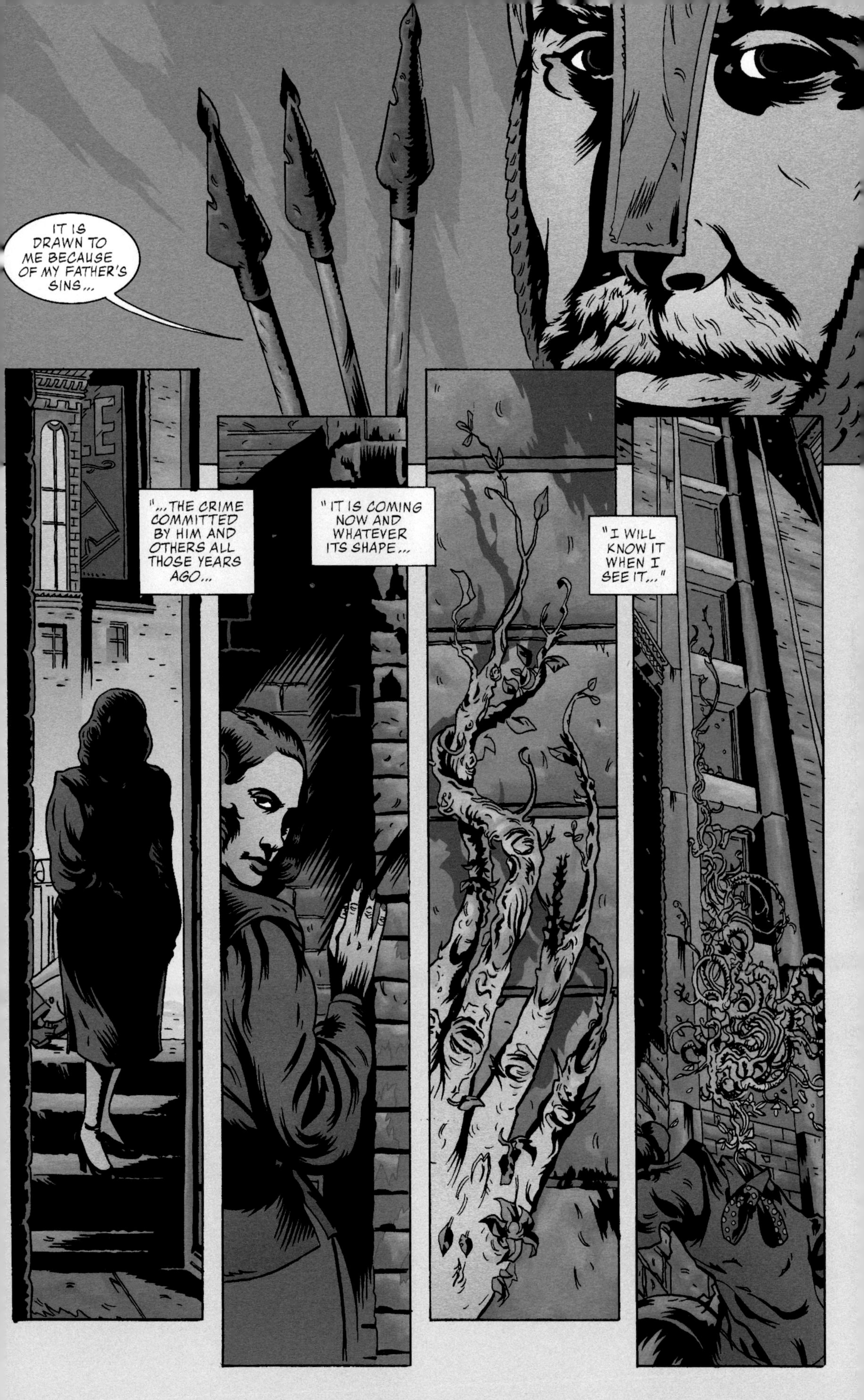
IT IS DRAWN TO ME BECAUSE OF MY FATHER'S SINS...
"...THE CRIME COMMITTED BY HIM AND OTHERS ALL THOSE YEARS AGO...
"IT IS COMING NOW AND WHATEVER ITS SHAPE...
"I WILL KNOW IT WHEN I SEE IT..."

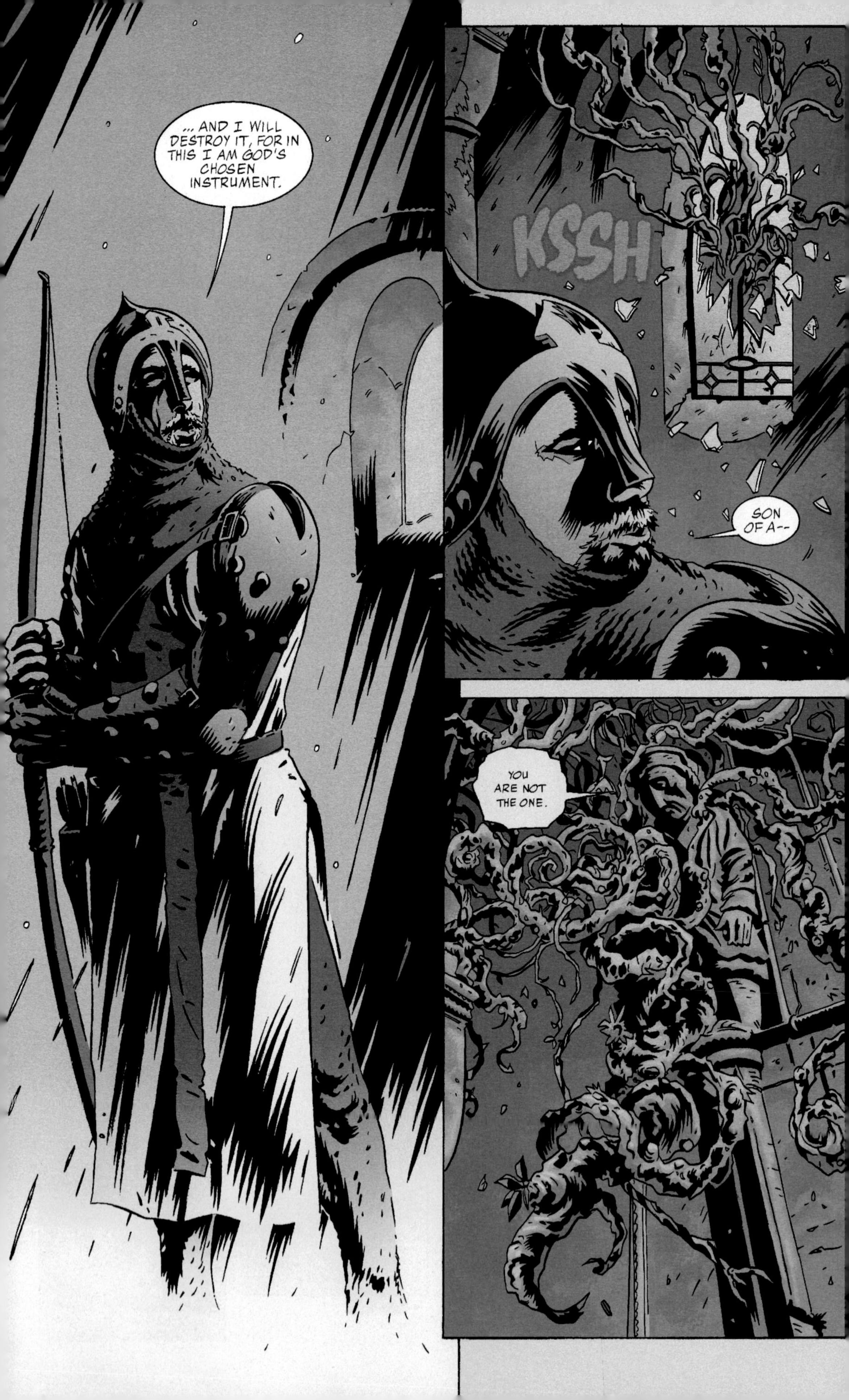
...AND I WILL DESTROY IT, FOR IN THIS I AM GOD'S CHOSEN INSTRUMENT.
KSSH
SON OF A--
YOU ARE NOT THE ONE.

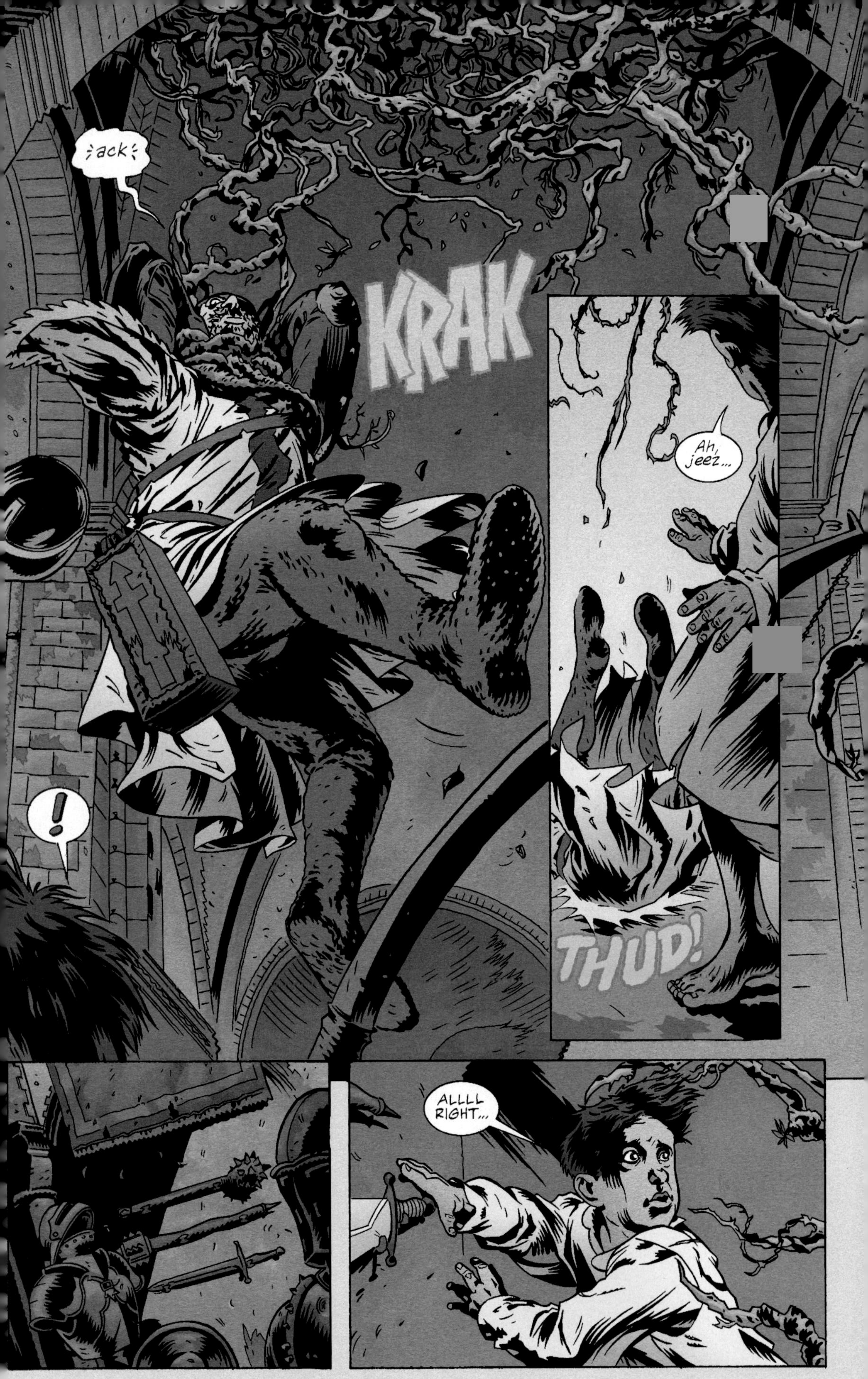
ack
KRAK
!
Ah, jeez...
THUD!
ALLLL RIGHT...

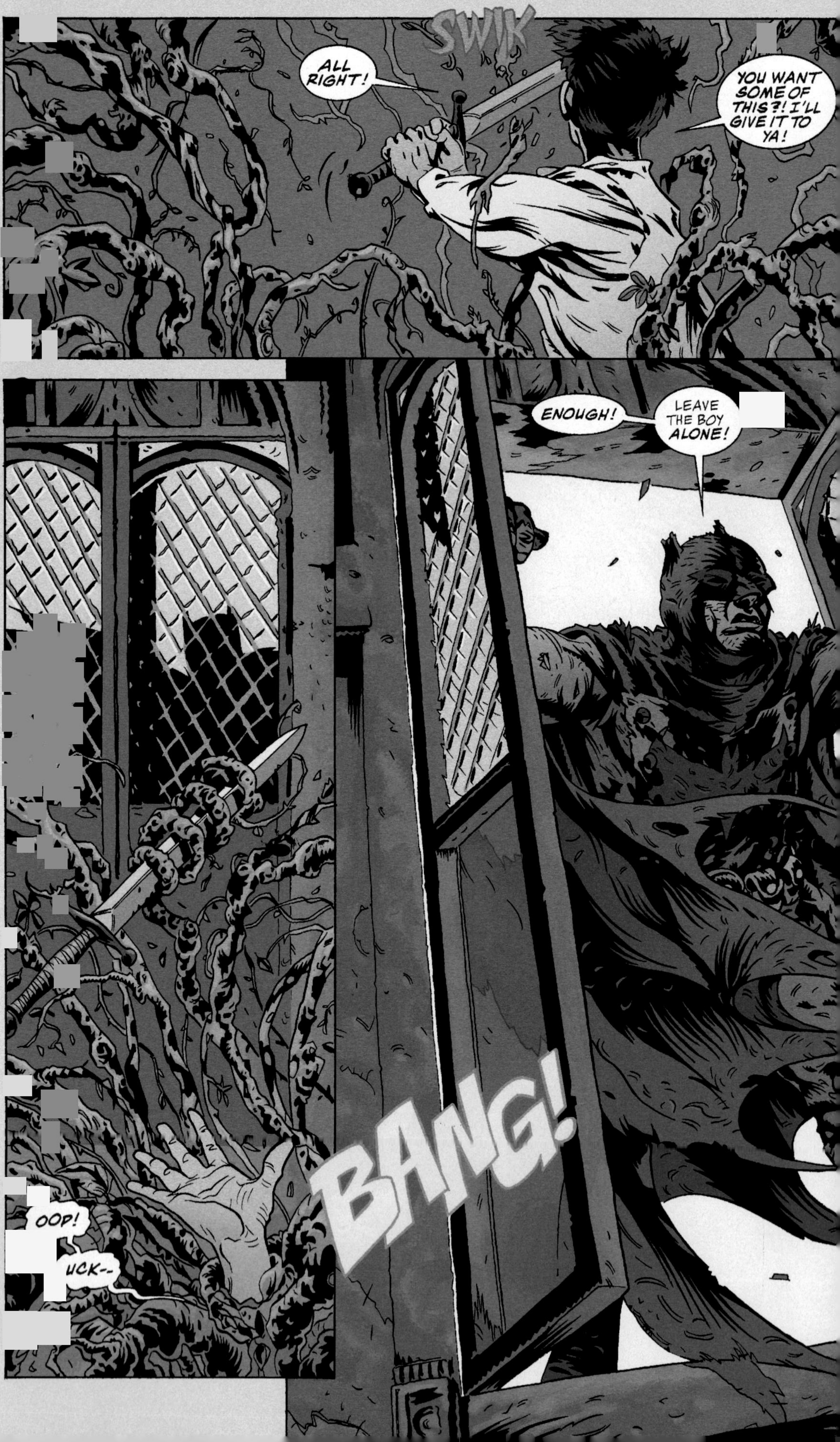
SWIK
ALL RIGHT!
YOU WANT SOME OF THIS?! I'LL GIVE IT TO YA!
ENOUGH!
LEAVE THE BOY ALONE!
BANG!
OOP!
UCK--

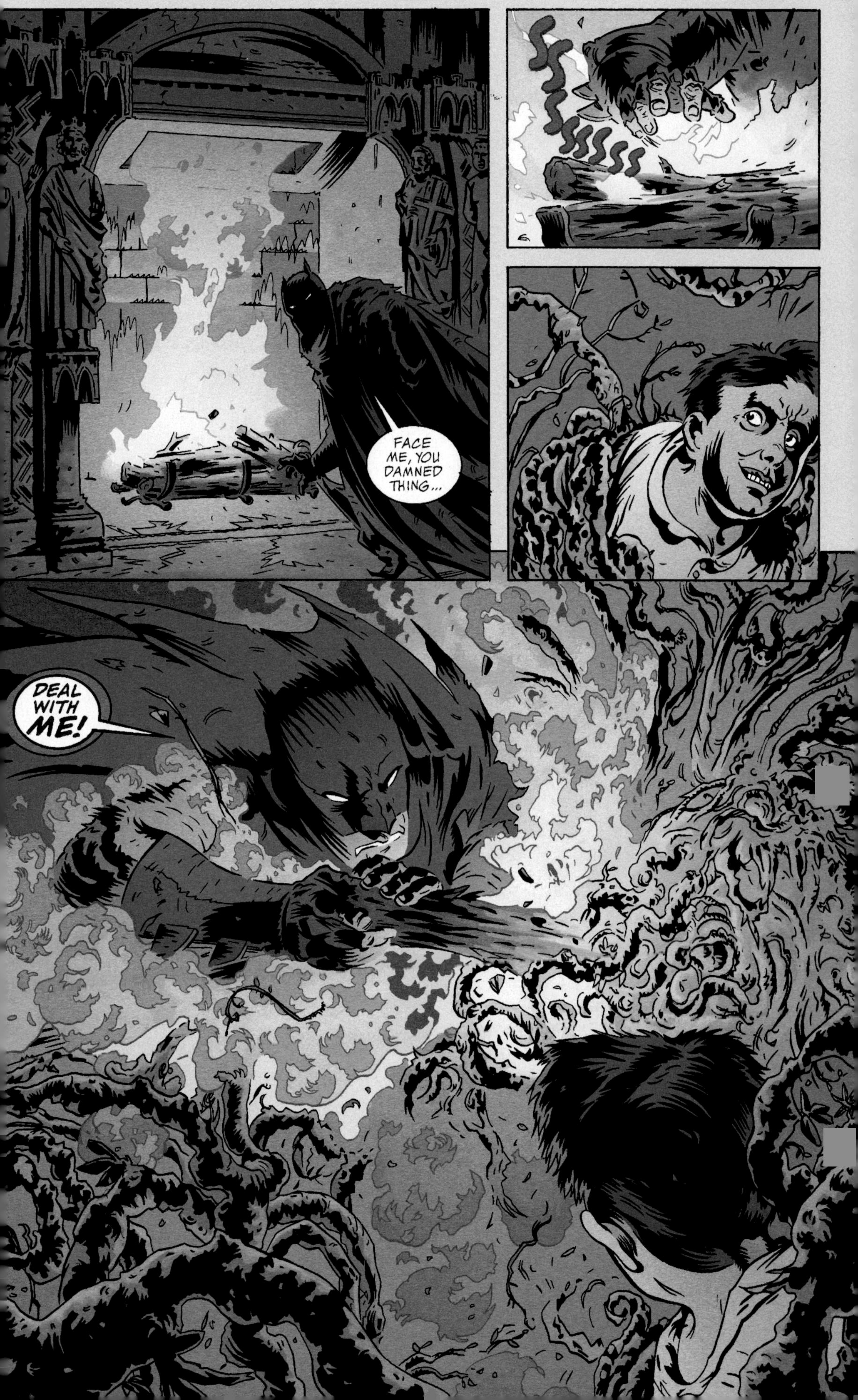
FACE ME, YOU DAMNED THING...
SSSSSSS
DEAL WITH ME!

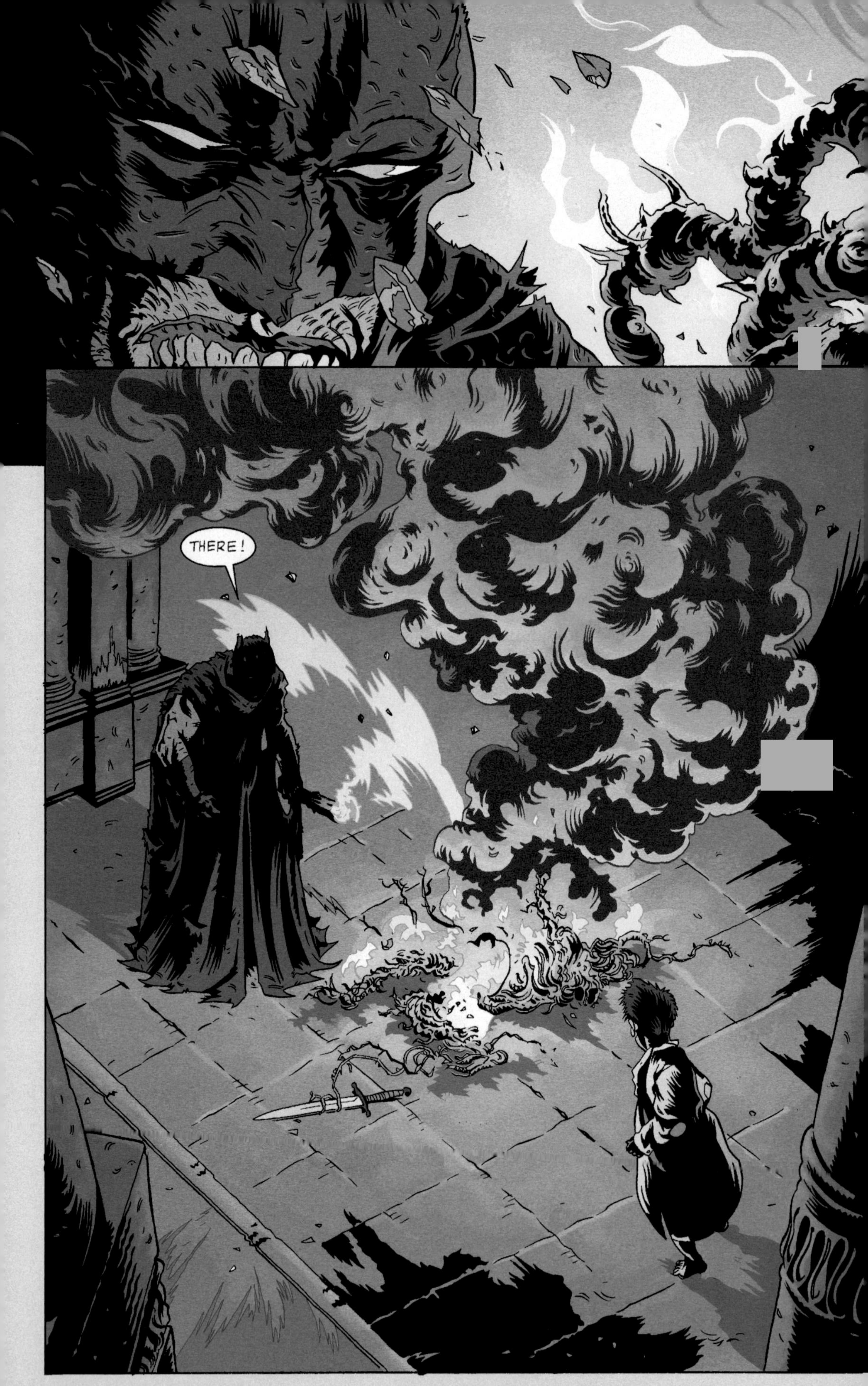
THERE!

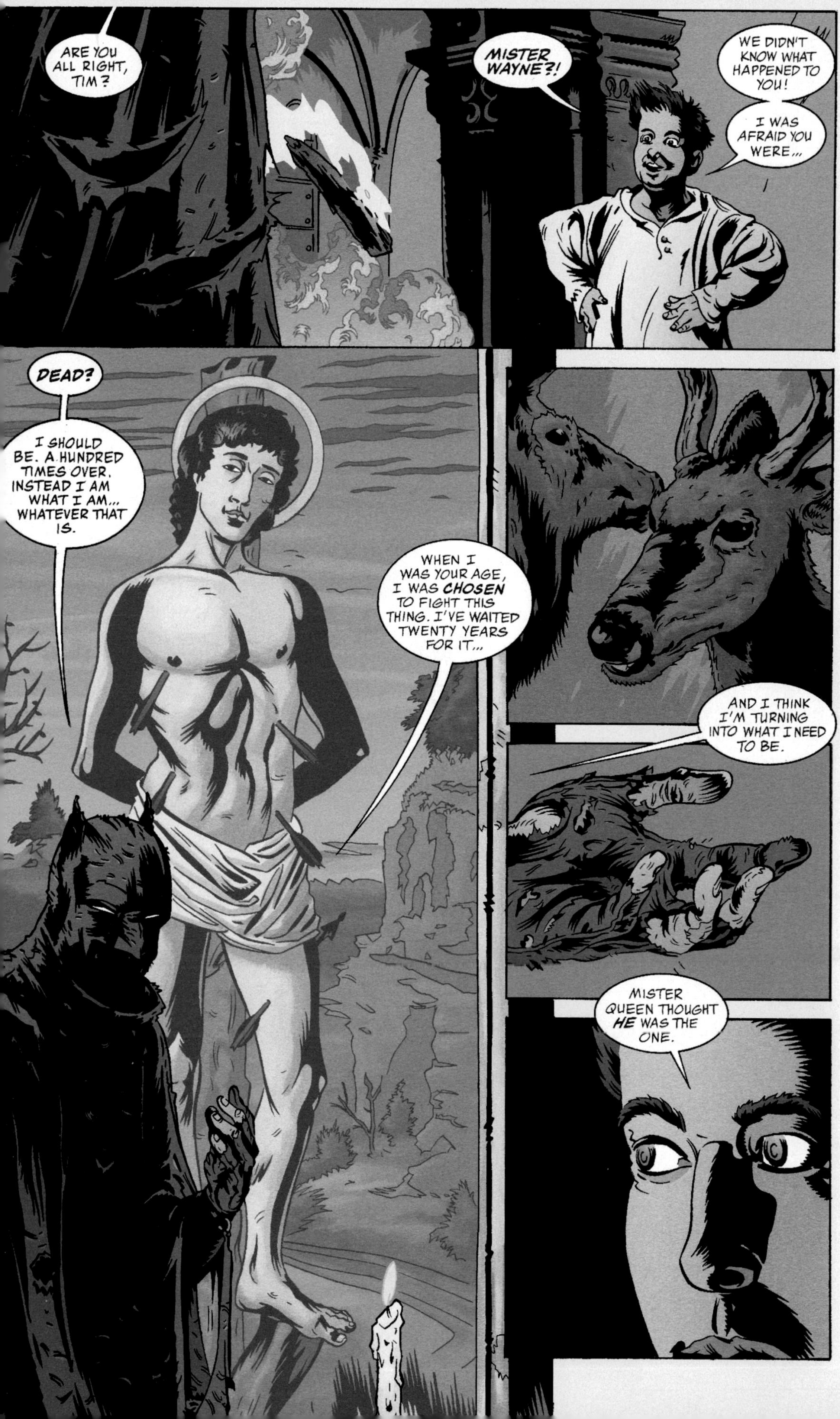
ARE YOU ALL RIGHT, TIM?
MISTER WAYNE?!
WE DIDN'T KNOW WHAT HAPPENED TO YOU!
I WAS AFRAID YOU WERE...
DEAD?
I SHOULD BE. A HUNDRED TIMES OVER. INSTEAD I AM WHAT I AM... WHATEVER THAT IS.
WHEN I WAS YOUR AGE, I WAS CHOSEN TO FIGHT THIS THING. I'VE WAITED TWENTY YEARS FOR IT...
AND I THINK I'M TURNING INTO WHAT I NEED TO BE.
MISTER QUEEN THOUGHT HE WAS THE ONE.

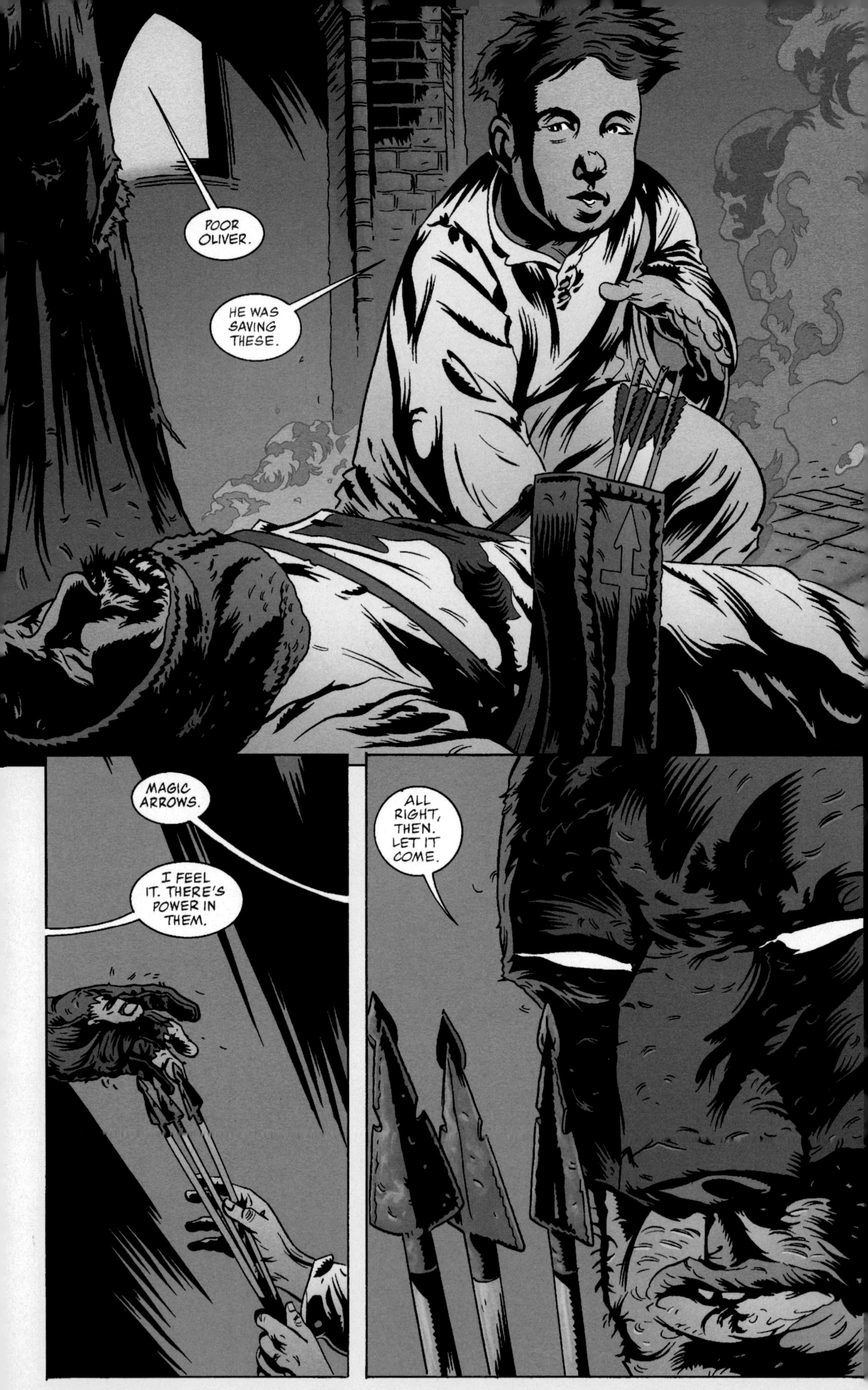
POOR OLIVER.
HE WAS SAVING THESE.
MAGIC ARROWS.
I FEEL IT. THERE'S POWER IN THEM.
ALL RIGHT, THEN. LET IT COME.

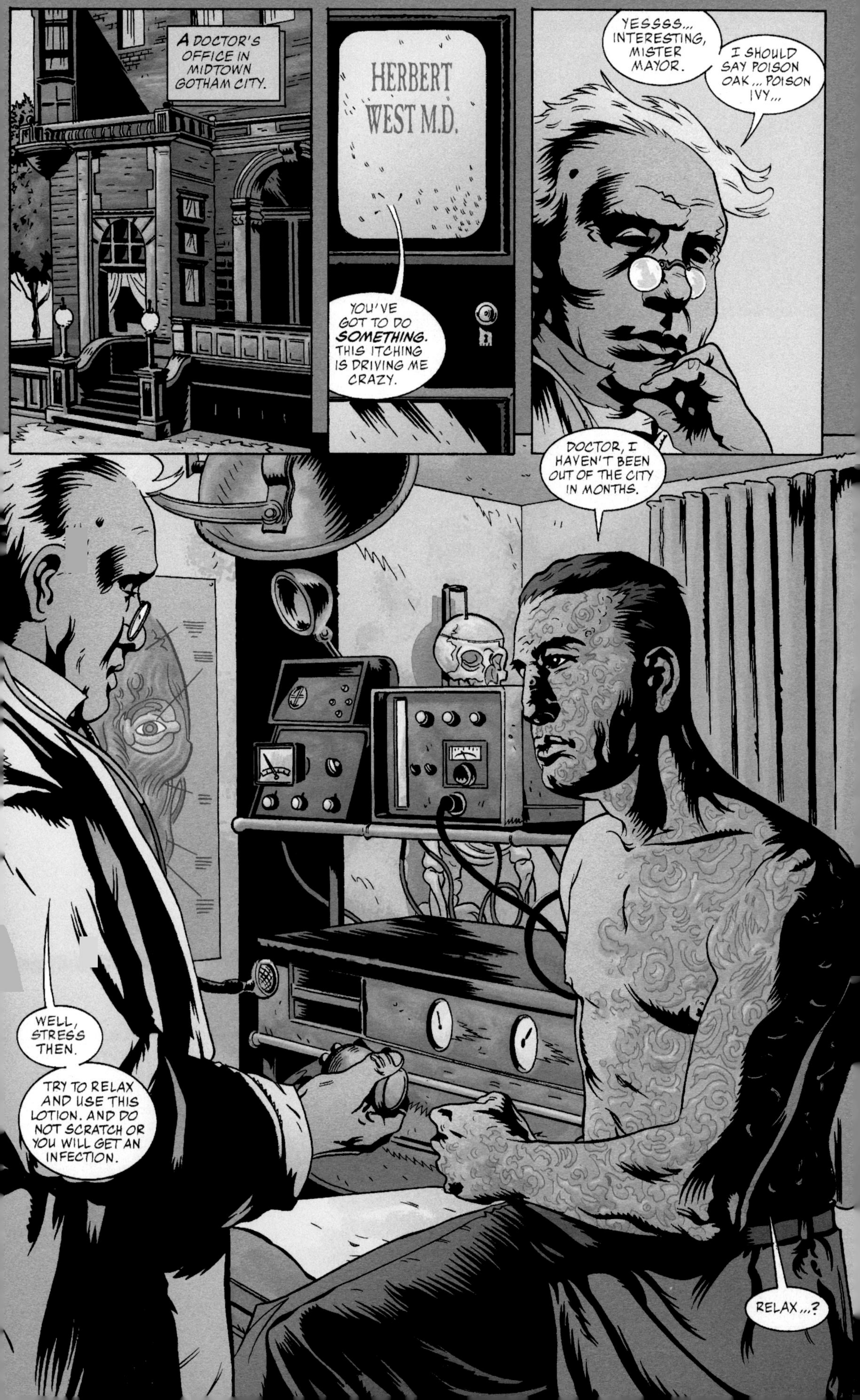
A DOCTOR'S OFFICE IN MIDTOWN GOTHAM CITY.
HERBERT WEST M.D.
YOU'VE GOT TO DO SOMETHING. THIS ITCHING IS DRIVING ME CRAZY.
YESSSS... INTERESTING, MISTER MAYOR.
I SHOULD SAY POISON OAK... POISON IVY...
DOCTOR, I HAVEN'T BEEN OUT OF THE CITY IN MONTHS.
WELL, STRESS THEN.
TRY TO RELAX AND USE THIS LOTION. AND DO NOT SCRATCH OR YOU WILL GET AN INFECTION.
RELAX...?

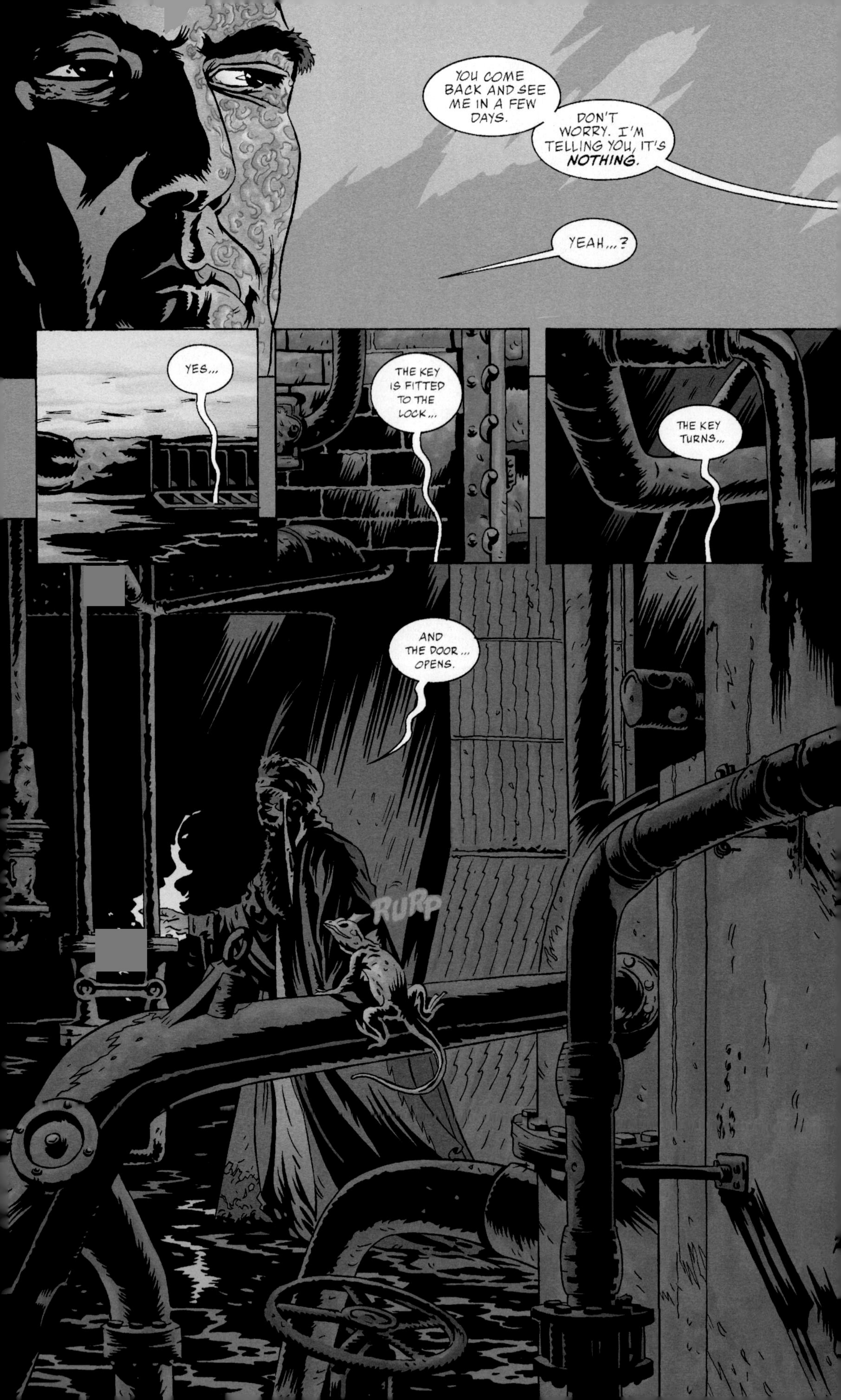
YOU COME BACK AND SEE ME IN A FEW DAYS.
DON'T WORRY. I'M TELLING YOU, IT'S NOTHING.
YEAH...?
YES...
THE KEY IS FITTED TO THE LOCK...
THE KEY TURNS...
AND THE DOOR... OPENS.
RURP

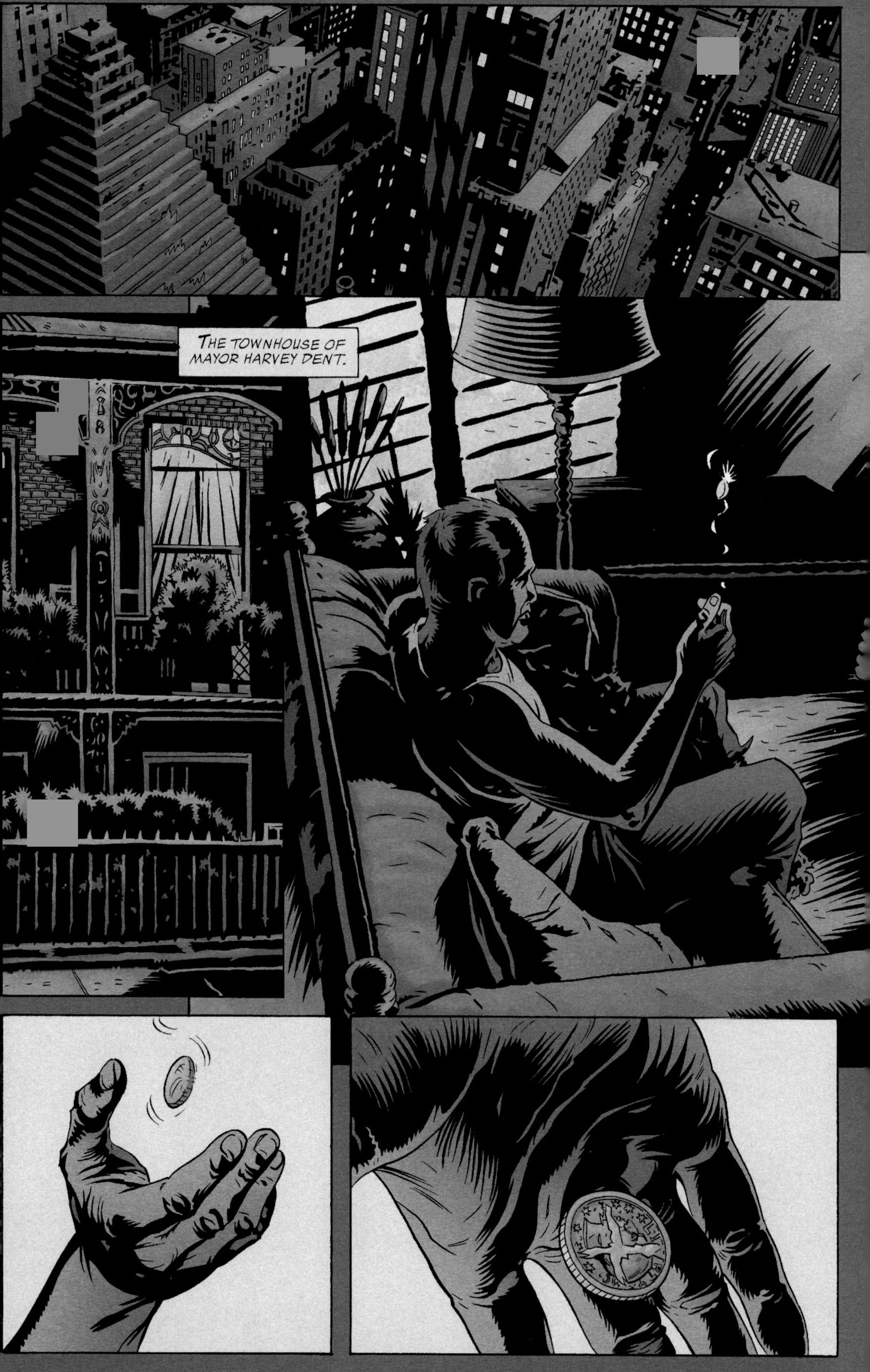
THE TOWNHOUSE OF MAYOR HARVEY DENT.

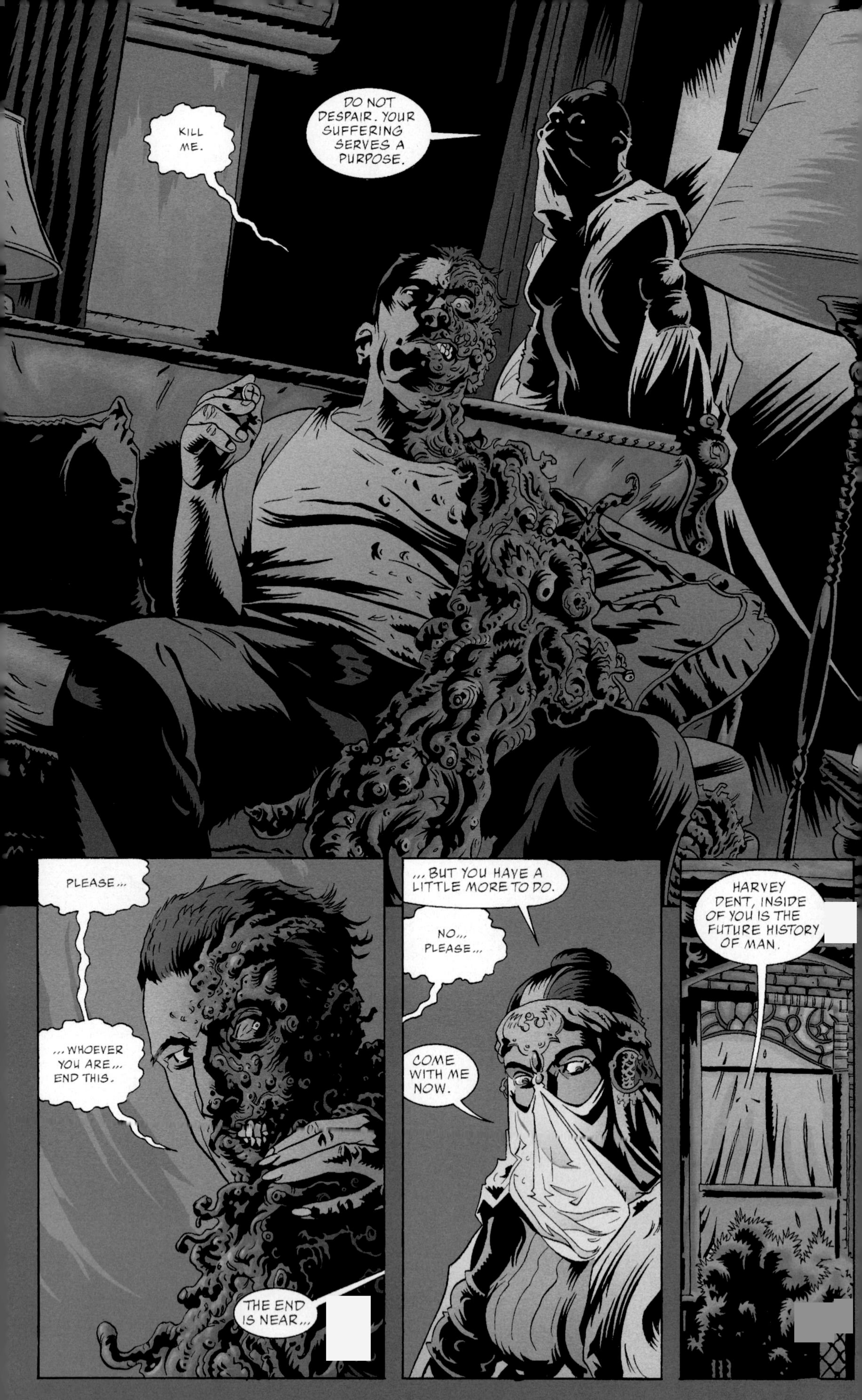
KILL ME.
DO NOT DESPAIR. YOUR SUFFERING SERVES A PURPOSE.
PLEASE...
...WHOEVER YOU ARE... END THIS.
THE END IS NEAR...
...BUT YOU HAVE A LITTLE MORE TO DO.
NO... PLEASE...
COME WITH ME NOW.
HARVEY DENT, INSIDE OF YOU IS THE FUTURE HISTORY OF MAN.

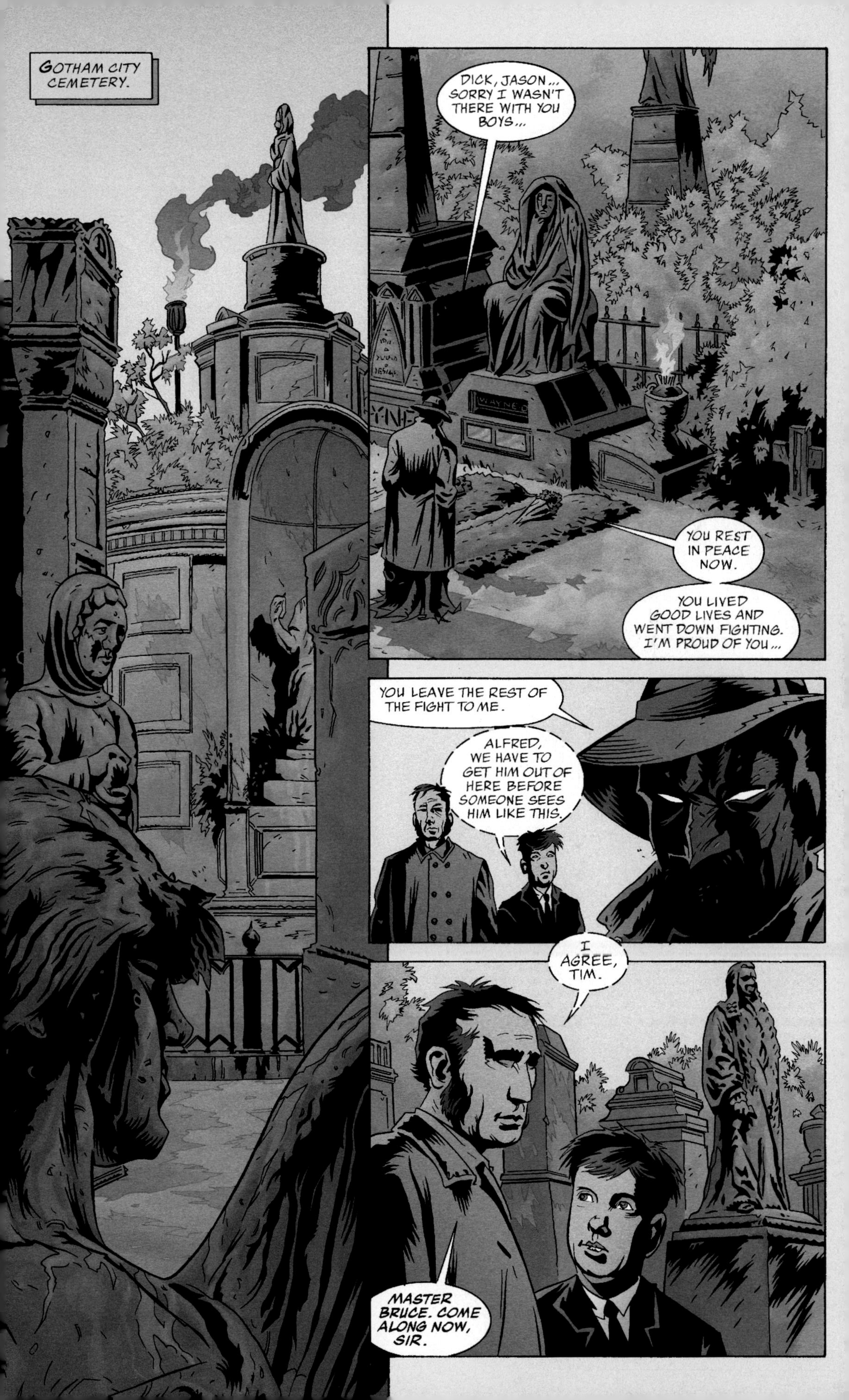
GOTHAM CITY CEMETERY.
DICK, JASON... SORRY I WASN'T THERE WITH YOU BOYS...
YOU REST IN PEACE NOW.
YOU LIVED GOOD LIVES AND WENT DOWN FIGHTING. I'M PROUD OF YOU...
YOU LEAVE THE REST OF THE FIGHT TO ME.
ALFRED, WE HAVE TO GET HIM OUT OF HERE BEFORE SOMEONE SEES HIM LIKE THIS.
I AGREE, TIM.
MASTER BRUCE. COME ALONG NOW, SIR.

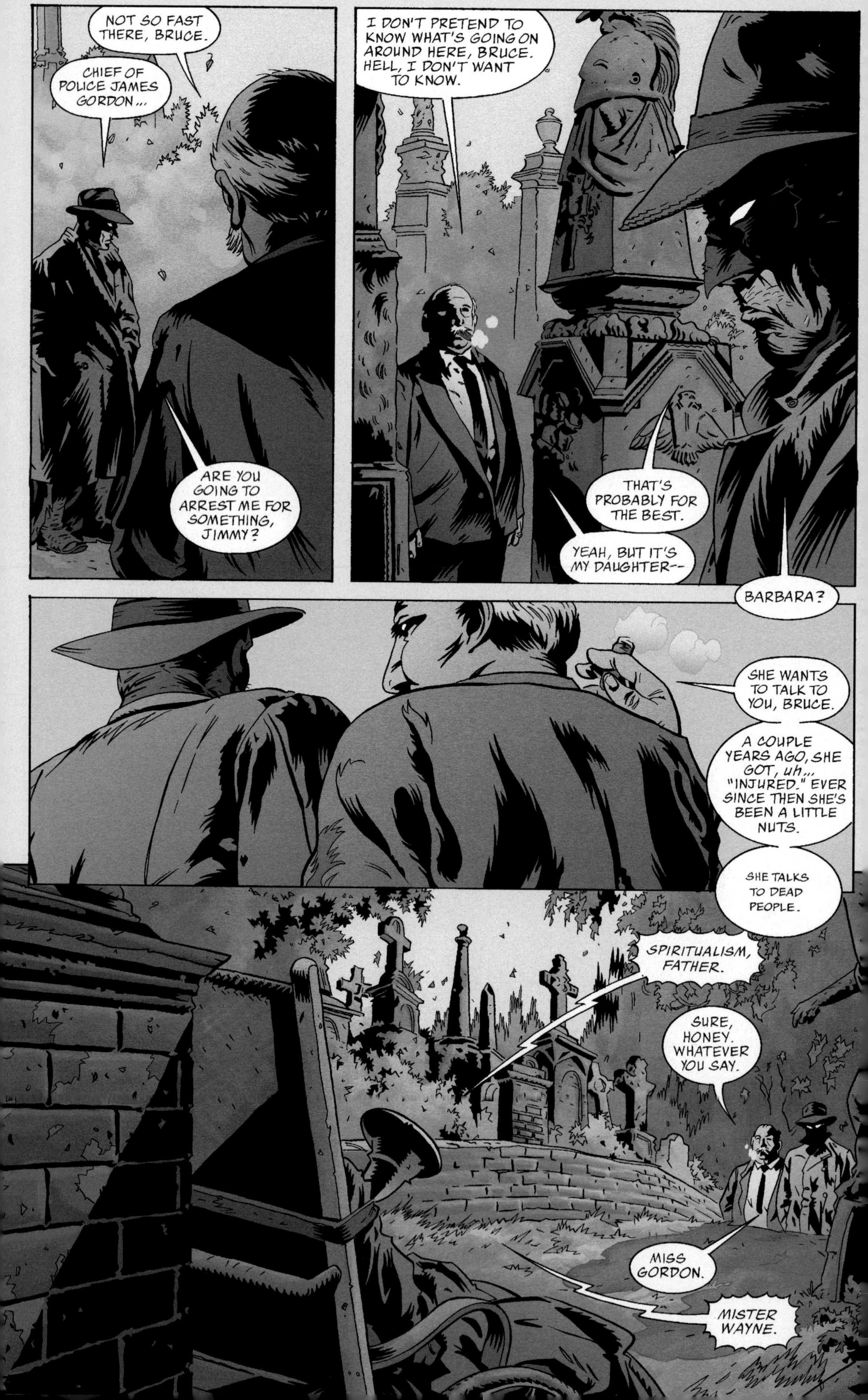
NOT SO FAST THERE, BRUCE.
CHIEF OF POLICE JAMES GORDON...
ARE YOU GOING TO ARREST ME FOR SOMETHING, JIMMY?
I DON'T PRETEND TO KNOW WHAT'S GOING ON AROUND HERE, BRUCE. HELL, I DON'T WANT TO KNOW.
THAT'S PROBABLY FOR THE BEST.
YEAH, BUT IT'S MY DAUGHTER--
BARBARA?
SHE WANTS TO TALK TO YOU, BRUCE.
A COUPLE YEARS AGO, SHE GOT, uh... "INJURED." EVER SINCE THEN SHE'S BEEN A LITTLE NUTS.
SHE TALKS TO DEAD PEOPLE.
SPIRITUALISM, FATHER.
SURE, HONEY. WHATEVER YOU SAY.
MISS GORDON.
MISTER WAYNE.

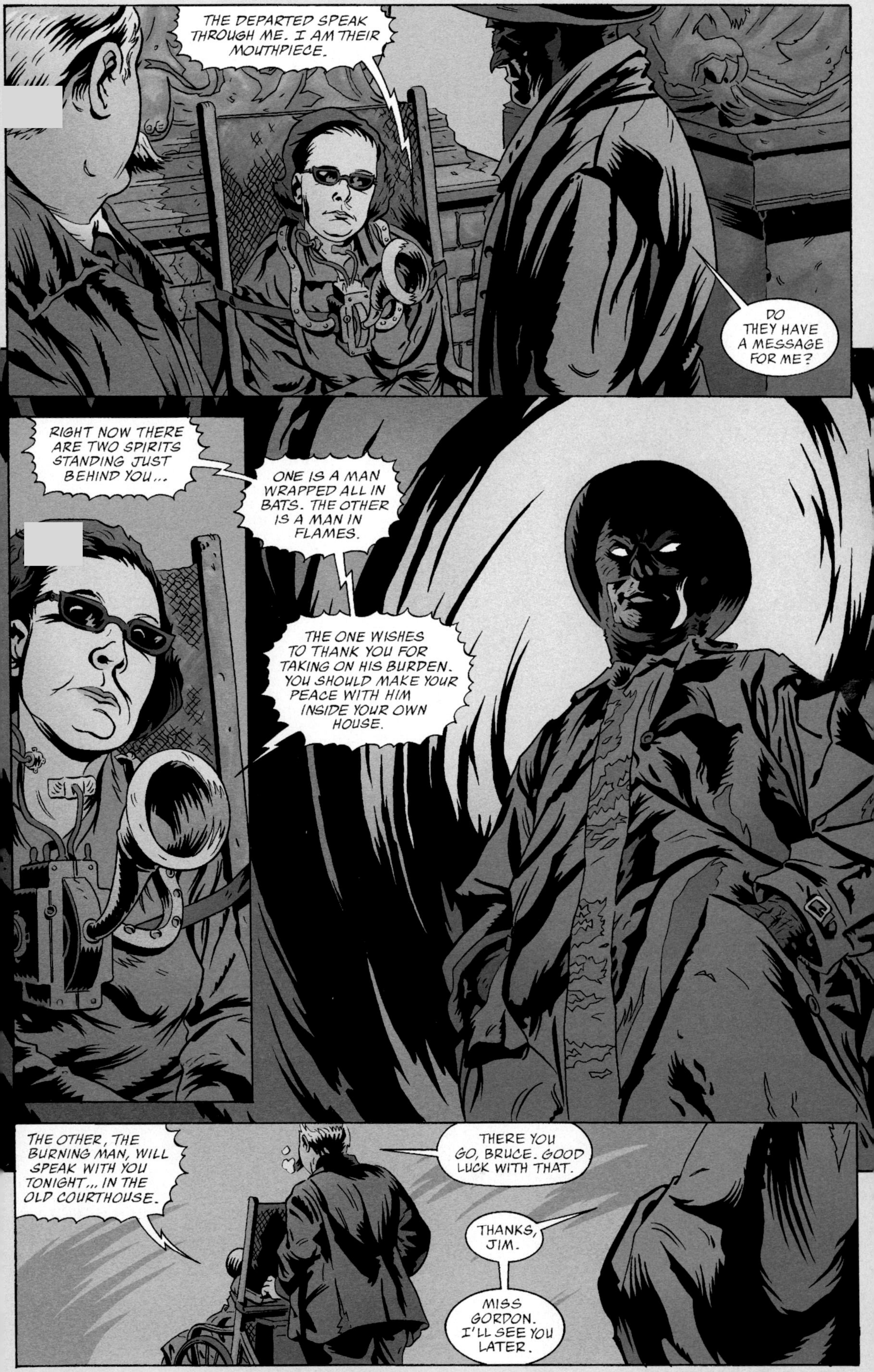
THE DEPARTED SPEAK THROUGH ME. I AM THEIR MOUTHPIECE.
DO THEY HAVE A MESSAGE FOR ME?
RIGHT NOW THERE ARE TWO SPIRITS STANDING JUST BEHIND YOU...
ONE IS A MAN WRAPPED ALL IN BATS. THE OTHER IS A MAN IN FLAMES.
THE ONE WISHES TO THANK YOU FOR TAKING ON HIS BURDEN. YOU SHOULD MAKE YOUR PEACE WITH HIM INSIDE YOUR OWN HOUSE.
THE OTHER, THE BURNING MAN, WILL SPEAK WITH YOU TONIGHT... IN THE OLD COURTHOUSE.
THERE YOU GO, BRUCE. GOOD LUCK WITH THAT.
THANKS, JIM.
MISS GORDON. I'LL SEE YOU LATER.

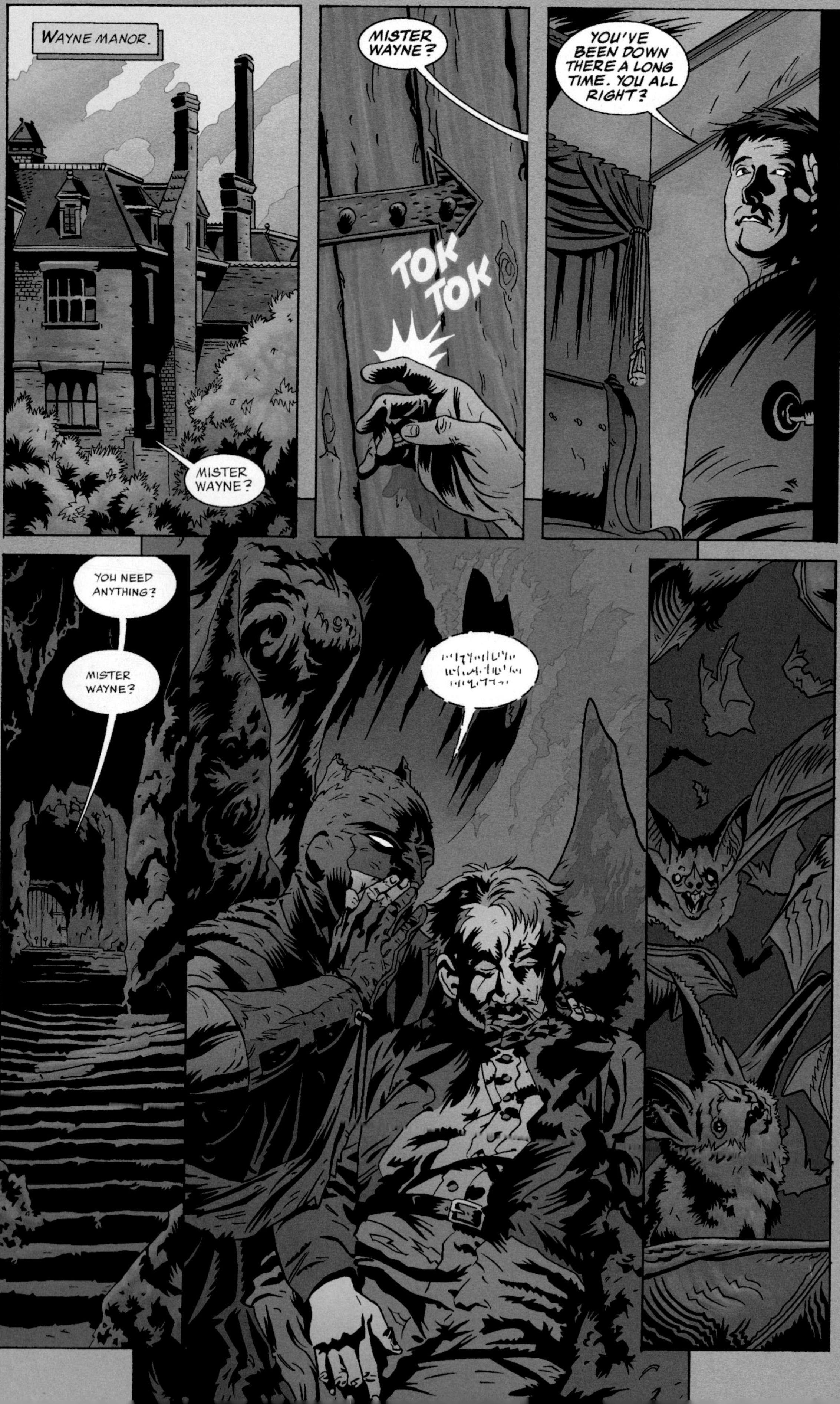

WAYNE MANOR.
MISTER WAYNE?
MISTER WAYNE?
TOK TOK
YOU'VE BEEN DOWN THERE A LONG TIME. YOU ALL RIGHT?
YOU NEED ANYTHING?
MISTER WAYNE?

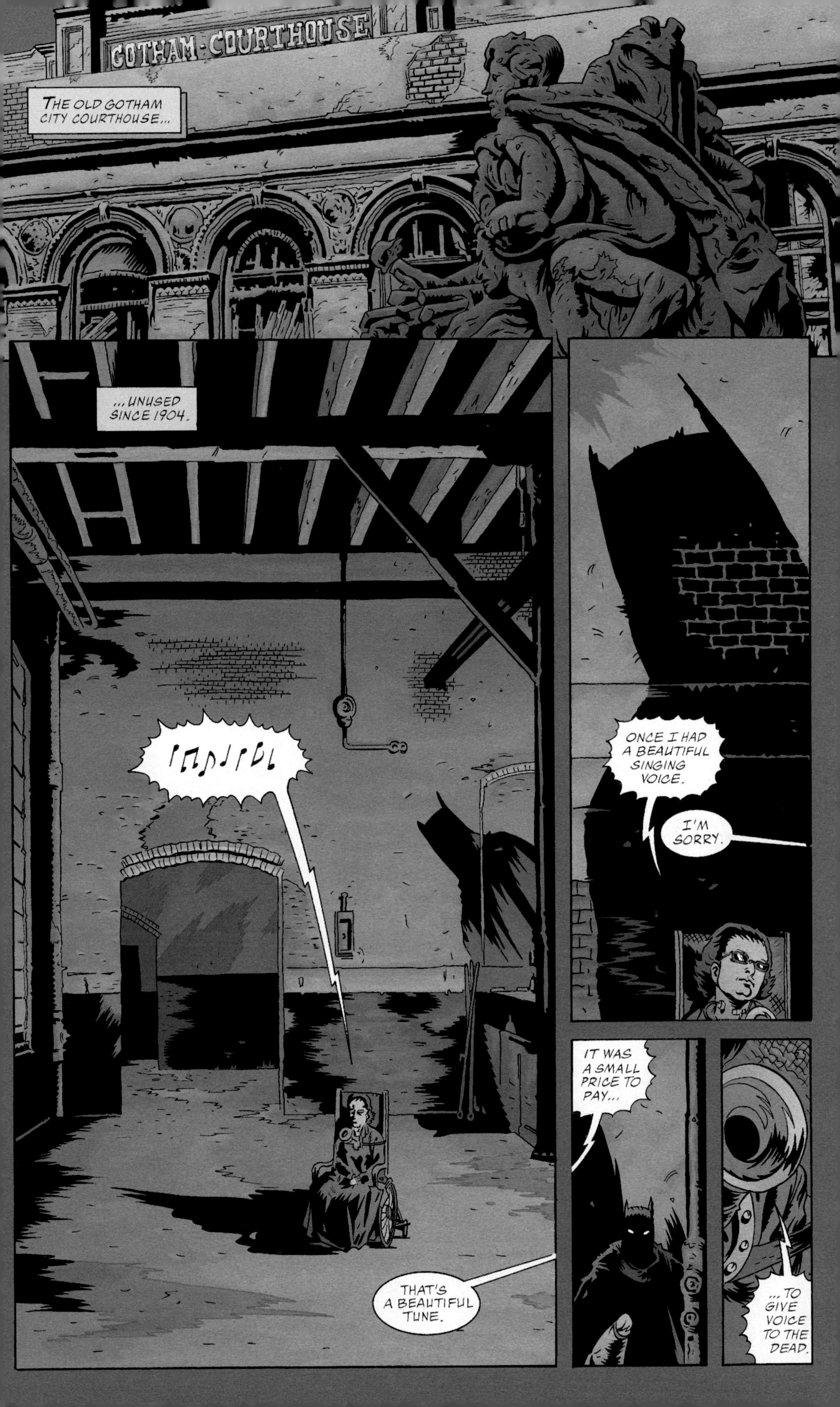
GOTHAM-COURTHOUSE
THE OLD GOTHAM CITY COURTHOUSE...
...UNUSED SINCE 1904.
ONCE I HAD A BEAUTIFUL SINGING VOICE.
I'M SORRY.
THAT'S A BEAUTIFUL TUNE.
IT WAS A SMALL PRICE TO PAY...
...TO GIVE VOICE TO THE DEAD.

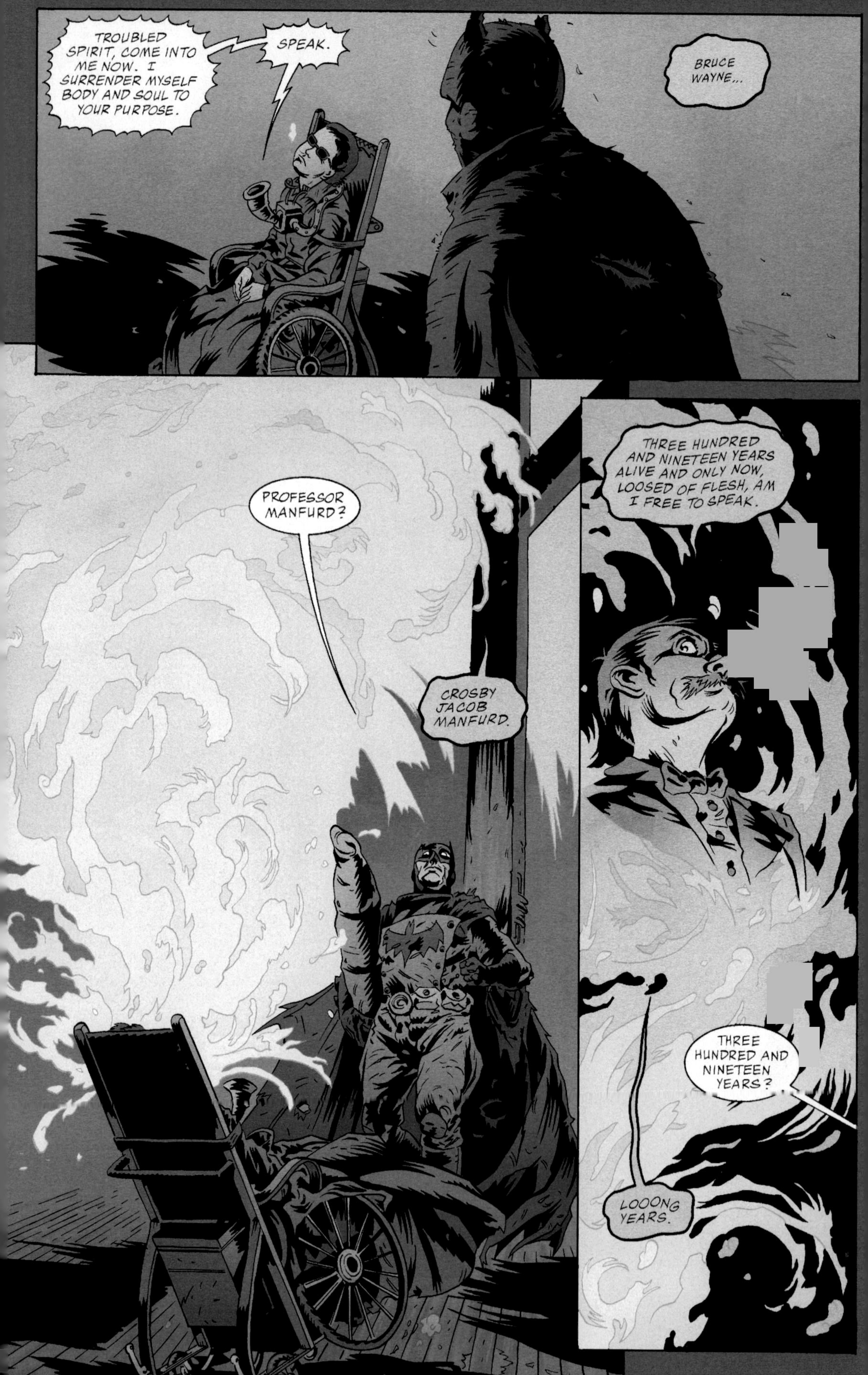
TROUBLED SPIRIT, COME INTO ME NOW. I SURRENDER MYSELF BODY AND SOUL TO YOUR PURPOSE.
SPEAK.
BRUCE WAYNE...
PROFESSOR MANFURD?
CROSBY JACOB MANFURD.
THREE HUNDRED AND NINETEEN YEARS ALIVE AND ONLY NOW, LOOSED OF FLESH, AM I FREE TO SPEAK.
THREE HUNDRED AND NINETEEN YEARS?
LOOONG YEARS.

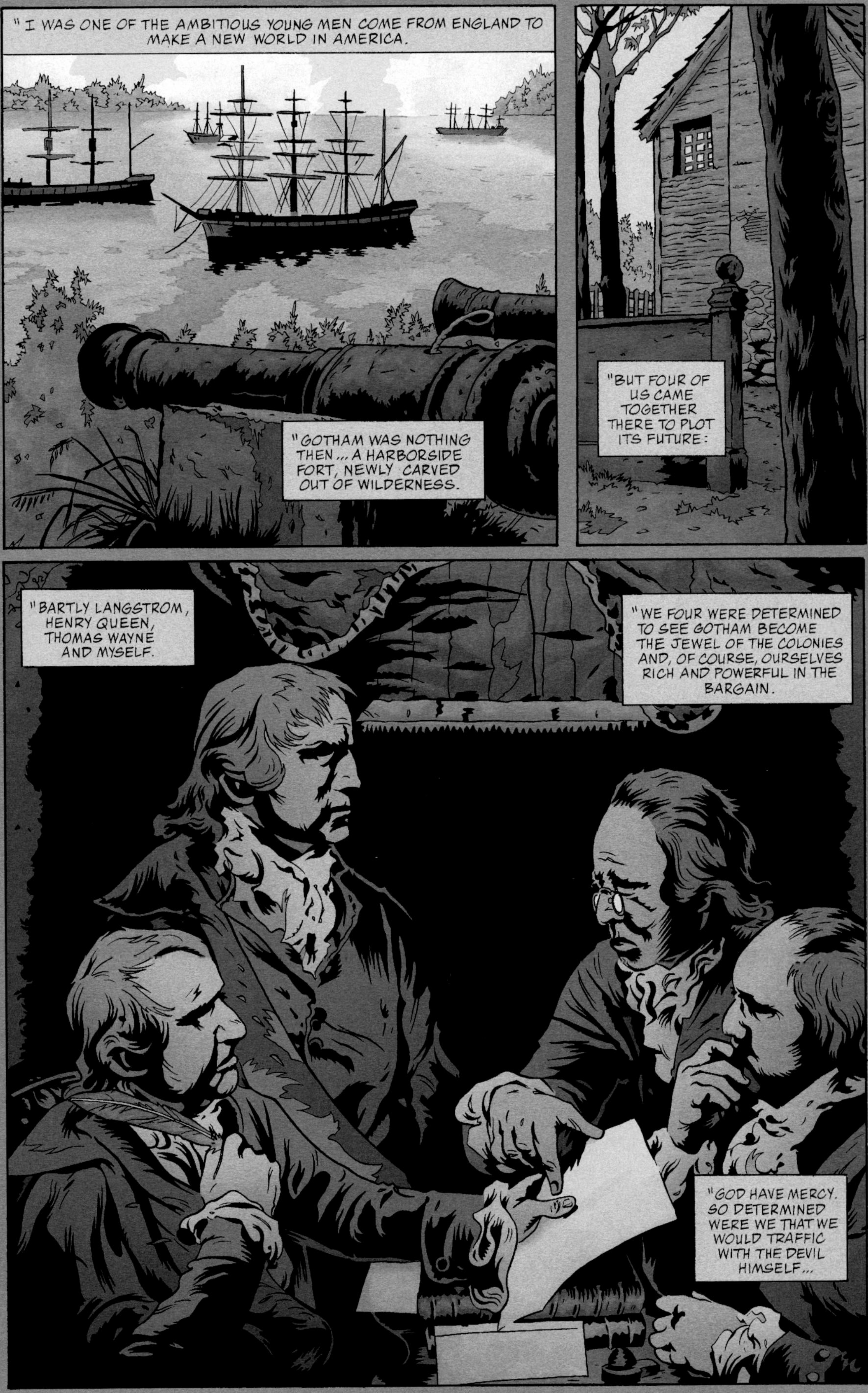
"I WAS ONE OF THE AMBITIOUS YOUNG MEN COME FROM ENGLAND TO MAKE A NEW WORLD IN AMERICA.
"GOTHAM WAS NOTHING THEN... A HARBORSIDE FORT, NEWLY CARVED OUT OF WILDERNESS.
"BUT FOUR OF US CAME TOGETHER THERE TO PLOT ITS FUTURE:
"BARTLY LANGSTROM, HENRY QUEEN, THOMAS WAYNE AND MYSELF.
"WE FOUR WERE DETERMINED TO SEE GOTHAM BECOME THE JEWEL OF THE COLONIES AND, OF COURSE, OURSELVES RICH AND POWERFUL IN THE BARGAIN.
"GOD HAVE MERCY. SO DETERMINED WERE WE THAT WE WOULD TRAFFIC WITH THE DEVIL HIMSELF...

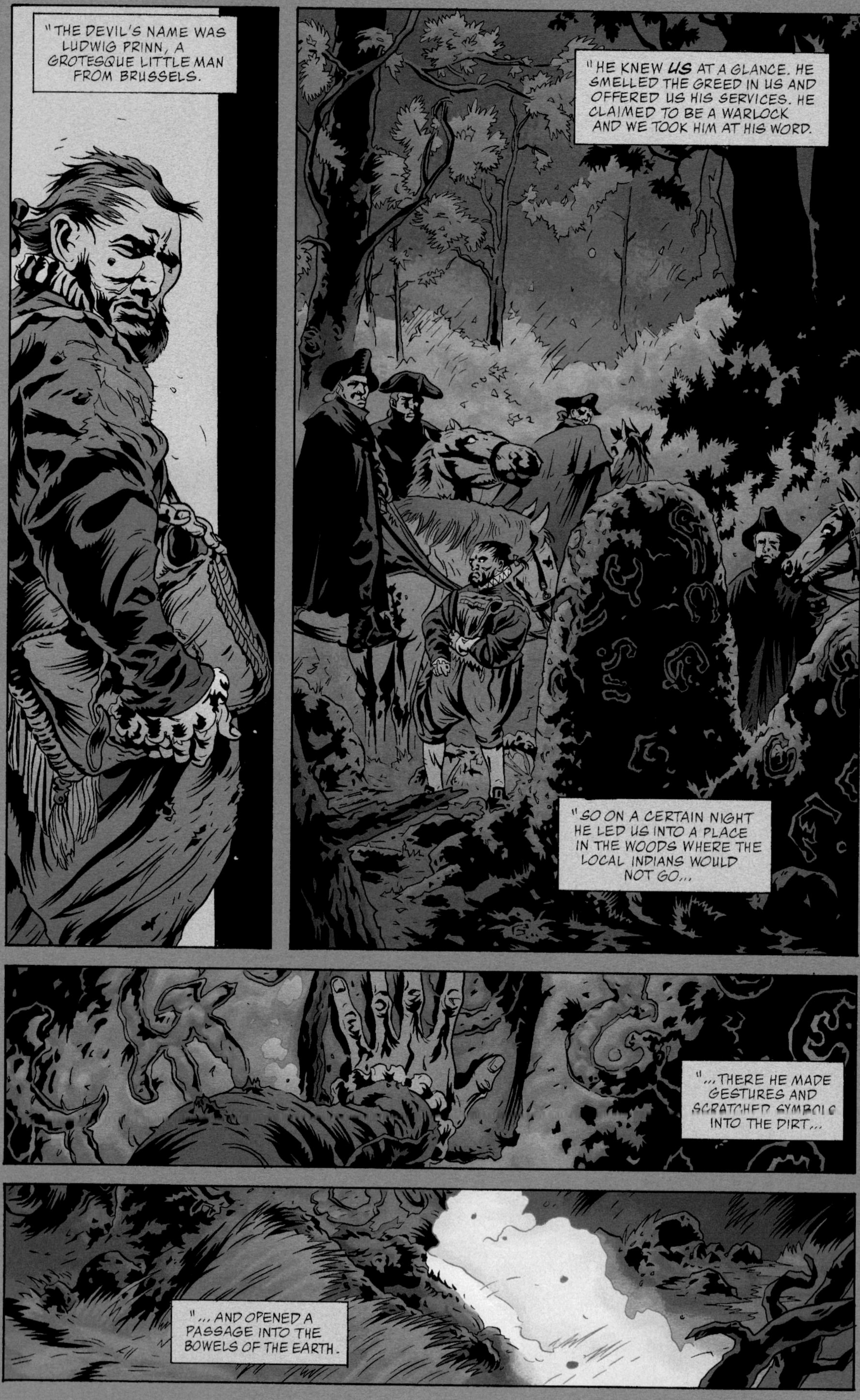

"THE DEVIL'S NAME WAS LUDWIG PRINN, A GROTESQUE LITTLE MAN FROM BRUSSELS.
"HE KNEW US AT A GLANCE. HE SMELLED THE GREED IN US AND OFFERED US HIS SERVICES. HE CLAIMED TO BE A WARLOCK AND WE TOOK HIM AT HIS WORD.
"SO ON A CERTAIN NIGHT HE LED US INTO A PLACE IN THE WOODS WHERE THE LOCAL INDIANS WOULD NOT GO...
"...THERE HE MADE GESTURES AND SCRATCHED SYMBOLS INTO THE DIRT...
"...AND OPENED A PASSAGE INTO THE BOWELS OF THE EARTH.

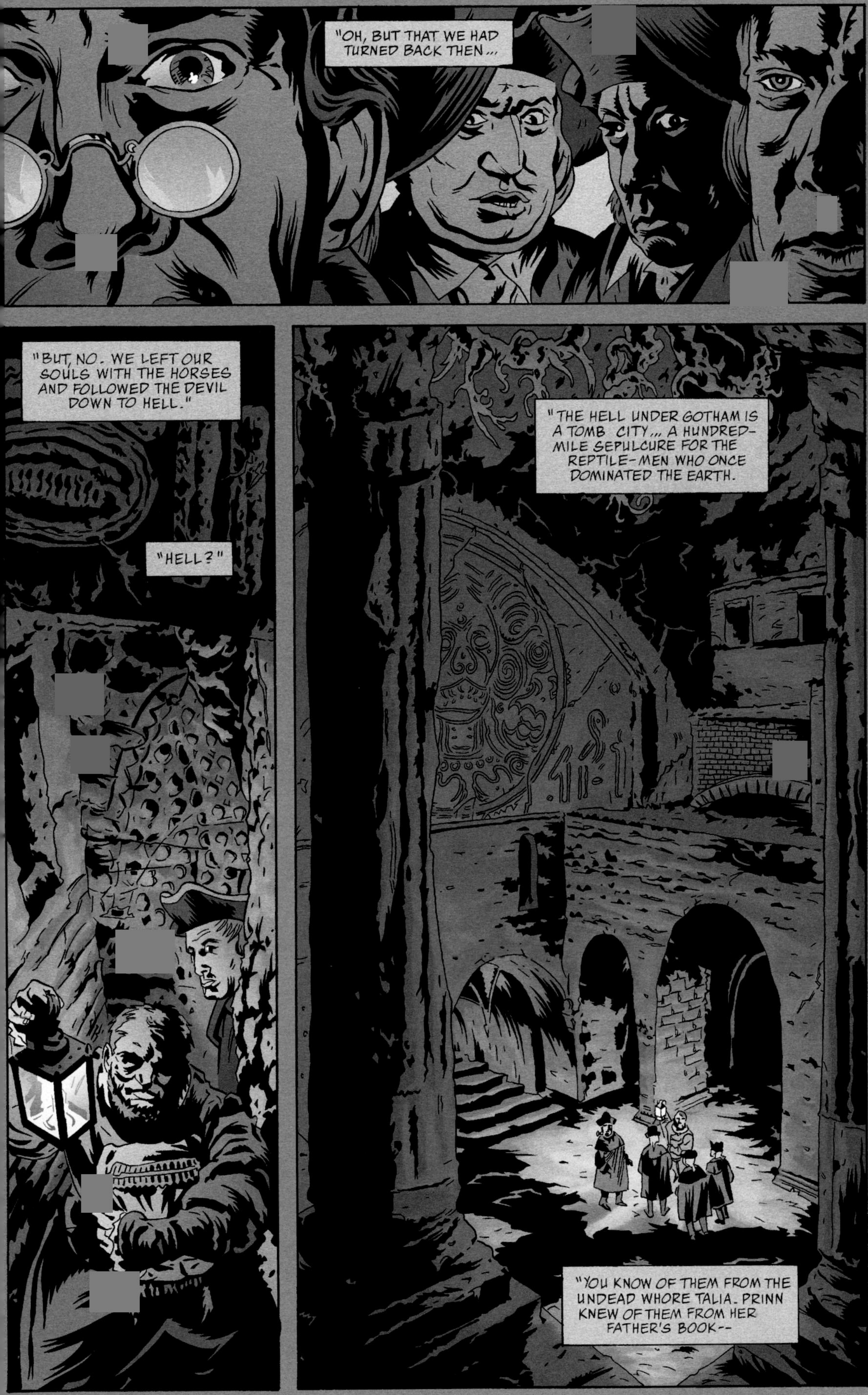
"OH, BUT THAT WE HAD TURNED BACK THEN...
"BUT, NO. WE LEFT OUR SOULS WITH THE HORSES AND FOLLOWED THE DEVIL DOWN TO HELL."
"HELL?"
"THE HELL UNDER GOTHAM IS A TOMB CITY... A HUNDRED-MILE SEPULCURE FOR THE REPTILE-MEN WHO ONCE DOMINATED THE EARTH.
"YOU KNOW OF THEM FROM THE UNDEAD WHORE TALIA. PRINN KNEW OF THEM FROM HER FATHER'S BOOK--

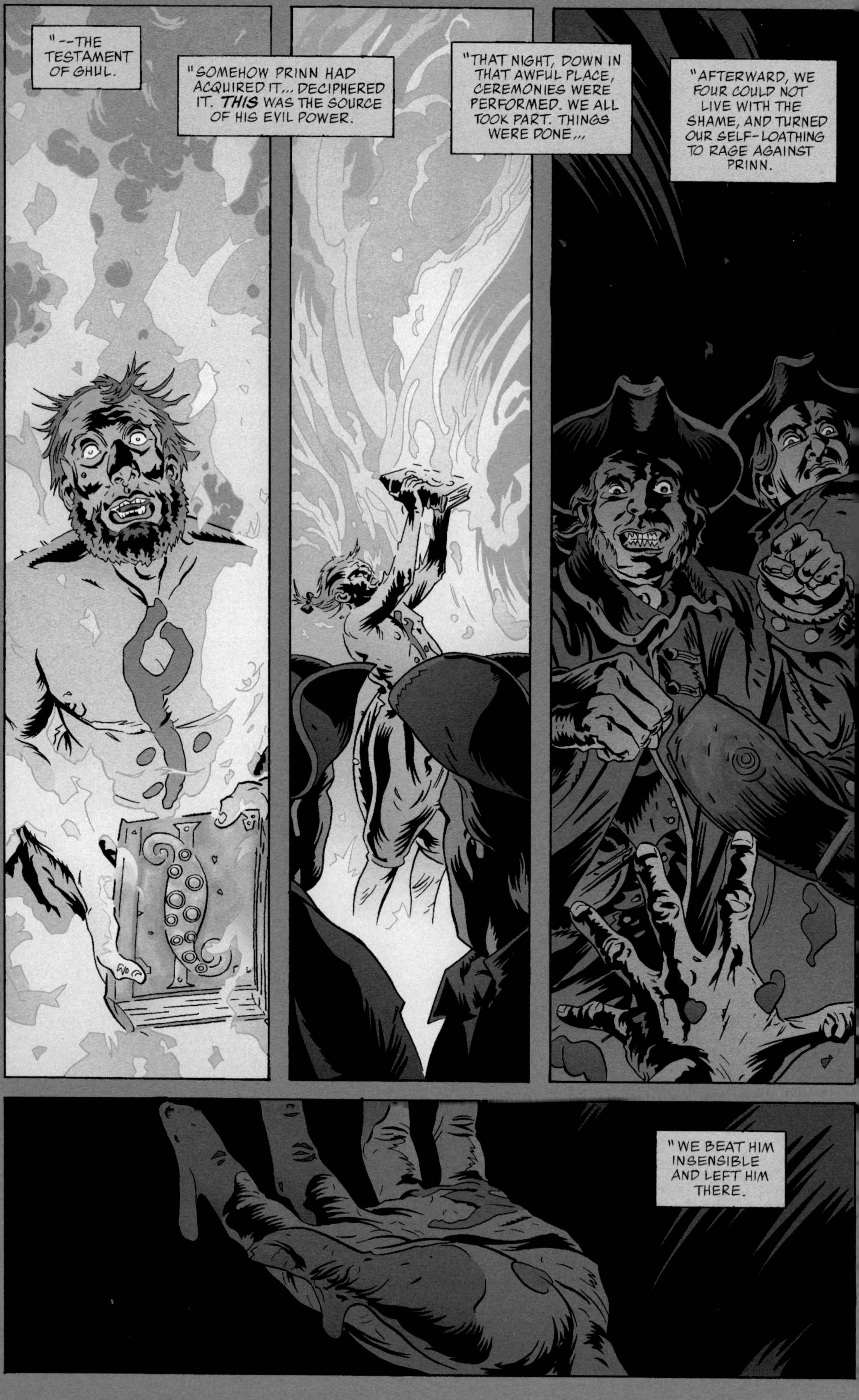
"--THE TESTAMENT OF GHUL.
"SOMEHOW PRINN HAD ACQUIRED IT... DECIPHERED IT. THIS WAS THE SOURCE OF HIS EVIL POWER.
"THAT NIGHT, DOWN IN THAT AWFUL PLACE, CEREMONIES WERE PERFORMED. WE ALL TOOK PART. THINGS WERE DONE...
"AFTERWARD, WE FOUR COULD NOT LIVE WITH THE SHAME, AND TURNED OUR SELF-LOATHING TO RAGE AGAINST PRINN.
"WE BEAT HIM INSENSIBLE AND LEFT HIM THERE.

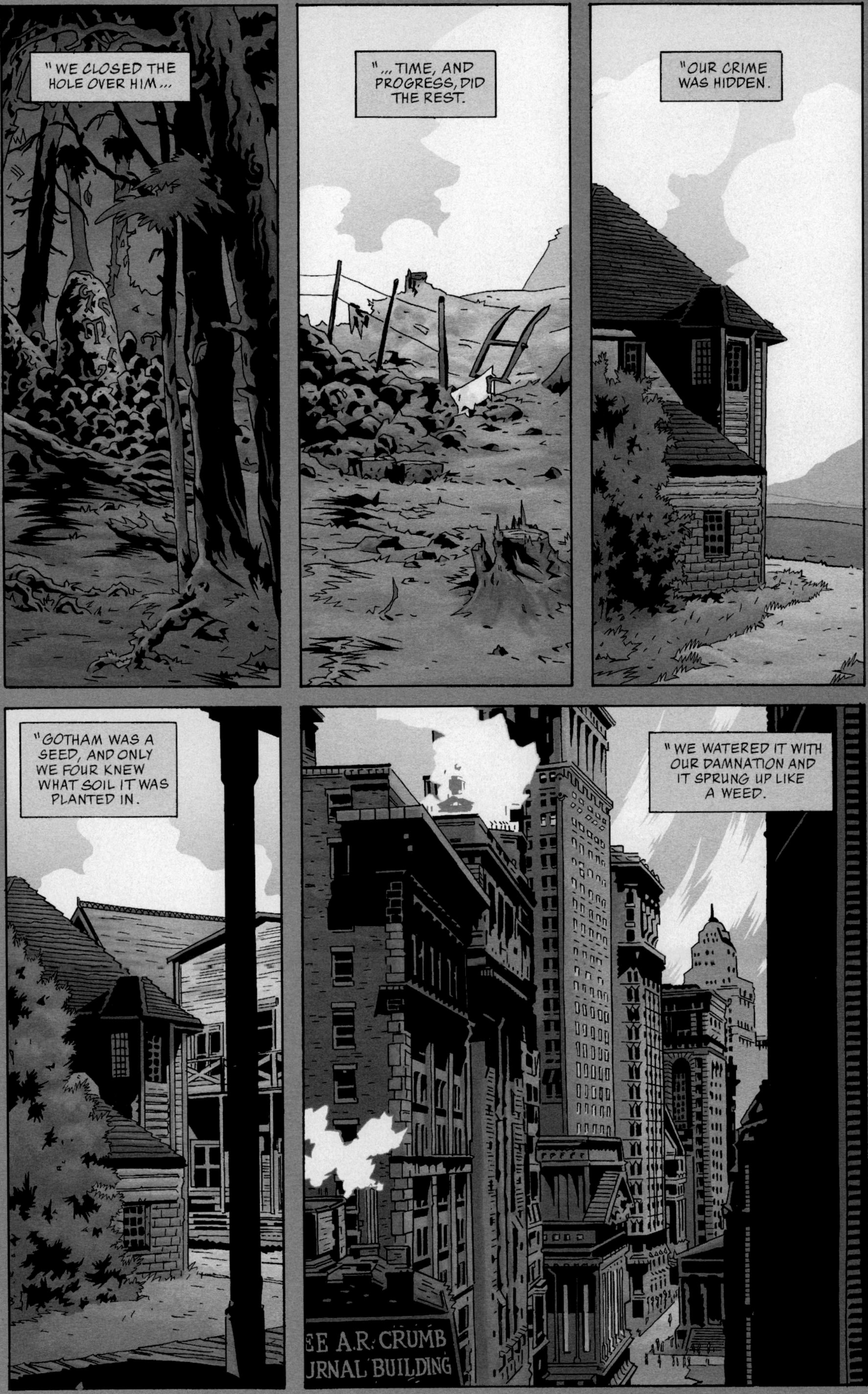
"WE CLOSED THE HOLE OVER HIM...
"...TIME, AND PROGRESS, DID THE REST.
"OUR CRIME WAS HIDDEN.
"GOTHAM WAS A SEED, AND ONLY WE FOUR KNEW WHAT SOIL IT WAS PLANTED IN.
"WE WATERED IT WITH OUR DAMNATION AND IT SPRUNG UP LIKE A WEED.
EE A.R. CRUMB
URNAL BUILDING

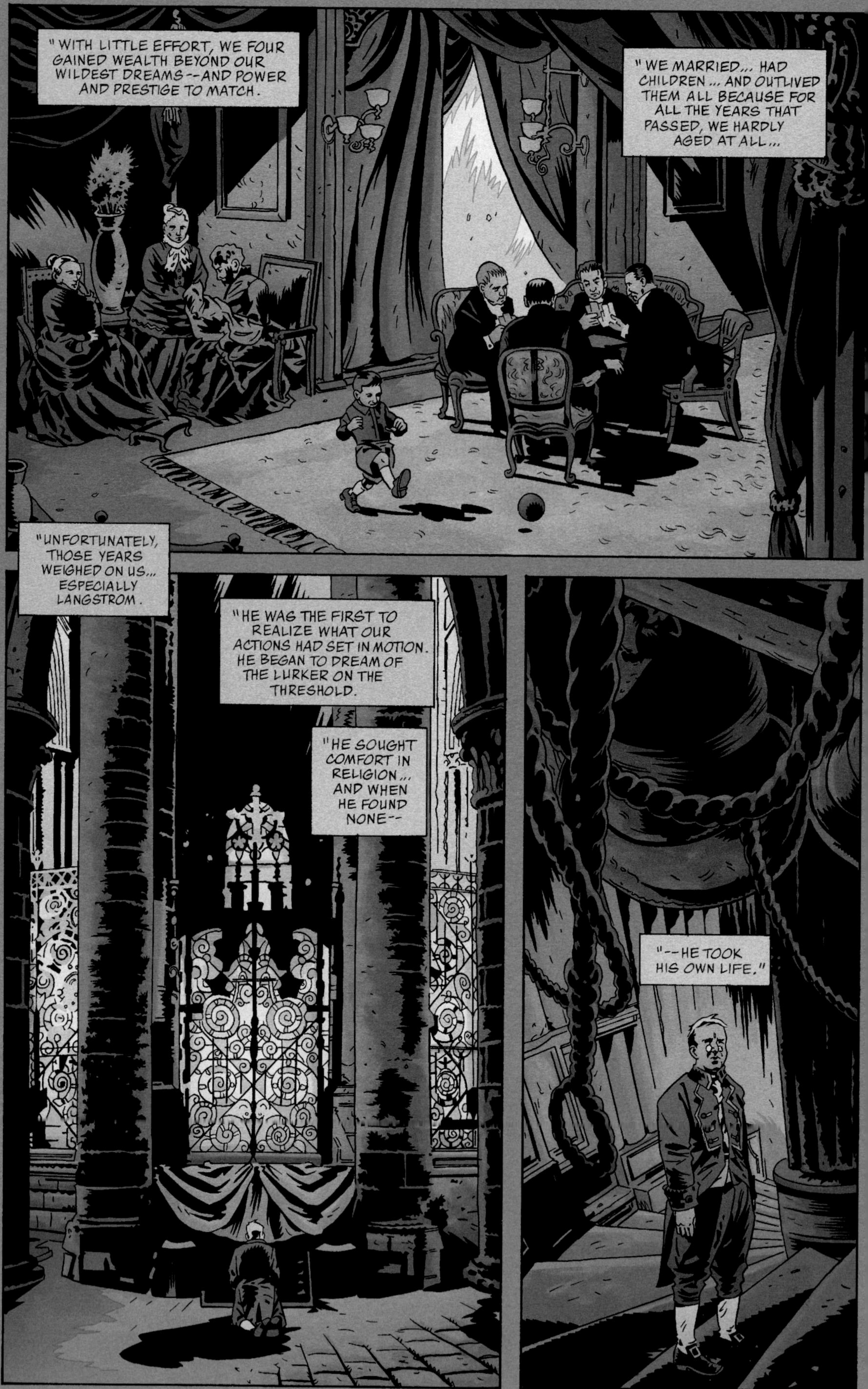
"WITH LITTLE EFFORT, WE FOUR GAINED WEALTH BEYOND OUR WILDEST DREAMS--AND POWER AND PRESTIGE TO MATCH.
"WE MARRIED... HAD CHILDREN ... AND OUTLIVED THEM ALL BECAUSE FOR ALL THE YEARS THAT PASSED, WE HARDLY AGED AT ALL...
"UNFORTUNATELY, THOSE YEARS WEIGHED ON US... ESPECIALLY LANGSTROM.
"HE WAS THE FIRST TO REALIZE WHAT OUR ACTIONS HAD SET IN MOTION. HE BEGAN TO DREAM OF THE LURKER ON THE THRESHOLD.
"HE SOUGHT COMFORT IN RELIGION... AND WHEN HE FOUND NONE--
"--HE TOOK HIS OWN LIFE."

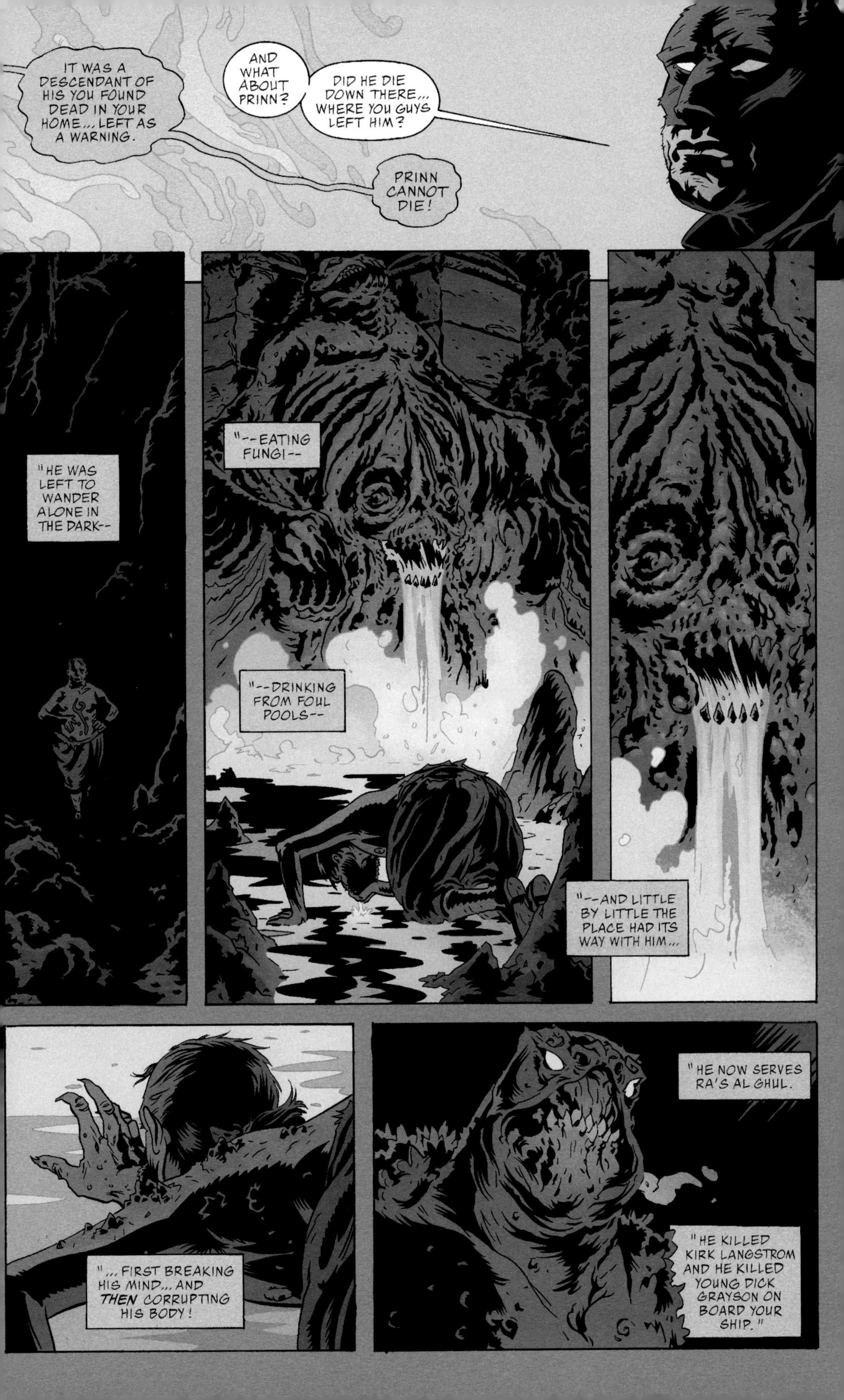
IT WAS A DESCENDANT OF HIS YOU FOUND DEAD IN YOUR HOME... LEFT AS A WARNING.
AND WHAT ABOUT PRINN?
DID HE DIE DOWN THERE... WHERE YOU GUYS LEFT HIM?
PRINN CANNOT DIE!
"HE WAS LEFT TO WANDER ALONE IN THE DARK--
"--EATING FUNGI--
"--DRINKING FROM FOUL POOLS--
"--AND LITTLE BY LITTLE THE PLACE HAD ITS WAY WITH HIM...
"...FIRST BREAKING HIS MIND... AND *THEN* CORRUPTING HIS BODY!
"HE NOW SERVES RA'S AL GHUL.
"HE KILLED KIRK LANGSTROM AND HE KILLED YOUNG DICK GRAYSON ON BOARD YOUR SHIP."

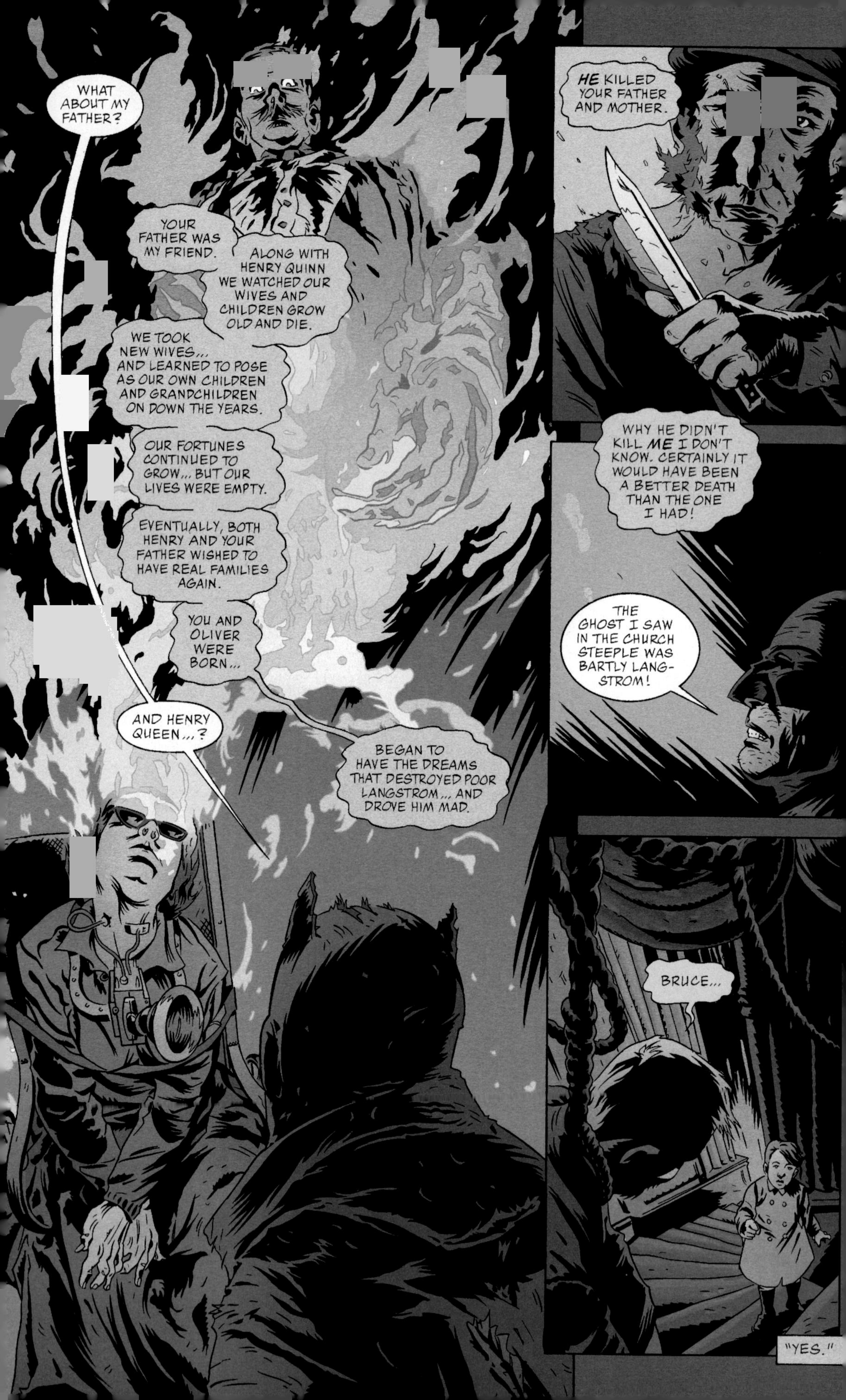

WHAT ABOUT MY FATHER?
YOUR FATHER WAS MY FRIEND.
ALONG WITH HENRY QUINN WE WATCHED OUR WIVES AND CHILDREN GROW OLD AND DIE.
WE TOOK NEW WIVES... AND LEARNED TO POSE AS OUR OWN CHILDREN AND GRANDCHILDREN ON DOWN THE YEARS.
OUR FORTUNES CONTINUED TO GROW... BUT OUR LIVES WERE EMPTY.
EVENTUALLY, BOTH HENRY AND YOUR FATHER WISHED TO HAVE REAL FAMILIES AGAIN.
YOU AND OLIVER WERE BORN...
AND HENRY QUEEN...?
BEGAN TO HAVE THE DREAMS THAT DESTROYED POOR LANGSTROM... AND DROVE HIM MAD.
HE KILLED YOUR FATHER AND MOTHER.
WHY HE DIDN'T KILL ME I DON'T KNOW. CERTAINLY IT WOULD HAVE BEEN A BETTER DEATH THAN THE ONE I HAD!
THE GHOST I SAW IN THE CHURCH STEEPLE WAS BARTLY LANG-STROM!
BRUCE...
"YES."

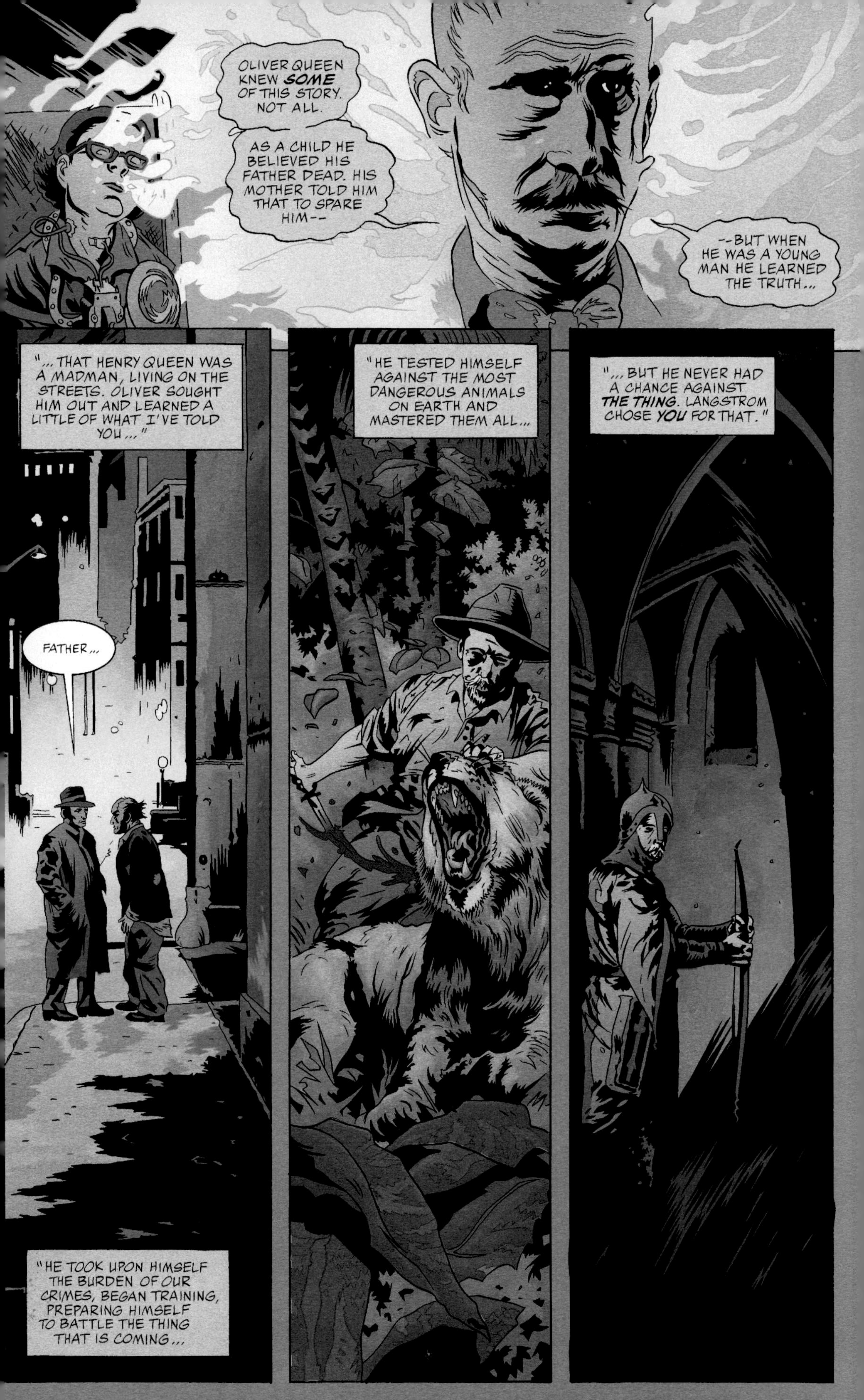
OLIVER QUEEN KNEW SOME OF THIS STORY. NOT ALL.
AS A CHILD HE BELIEVED HIS FATHER DEAD. HIS MOTHER TOLD HIM THAT TO SPARE HIM--
--BUT WHEN HE WAS A YOUNG MAN HE LEARNED THE TRUTH...
"...THAT HENRY QUEEN WAS A MADMAN, LIVING ON THE STREETS. OLIVER SOUGHT HIM OUT AND LEARNED A LITTLE OF WHAT I'VE TOLD YOU..."
FATHER...
"HE TOOK UPON HIMSELF THE BURDEN OF OUR CRIMES, BEGAN TRAINING, PREPARING HIMSELF TO BATTLE THE THING THAT IS COMING...
"HE TESTED HIMSELF AGAINST THE MOST DANGEROUS ANIMALS ON EARTH AND MASTERED THEM ALL...
"...BUT HE NEVER HAD A CHANCE AGAINST THE THING. LANGSTROM CHOSE YOU FOR THAT."

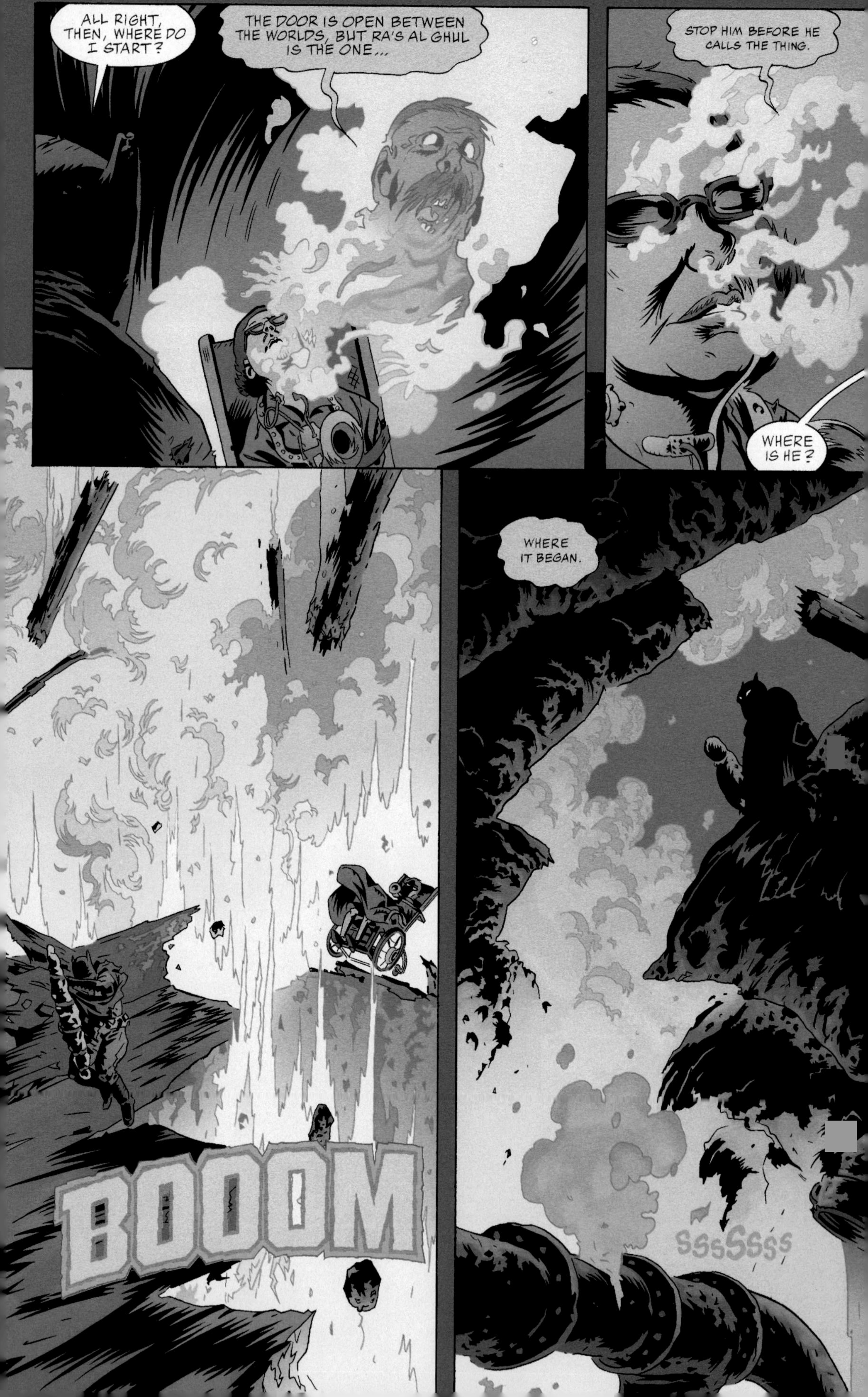
ALL RIGHT, THEN, WHERE DO I START?
THE DOOR IS OPEN BETWEEN THE WORLDS, BUT RA'S AL GHUL IS THE ONE...
STOP HIM BEFORE HE CALLS THE THING.
WHERE IS HE?
BOOOM
WHERE IT BEGAN.
SSSSSSS

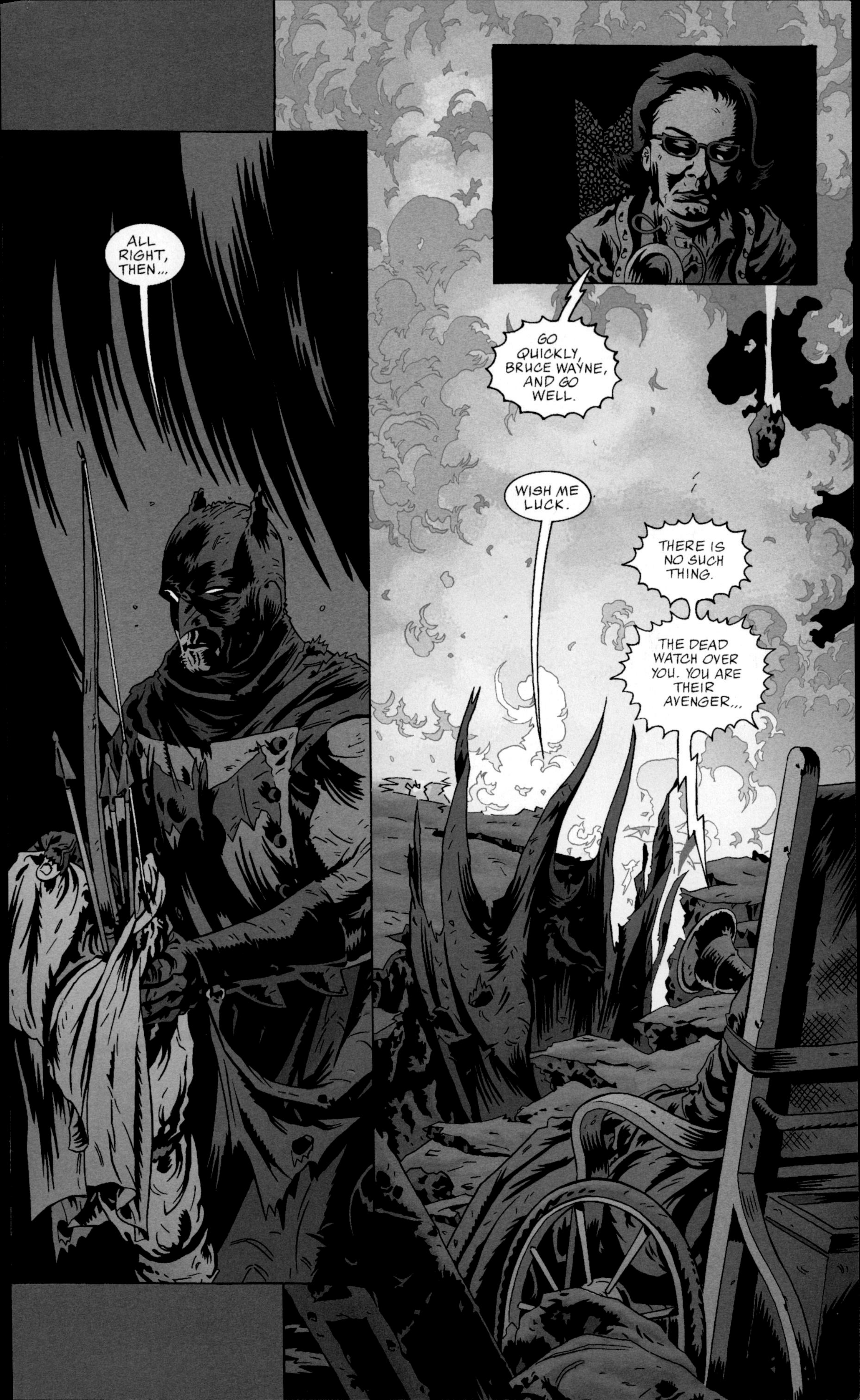
ALL RIGHT, THEN...
GO QUICKLY, BRUCE WAYNE, AND GO WELL.
WISH ME LUCK.
THERE IS NO SUCH THING.
THE DEAD WATCH OVER YOU. YOU ARE THEIR AVENGER...

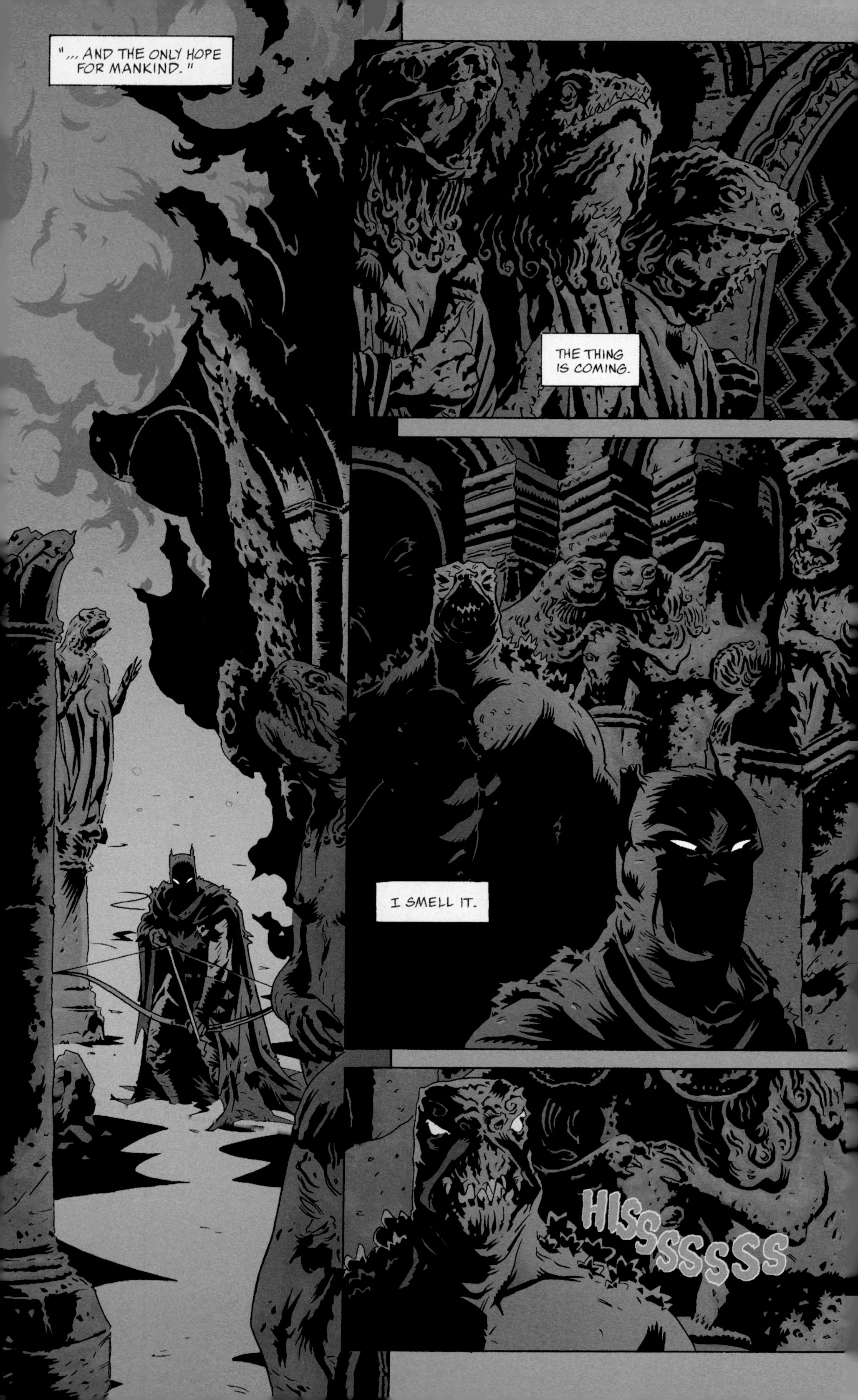
"... AND THE ONLY HOPE FOR MANKIND."
THE THING IS COMING.
I SMELL IT.
HISSSSSSSS

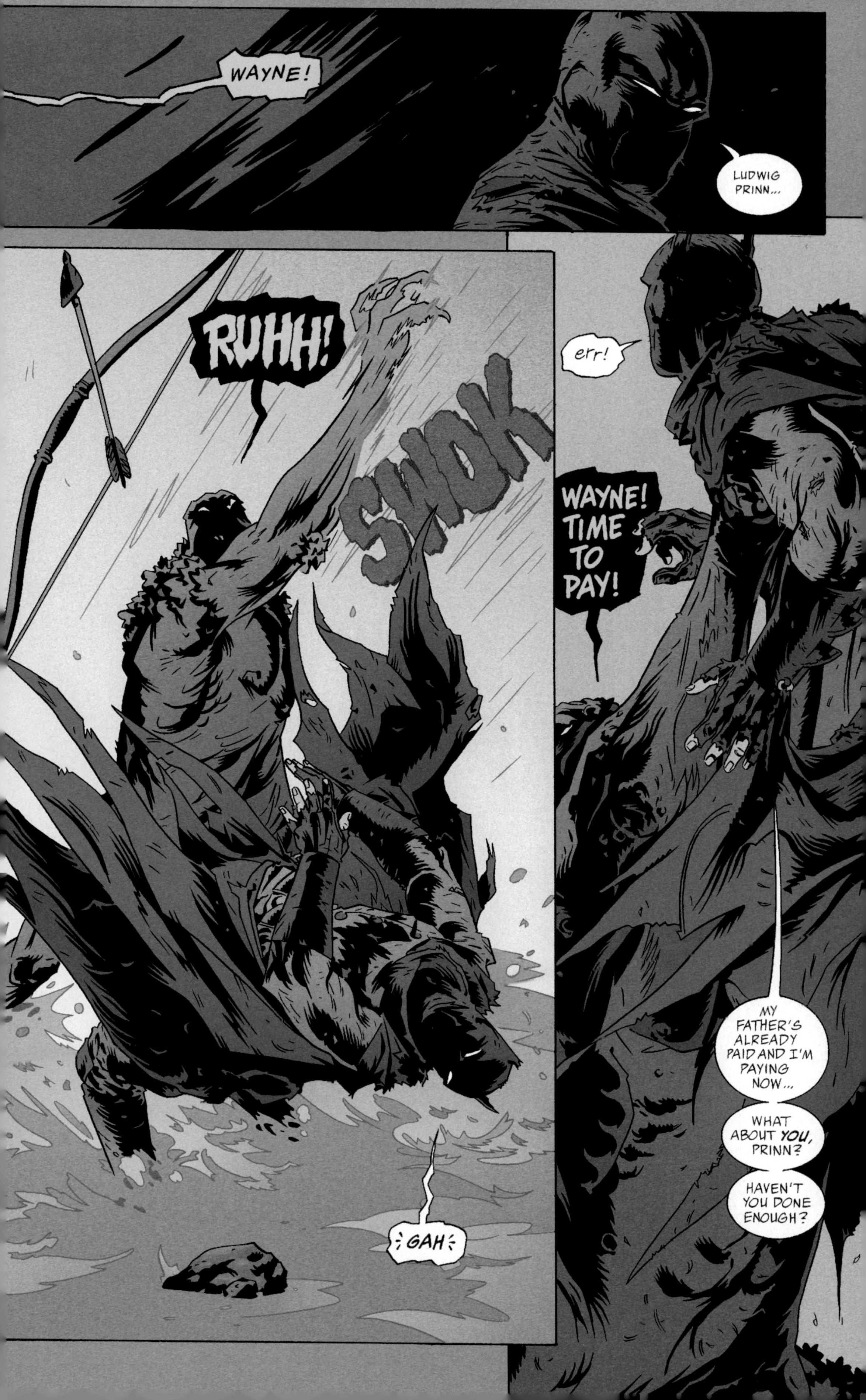
WAYNE!
LUDWIG PRINN...
RUHH!
SHOK
GAH
err!
WAYNE! TIME TO PAY!
MY FATHER'S ALREADY PAID AND I'M PAYING NOW...
WHAT ABOUT *YOU*, PRINN?
HAVEN'T YOU DONE ENOUGH?

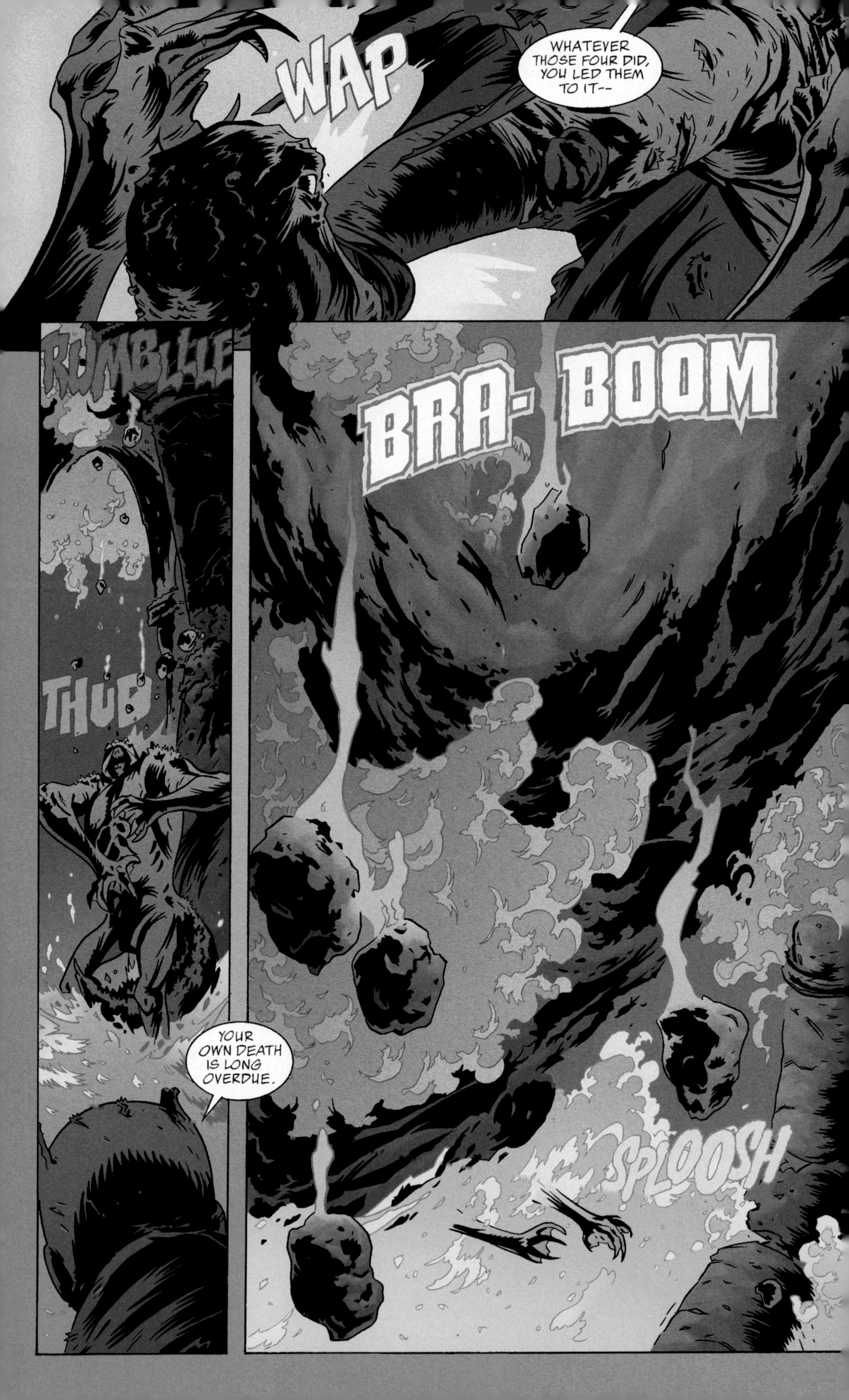
WAP
WHATEVER THOSE FOUR DID, YOU LED THEM TO IT--
RUMBLLLE
THUD
YOUR OWN DEATH IS LONG OVERDUE.
BRA-BOOM
SPLOOSH

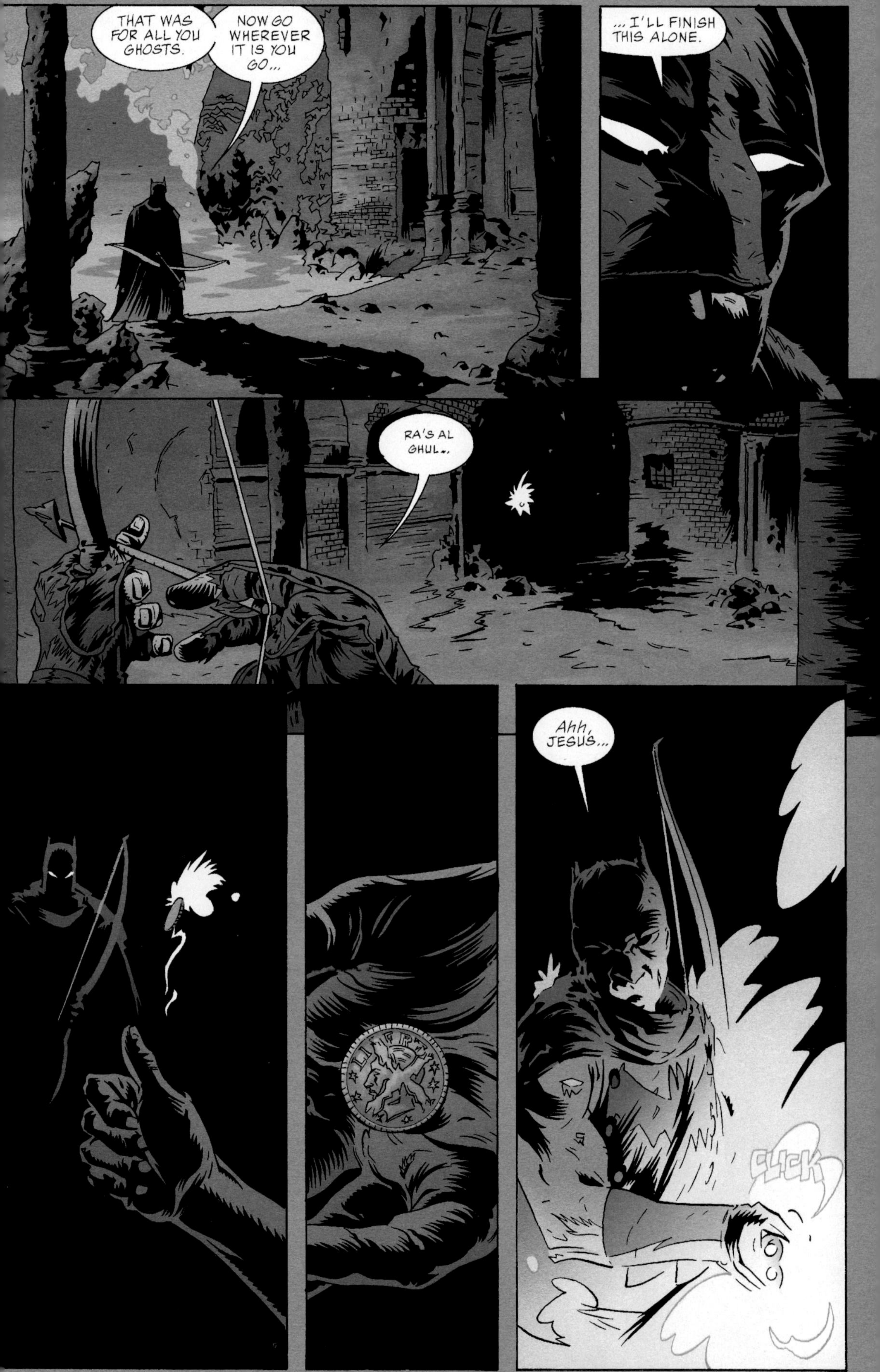
THAT WAS FOR ALL YOU GHOSTS.
NOW GO WHEREVER IT IS YOU GO...
...I'LL FINISH THIS ALONE.
RA'S AL GHUL..
Ahh, JESUS...
CLICK

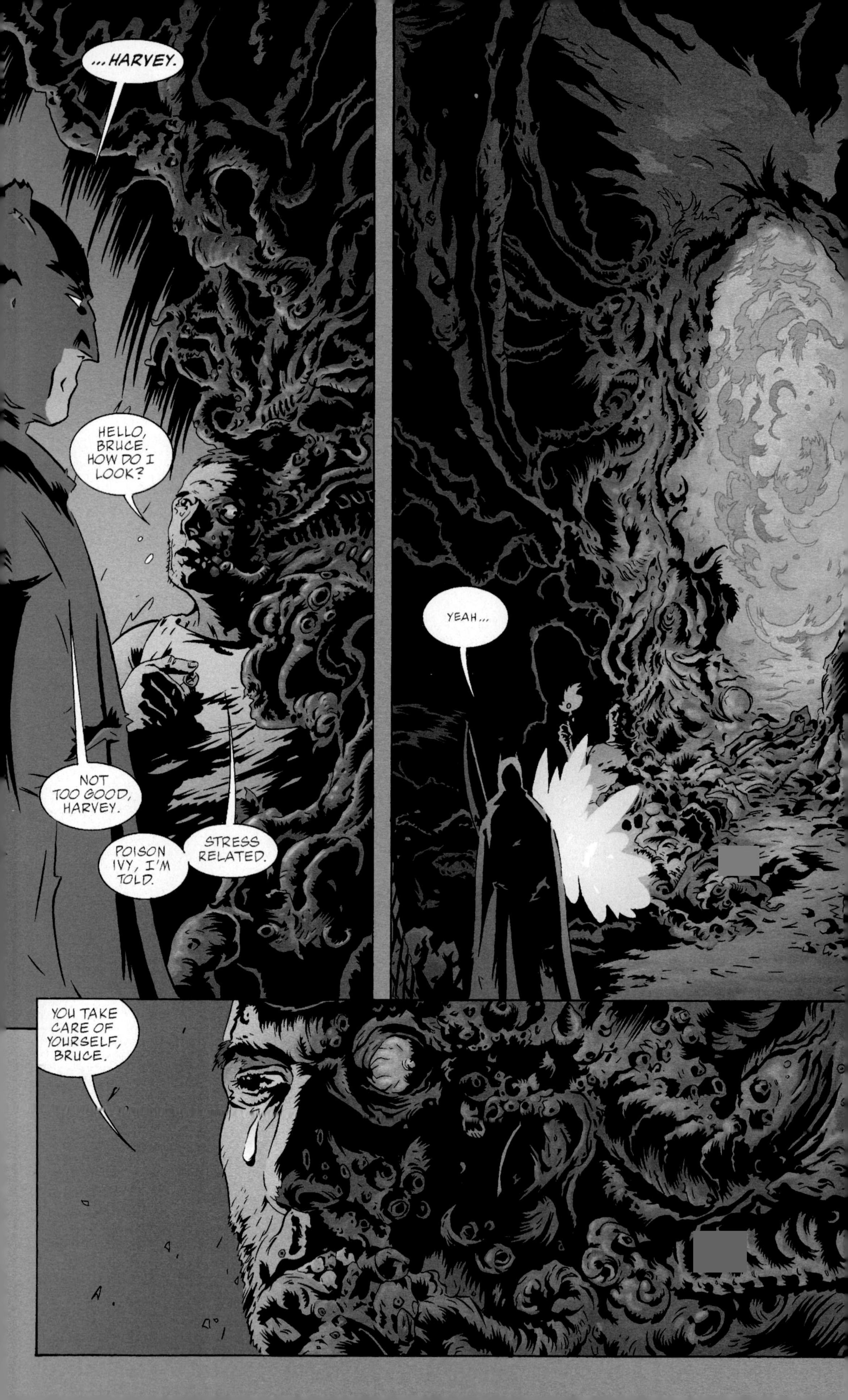
...HARVEY.
HELLO, BRUCE. HOW DO I LOOK?
NOT TOO GOOD, HARVEY.
POISON IVY, I'M TOLD.
STRESS RELATED.
YEAH...
YOU TAKE CARE OF YOURSELF, BRUCE.

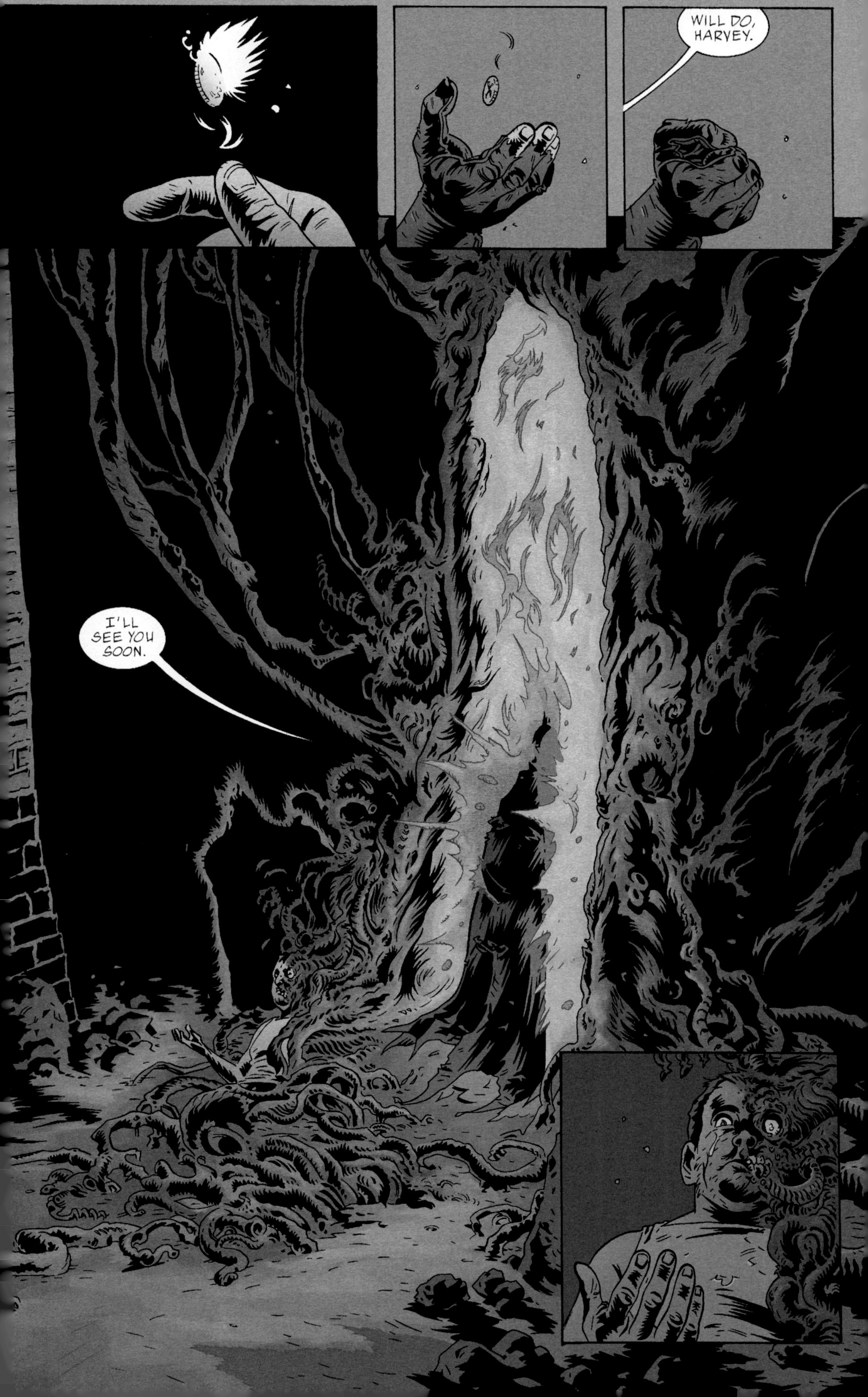
WILL DO, HARVEY.
I'LL SEE YOU SOON.

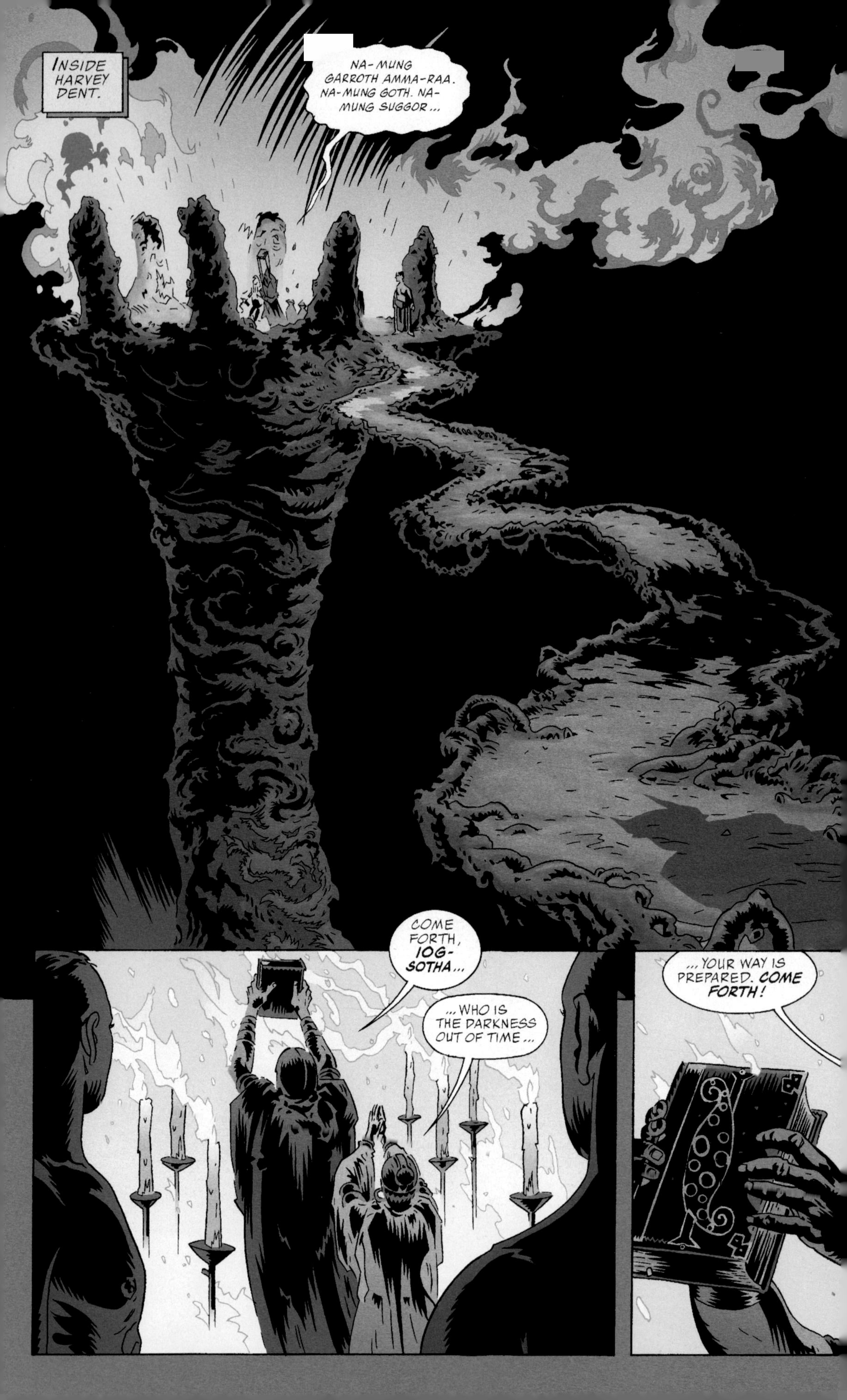
INSIDE HARVEY DENT.
NA-MUNG GARROTH AMMA-RAA. NA-MUNG GOTH. NA-MUNG SUGGOR...
COME FORTH, IOG-SOTHA...
...WHO IS THE DARKNESS OUT OF TIME...
...YOUR WAY IS PREPARED. COME FORTH!

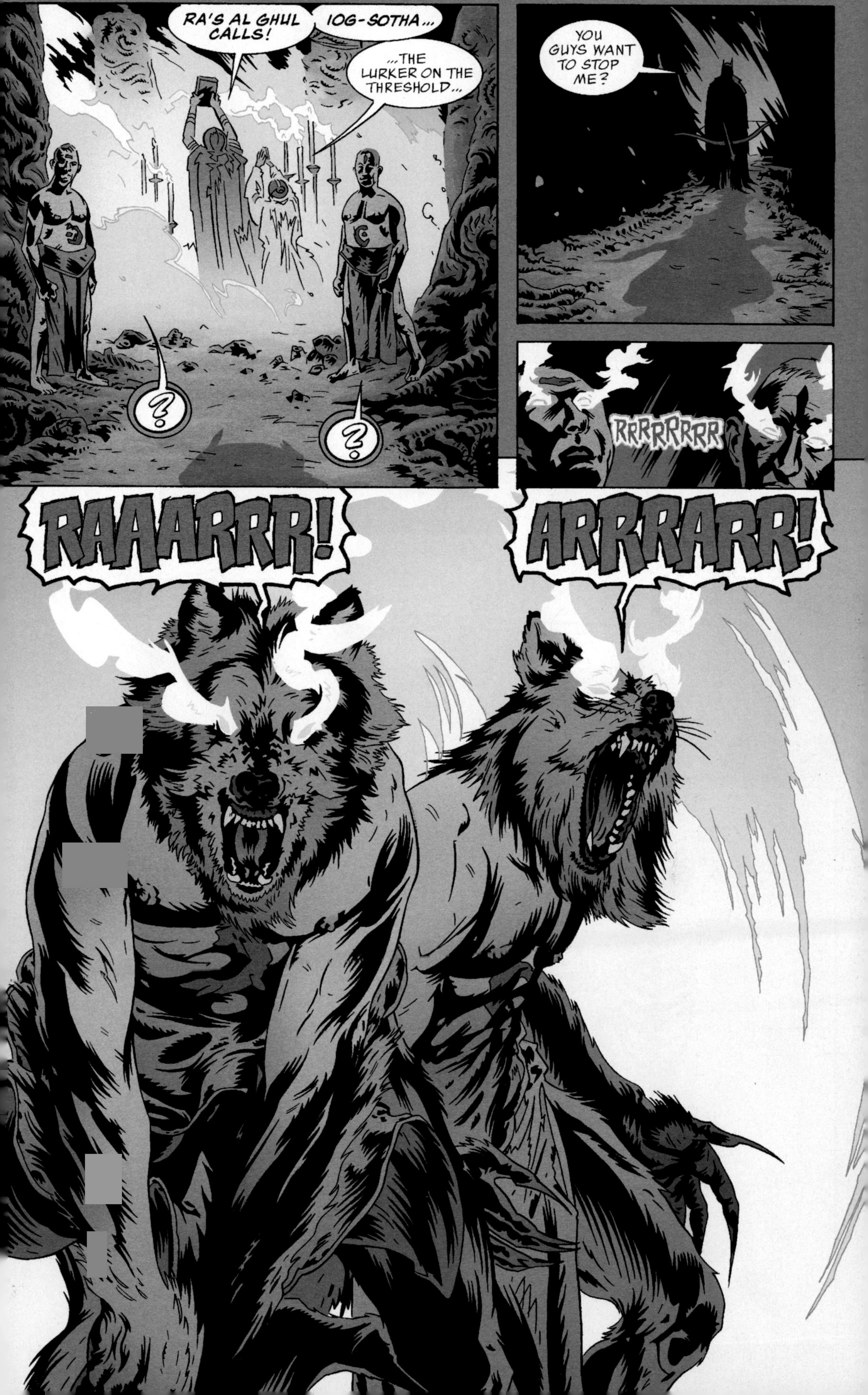
RA'S AL GHUL CALLS!
IOG-SOTHA...
...THE LURKER ON THE THRESHOLD...
?
?
YOU GUYS WANT TO STOP ME?
RRRRRRRR
RAAARRRR!
ARRRARR!

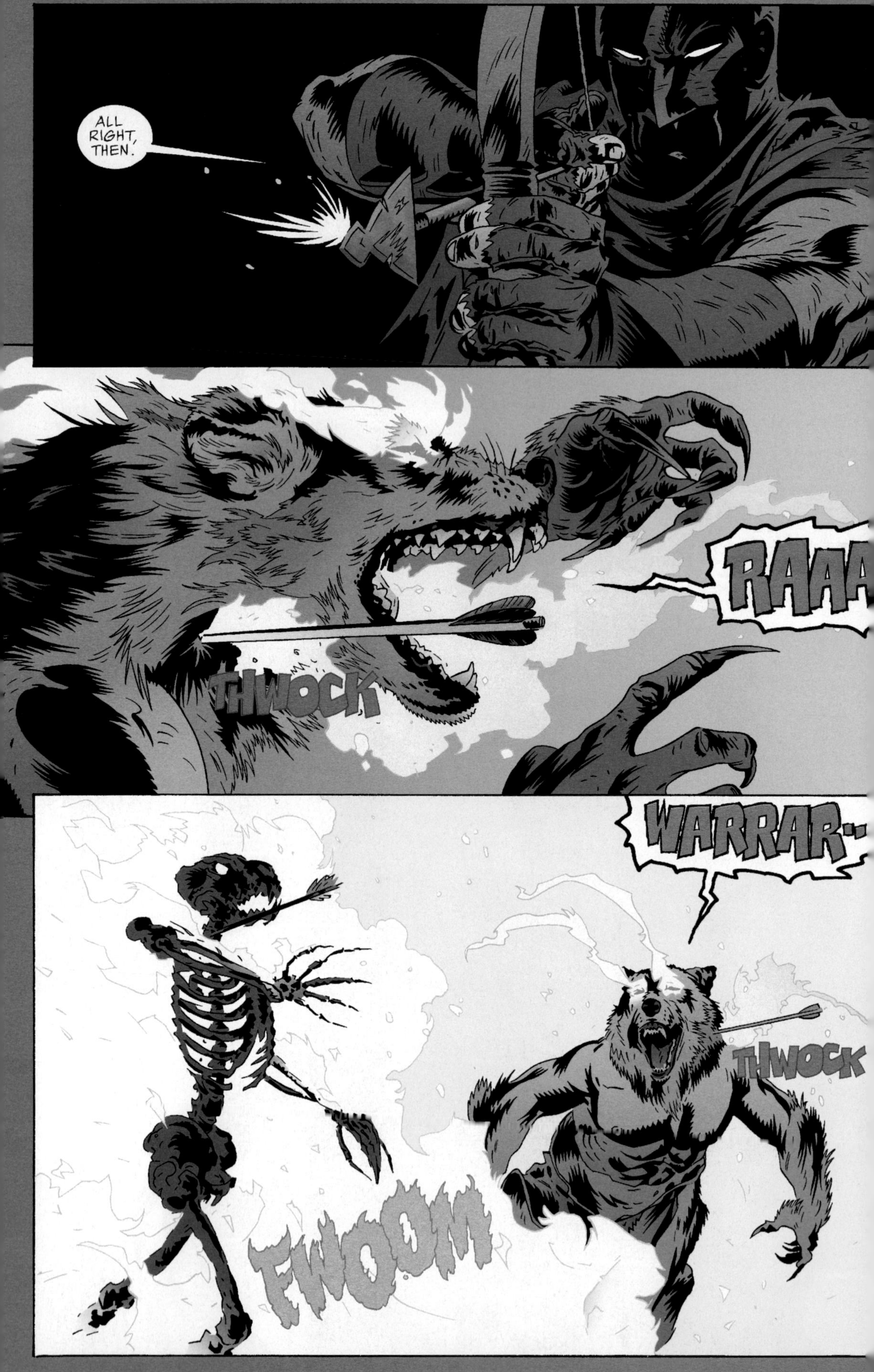
ALL RIGHT, THEN.
RAAA
THWOCK
WARRAR--
THWOCK
FWOOM

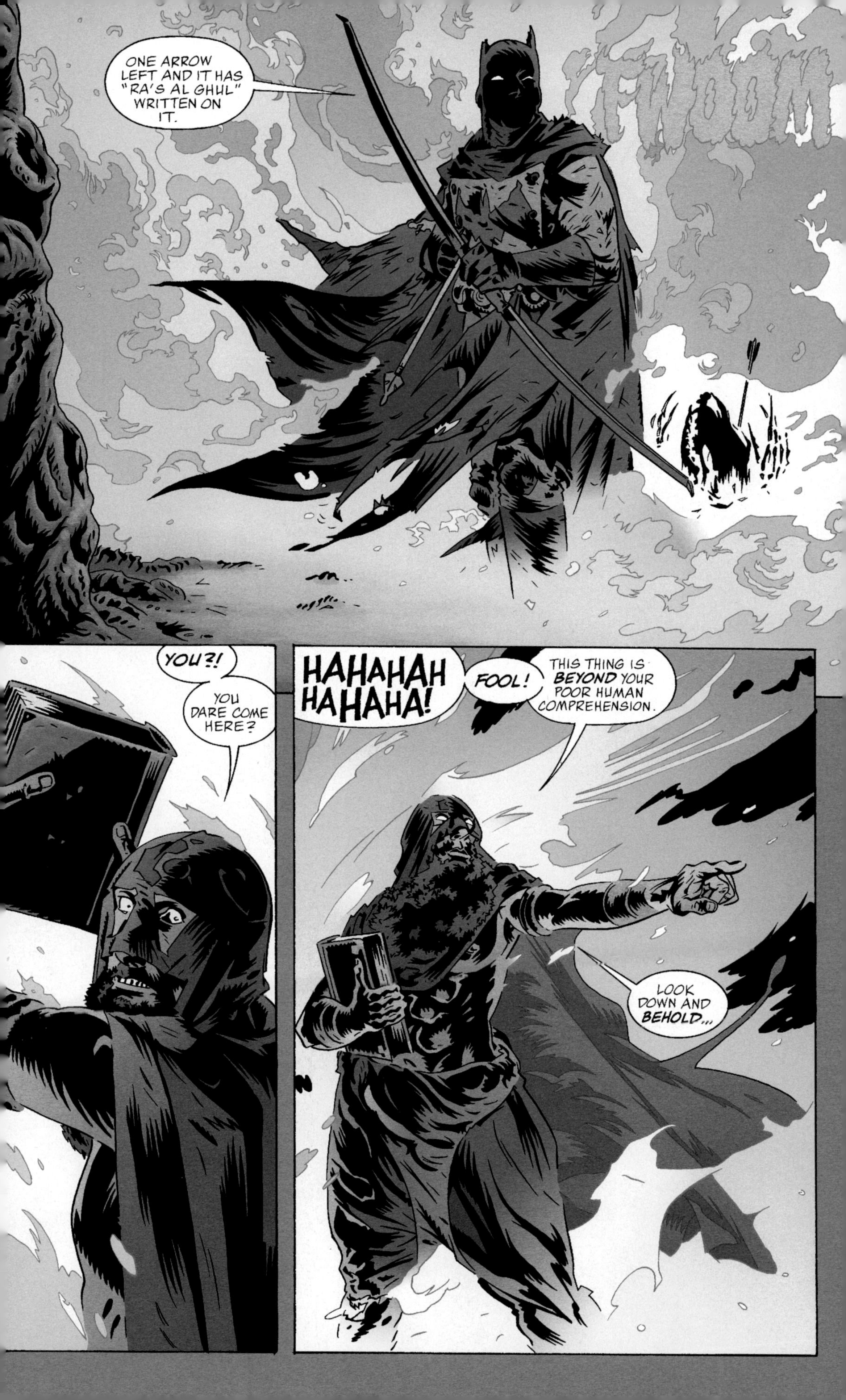
ONE ARROW LEFT AND IT HAS "RA'S AL GHUL" WRITTEN ON IT.
FWOOM
YOU?!
YOU DARE COME HERE?
HAHAHAH HAHAHA!
FOOL!
THIS THING IS BEYOND YOUR POOR HUMAN COMPREHENSION.
LOOK DOWN AND BEHOLD...

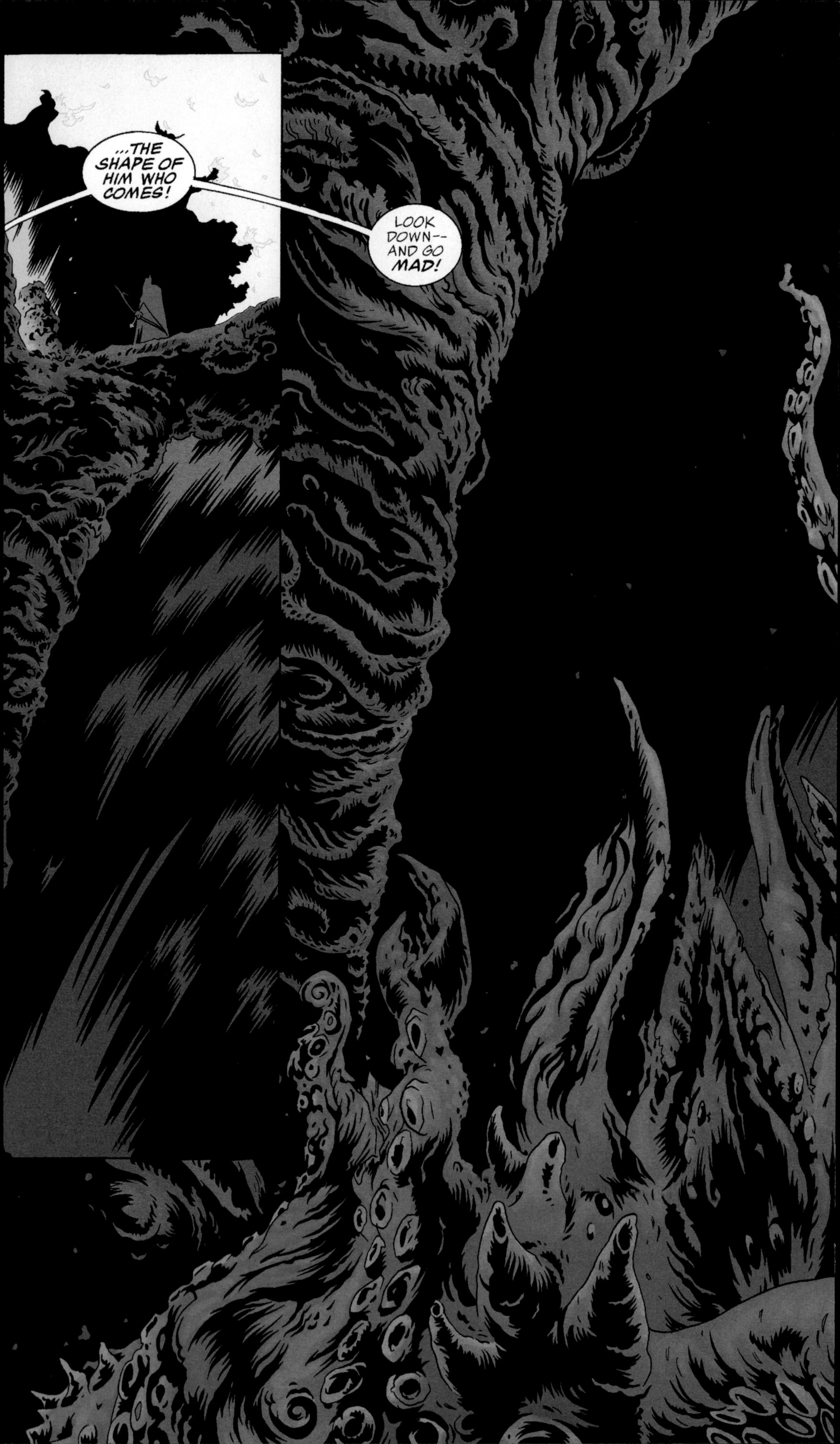
...THE SHAPE OF HIM WHO COMES!
LOOK DOWN-- AND GO MAD!

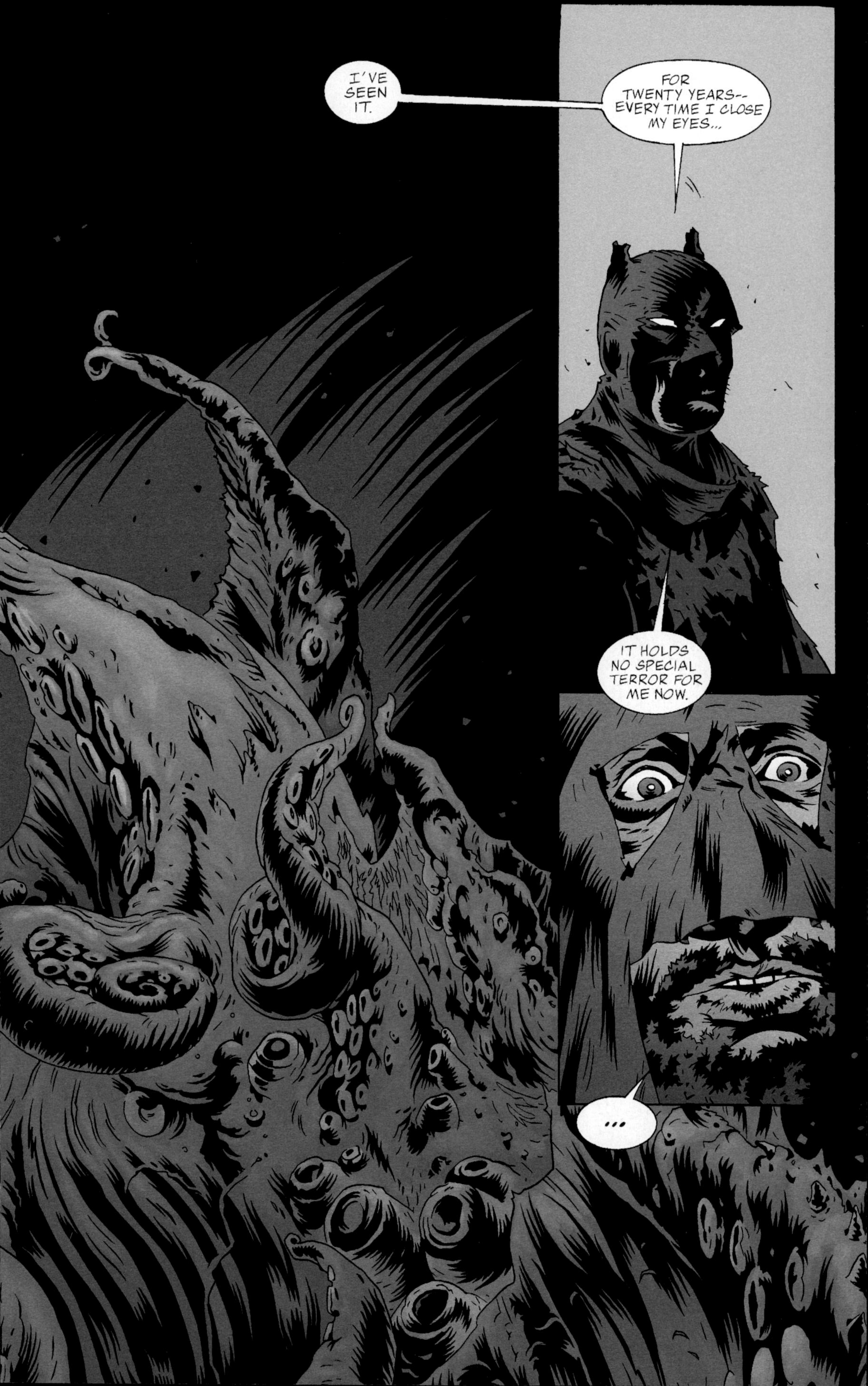
I'VE SEEN IT.
FOR TWENTY YEARS-- EVERY TIME I CLOSE MY EYES...
IT HOLDS NO SPECIAL TERROR FOR ME NOW.
...

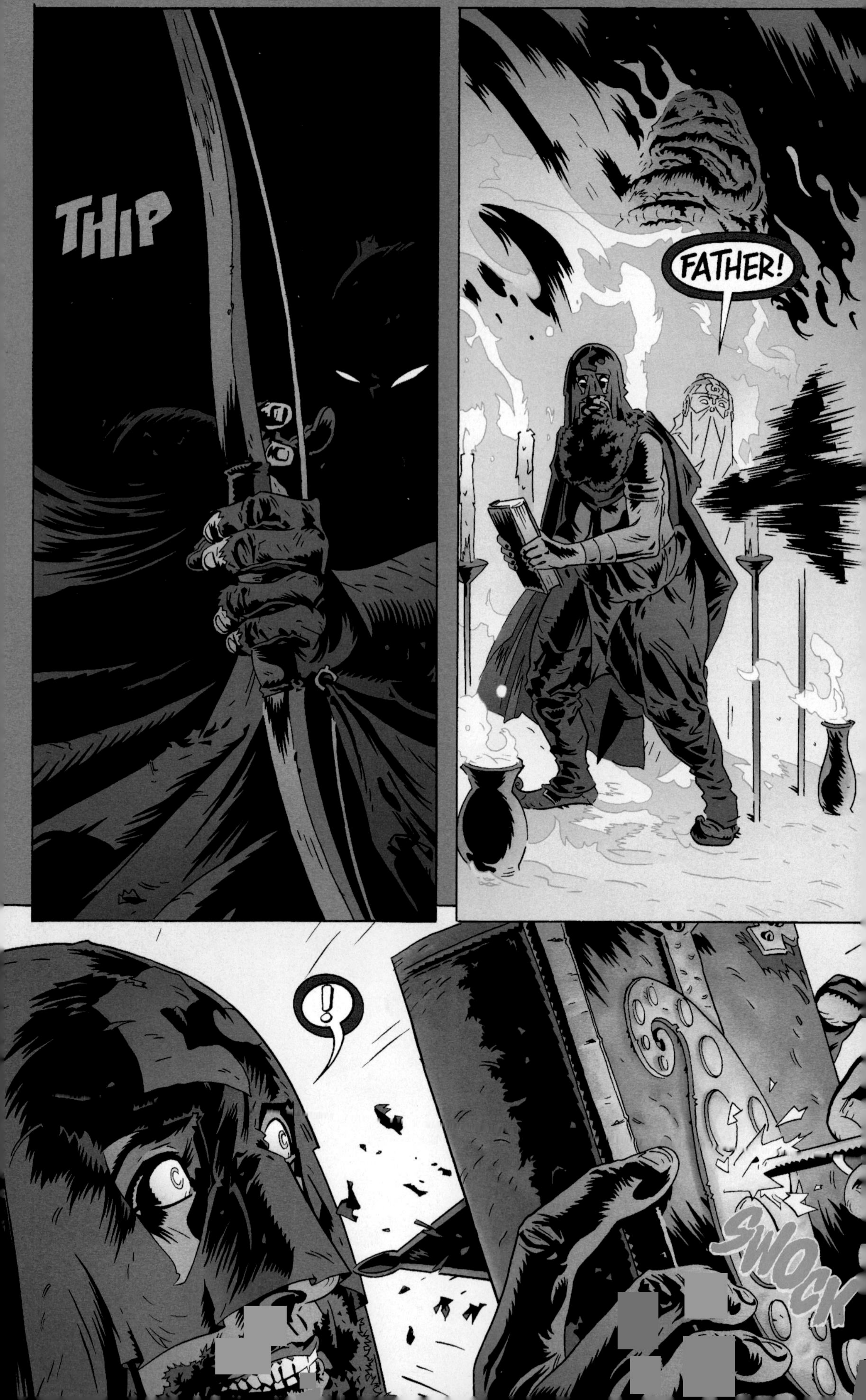

THIP
FATHER!
!
SWOCK

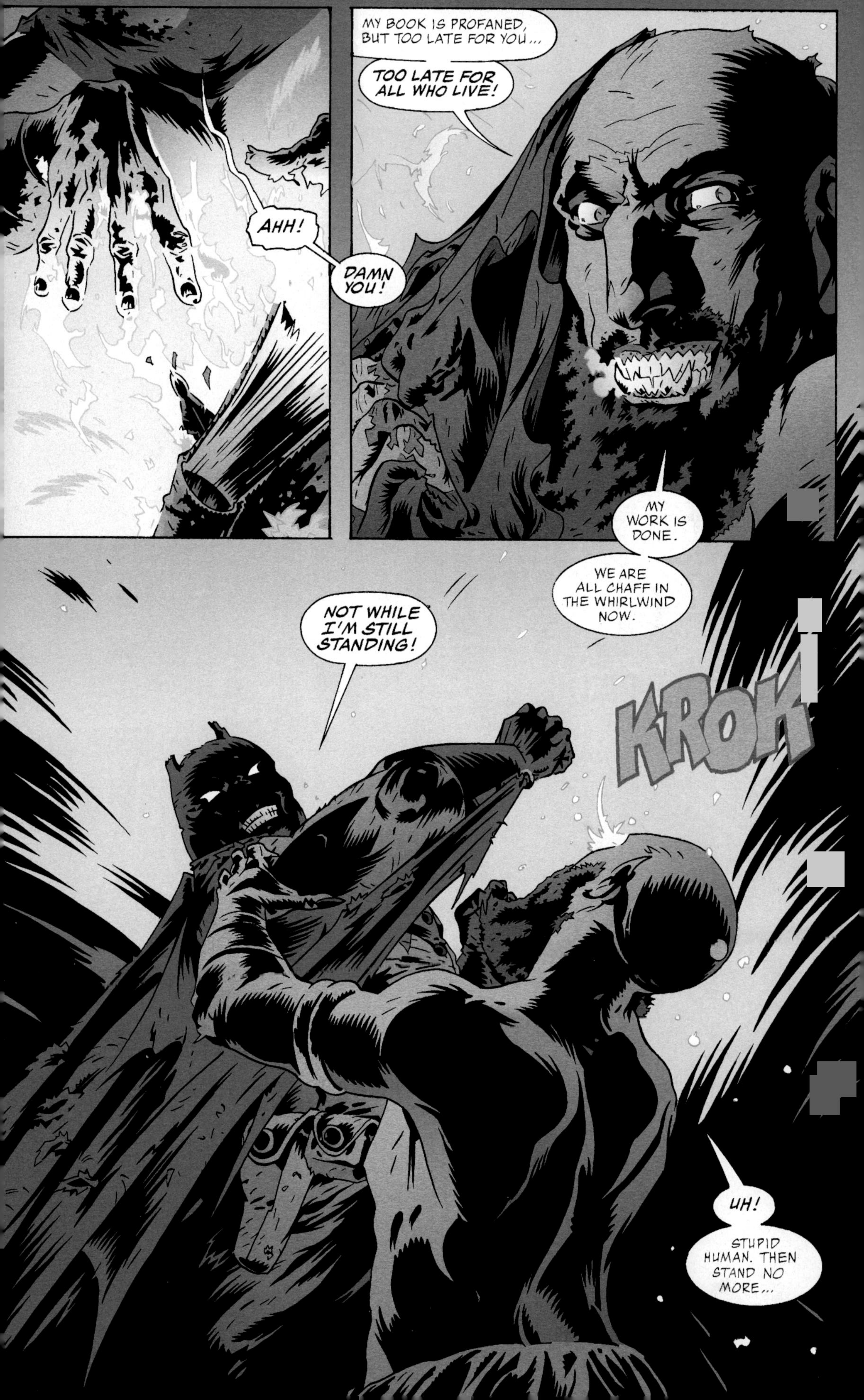
AHH!
DAMN YOU!
MY BOOK IS PROFANED, BUT TOO LATE FOR YOU...
TOO LATE FOR ALL WHO LIVE!
MY WORK IS DONE.
WE ARE ALL CHAFF IN THE WHIRLWIND NOW.
NOT WHILE I'M STILL STANDING!
KROK
UH!
STUPID HUMAN. THEN STAND NO MORE...

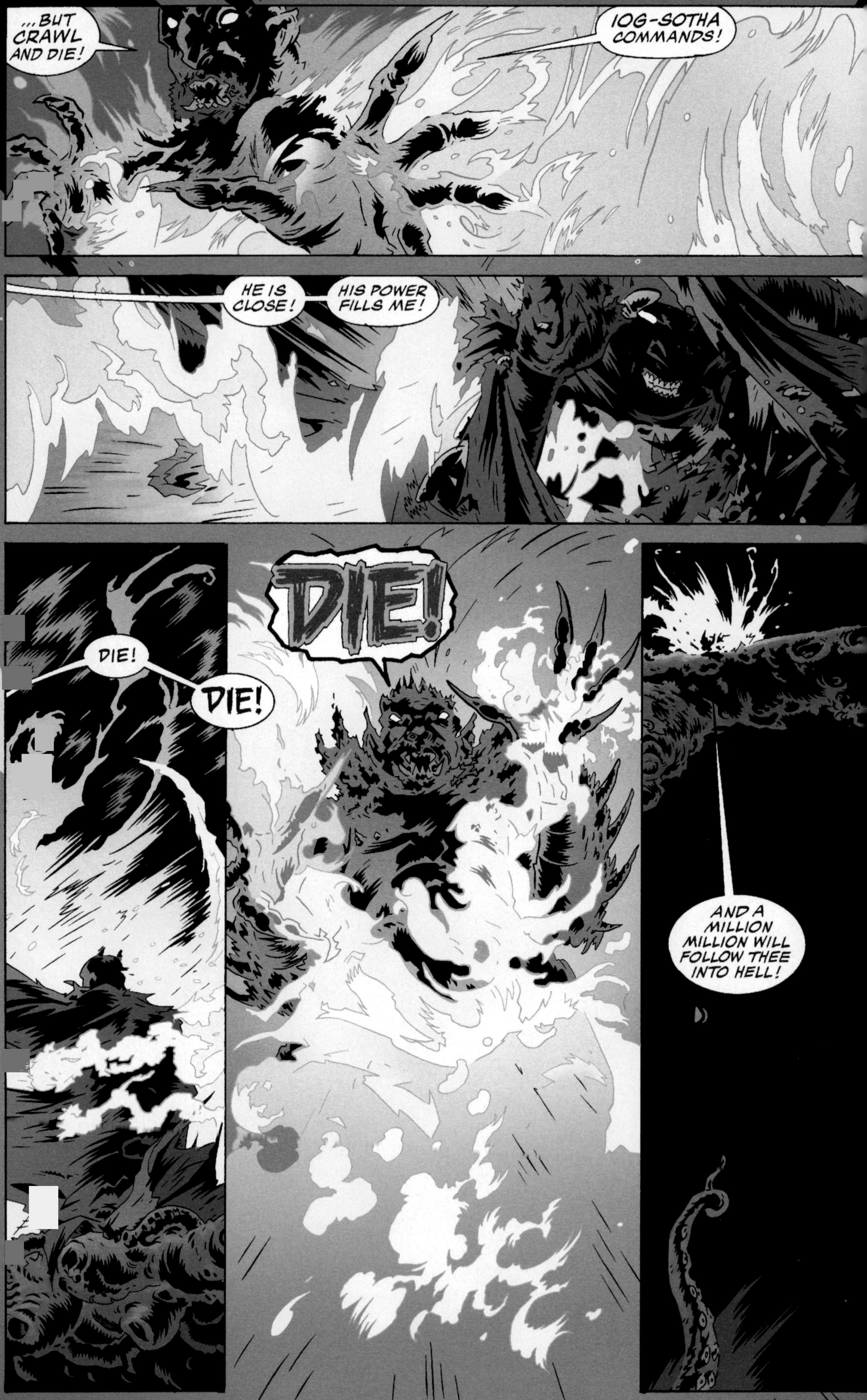
...BUT CRAWL AND DIE!
IOG-SOTHA COMMANDS!
HE IS CLOSE!
HIS POWER FILLS ME!
DIE!
DIE!
DIE!
AND A MILLION MILLION WILL FOLLOW THEE INTO HELL!

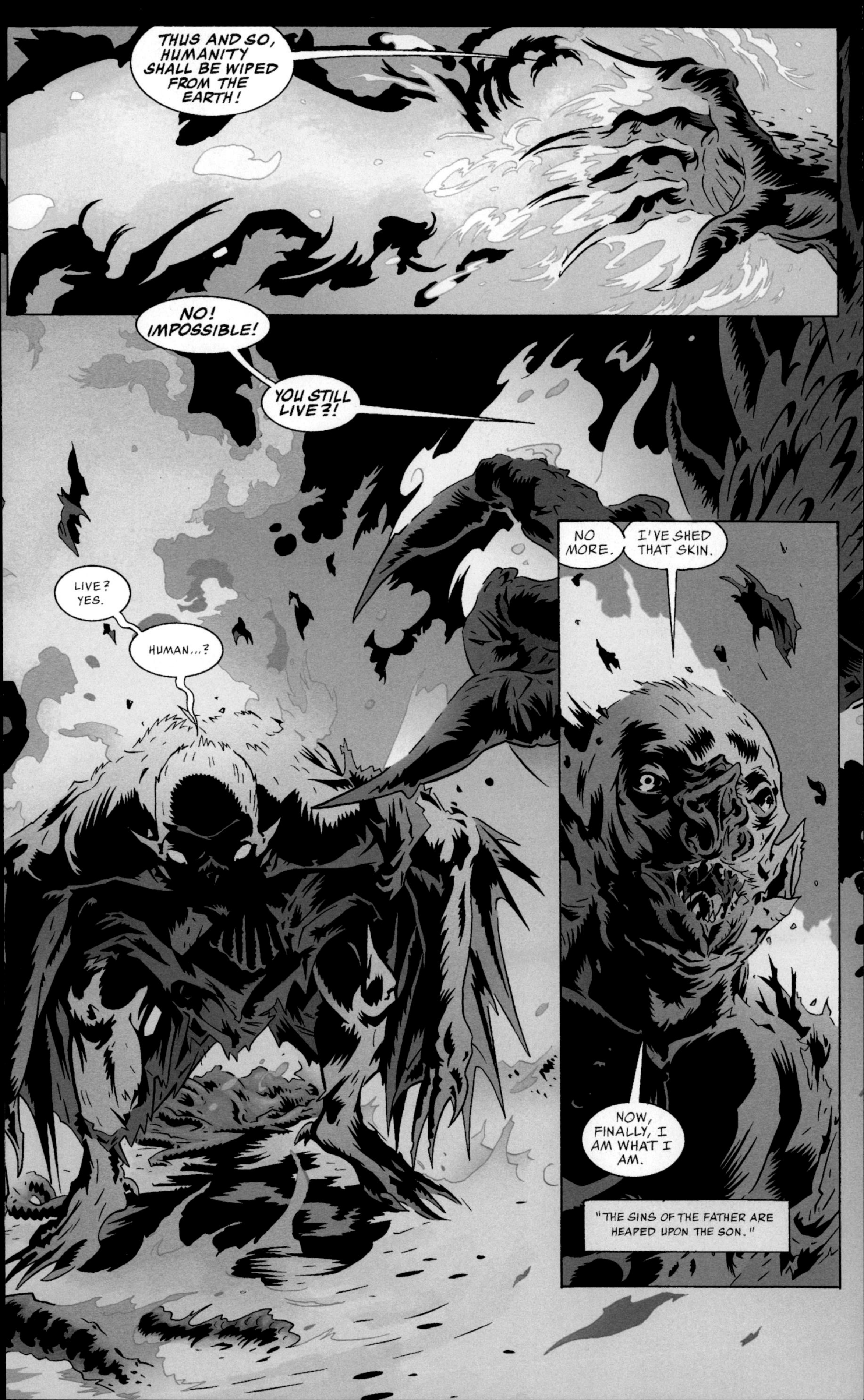
THUS AND SO, HUMANITY SHALL BE WIPED FROM THE EARTH!
NO! IMPOSSIBLE!
YOU STILL LIVE?!
LIVE? YES.
HUMAN...?
NO MORE.
I'VE SHED THAT SKIN.
NOW, FINALLY, I AM WHAT I AM.
"THE SINS OF THE FATHER ARE HEAPED UPON THE SON."

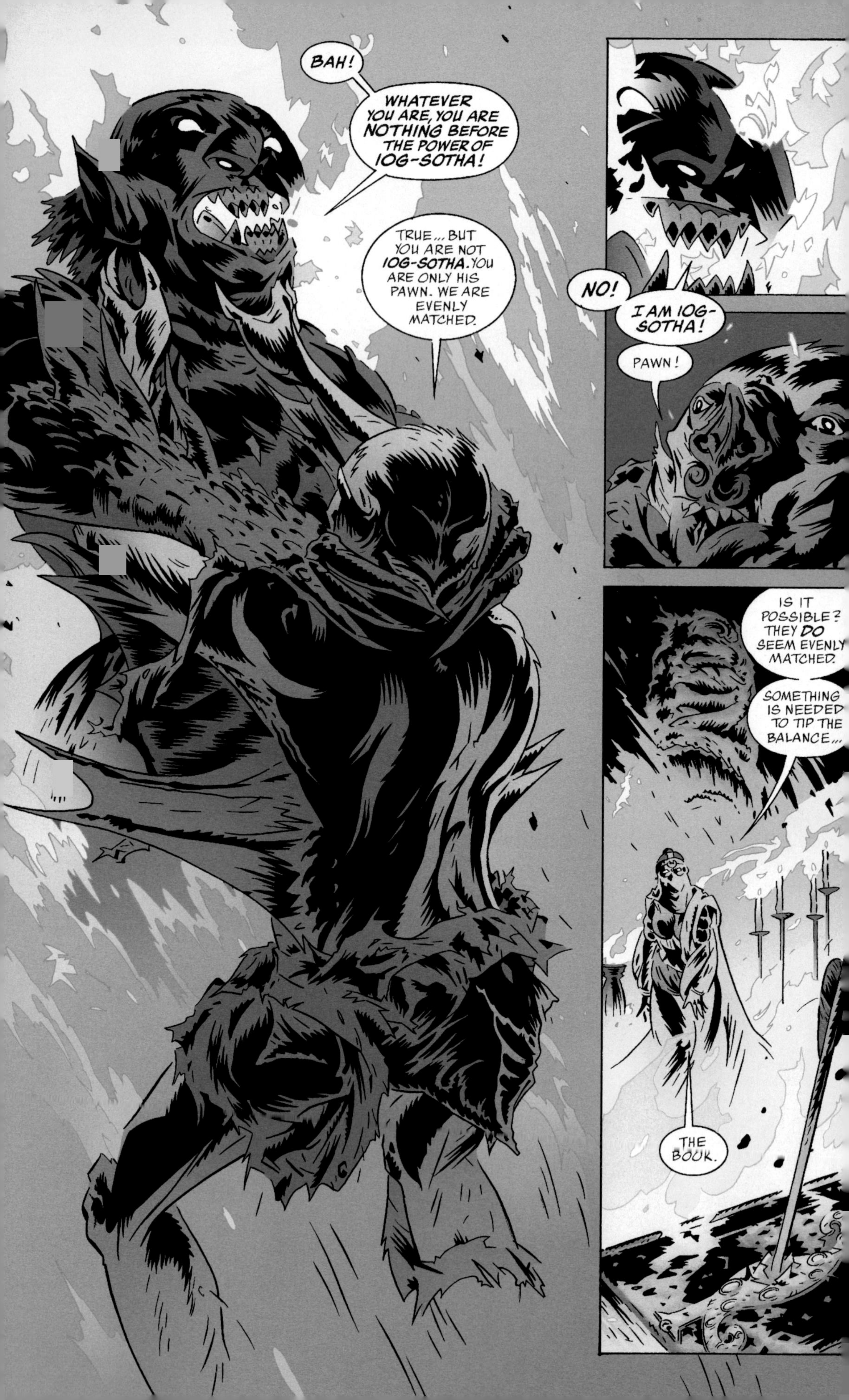
BAH!
WHATEVER YOU ARE, YOU ARE NOTHING BEFORE THE POWER OF IOG-SOTHA!
TRUE... BUT YOU ARE NOT IOG-SOTHA. YOU ARE ONLY HIS PAWN. WE ARE EVENLY MATCHED.
NO!
I AM IOG-SOTHA!
PAWN!
IS IT POSSIBLE? THEY DO SEEM EVENLY MATCHED.
SOMETHING IS NEEDED TO TIP THE BALANCE...
THE BOOK.

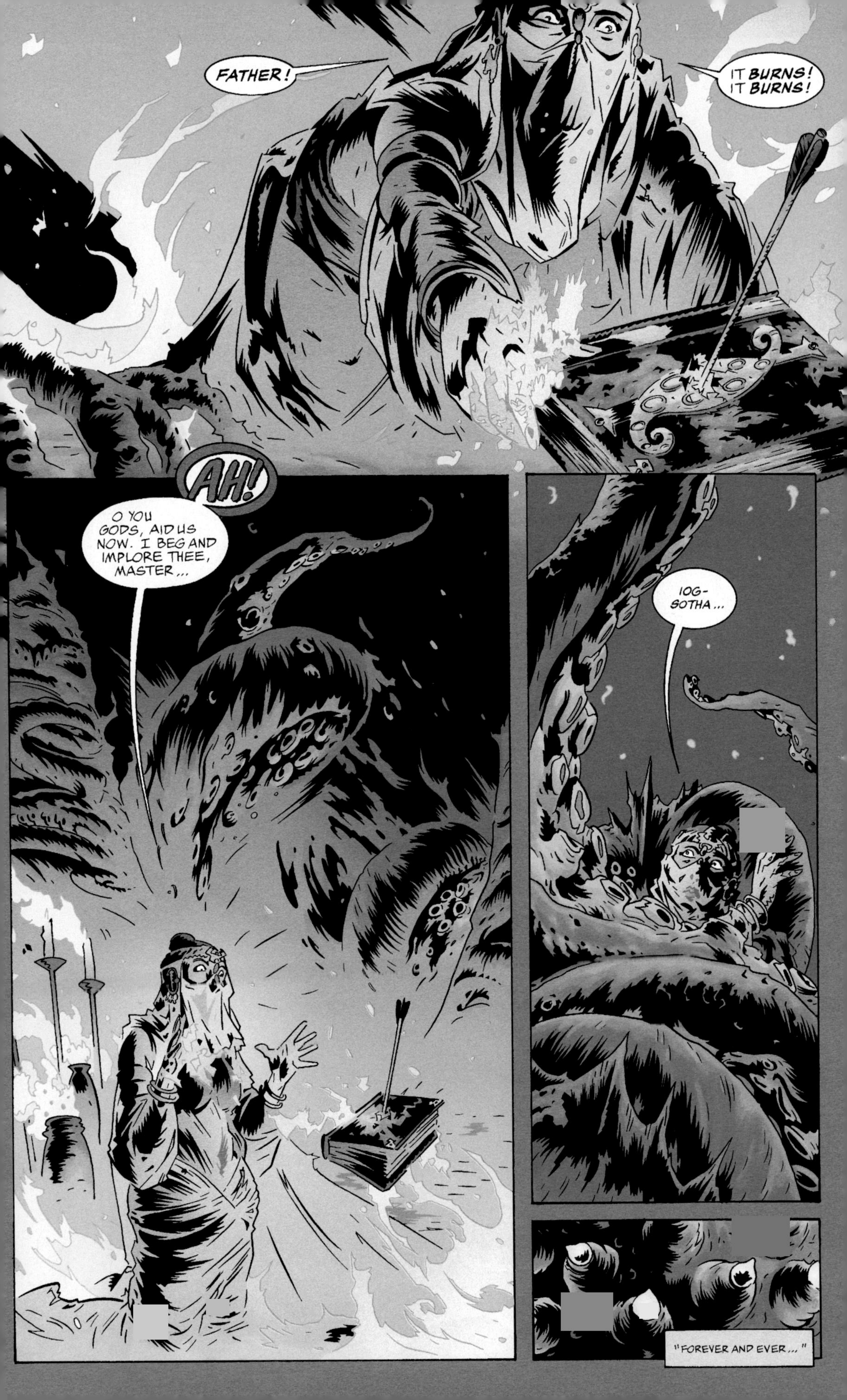
FATHER!
IT BURNS! IT BURNS!
AH!
O YOU GODS, AID US NOW. I BEG AND IMPLORE THEE, MASTER...
IOG-SOTHA...
"FOREVER AND EVER..."

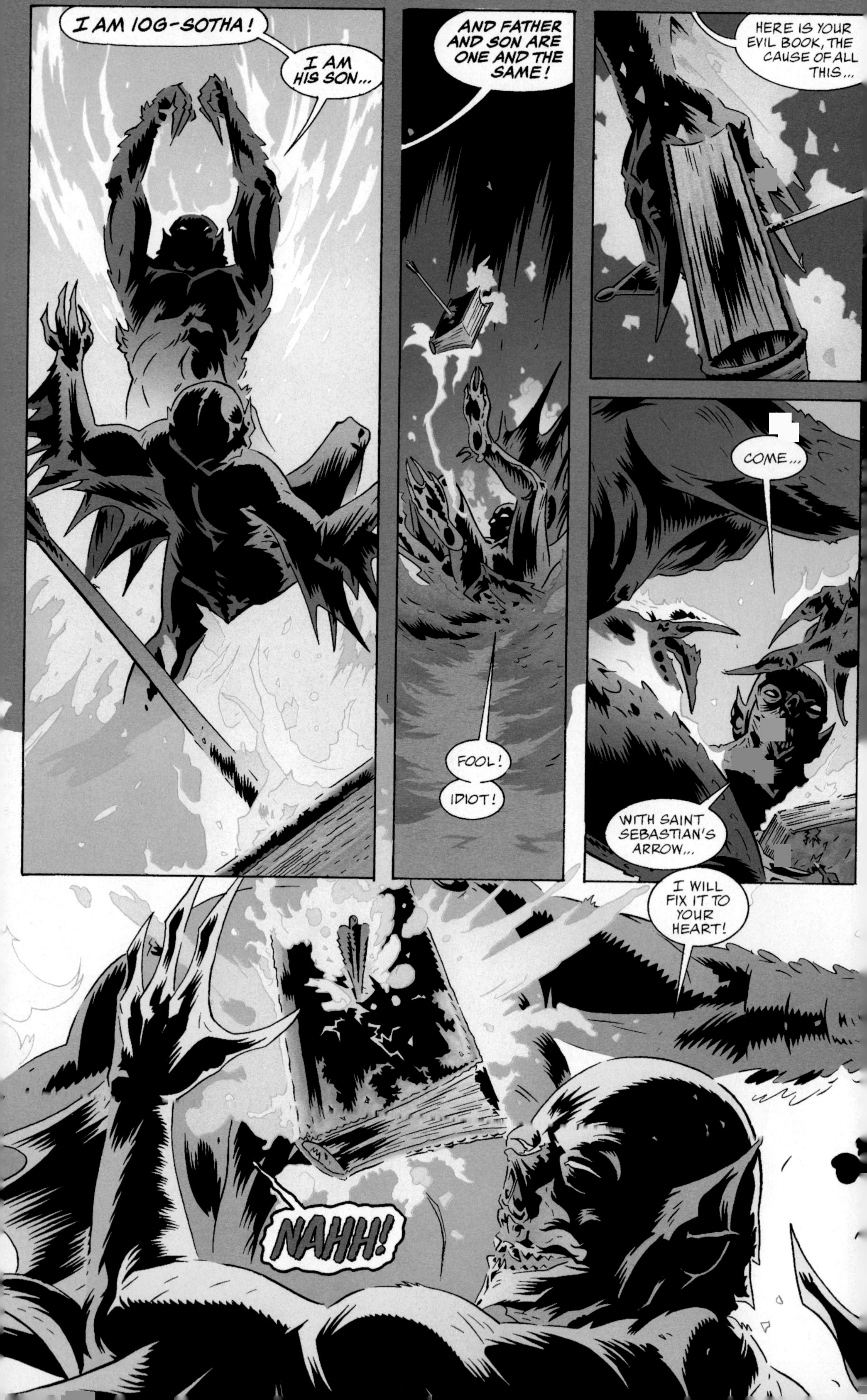
I AM IOG-SOTHA!
I AM HIS SON...
AND FATHER AND SON ARE ONE AND THE SAME!
FOOL!
IDIOT!
HERE IS YOUR EVIL BOOK, THE CAUSE OF ALL THIS...
COME...
WITH SAINT SEBASTIAN'S ARROW...
I WILL FIX IT TO YOUR HEART!
NAHH!

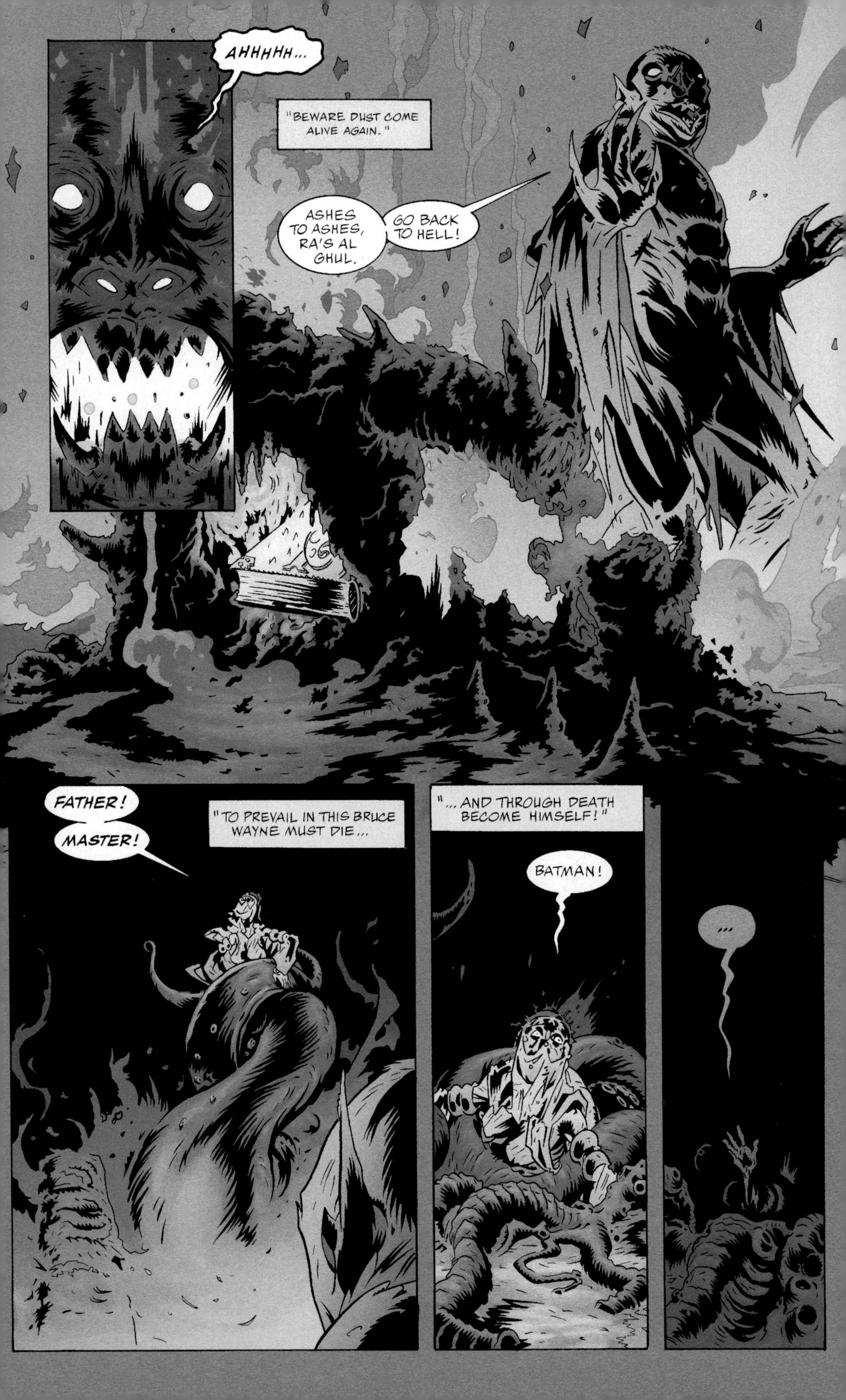
AHHHHH...
"BEWARE DUST COME ALIVE AGAIN."
ASHES TO ASHES, RA'S AL GHUL.
GO BACK TO HELL!
FATHER!
MASTER!
"TO PREVAIL IN THIS BRUCE WAYNE MUST DIE...
"...AND THROUGH DEATH BECOME HIMSELF!"
BATMAN!
...

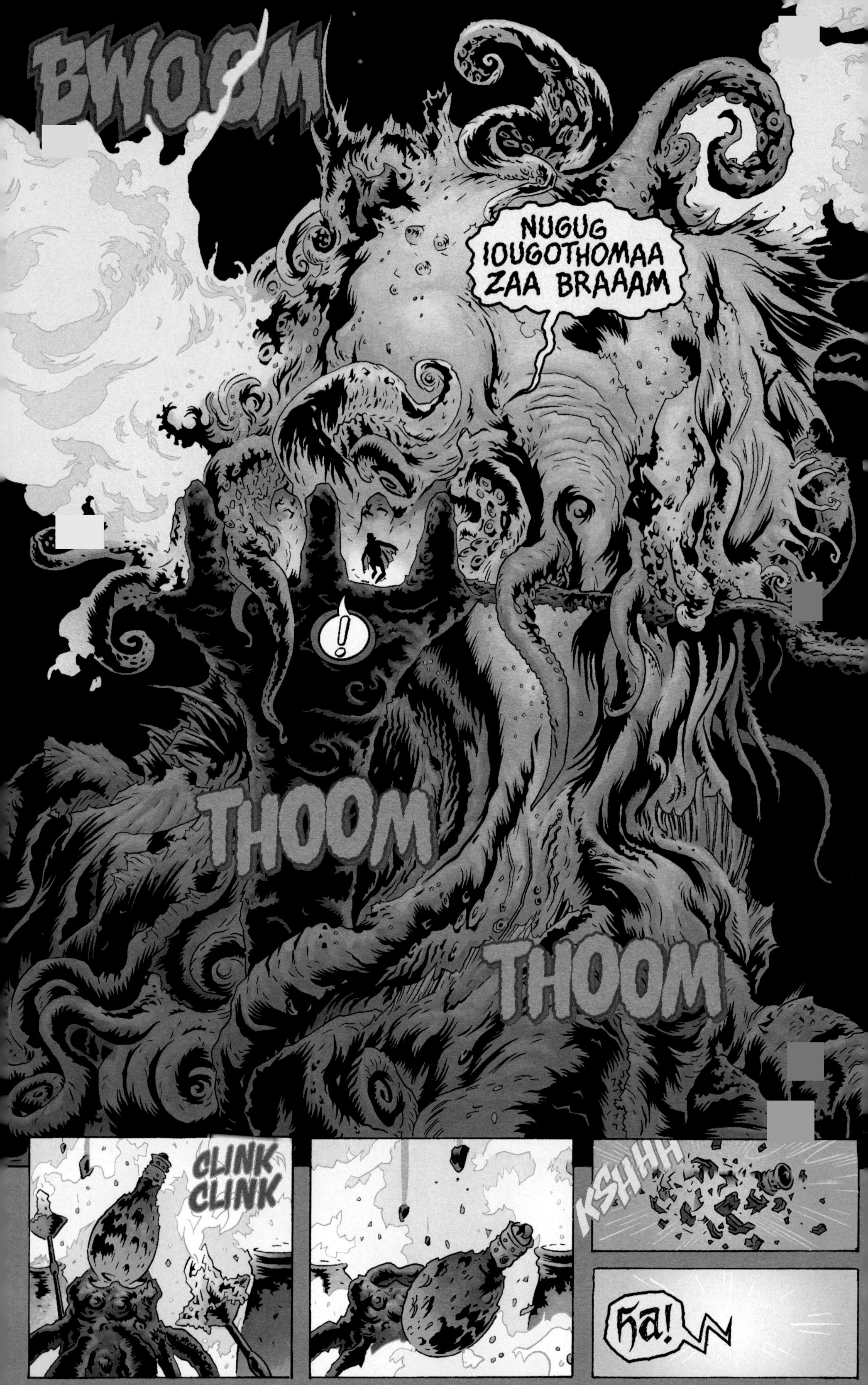
BWOOM
NUGUG IOUGOTHOMAA ZAA BRAAAM
!
THOOM
THOOM
CLINK CLINK
KSHHH
ha!

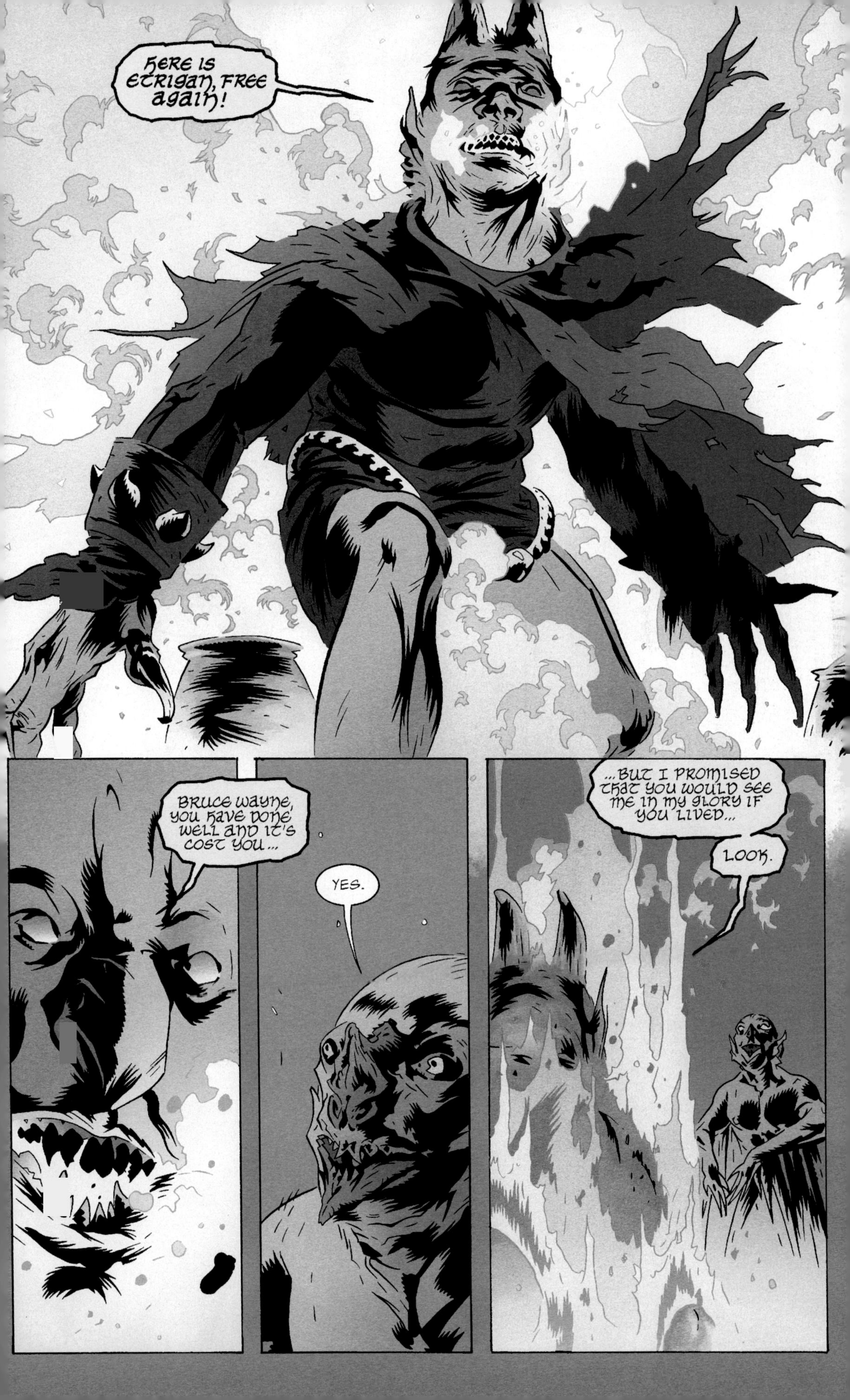
HERE IS ETRIGAN, FREE AGAIN!
BRUCE WAYNE, YOU HAVE DONE WELL AND IT'S COST YOU...
YES.
...BUT I PROMISED THAT YOU WOULD SEE ME IN MY GLORY IF YOU LIVED...
LOOK.

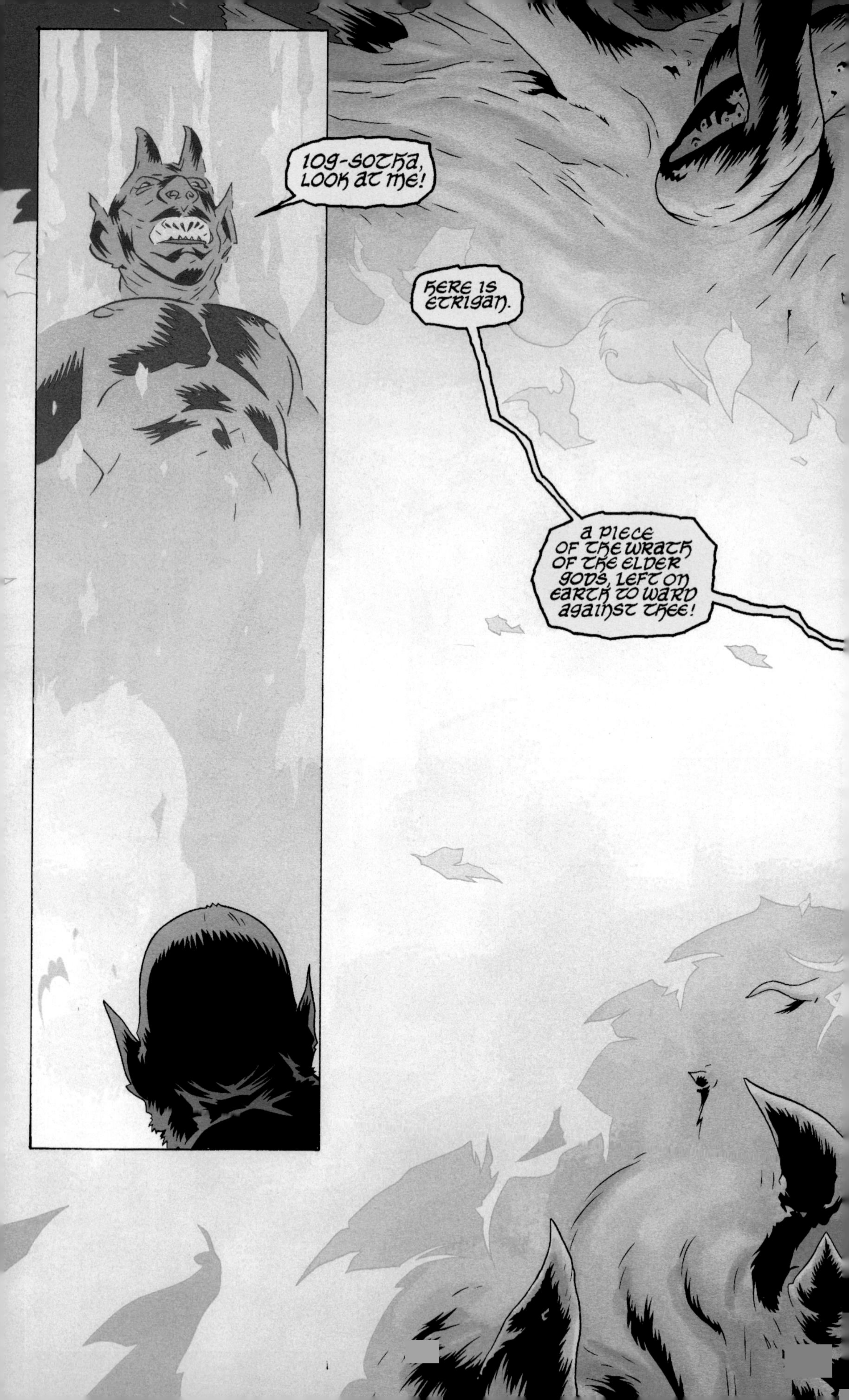
YOG-SOTHA, LOOK AT ME!
HERE IS ETRIGAN.
A PIECE OF THE WRATH OF THE ELDER GODS, LEFT ON EARTH TO WARD AGAINST THEE!

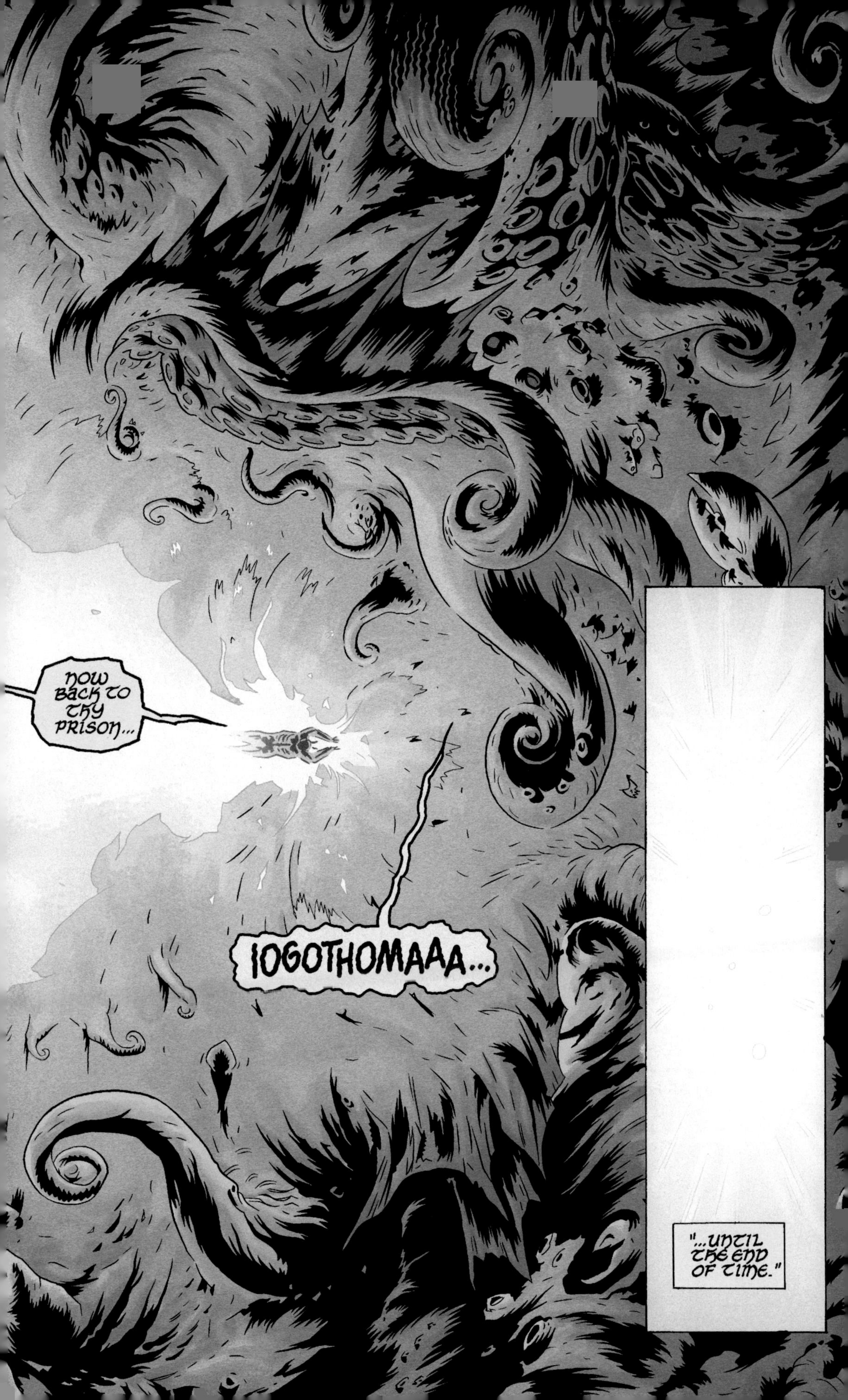

NOW BACK TO THY PRISON...
IOGOTHOMAAA...
"...UNTIL THE END OF TIME."

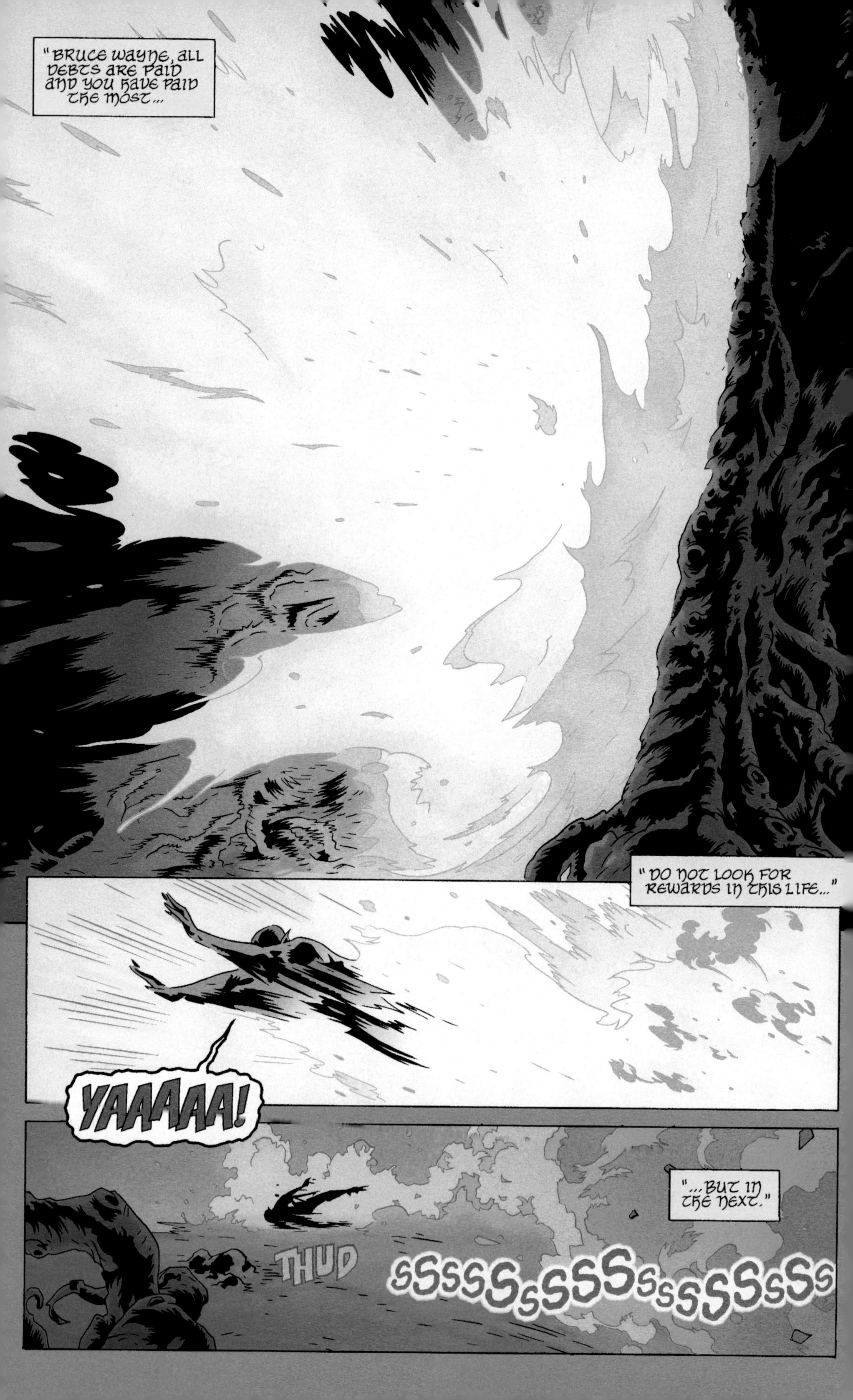
"BRUCE WAYNE, ALL DEBTS ARE PAID AND YOU HAVE PAID THE MOST...
"DO NOT LOOK FOR REWARDS IN THIS LIFE..."
YAAAAA!
"...BUT IN THE NEXT."
THUD
SSSSSSSSSSSSSSSSSSS

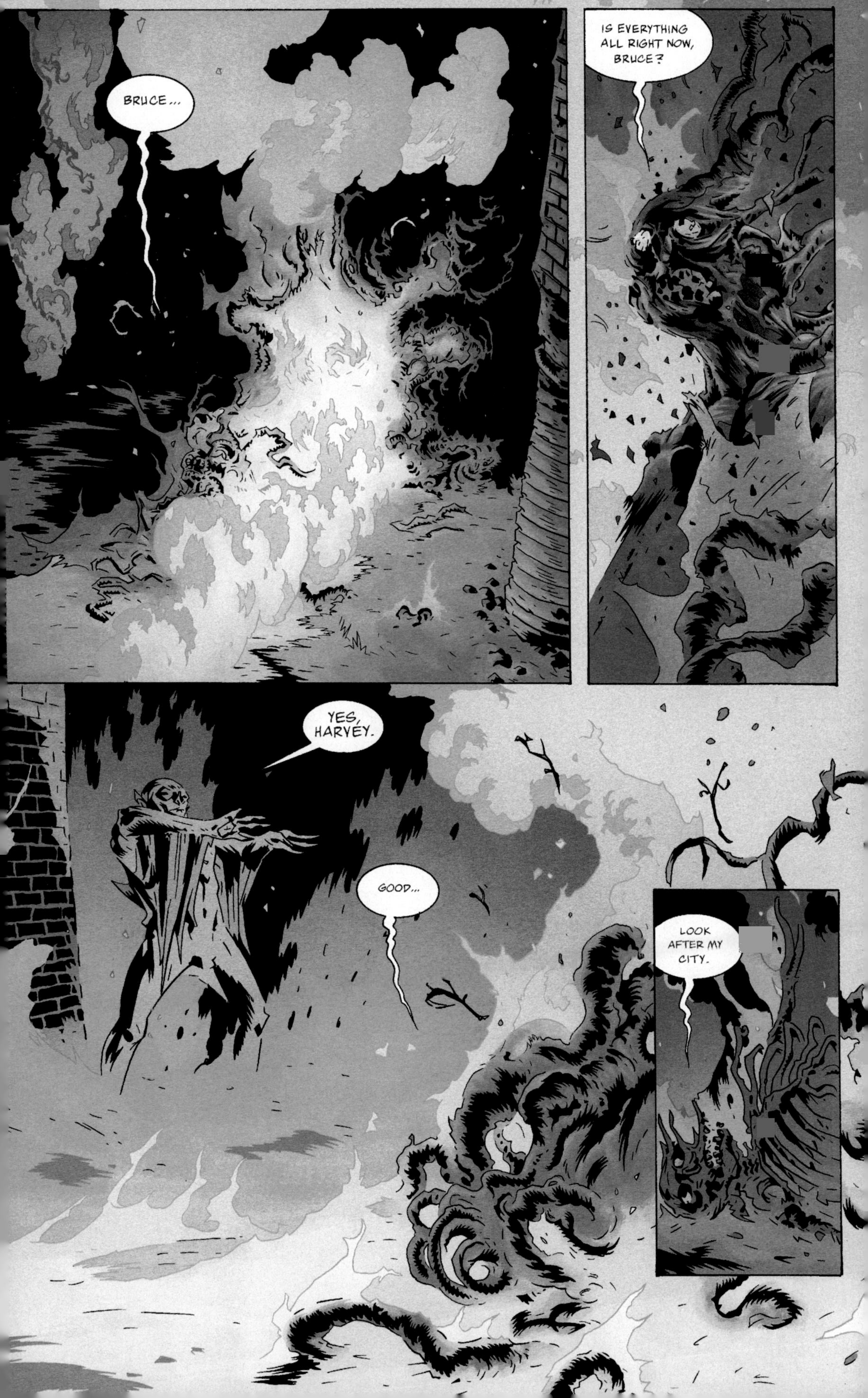
BRUCE...
IS EVERYTHING ALL RIGHT NOW, BRUCE?
YES, HARVEY.
GOOD...
LOOK AFTER MY CITY.

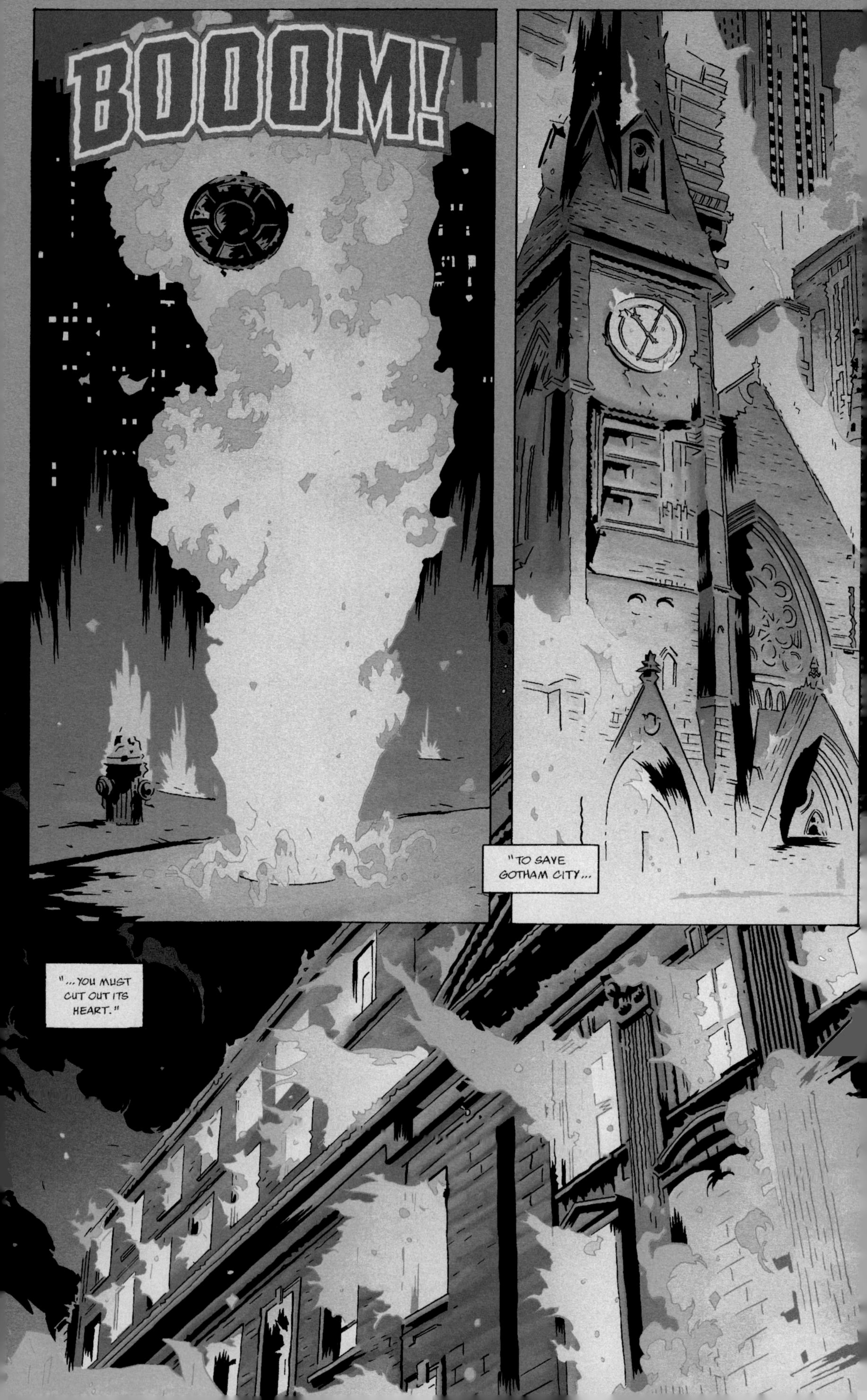
BOOOM!
"TO SAVE GOTHAM CITY...
"...YOU MUST CUT OUT ITS HEART."

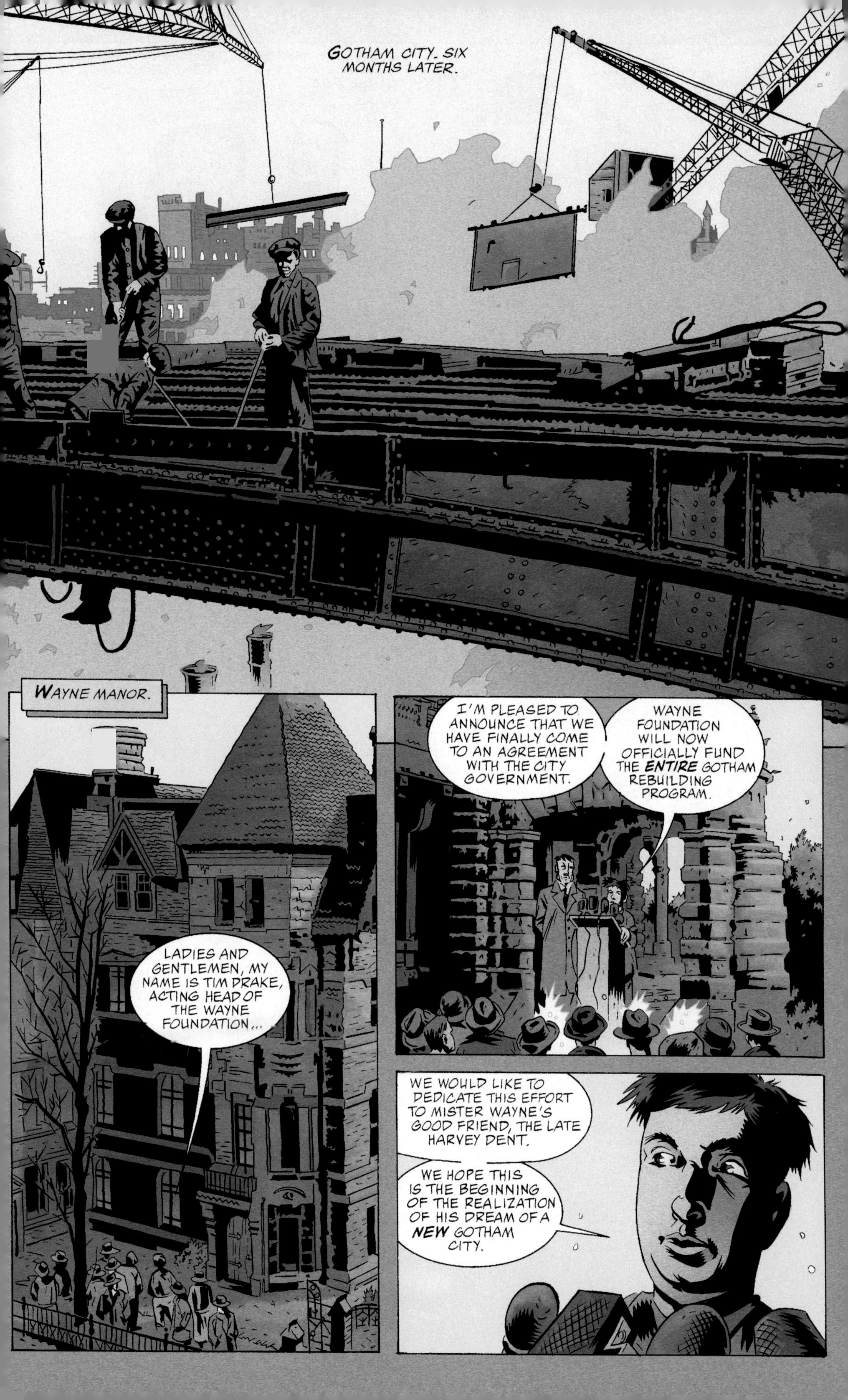
GOTHAM CITY. SIX MONTHS LATER.
WAYNE MANOR.
LADIES AND GENTLEMEN, MY NAME IS TIM DRAKE, ACTING HEAD OF THE WAYNE FOUNDATION...
I'M PLEASED TO ANNOUNCE THAT WE HAVE FINALLY COME TO AN AGREEMENT WITH THE CITY GOVERNMENT.
WAYNE FOUNDATION WILL NOW OFFICIALLY FUND THE *ENTIRE* GOTHAM REBUILDING PROGRAM.
WE WOULD LIKE TO DEDICATE THIS EFFORT TO MISTER WAYNE'S GOOD FRIEND, THE LATE HARVEY DENT.
WE HOPE THIS IS THE BEGINNING OF THE REALIZATION OF HIS DREAM OF A *NEW* GOTHAM CITY.

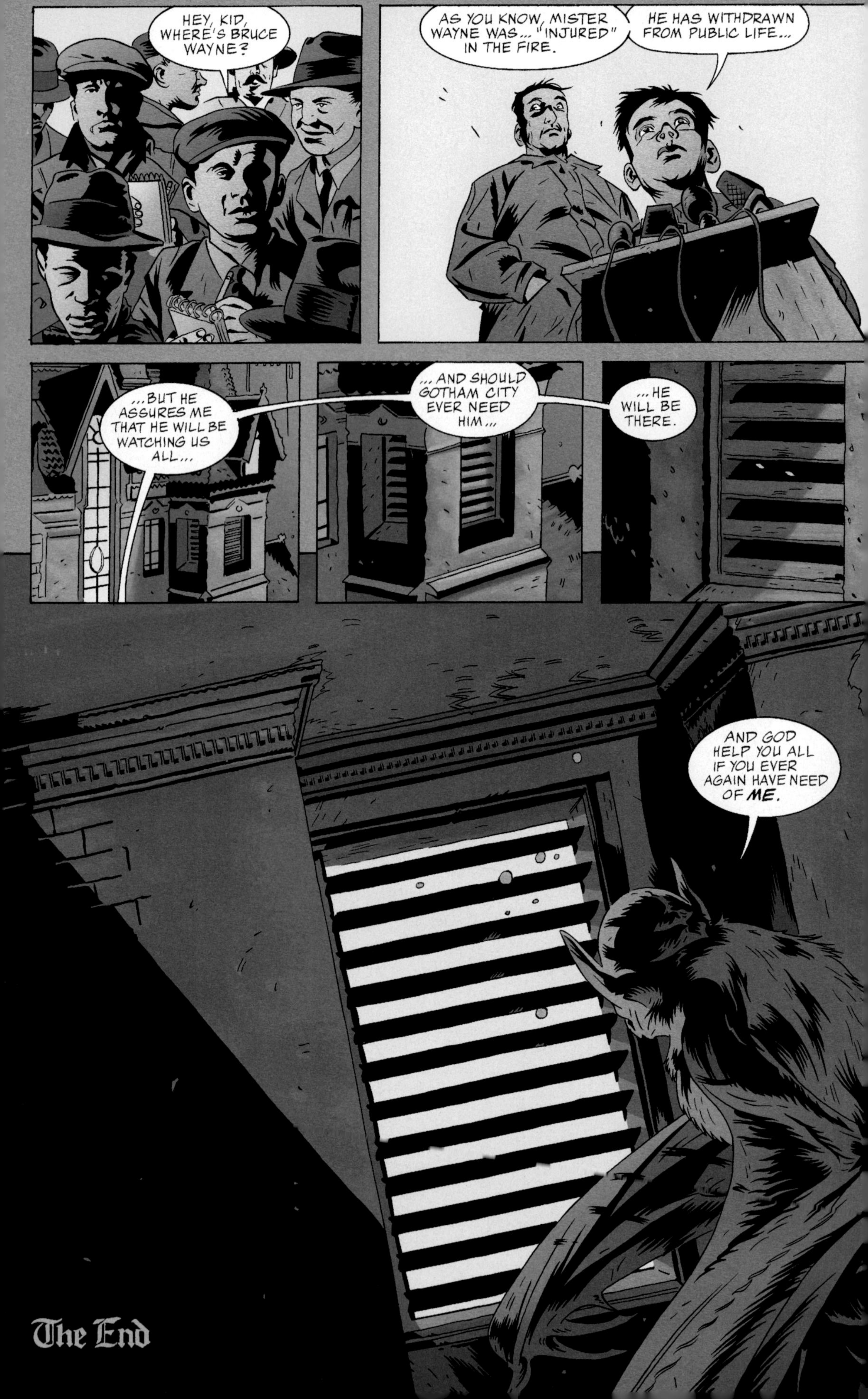
HEY, KID, WHERE'S BRUCE WAYNE?
AS YOU KNOW, MISTER WAYNE WAS... "INJURED" IN THE FIRE.
HE HAS WITHDRAWN FROM PUBLIC LIFE...
...BUT HE ASSURES ME THAT HE WILL BE WATCHING US ALL...
...AND SHOULD GOTHAM CITY EVER NEED HIM...
...HE WILL BE THERE.
AND GOD HELP YOU ALL IF YOU EVER AGAIN HAVE NEED OF ME.
The End

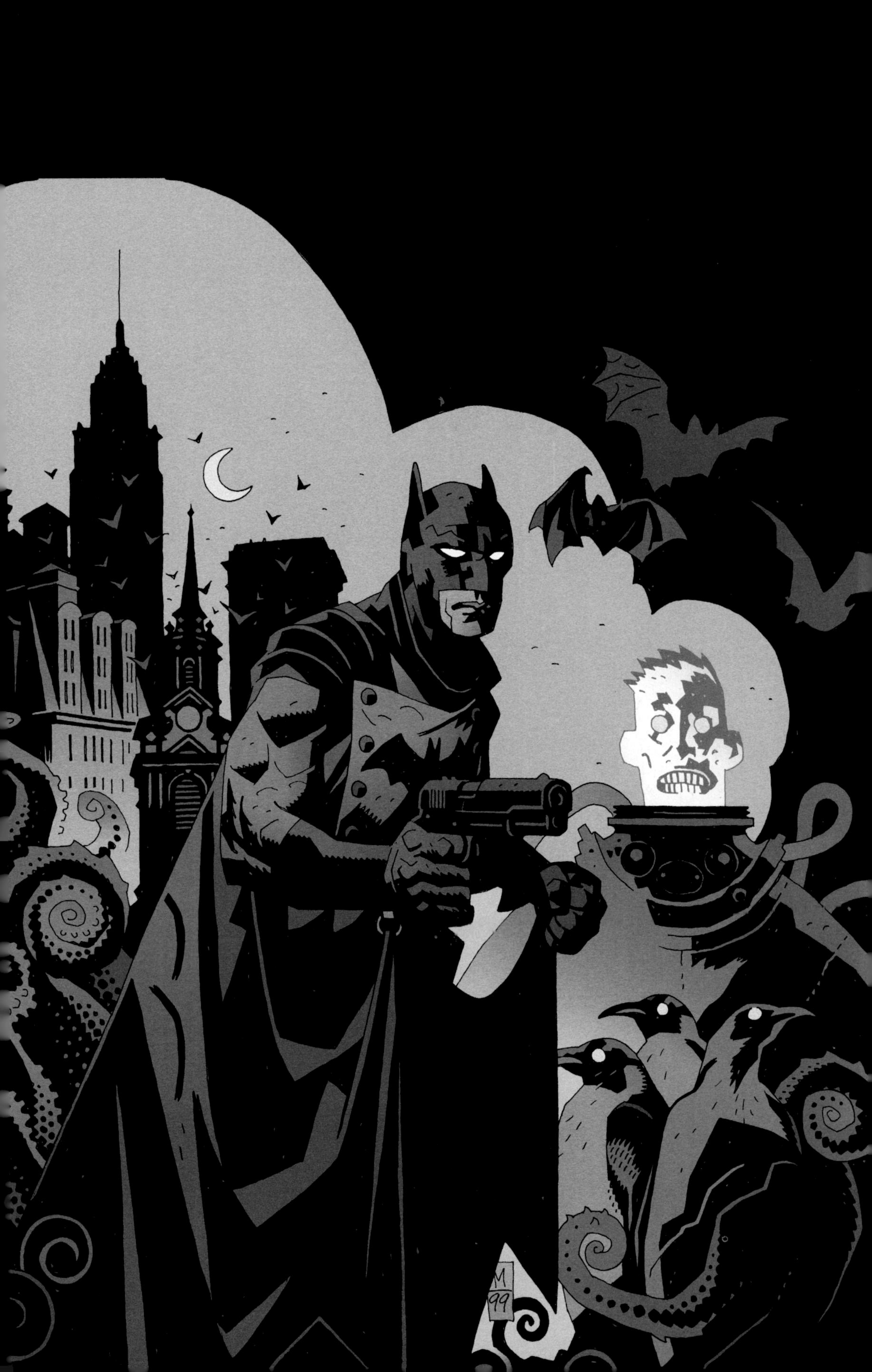

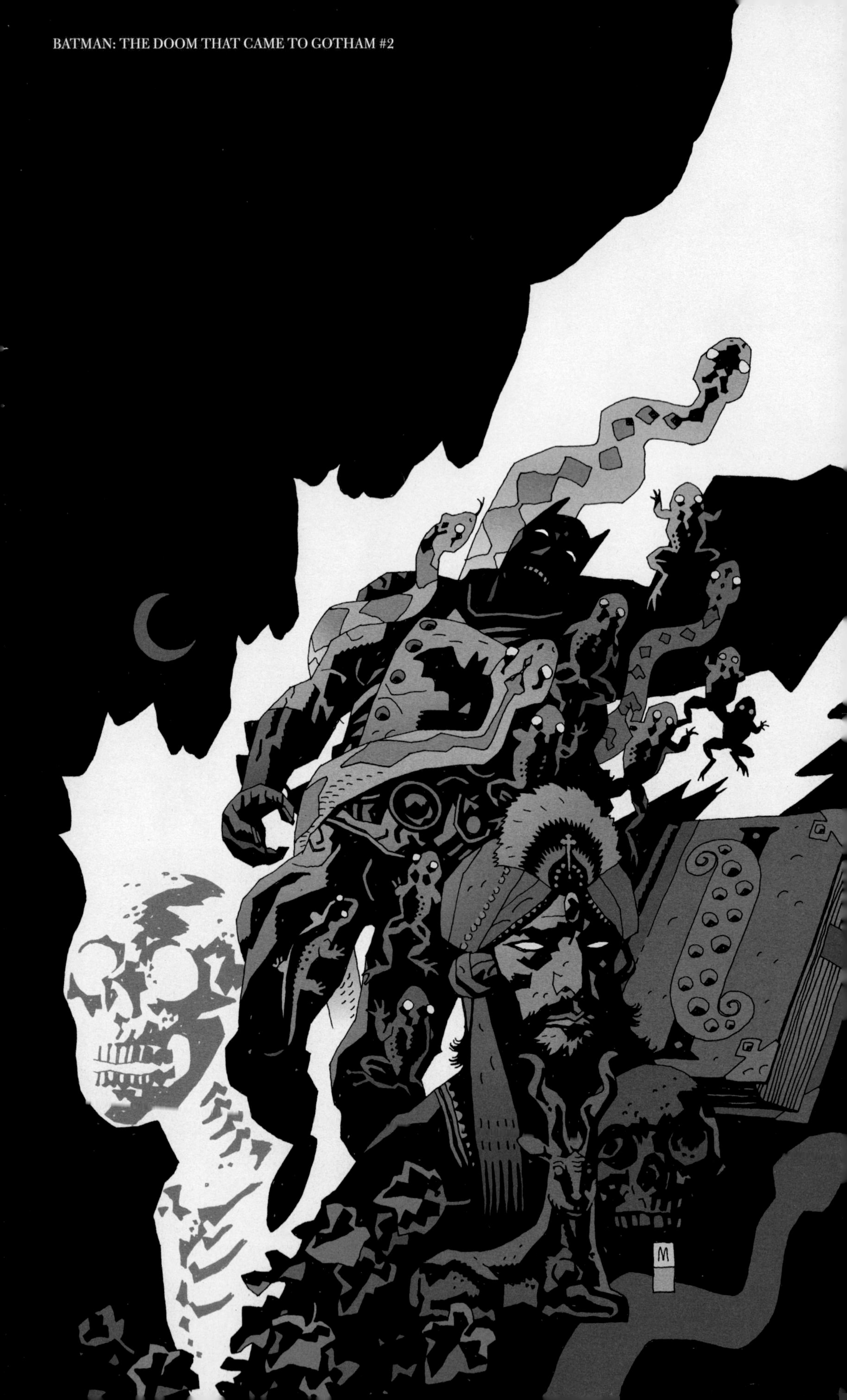
M

BATMAN: THE DOOM THAT CAME TO GOTHAM #3

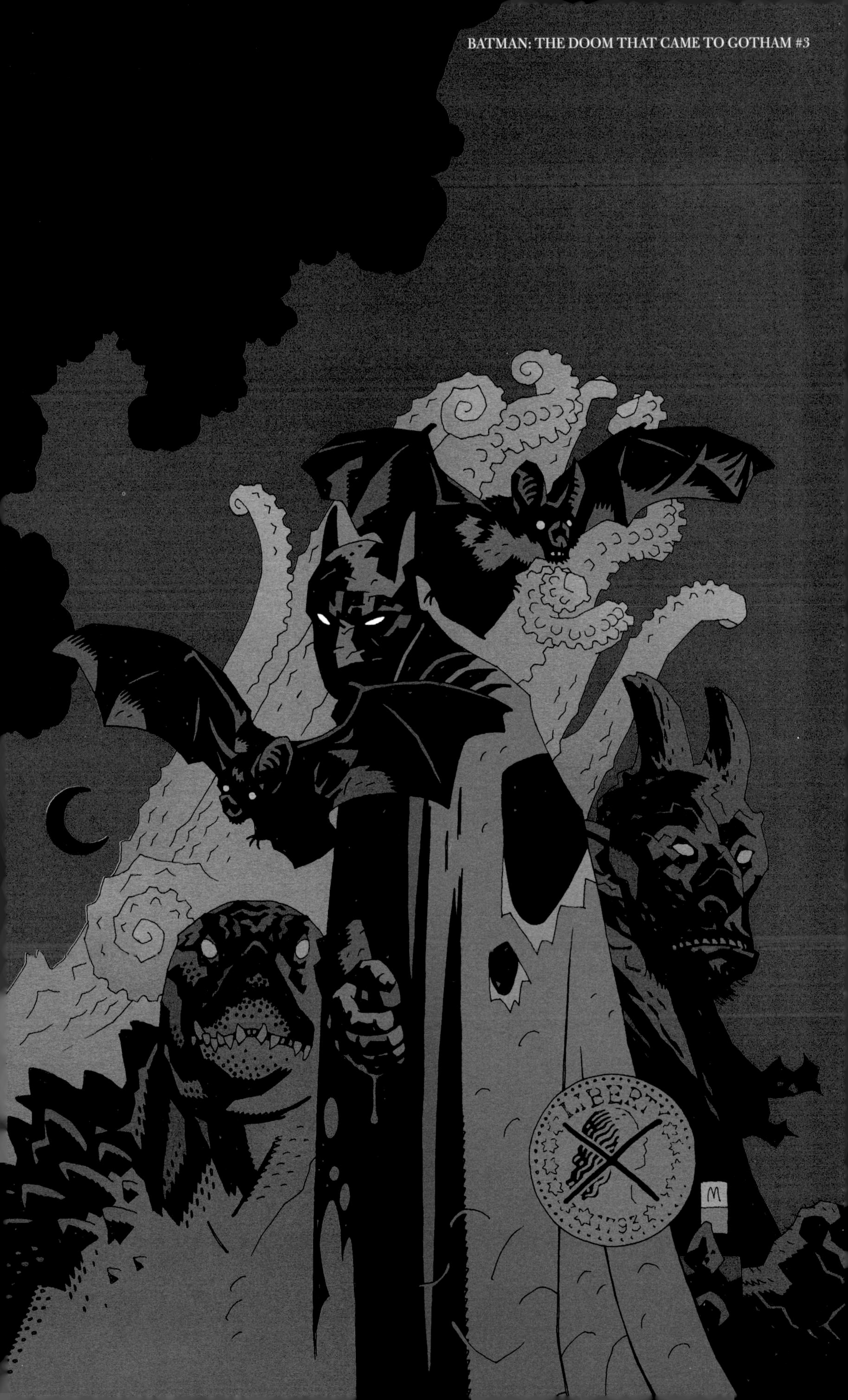

Conceptualized by Richard Pace and Mike Mignola and pitched to Archie Godwin, BATMAN: THE DOOM THAT CAME TO GOTHAM was originally slated to be written by Richard and Mike with Richard penciling. Though some things never quite work out, and Troy Nixey and Dennis Janke were brought on board to pencil and ink the book. What follows are some of Richard's original pencils from issue #1.

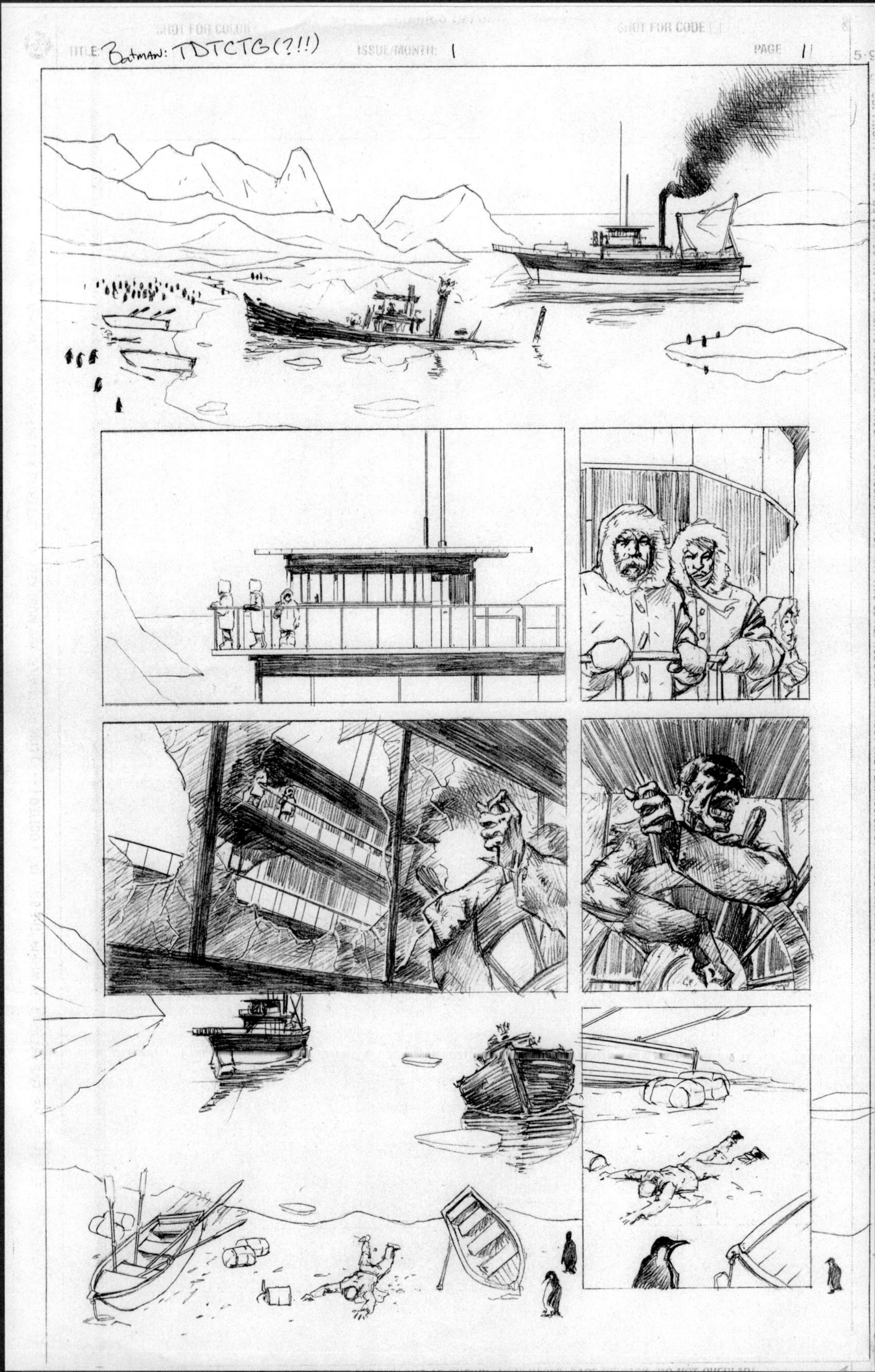
SHOT FOR COLOR
SHOT FOR CODE
TITLE: Batman: TDTCTG(?!!)
ISSUE/MONTH: 1
PAGE 11

TITLE: Batman: Doom... Gotham ISSUE/MONTH: 1 PAGE 3

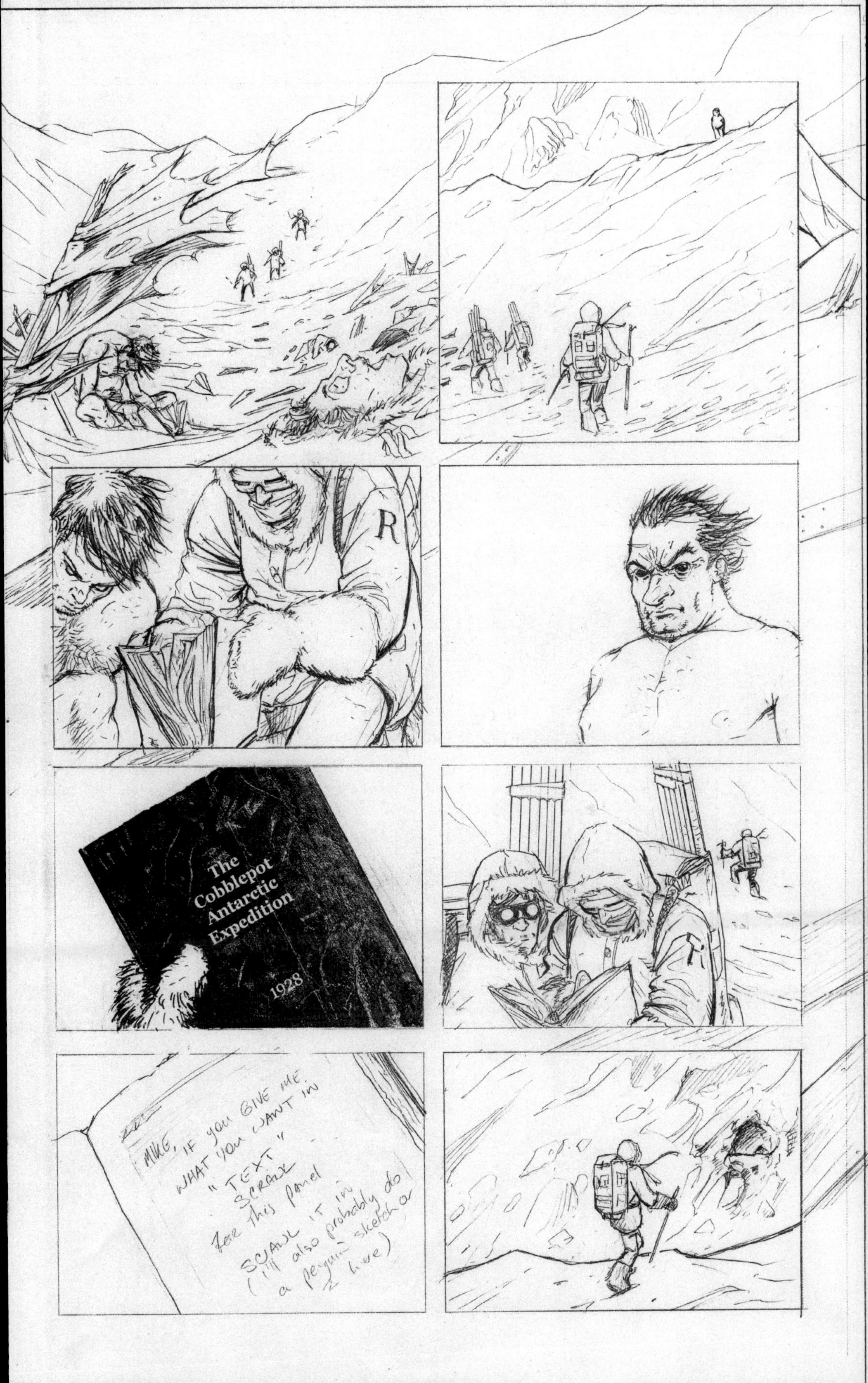
The Cobblepot Antarctic Expedition
1928
MIKE, IF YOU GIVE ME WHAT YOU WANT IN "TEXT SCRAWL" for this panel SCRAWL IT IN (I'll also probably do a penguin sketch or 2 here)

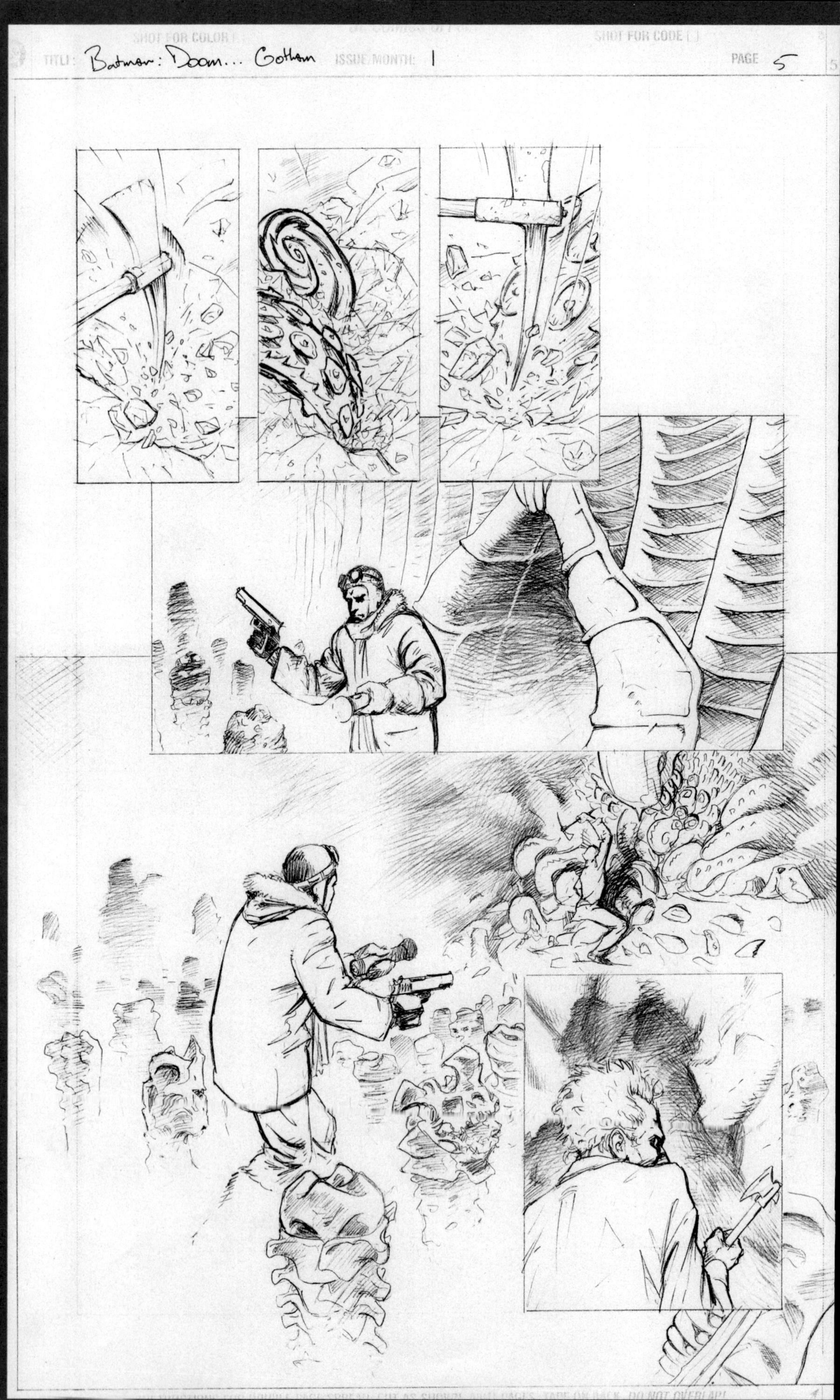
SHOT FOR COLOR
SHOT FOR CODE
TITLE: Batman: Doom... Gotham
ISSUE/MONTH: 1
PAGE 5

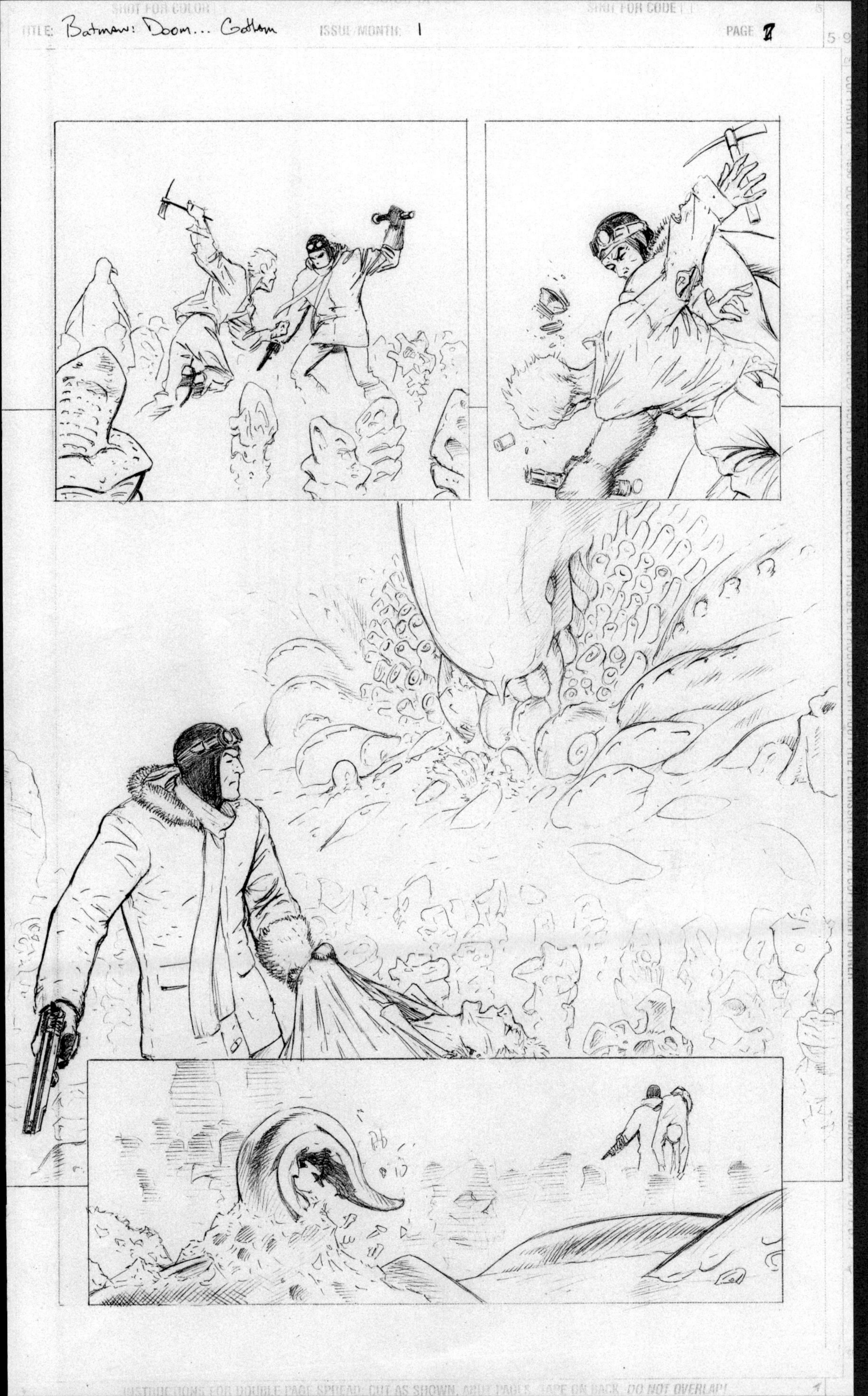
TITLE: Batman: Doom... Gotham
ISSUE/MONTH: 1
PAGE

SHOT FOR COLOR
SHOT FOR CODE
TITLE: Batman: Doom... Gotham ISSUE/MONTH: 1 PAGE 12

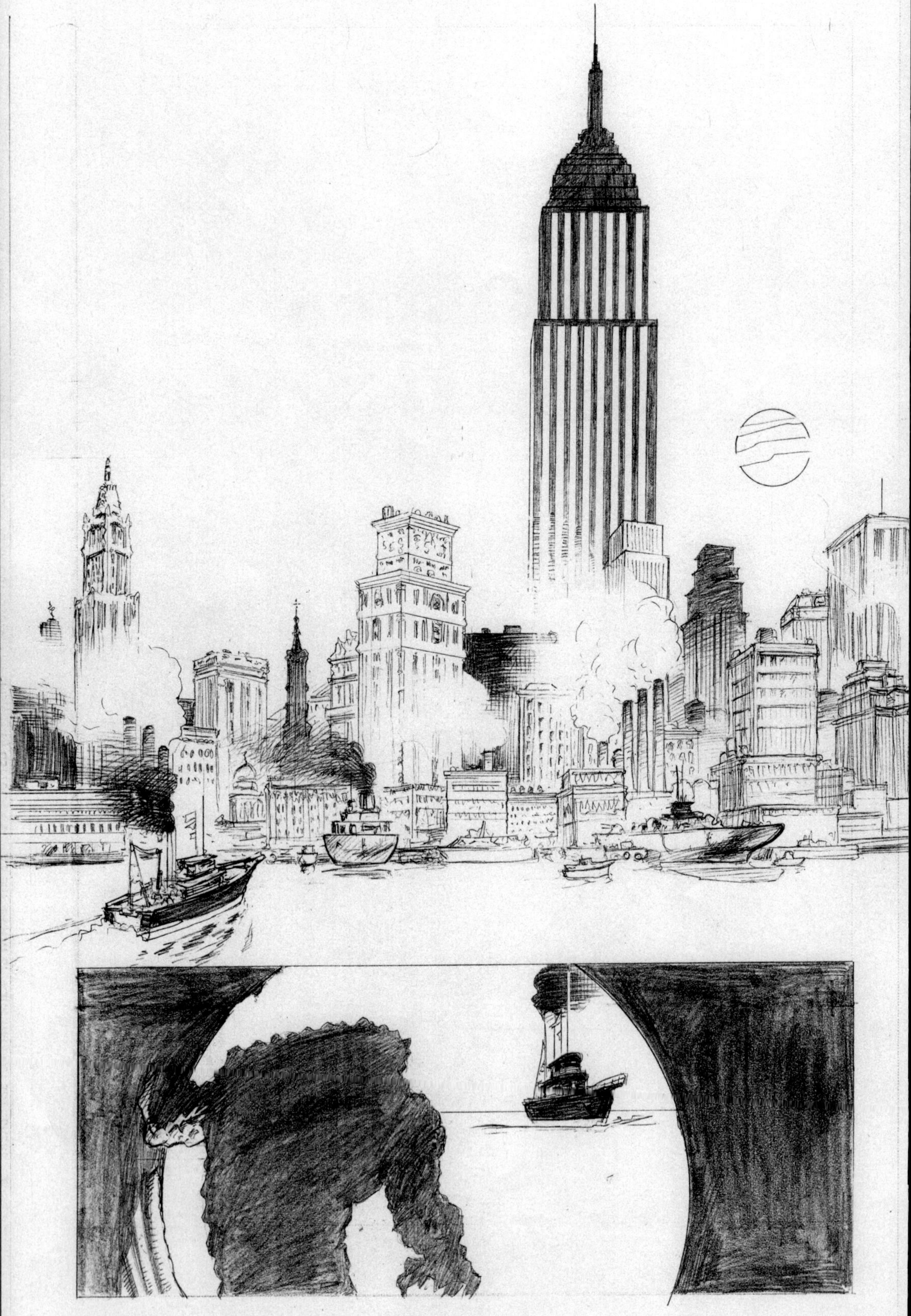

INSTRUCTIONS FOR DOUBLE-PAGE SPREAD: CUT AS SHOWN, ABUT PAGES, TAPE ON BACK. DO NOT OVERLAP!

The following pages are Troy Nixey's original rough layouts and their accompanying final pages.

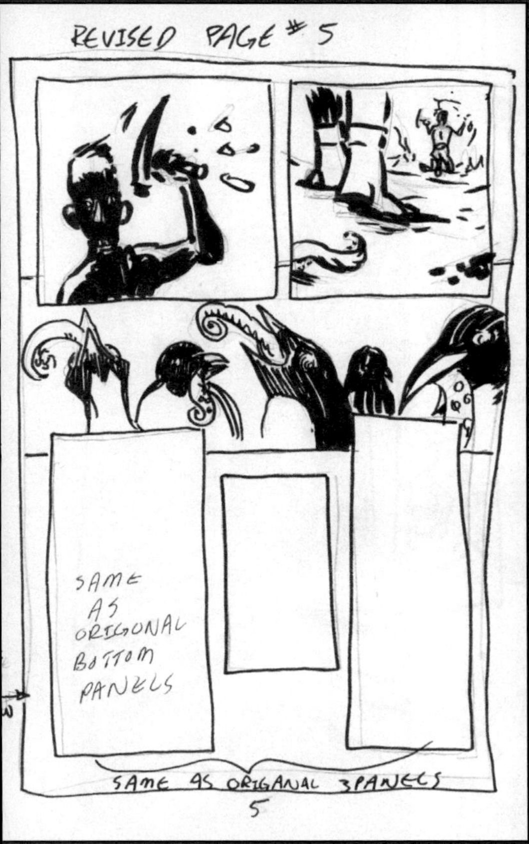
REVISED PAGE #5
SAME AS ORIGONAL BOTTOM PANELS
SAME AS ORIGANAL 3PANELS
5

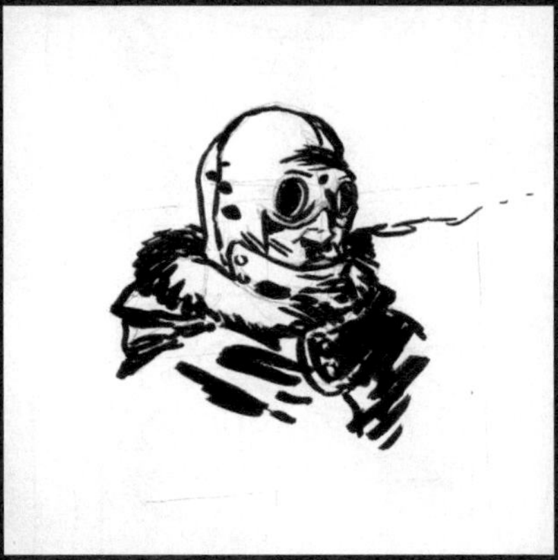

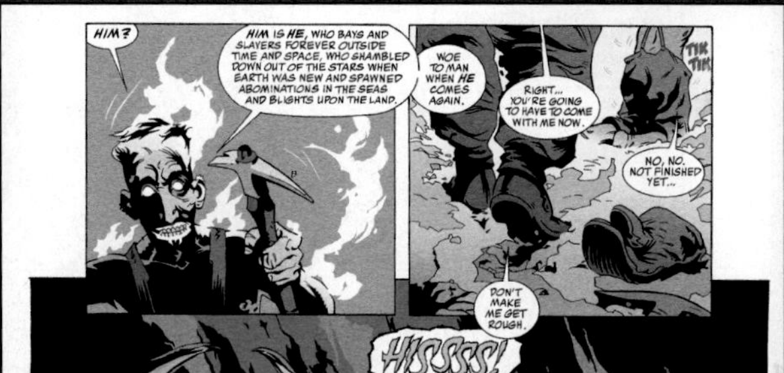
HIM?
HIM IS HE, WHO BAYS AND SLAYERS FOREVER OUTSIDE TIME AND SPACE, WHO SHAMBLED DOWN OUT OF THE STARS WHEN EARTH WAS NEW AND SPAWNED ABOMINATIONS IN THE SEAS AND BLIGHTS UPON THE LAND.
WOE TO MAN WHEN HE COMES AGAIN.
TIK TIK
RIGHT... YOU'RE GOING TO HAVE TO COME WITH ME NOW.
NO, NO. NOT FINISHED YET...
DON'T MAKE ME GET ROUGH.
HISSSS!
YAK YAK YAK
AHH!
BLAM
BLAM
WUK WUK WOK WOK WUK
WUK WUK WUK

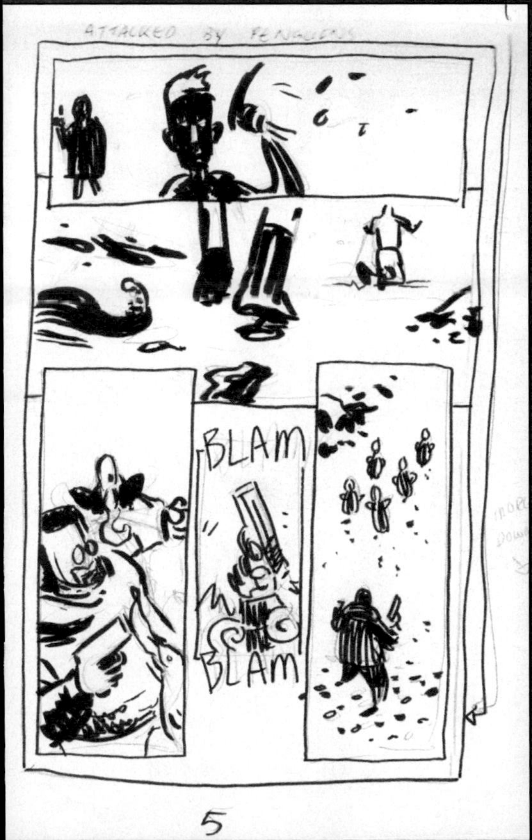
BLAM
BLAM
5

Issue #1, Page 5

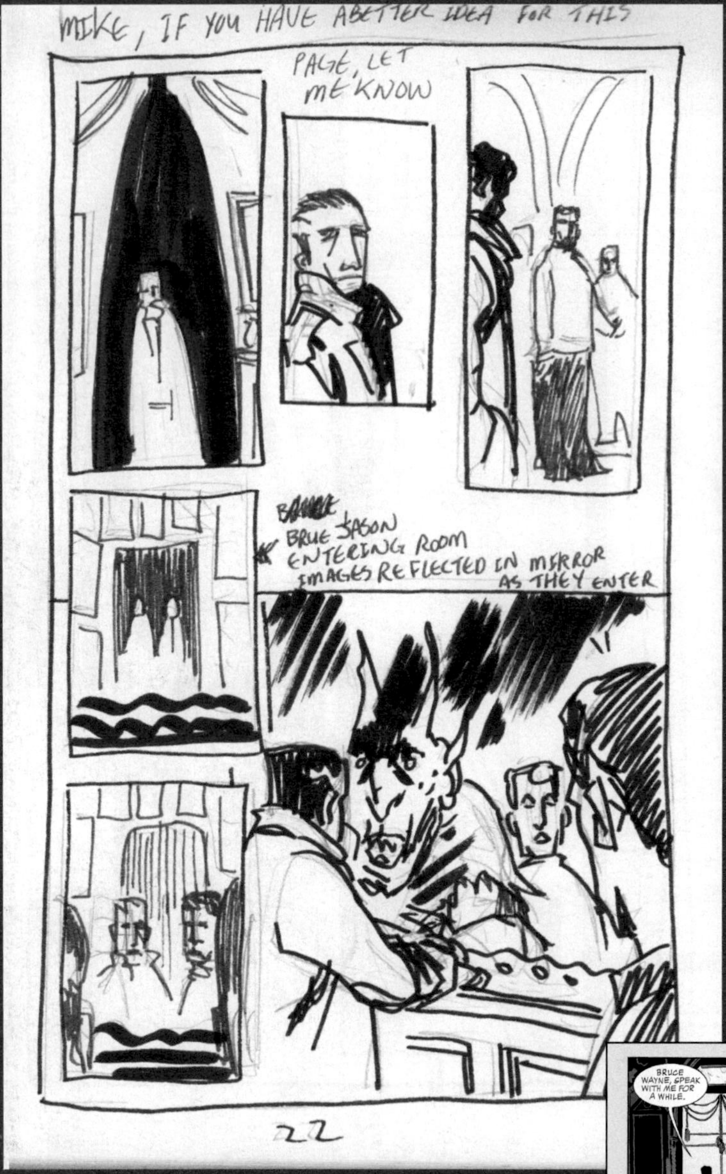

MIKE, IF YOU HAVE A BETTER IDEA FOR THIS PAGE, LET ME KNOW
BRUE JASON ENTERING ROOM
IMAGES REFLECTED IN MIRROR AS THEY ENTER
22

Issue #1, Page 22

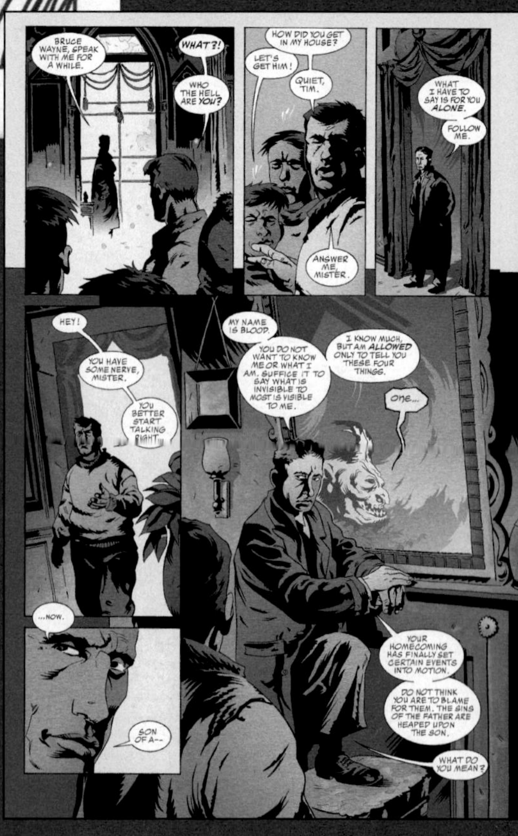

BRUCE WAYNE, SPEAK WITH ME FOR A WHILE.
WHAT?!
WHO THE HELL ARE *YOU*?
HOW DID YOU GET IN MY HOUSE?
LET'S GET HIM!
QUIET, TIM.
ANSWER ME, MISTER.
WHAT I HAVE TO SAY IS FOR YOU *ALONE*.
FOLLOW ME.
HEY!
YOU HAVE SOME NERVE, MISTER.
YOU BETTER START TALKING RIGHT
...NOW.
MY NAME IS BLOOD.
YOU DO NOT WANT TO KNOW ME OR WHAT I AM. SUFFICE IT TO SAY WHAT IS INVISIBLE TO MOST IS VISIBLE TO ME.
I KNOW MUCH, BUT AM *ALLOWED* ONLY TO TELL YOU THESE FOUR THINGS.
One...
YOUR HOMECOMING HAS FINALLY SET CERTAIN EVENTS INTO MOTION.
DO NOT THINK YOU ARE TO BLAME FOR THEM. THE SINS OF THE FATHER ARE HEAPED UPON THE SON.
SON OF A--
WHAT DO YOU MEAN?

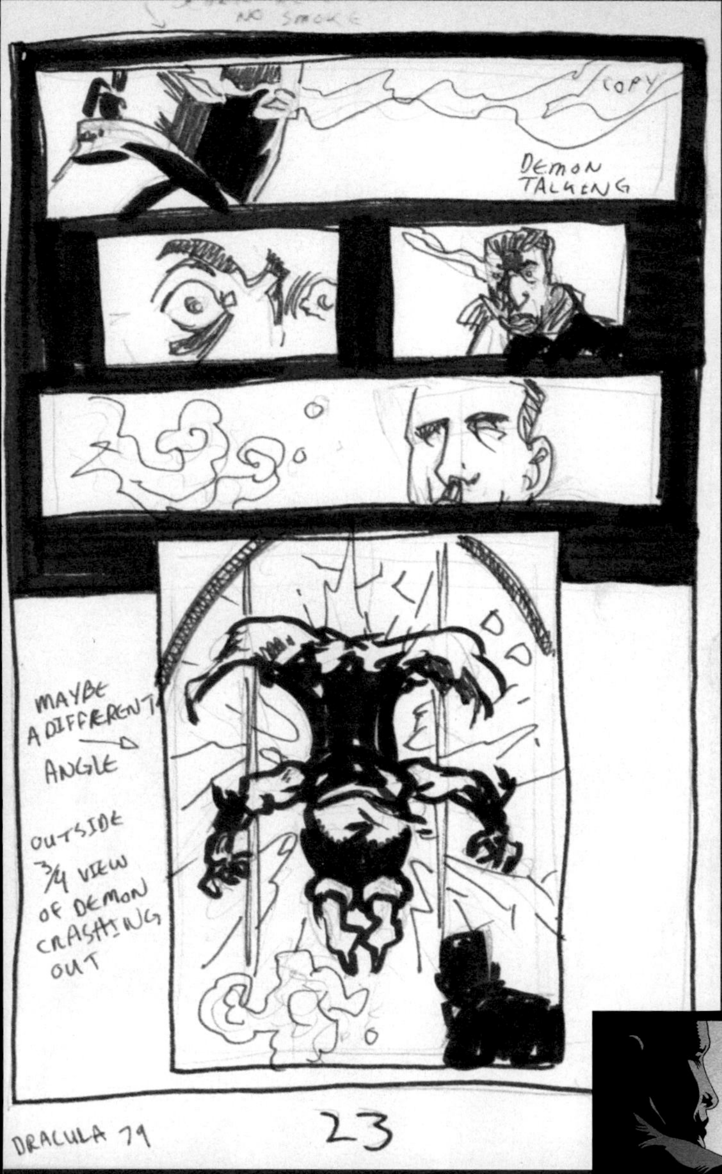
NO SMOKE
COPY
DEMON TALKING
MAYBE A DIFFERENT ANGLE
OUTSIDE 3/4 VIEW OF DEMON CRASHING OUT
DRACULA 79
23

Issue #1, Page 23

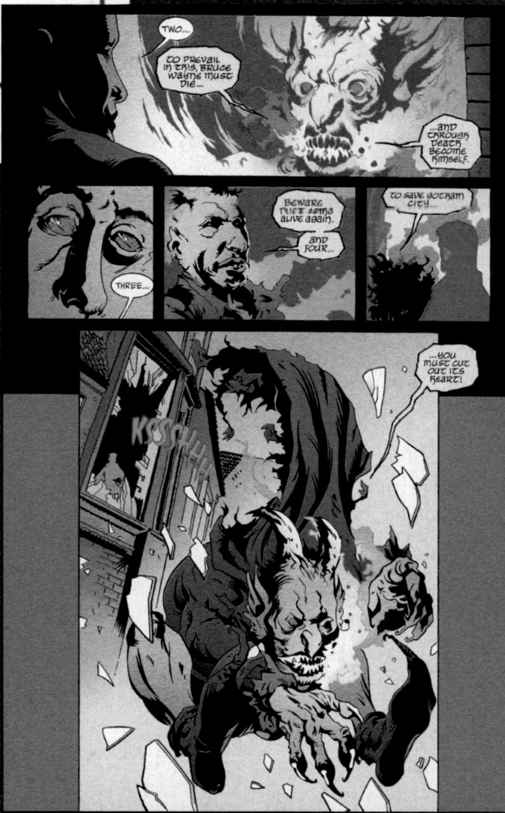
TWO...
TO PREVAIL IN THIS, BRUCE WAYNE MUST DIE...
...AND THROUGH DEATH BECOME HIMSELF.
THREE...
AND FOUR...
TO SAVE GOTHAM CITY...
KSSSHHH
...YOU MUST CUT OUT ITS HEART!

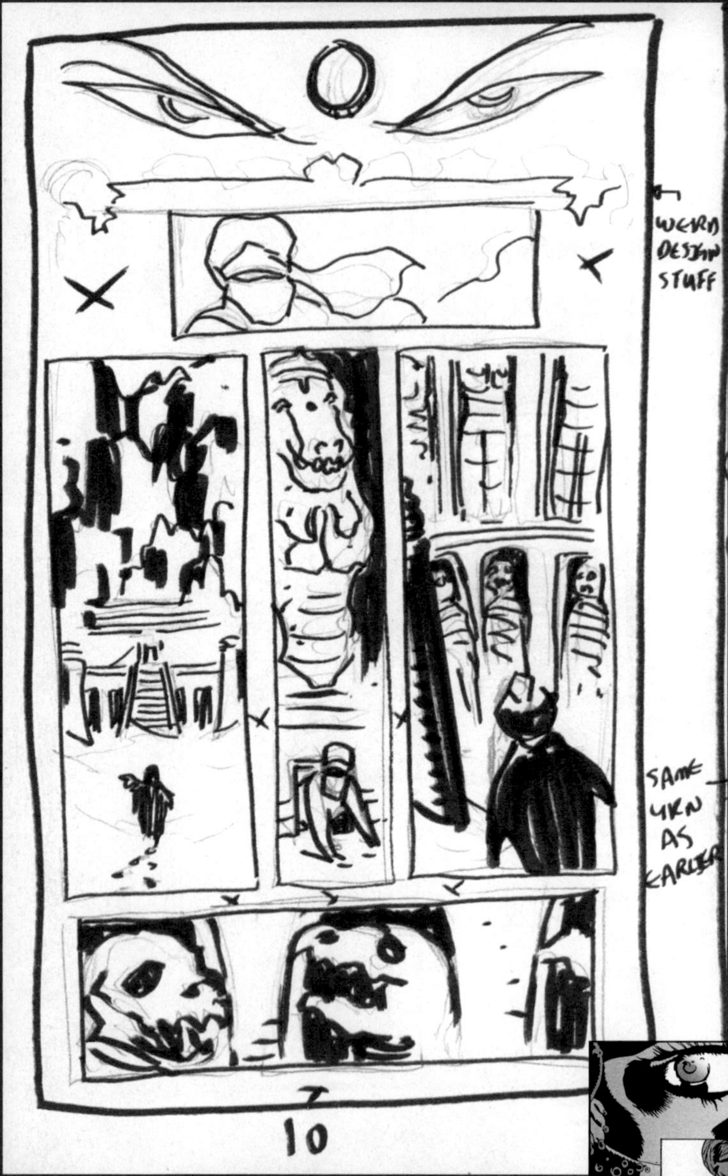
WEIRD DESIGN STUFF
SAME
AS
EARLIER
10

Issue #2, Page 10

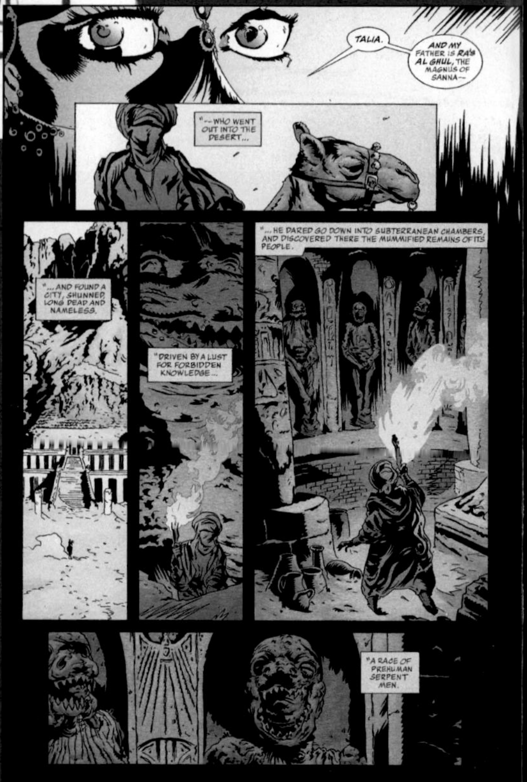
TALIA.
AND MY FATHER IS RA'S AL GHUL, THE MAGNUS OF SANNA--
"--WHO WENT OUT INTO THE DESERT...
"...AND FOUND A CITY, SHUNNED, LONG DEAD AND NAMELESS.
"DRIVEN BY A LUST FOR FORBIDDEN KNOWLEDGE...
"...HE DARED GO DOWN INTO SUBTERRANEAN CHAMBERS, AND DISCOVERED THERE THE MUMMIFIED REMAINS OF ITS PEOPLE.
"A RACE OF PREHUMAN SERPENT MEN.